NBER
Macroeconomics
Annual 2002

NBER
Macroeconomics
Annual 2002

Editors
Mark Gertler and
Kenneth Rogoff

THE MIT PRESS
Cambridge, Massachusetts
London, England

NBER/Macroeconomics Annual, Number 17, 2002
ISSN: 0889-3365
ISBN: Hardcover 0-262-07246-7
ISBN: Paperback 0-262-57173-0

Published annually by The MIT Press, Cambridge, Massachusetts 02142-1407

Standing orders/subscriptions are available. Inquiries, and changes to subscriptions and addresses should be addressed to MIT Press Standing Order Department/BB, Five Cambridge Center, Cambridge, MA 02142-1407, phone 617-258-1581, fax 617-253-1709, email standing-orders@mitpress.mit.edu

In the United Kingdom, continental Europe, and the Middle East and Africa, send single copy and back volume orders to: The MIT Press Ltd., Fitzroy House, 11 Chenies Street, London WC1E 7ET England, phone 44-020-7306-0603, fax 44-020-7306-0604, email info@hup-MITpress.co.uk, website http://mitpress.mit.edu

In the United States and for all other countries, send single copy and back volume orders to: The MIT Press c/o Triliteral, 100 Maple Ridge Drive, Cumberland, RI 02864, phone 1-800-405-1619 (U.S. and Canada) or 401-658-4226, fax 1-800-406-9145 (U.S. and Canada) or 401-531-2801, email mitpress-orders@mit.edu, website http://mitpress.mit.edu

This book was set in Palatino by Achorn Graphic Services, Inc., Worcester, Massachusetts and was printed and bound in the United States of America.

10 9 8 7 6 5 4 3 2 1

Relation of the Directors to the
Work and Publications of the
NBER

1. The object of the NBER is to ascertain and present to the economics profession, and to the public more generally, important economic facts and their interpretation in a scientific manner without policy recommendations. The Board of Directors is charged with the responsibility of ensuring that the work of the NBER is carried on in strict conformity with this object.

2. The President shall establish an internal review process to ensure that book manuscripts proposed for publication do not contain policy recommendations. This shall apply both to the proceedings of conferences and to manuscripts by a single author or by one or more co-authors but shall not apply to authors of comments at NBER conferences who are not NBER affiliates.

3. No book manuscript reporting research shall be published by the NBER until the President has sent to each member of the Board a notice that a manuscript is recommended for publication and that in the President's opinion it is suitable for publication in accordance with the above principles of the NBER. Such notification will include a table of contents and an abstract or summary of the manuscript's content, a list of contributors if applicable, and a response form for use by Directors who desire a copy of the manuscript for review. Each manuscript shall contain a summary drawing attention to the nature and treatment of the problem studied and the main conclusions reached.

4. No volume shall be published until forty-five days have elapsed from the above notification of intention to publish it. During this period a copy shall be sent to any Director requesting it, and if any Director objects to publication on the grounds that the manuscript contains policy recommendations, the objection will be presented to the author(s) or editor(s). In case of dispute, all members of the Board shall be notified, and the President shall appoint an ad hoc committee of the Board to decide the matter; thirty days additional shall be granted for this purpose.

5. The President shall present annually to the Board a report describing the internal manuscript review process, any objections made by Directors before publication or by anyone after publication, any disputes about such matters, and how they were handled.

6. Publications of the NBER issued for informational purposes concerning the work of the Bureau, or issued to inform the public of the activities at the Bureau, including but not limited to the NBER Digest and Reporter, shall be consistent with the object stated in paragraph 1. They shall contain a specific disclaimer noting that they have not passed through the review procedures required in this resolution. The Executive Committee of the Board is charged with the review of all such publications from time to time.

7. NBER working papers and manuscripts distributed on the Bureau's web site are not deemed to be publications for the purpose of this resolution, but they shall be consistent with the object stated in paragraph 1. Working papers shall contain a specific disclaimer noting that they have not passed through the review procedures required in this resolution. The NBER's web site shall contain a similar disclaimer. The President shall establish an internal review process to ensure that the working papers and the web site do not contain policy recommendations, and shall report annually to the Board on this process and any concerns raised in connection with it.

8. Unless otherwise determined by the Board or exempted by the terms of paragraphs 6 and 7, a copy of this resolution shall be printed in each NBER publication as described in paragraph 2 above.

Contents

Editorial: *Mark Gertler and Kenneth Rogoff* 1

Abstracts 5

"RULES VS. DISCRETION" AFTER TWENTY-FIVE YEARS 9
Nancy L. Stokey
COMMENTS: Peter N. Ireland 46
             Lars E. O. Svensson 54
DISCUSSION 62

CURRENT ACCOUNTS IN THE LONG AND THE SHORT RUN 65
Aart Kraay and Jaume Ventura
COMMENTS: Fabrizio Perri 94
             Eric van Wincoop 105
DISCUSSION 110

PRODUCTIVITY GROWTH IN THE 2000S 113
J. Bradford DeLong
COMMENTS: Susanto Basu 145
             Boyan Jovanovic 150
DISCUSSION 155

HAS THE BUSINESS CYCLE CHANGED AND WHY? 159
James H. Stock and Mark W. Watson
COMMENTS: Jordi Galí 219
             Robert E. Hall 224
DISCUSSION 228

EXPENDITURE SWITCHING AND EXCHANGE-RATE POLICY   231
Charles Engel
COMMENTS: Karen K. Lewis   272
                   Pierre-Olivier Gourinchas   281
DISCUSSION   298

OPTIMAL CURRENCY AREAS   301
Alberto Alesina, Robert J. Barro, and Silvana Tenreyro
COMMENTS: Rudiger Dornbusch   345
                   Andrew K. Rose   349
DISCUSSION   353

Editorial, NBER Macroeconomics Annual 2002

The year 2001 witnessed the first global recession in nearly a decade. Although the 2001 downturn had much in common with earlier global recessions, two features stood out. First, productivity growth in the United States remained strong in comparison with previous recessions, despite the sharp slowdown in employment. Second, even after recent data revisions the downturns in both the United States and Europe have been mild in comparison with the recessions of the 1970s and early 1980s, in keeping with a longer-term trend, especially pronounced since 1985, towards milder fluctuations in output. This trend is not universal (Japan is an exception), but it is widespread and certainly especially pronounced in the United States. Has the recent experience been merely an aberration, or does it result from changes in the underlying economy? Are markets better at managing risk? To what extent are improvements in macroeconomic policy management responsible, especially monetary policy? Going forward, how does the world monetary regime need to evolve if this downward trend in business cycle fluctuations is to continue? The papers in this volume of the *NBER Macroeconomics Annual* show that modern economic analysis can help provide considerable insights into these issues, and that thinking on these topics has evolved quite a bit, even from just five years back.

Brad DeLong tackles the question of the day: Is the recent U.S. productivity boom going to be a long-lasting one, or will it fizzle like an Internet bubble stock? For some time, the evidence has been mixed, with many skeptics arguing that there is little evidence of a productivity boom outside the information technology (IT) and telecommunications sectors. DeLong's assessment is that the delay seen in the spread of IT productivity benefits to the rest of the economy is quite normal for major transforming inventions; he brings to bear the recent results of many other young researchers to buttress his conclusions. He argues that the social returns to technology would have to drop precipitously for the boom to suddenly taper off, and that a more detailed look at investment patterns only strengthens the case of the productivity optimists.

While DeLong's paper assesses the trend behavior of U.S. output, James Stock and Mark Watson focus on the cycle. They carefully analyze both the nature and the sources of the decline in cyclical volatility. They show that not only has there been a decline in the variability of GDP growth, but that the decline has been across the board: The major components of GDP and the major sectors of the economy have all experienced a drop in volatility, suggesting that this phenomenon is not an artifact of shifting composition of output (e.g., from manufacturing to services). They also show that the reduction in volatility was likely the outcome of a sharp break around 1984, consistent with the evidence in Kim and Nelson (1999) and McConnell and Perez-Quiros (2000), as opposed to a smooth decline over the postwar period. They then take up the daunting issue of identifying the sources of the moderated cycle, focusing on three potential explanations: (1) good luck (i.e., smaller shocks), (2) good monetary policy management, and (3) technological change (e.g., improved inventory management). They find that improved monetary policy could account for 20% to 30% of the volatility reduction, but that smaller shocks probably account for most of the rest, in keeping with the hypothesis of Blanchard and Simon (2001) and Ahmed, Levin, and Wilson (2002). The authors stress, however, that their conclusions are tentative and that the issue is wide open for further investigation.

Twenty-five years ago, when Kydland and Prescott in their landmark paper first emphasized the time-consistency problem in the formulation of economic policy, it appeared that the inability to commit monetary policy was a major source of instability in the economy. Indeed, many concluded (most famously, Rudiger Dornbusch in his celebrated overshooting and exchange-rates paper) that as far as stabilization policy goes, monetary policy is part of the problem rather than part of the solution. How can things have changed so much in 25 years? Nancy Stokey revisits Kydland and Prescott's analysis, bringing her own modern perspective to the issues. Acknowledging that institutional innovation may arise to address the credibility problem (e.g., independent and inflation-conservative central bankers, inflation targeting), Stokey also emphasizes the role of reputation. She develops a simple model in which reputation is intimately interlinked with social consensus, a phenomenon well documented in many industrialized countries and emerging markets. She also notes that the choice of monetary instrument has fundamental strategic implications in a world where reputation underpins monetary stability and imperfect information always threatens to undermine reputation. In addition to the policy significance of Stokey's paper, it gives an extremely useful introduction to recent research on time consistency and monetary policy.

How can it be that macroeconomic volatility has gone down when exchange-rate volatility, at least among the largest three currencies (euro, yen, and dollar) remains so significant? The basic answer, offered by Maurice Obstfeld and Kenneth Rogoff in their *Macroeconomics Annual 2000* paper, is that there appears to be a disconnect between macroeconomic variables and exchange rates. Obstfeld and Rogoff argue that a major reason is that due to various trade costs, the effective share of nontraded goods in the largest modern industrialized economies is much bigger than we formerly believed. They do not, however, provide a detailed model of the transmission mechanism. The starting point for Engel's analysis is "new open-economy macroeconomics" models that essentially developed in parallel with dynamic new Keynesian models that are prevalent in macroeconomic policy analysis today. Closed-economy theorists have debated for some time whether it is more realistic to model prices or wages as the principal source of nominal rigidity in the economy. International economists have long since moved past this debate; the evidence of price rigidities is overwhelming in the international context (the evidence famously stemming from Mussa's 1986 paper). Rather, the core issue today is whether prices are sticky in the exporter's or the importer's currency. The classic debates of Keynes and Ohlin and others took as given that nominal rigidities were mainly in terms of prices denominated in the exporter's currency (we know today that this is consistent with a world in which nominal wages are the main underlying source of rigidity). Engel cites a wide range of recent evidence showing that for many countries this is not the case; the prices are more accurately described as sticky in the importer's currency. As Engel shows, the differences between the two cases can be quite fundamental: if there is "pricing to market with local-currency pricing" (the new view), the classical transmission channels analyzed by Keynes and Ohlin are not operative. There is a great deal of debate raging in the field, including about whether intermediate products might be characterized by producer currency pricing even if final goods are not. Engel's paper gives an interesting overview of the issues and shows how important the questions of pricing practices are for understanding the efficacy of alternative exchange-rate regimes.

Alberto Alesina, Robert Barro, and Silvana Tenreyro carry the link between exchange rate and output volatility one step further, asking how the future map of world currencies ought to look if economic boundaries ever came to supersede political ones, at least for purposes of monetary policy. Certainly, they must be right that some day, as economies become more open and more integrated, there will have to be more experimentation with multicountry currency unions along the lines of the euro. One of their most interesting observations is that there are many more countries that have a natural currency-union partner—in terms of trade links, output correlations, etc.—in the dollar or the euro than in the yen. The authors make an effort to account for the endogeneity of optimal currency areas, that is, the fact that economies may adapt to circumstances if faced with a currency union. In his insightful comments (which were transcribed from the conference discussion), the late Rudiger Dornbusch claimed that in spite of plausible calculations such as Alesina, Barro, and Tenreyro present, many variants of currency unions are being contemplated in Asia. He also argued that some types of currency unions might be along very different lines than the authors consider, say a currency union of countries that are major non-oil commodity exporters, such as New Zealand, Canada, and Australia. Alesina, Barro, and Tenreyro package their findings in terms of a provocative map of a possible future configuration of currency unions.

Finally, market completeness plays a critical role both in the dynamics of business cycles and in their international transmission. Aart Kraay and Jaume Ventura present a model in which current account shifts are intimately linked to portfolio shifts. Their model, though radical in some of its conclusions, appears to accord well with recent U.S. experience where portfolio shifts have played a significant role in shaping current account cycles. There was some debate at the conference over whether their results would hold in a much broader class of growth models, at least in the long run. Certainly, Kraay and Ventura's perspective is novel compared to 1980s research on the intertemporal approach to the current account, where portfolio considerations were secondary.

The authors would like to take this opportunity to thank Martin Feldstein and the National Bureau of Economic Research for this continued support of the *NBER Macroeconomics Annual* and its associated conference; the NBER's conference staff, especially Rob Shannon, for excellent logistical support; and the National Science Foundation for financial assistance. Doireann Fitzgerald did an excellent job again as conference rapporteur and editorial assistant for this volume.

This volume is Mark Gertler's first as coeditor; he replaces Ben Bernanke. Finally, we are very sorry indeed that this macroeconomic annual conference will be the last one to feature the late Rudiger Dornbusch. His passing is a great loss to our profession. We are fortunate though to be able to present his comments from the conference (see Alesina, Barro, and Tenreyro's session), which feature the wit, humor, and sparkling insight for which he was so justly renowned.

Mark Gertler and Kenneth Rogoff

Abstracts

"Rules vs. Discretion" after Twenty-five Years
NANCY L. STOKEY

Two models of government policy are presented. In the first the choice of an instrument for conducting monetary policy is analyzed. The ease of observing policy under an exchange-rate regime is shown to confer an advantage on it compared with a regime that targets the money growth rate. In the second a discretionary fiscal regime is compared with one that mandates a simple policy rule restricting capital taxation. The discretionary regime is preferred under a Ramsey government, but the rule confers an advantage if the type of government is uncertain and the probability of a myopic administration is high enough.

Current Accounts in the Long and the Short Run
AART KRAAY AND JAUME VENTURA

Faced with income fluctuations, countries smooth their consumption by raising (lowering) savings when income is high (low). How much of these savings do countries invest at home and abroad? In other words, what are the effects of fluctuations in savings on domestic investment and the current account? In the long run, we find that countries invest the marginal unit of savings in domestic and foreign assets in the same proportions as in their initial portfolio, so that the latter is remarkably stable. In the short run, we find that countries invest the marginal unit of savings mostly in foreign assets, and only gradually do they rebalance their portfolio back to its original composition. This means that countries try to smooth not only consumption, but also domestic investment. To achieve this, they use foreign assets as a buffer stock.

Productivity Growth in the 2000s
J. BRADFORD DeLONG

A near-consensus sees the cause of the productivity speedup of the 1990s in the information technology (IT) sector. The pace of invention and innovation in that sector generated real price declines of between ten and twenty percent per year for decades. Increased productivity in the IT capital-goods-producing sector, coupled with real capital deepening as the quantity of investment bought by a dollar of nominal savings grows, has driven the productivity speedup. Will this higher level of productivity growth persist? The answer appears to be "probably." The most standard of applicable growth models predicts that the social return to IT investment would have to suddenly drop to near zero for the upward jump in productivity growth to reverse itself. More complicated models that focus in more detail on the determinants of investment spending or on the sources of increased total factor productivity strengthen, not weaken, forecasts of productivity growth over the next decade.

Has the Business Cycle Changed and Why?
JAMES H. STOCK AND MARK W. WATSON

From 1960 to 1983, the standard deviation of annual growth rates in real GDP in the United States was 2.7%. From 1984 to 2001, the corresponding standard deviation was 1.6%. This paper investigates this large drop in the cyclical volatility of real economic activity. The paper has two objectives. The first is to provide a comprehensive characterization of the decline in volatility using a large number of U.S. economic time series and a variety of methods designed to describe time-varying time-series processes. In so doing, the paper reviews the literature on the moderation and attempts to resolve some of its disagreements and discrepancies. The second objective is to provide new evidence on the quantitative importance of various explanations for this "great moderation." Taken together, we estimate that the moderation in volatility is attributable to a combination of improved policy (20–30%), identifiable good luck in the form of productivity and commodity price shocks (20–30%), and other unknown forms of good luck that manifest themselves as smaller reduced-form forecast errors (40–60%).

Expenditure Switching and Exchange-Rate Policy
CHARLES ENGEL

Changes in nominal exchange rates can lead to *expenditure switching* when they change relative international prices. A traditional argument for flexible nominal exchange rates posits that when prices are sticky in producers' currencies, nominal-exchange-rate movements can change relative prices between home and foreign goods. But if prices are fixed ex ante in consumers' currencies, nominal exchange-rate flexibility cannot achieve any relative price adjustment. In that case nominal-exchange-rate fluctuations have the undesirable feature that they lead to deviations from the law of one price. The case for floating exchange rates is weakened if prices are sticky in this way. The empirical literature appears to support the notion that prices are sticky in consumers' currencies. Here, additional support for this conclusion is provided. We then review some new approaches in the theoretical literature that imply an important expenditure-switching role even when consumer prices are sticky in consumers' currencies. Further empirical research is needed to resolve the quantitative importance of the expenditure-switching role for nominal exchange rates.

Optimal Currency Areas
ALBERTO ALESINA, ROBERT J. BARRO, AND SILVANA TENREYRO

As the number of independent countries increases and their economies become more integrated, we would expect to observe more multicountry currency unions. This paper explores the pros and cons for different countries to adopt as an anchor the dollar, the euro, or the yen. Although there appear to be reasonably well-defined euro and dollar areas, there does not seem to be a yen area. We also address the question of how trade and comovements of outputs and prices would respond to the formation of a currency union. This response is important because the decision of a country to join a union would depend on how the union affects trade and comovements.

Nancy L. Stokey
UNIVERSITY OF CHICAGO

"Rules vs. Discretion" after Twenty-five Years

1. Introduction

From time immemorial citizens have complained about their governments. When the government is a greedy despot or the society is composed of private agents with conflicting goals, it is easy to see why complaints arise. Twenty-five years ago Kydland and Prescott (1977) showed something more surprising: even in a society with identical households (with identical tastes and opportunities, and the same choices to make) and a perfectly benevolent government (one that wants to maximize the utility of this representative household), in some circumstances bad outcomes may occur. These situations seem to involve no conflict of interest, either among different groups of households or between the private sector and the government, and the outcomes are "bad" in the sense that better alternatives are obviously available and seem to be—almost—within reach. Settings where this paradox arises include patent protection, capital levies, default on debt, disaster relief, and monetary policy.

Two elements are needed to create such a situation. First, anticipations about future government policy must be important in shaping current decisions in the private sector. Second, there must be a public-good aspect—an *external effect*—of the private-sector choices that are influenced by anticipated policy.

In a setting with these two features, even a benevolent government typically has an incentive to mislead the private sector about the policies that will be implemented in the future, in order to manipulate their cur-

I am grateful to Fernando Alvarez, V. V. Chari, Patrick Kehoe, Robert Lucas, Roger Myerson, and Christopher Phelan for useful discussions, and to the Research Division of the Federal Reserve Bank of Minneapolis for hosting me during a visit where much of this work was done.

rent decisions and enhance the external effect. After the private-sector choices have been made, the government's incentives put weight on only the direct (contemporaneous) effect of the policy. Thus, it has an incentive to implement a different policy from the one announced. If private-sector agents are rational, however, they foresee that the government's incentives will change and refuse to be misled in the first place. The resulting outcome seems bad if the enhanced external effect, which must be forgone, is large. All agents would all be better off if all could be fooled, but rational behavior precludes this possibility: in equilibrium the private sector must anticipate correctly the policymaker's incentives and choices. Thus, the time-consistency problem offers an explanation for what seem to be paradoxically bad policy outcomes.[1]

A key issue in settings where the time-consistency problem arises is the ability or inability of the government to make binding commitments about future policy: *Rules* imply commitment, while *discretion* implies its absence. Commitment is important if anticipations about future government actions influence the current choices of the private agents in the economy. With the ability to commit, the government can tie the hands of its successors in a way that may improve outcomes. Without that ability the private sector fears—with good reason—that today's government will make promises that its successors will refuse to honor.

If commitment is lacking, a framework that incorporates game-theoretic elements is needed to model the policymaker's incentives.[2] And as Barro and Gorden (1983) showed early on, such a formulation also points the way to a resolution of the problem: within a game-theoretic framework it is easy to show that if the game is repeated and agents are not too impatient, there are reputation equilibria in which the "good" outcome prevails along the equilibrium path. That is, a policymaker can be disciplined by reputation considerations even if he has discretion.

The time-consistency issue has been intensively studied over the past twenty-five years, and many of the main theoretical issues have been resolved. Interesting substantive applications are, of course, still being developed. But rather than review the theoretical literature again[3] or attempt

---

1. If the government is not benevolent—if it has objectives different from those of the private sector—the same incentive to mislead can arise. But with conflicting objectives that is unsurprising. What is astonishing about Kydland and Prescott's examples is that all parties seem to share the same objectives. This appearance is somewhat illusory, in the sense that the payoffs of the private sector agents are symmetric, not identical: the private sector is not a "team." See Chari, Kehoe, and Prescott (1989) for a more detailed discussion.
2. Chari and Kehoe (1990) and Stokey (1991) offer two slightly different general frameworks.
3. See Rogoff (1987, 1989) for an excellent survey of the early literature, Persson and Tabellini (1994) for a discussion of many applied questions, and McCallum (1999) for a discussion of issues related to monetary policy.

to survey the applications (which are too numerous even to list), we will look at two issues that remain. Both deal with choices about the policy regime to be used.

The first issue is reputation building. A policy instrument that can be monitored more closely implies less frequent breakdowns in a reputation equilibrium. Thus, ease of observability is one criterion involved in the choice among discretionary instruments. Here we will look at a central bank deciding whether to peg an exchange rate or to set a rate of money growth. The model focuses on the trade-off between *observability*, the accuracy with which the private sector can monitor the central bank's actions, and *tightness*, how closely the instrument is linked to the object of ultimate interest, the inflation rate. We will show that the ease of monitoring an exchange-rate policy may outweigh other costs it imposes relative to a money growth policy.

The second issue is the robustness of a policy mechanism against mismanagement. One reason to prefer rules over discretion is that governments are not always as intelligent, benevolent, and farsighted as the Ramsey government found in theoretical discussions of policy. Policymakers who are misguided, greedy, or myopic sometimes hold office. Rules that are hard to change may offer protection against these less than ideal types of government officials. The robustness argument is one of the motivations in Friedman's (1948) recommendations on aggregative policy, and it is one that seems worth reviving. Many of the biggest policy blunders seems to arise from incompetence or special-interest-group pressures, rather than the classic time-consistency issue.[4]

Here we will look at robustness using a model in which the type of government in power, Ramsey or myopic, changes randomly from period to period. In this setting the (farsighted) Ramsey government faces an especially difficult task, since the possibility of the myopic type adversely affects private-sector behavior. Hence when the Ramsey government is in power it must distort its own policy in a way that offsets the policy of the myopic type. If the probability of the myopic type is high enough, a simple policy rule can be advantageous. A well-designed rule places an important restriction on the policy of the myopic type, while leading to only a mild change in the policy of the Ramsey type.

---

4. There are many examples of policy that was arguably well intentioned but surely misguided. Cole and Ohanian (2001) argue that the National Labor Relations Act was important in prolonging the Great Depression by keeping wage rates too high. The inflationary episodes experienced in many countries during the 1970s may offer another example. See Ireland (1999) and Clarida, Gali, and Gertler (1999) for a further discussion. Phelan (2001) offers an interesting model in which a government that is greedy, but also intelligent and patient, may for long episodes behave like one that is benevolent.

These two issues are examined in next two sections. The concluding section discusses some of the results.

2. Reputation Building

The ability of a government policymaker to establish and maintain a reputation for reliable conduct depends on how well the public can observe his actions. A policy instrument that is more easily monitored—one that allows the private sector to detect deviations from announced policy rules more easily—has an obvious advantage in allowing the policymaker to build and keep a reputation. Hence observability is often a key issue. But a policy instrument that is more observable may be less tightly connected to the ultimate target, and consequently there is a tension between observability and tightness.[5]

In a recent paper Atkeson and Kehoe (2001) look at the problem of a central bank choosing between two instruments for conducting monetary policy. The bank's options are to peg an exchange rate or to target the rate of money growth. If it pegs an exchange rate, realized inflation is equal to the rate of depreciation in the exchange rate plus an exogenous shock term that represents the foreign rate of inflation. If the bank targets money growth, realized inflation is equal to the rate of money growth plus an exogenous shock term that represents a domestic velocity shock. The central bank chooses its instrument period by period and may switch instruments at any time. If any reversions occur along the equilibrium path, the most severe punishment is implemented.

Notice that with either instrument the object of interest—the inflation rate—is imperfectly related to the bank's action. The exogenous shock terms—the foreign rate of inflation in the first case and the domestic velocity shock in the second—are beyond the bank's control and are unknown when the bank is making its policy decision. In general the two shocks will have different variances, and those variances are important inputs into the banks decision.

The two instruments also differ along a second dimension. The public is assumed to observe the exchange rate directly, so any deviation is immediately detected. That is, the exchange rate is assumed to be a perfectly observable instrument. Consequently, with the exchange rate as the in-

---

5. Observability is different from what most authors call transparency. In discussions of monetary policy the latter is typically used to refer to the clarity with which the private sector can observe the central bank's *objectives*. The term observability will be used here to refer to the clarity with which the private sector can observe the bank's *actions*.

strument there exist equilibria in which the *threat* of reversion disciplines central-bank behavior, but no reversions actually occur along the equilibrium path.

The money growth rate, on the other hand, is not directly observed. Thus, if the central bank uses the money growth rate for its instrument, the private sector can only infer something about its behavior by looking at the realized rate of inflation. Hence, under a money-growth regime, (accidental) reversions cannot be avoided. As in Green and Porter's (1984) cartel model, the imperfect monitoring technology is the source of these reversions.

Atkeson and Kehoe show that if the central bank can commit to a policy, then it chooses the instrument with the smaller variance for its shock. That is, with commitment only tightness is valued. They also show that if the central bank cannot commit, then it prefers to use the perfectly observable instrument, the exchange rate, even if the variance of the foreign inflation shock is somewhat larger than the variance of the domestic velocity shock.[6]

In this section we will look at a slightly modified version of Atkeson and Kehoe's model that highlights the main conclusions. First, we will require the government to make a one-time decision about which instrument to use, instead of choosing the instrument period by period. Second, we will use reversions to the one-shot Nash equilibrium instead of the most-severe-punishment path. Third, we will formulate the model in the classic Ramsey tradition, as one in which the government's objective is to maximize the utility of the representative household. Finally, we will allow an alternative version of the inflation process under a money-growth rule.

2.1 THE ECONOMY

Consider a central bank choosing between money growth and an exchange rate as the instrument for conducting monetary policy. Suppose

$$\mu + v = \pi = e + \zeta,$$

where μ is the money growth rate, v is a velocity shock, π is the inflation rate, e is the rate of depreciation in the exchange rate, and ζ is the foreign rate of inflation, all in logs. Assume that the shocks v, ζ are i.i.d. and

---

6. Of course, many other issues affect this choice as well. For example, in an early contribution Poole (1970) focuses on the sources of shocks.

Figure 1 REALIZED INFLATION RATE: (a) MONEY-GROWTH REGIME,
(b) EXCHANGE-RATE REGIME

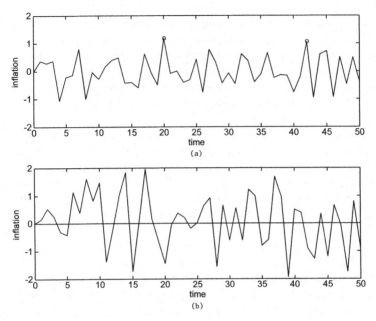

independent of each other, with means of zero and variances σ_v^2, $\sigma_\zeta^2 > 0$.
Assume that π and e are observed.[7]

Under a money-growth policy the instrument is μ, the (noisy) signal is
π, and the velocity shock v affects the realized inflation rate. Although
$e = \pi - \zeta$ is observed, it is not useful in assessing the central bank's performance: e is a noisy signal about π, and π is observed directly. Under an
exchange-rate policy the instrument is e, the (noiseless) signal is e, and
the foreign inflation rate ζ affects the realized inflation rate.

Figure 1 illustrates the trade-off. Figure 1a displays the realized rate of

7. To incorporate serial correlation in the shocks, define μ and e to include expected changes
in velocity and foreign inflation, respectively. Then v and ζ, interpreted respectively as
innovations in velocity and exchange-rate depreciation, are serially uncorrelated and have
means of zero. With serial correlation we must also ask whether it remains reasonable
to assume that e is perfectly observable. If the foreign rate of inflation is serially correlated,
then e is observable only if $E[\pi^f]$, the central bank's forecast of the foreign inflation rate,
is observable. If the central bank announces its estimate $E[\pi^f]$ each period, and if the
private sector can verify this forecast independently, then the model goes through without
change. As Goodfriend (1986) notes, a central bank's main forecasting advantage derives
from its earlier access to data. But presumably the domestic central bank has little advantage in acquiring the data relevant for the foreign inflation rate. Hence the assumption
that the private sector can verify the bank's announcement seems reasonable.

inflation under a money-growth rule. Since the actual rate of money growth (which is always zero in equilibrium) is not observed by the private sector, the reputation equilibrium involves reversions when the realized inflation rate exceeds some (optimally chosen) threshold. The small circles depict situations where a reversion is triggered.

Figure 1b displays the situation under an exchange-rate rule. The horizontal line is the actual rate of depreciation in the exchange rate, and the fluctuations around it depict the realized rate of inflation. The variance of realized inflation is larger than under a money-growth rule, but since the exchange rate is observed directly, no reversions occur. Thus, the optimal choice trades off the higher ongoing cost of larger fluctuations under the exchange-rate regime against the cost of occasional reversions under a money-growth regime.

A slightly more complicated model of money growth incorporates output growth. Suppose

$$\pi = (\hat{\mu} - g) + u,$$

where $\hat{\mu}$ is money growth, g is real GDP growth over the period, and u is a velocity shock. Let

$$g^e = g + \varepsilon$$

be the central bank's (imperfect) forecast of real growth, where ε is the forecast error. Assume that the shocks ε, u, ζ are i.i.d. and independent of each other, with means of zero and variances σ_ε^2, σ_u^2, $\sigma_\zeta^2 > 0$. Under a money-growth policy the bank can be viewed as choosing

$$\mu = \hat{\mu} - g^e,$$

the excess of money growth over expected real growth. For simplicity we will continue to call μ the rate of money growth. Assume that the private sector cannot observe g^e, but does observe $\hat{\mu}$ and g. Then

$$\hat{\mu} - g = \mu + \varepsilon$$

is its signal about the bank's action, and

$$\pi = \mu + \varepsilon + u$$

is the realized inflation rate.[8]

---

8. Our second model of money growth is similar in spirit to Canzoneri's (1985) model. There the central bank was assumed to have private information about a velocity shock; here it has private information about real output growth.

Thus, in both models of money growth the signal about the central bank's action is noisy, so reputation equilibria involve reversions ("punishments") along equilibrium outcome paths. In the first model the realized inflation rate is itself the signal, while in the second the inflation rate is the signal plus additional noise. To capture both models of money growth, the framework analyzed here allows two shocks. For the first interpretation one shock is set identically to zero.

In the next two sections we will characterize a certain class of reputation equilibria and calculate expected payoffs along the equilibrium outcome paths. These equilibria are then compared with those for the exchange-rate model. Since the signal is noiseless under an exchange-rate regime, no reversions occur along the equilibrium outcome path.

2.2 HOUSEHOLD BEHAVIOR

Under a money-growth rule the timing of events within each period is:

1. the government sets the money growth rate μ;
2. each household chooses w, interpreted as a rate of wage growth, in anticipation of the current inflation rate;
3. the signal

$$s = \mu + \varepsilon$$

and the inflation rate

$$\pi = \mu + \varepsilon + u$$

are observed, where ε and u are the exogenous shocks. In the simple model $\varepsilon \equiv v$ and $u \equiv 0$.

Let $\bar{w}$ denote the average rate of wage growth in the economy. The one-period loss for a household that sets the wage w is

$$L(w, \bar{w}, \pi) = \frac{a}{2} \pi^2 + \frac{b}{2}(\bar{w} - \pi)^2 + \frac{d}{2}(w - \alpha - \pi)^2,$$

where $\alpha > 0$, and where $a, b, d > 0$ with $(a + b + d)/2 = 1$ are relative weights.

The household's loss function has a "new Keynesian" interpretation.[9] Suppose each household is the monopolistic supplier of a differentiated commodity produced with labor as the only input. Since households set

9. See Ireland (1997) for a more detailed justification of a similar payoff function.

wages before the current inflation rate is known, wages are sticky for one period.

Suppose each household's target wage is $W = (1 + \hat{\alpha}) P$, where P is the average price level in the economy and $\hat{\alpha}$ is the desired markup. It is convenient to renormalize units each period so $P_{-1} = 1$, and let $w = \ln W$, $\pi = \ln P$, and $\alpha = \ln(1 + \hat{\alpha})$.

The first term in the loss function represents the "shoe leather" cost of inflation. It depends only on the actual rate of inflation P/P_{-1}, and with the chosen normalization it is proportional to $[\ln(P/P_{-1})]^2 = \pi^2$.

The second term represents the household's interests as a consumer. Its surplus is maximized if other producers set wages at $\bar{W} = P$, and its relative loss is proportional to $[\ln(\bar{W}/P)]^2 = (\bar{w} - \pi)^2$.

The last term represents the household's interests as a producer. Its surplus is maximized if its wage equals the target value, and its relative loss is proportional to

$$\left[\ln\left(\frac{W}{(1 + \hat{\alpha})P} \right) \right]^2 = (w - \alpha - \pi)^2.$$

Notice that $\mu = E[\pi|\mu]$ is the expected rate of inflation, conditional on the value μ for money growth. Let μ^a denote the rate of money growth anticipated by households. Then μ^a is also the inflation rate expected by households, where the word "expected" encompasses uncertainty about the central bank's action as well as uncertainty about the shock.

Consider the expected value of the current period loss if μ^a is anticipated and μ is carried out. Households set wages at $w = \mu^a + \alpha$, so the expected loss is

$$\Lambda(\mu^a, \mu) = E[L(\mu^a + \alpha, \mu^a + \alpha, \mu + \varepsilon + u)]$$

$$= \frac{a}{2} \mu^2 - b\alpha(\mu - \mu^a) + \frac{b + d}{2}(\mu - \mu^a)^2 + M, \tag{1}$$

where

$$M \equiv \sigma_\varepsilon^2 + \sigma_u^2 + \frac{b}{2}\alpha^2$$

is an unavoidable part of the expected loss. The first two terms in Λ, which are exactly as in Barro and Gordon (1983), are important for the incentive constraints for the central bank. The third term and its derivative vanish when households correctly anticipate the action of the central bank, $\mu^a = \mu$, as they do in equilibrium. The last term, M, is important for cost comparisons across instruments.

The second term in Λ can be interpreted as a Phillips-curve coefficient. If households anticipate an average rate of inflation μ^a, then the central bank can reduce this part of the expected loss by setting the money growth rate a little higher, $\mu > \mu^a$. Of course, a higher value for μ increases the first and third terms in Λ, putting a bound on the net gain from unanticipated inflation.

In equilibrium households correctly anticipate the action of the central bank, $\mu^a = \mu$, so the expected loss is

$$\Lambda(\mu, \mu) = \frac{a}{2}\mu^2 + M.$$

Consequently, if the central bank could precommit, it would set $\mu = 0$ to minimize this loss. Call $\mu = 0$ the *Ramsey rate* of money growth. For the reasons noted above, if $\mu^a = 0$ is anticipated, short-run considerations tempt the central bank to set $\mu > 0$.

Define μ^N to be the unique rate of money growth with the property that if μ^N is anticipated by households, so they set wages at $w = \mu^N + \alpha$, then the central bank has no short-run temptation to deviate. The latter requires $\Lambda_2(\mu^N, \mu^N) = 0$, so

$$\mu^N = \frac{b\alpha}{a}.$$

Call μ^N the *Nash rate* of money growth.

Let

$$\delta \equiv \Lambda(\mu^N, \mu^N) - \Lambda(0, 0) = \frac{\alpha}{2}(\mu^N)^2 = \frac{(b\alpha)^2}{2a}$$

denote the difference between the expected losses (over one period) under the Nash and Ramsey money growth rates.

2.3 MARKOV EQUILIBRIA

The game described above is infinitely repeated, and future losses are discounted by the constant factor $\beta \in (0, 1)$ per period. If β is close to one, as we will assume here, the repeated game has many subgame-perfect equilibria. We will focus on a particular subset: Markov equilibria in which there are two states, *good* and *bad*, that also satisfy some other restrictions. In the rest of this section we will briefly describe this set of equilibria and sketch the argument for characterizing the subset that minimize expected discounted losses. A more detailed discussion is provided in Appendix A.

Each equilibrium in the class we are considering is characterized by rates of money growth (μ^g, μ^b) for the central bank and rates of wage growth (w^g, w^b) for the representative household for each state, and rules for updating the state at the end of each period. These must satisfy the usual equilibrium conditions. The additional restrictions are twofold.

First, we will focus on equilibria in which the central bank chooses the Ramsey rate of money growth in the good state, $\mu^g = 0$, and the Nash rate in the bad state, $\mu^b = \mu^N$. It then follows immediately that the rates of wage growth chosen by households are $w^g = 0 + \alpha$ and $w^b = \mu^N + \alpha$.

Second, we will restrict the class of rules for updating the state. We will assume that only the current signal s is used and that it is used in a particular way in each state. Specifically, if the economy is currently in the good state, households compare the signal with a one-sided threshold S^g, and the state remains good in the next period if and only if $s \leq S^g$. If the economy is currently in the bad state, households check whether the signal lies in a symmetric interval around μ^N, and the state reverts to good in the next period if and only if $s \in [\mu^N - \varepsilon^b, \mu^N + \varepsilon^b]$. The simple structure of these equilibria makes them appealing candidates for attention.

The pair of thresholds (S^g, ε^b) must also satisfy incentive compatibility (IC) constraints for the central bank in each state. These constraints ensure that any deviation from the equilibrium rate of money growth, 0 or μ^N, is unattractive to the bank.

DEFINITION   *Simple two-state Markov equilibria* are characterized by money growth rates $\mu^g = 0$ and $\mu^b = \mu^N$, rates of wage growth $w^g = 0 + \alpha$ and $w^b = \mu^N + \alpha$, and updating rules that use only the current signal. Depending on the current state, the state next period is good if and only if $s \leq S^g$ or $s \in [\mu^N - \varepsilon^b, \mu^N + \varepsilon^b]$, where the critical values S^g, $\varepsilon^b \geq 0$ satisfy the IC constraints for the central bank.

The symmetric form of the test in the bad state ensures that the IC constraint holds in that state. The IC constraint in the good state imposes an additional restriction on the pair (S^g, ε^b). We turn next to a brief discussion of that constraint.

Instead of using S^g and ε^b, it is convenient to analyze the model in terms of the corresponding probabilities p of a reversion from the good state to the bad and q of a return in the other direction. It is also useful to place a mild restriction on the distribution of the shock ε.

ASSUMPTION 1 ε has a continuous, symmetric, unimodal density $f(\varepsilon)$ with mean zero, whose support is all of **R**.

Under Assumption 1 the reversion probability p can be adjusted continuously from 0 to $\frac{1}{2}$ by adjusting S^g from 0 to $+\infty$; and the return probability q can be adjusted continuously from 0 to 1 by adjusting ε^b from 0 to $+\infty$. Normal distributions with mean zero satisfy this assumption and will be used in the examples.[10]
It is useful to define the function

$$\gamma(p) \equiv f(F^{-1}(1 - p)), \qquad p \in (0, 1),$$

where F is the c.d.f. for f. Then $\varepsilon = F^{-1}(1 - p)$ is the value for the shock that leaves probability p in the upper tail, and $f(\varepsilon)$ is the height of the density function at this point. Thus, $\gamma(\cdot)$ maps probabilities in the upper tail into levels for the density function. We will also use the hazard function, $h(p) = \gamma(p)/p$.
Fix β and define the function

$$\psi(p, q; \beta) = \frac{1}{1 - \beta(1 - p - q)}.$$

Recall that δ is the incremental expected loss from being in the bad state rather than the good in the current period. If the switching probabilities are (p, q), then $\delta\psi(p, q)$ is the expected discounted value of the (current and future) incremental losses from being (currently) in the bad state. That is, $\psi(p, q)$ takes account of all future switches back and forth between states, discounting and weighting them appropriately. Note that ψ is decreasing in p and q: higher switching probabilities reduce the difference between the states.
Fix the parameters (a, b, α) and the density f; let $\mu^N = b\alpha/a$ be the Nash inflation rate, and let γ, h be the functions defined above. The set of probabilities $(p, q) \in (0, \frac{1}{2}] \times [0, 1]$ that satisfy the central bank's IC constraint in the good state are those for which

$$\gamma(p)\beta\delta\psi(p, q) \geq b\alpha.$$

---

10. If there are equilibria with $p > \frac{1}{2}$, then there are also equilibra with $p \leq \frac{1}{2}$, and the latter have lower costs. Hence we focus on them.

The interpretation is as follows: increasing the money growth rate above $\mu^s = 0$ leads to a marginal gain of $b\alpha$ in the current period and a marginal increase of $\gamma(p)$ in the probability of reversion to the bad state. The latter is multiplied by $\beta\delta\psi(p, q)$, the expected discounted loss if a reversion occurs. Using h instead of γ and rearranging terms, we can rewrite this constraint as

$$\beta\delta p\psi(p, q) \geq \frac{b\alpha}{h(p)}. \tag{2}$$

Suppose the pair (p, q) satisfies (2). If the economy is currently in the good state, the expected discounted cost of future reversions is $\beta\delta p\psi(p, q)$. Hence the equilibria that minimize expected discounted losses are those that solve

$$\min_{p,q \in (0, 1/2] \times [0, 1]} \beta\delta p\psi(p, q) \quad \text{s.t. (2).} \tag{3}$$

Proposition 1 characterizes the set of equilibria that minimize expected losses among all simple two-state Markov equilibria.

PROPOSITION   Let $f(\varepsilon)$ satisfy Assumption 1. Then

(i)   any pair $(p, q) \in (0, \frac{1}{2}] \times [0, 1]$ satisfying (2) characterizes a simple two-state Markov equilibrium;
(ii)   the set of such equilibria is nonempty if and only if (2) holds for $q = 0$, for some $p \in (0, \frac{1}{2}]$;
(iii) a pair (p^*, q^*) attains the minimum expected loss if and only if it solves (3), and a solution exists if the set of equilibria is nonempty;
(iv)   if (p^*, q^*) is a loss-minimizing pair and $q^* < 1$, then the expected loss per period, conditional on starting in the good state, is

$$C = \Lambda(0, 0) + \frac{b\alpha}{h(p^*)}; \tag{4}$$

(v)   if $f(\varepsilon)$ is a normal density, then the solution (p^*, q^*) is unique (if one exists) and $q^* = 0$.

The first and third claims summarize the discussion of (2) and (3). The second claim follows from the fact that ψ is decreasing in q. The fourth follows from the fact that if (p^*, q^*) is loss-minimizing and $q^* < 1$, then (2) holds with equality. If it did not, q^* could be increased, shortening

Figure 2 EQUILIBRIUM REVERSION PROBABILITIES

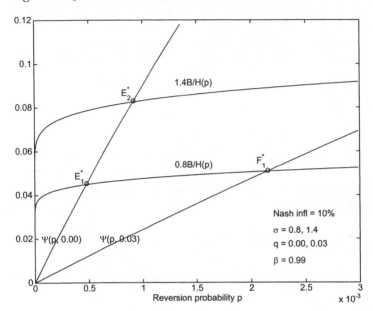

reversions and further reducing expected losses. To illustrate the last claim we turn to an example.

If $f_i(\cdot)$ is a normal $(0, \sigma_i^2)$ density, the associated hazard function is $h_i(p) = H(p)/\sigma_i$, where H is the hazard function for a normal $(0, 1)$. The function H is decreasing for $p \leq \frac{1}{2}$. (Recall that p is the probability in the *upper* tail.)

Figure 2 displays the function $\Psi(p, q; \beta) = \beta p \psi(p, q; \beta)$, for $\beta = 0.99$ and $q = 0.0, 0.03$; and the function $b\alpha/\delta h_i(p) = 2/\mu^N h_i(p)$, for $\mu^N = 10\%$ and $\sigma_i = 0.8, 1.4$. Suppose $\sigma = \sigma_1 = 0.8$. The points E_1^* and F_1^* occur where the $2/\mu^N h_1(p)$ curve crosses the $\Psi(p, q)$ curves, for $q = 0$ and 0.03. Call the x-coordinates of these points $p_1^{min}(q)$. For each q, the IC constraint (2) holds to the right of this point, so there are equilibria for $p \geq p_1^{min}(q)$. Reducing q extends the feasible range for p downward, reflecting the fact that the central bank's IC constraint involves a trade-off: longer punishments (lower q) permit less frequent punishments (lower p).

For each fixed q, the pair $(p_1^{min}(q), q)$ minimizes expected discounted costs. And since a pair of this form satisfies the IC constraint with equality, the expected discounted cost of future reversions is proportional to the quantity on the vertical axis. Hence the minimum expected loss overall is attained at $E_1^* = (p_1^*, q_1^*) = (p_1^{min}(0), 0)$.

The figure is qualitatively the same for any parameter values, provided the shock ε has a normal distribution, establishing claim (v). For $\sigma = \sigma_2$ $= 1.4$ the (unique) minimum-cost equilibrium occurs at the crossing point E_2^*, again with $q^* = 0$. Notice that increasing σ raises the minimum expected cost: a less informative signal requires a higher reversion probability p^*.

Figure 3a displays the optimal reversion probability p^* as a function of the standard deviation σ, for Nash inflation rates of 3%, 5%, 10%, and 20%. Looking along each curve, we see that increasing the standard deviation of the shock—reducing the accuracy of the signal—leads to more frequent reversions. Looking across curves, we see that increasing the Nash inflation rate—raising the cost of reversions—reduces the frequency of reversions. Figure 3b displays the corresponding thresholds for the inflation rate.

The conclusion that $q^* = 0$ is a direct consequence of the fact that the hazard function $h(p)$ for a normal density is a decreasing function. It holds for other distributions with that property, but not in general. For example, suppose $f(\varepsilon)$ has an exponential distribution in the relevant range,

$$f(\varepsilon) = \frac{1}{2}\eta e^{-\eta\varepsilon}, \qquad \varepsilon \geq 0.$$

Then the hazard rate is constant in the region of interest: $h(p) = \eta$, $p \leq \frac{1}{2}$. For this distribution the curve $2/\mu^N h(p)$ in Figure 2a is a horizontal line. Hence if there are any equilibria at all, there are many that attain the minimum expected cost, each with the form $(p^{\min}(q), q)$, $q \in Q^*$. These equilibria have switching probabilities that rise and fall together.

Alternatively, if f has an increasing hazard rate in the relevant range, then the cost-minimizing equilibrium is again unique and has $q = 1$.

2.4. OBSERVABILITY AND TIGHTNESS

With the characterization of the least-cost equilibria in hand, we can return to the central bank's problem of choosing between the two potential policy instruments, money growth and the exchange rate. Recall from (1) that $\Lambda(0, 0) = M = \sigma_\varepsilon^2 + \sigma_u^2 + b\alpha^2/2$ is the expected loss per period, ignoring reversions. Since no reversions occur under the exchange-rate regime and there is only one shock, the expected loss per period is simply

$$C^{\text{ex}} = \sigma_\zeta^2 + \frac{1}{2}b\alpha^2.$$

Figure 3 (a) OPTIMAL REVERSION PROBABILITIES; (b) OPTIMAL
INFLATION THRESHOLDS

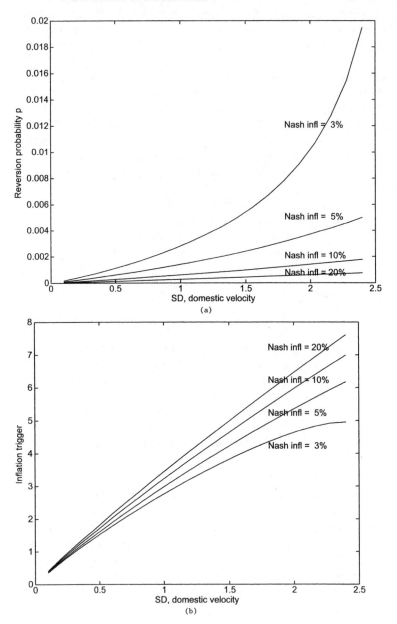

(a)

(b)

Under a money-growth regime the expected cost of reversions must also be included. Consider first the simple model of money growth. The velocity shock intervenes between the money growth rate and the signal, $s = \pi = \mu + v$, and it is the only shock. Hence $\varepsilon = v$ and $u = 0$, and Assumption 1 must hold for the velocity shock. Let h_v^* denote the hazard rate in a cost-minimizing equilibrium. Then the expected cost per period is

$$C^{mg} = \sigma_v^2 + \frac{1}{2}b\alpha^2 + \frac{b\alpha}{h_v^*}.$$

Comparing the two costs, we find that the exchange rate is preferred to money growth as an instrument if and only if

$$\sigma_\zeta^2 \leq \sigma_v^2 + \frac{b\alpha}{h_v^*}.$$

If $\sigma_\zeta^2 \leq \sigma_v^2$, then the exchange rate is obviously preferred: it is both tighter and more observable. If $\sigma_\zeta^2 > \sigma_v^2$, then the exchange rate is the preferred instrument if and only if the higher cost from its looser relationship with the target (the higher variance of its shock) is more than offset by the expected cost of reversions under a money-growth policy.

Figure 4 displays the tradeoff for $\beta = 0.99$, a Nash inflation rate of $\mu^N =$

Figure 4 INSTRUMENT CHOICE

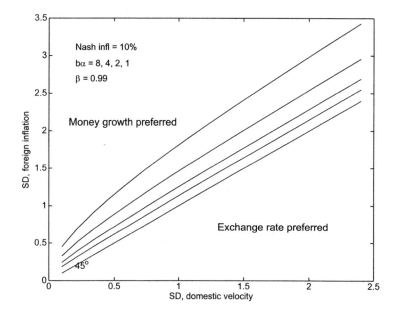

$b\alpha/a = 10\%$, and the four values $b\alpha = 1, 2, 4, 8$ for the Phillips-curve coefficient. [The corresponding weights on the shoe-leather cost of inflation, the first term in (1), are $a = 0.1, 0.2, 0.4, 0.8.$] The exchange rate is the preferred instrument along and below the 45° line, where the standard deviation of the foreign inflation shock is no greater than that of the domestic velocity shock. In addition it is preferred if the former is somewhat larger than the latter, with the exact position of the separating curve depending on the parameters.

A higher value for the Phillips-curve coefficient $b\alpha$ increases the central bank's incentive to deviate under a money-growth regime, increasing the size of the region where the exchange rate is preferred instrument. That coefficient measures the gain from surprise inflation, which in the model here is interpreted as arising because of monopolistic (rather than perfect) competition among producers (households). But it can have other interpretations as well. For example, it might represent the value of additional seignorage revenue, or the benefit from devaluing outstanding (nominal) debt.

For the complex model of money growth the signal is $s = \mu + \varepsilon$, where ε is the error in the bank's forecast of GDP growth, and Assumption 1 must hold for ε. Repeating the argument above and letting h_ε^* denote the optimal hazard rate, we find that

$$C^{\mathrm{mg}} = \sigma_\varepsilon^2 + \sigma_u^2 = \frac{1}{2}b\alpha^2 + \frac{b\alpha}{h_\varepsilon^*},$$

so the exchange rate is the preferred instrument if and only if

$$\sigma_\zeta^2 - \sigma_u^2 \le \sigma_\varepsilon^2 + \frac{b\alpha}{h_\varepsilon^*}.$$

If $\sigma_\zeta^2 \le \sigma_\varepsilon^2 + \sigma_u^2$, then the exchange rate is obviously preferred. Otherwise there is, as before, a trade-off between tightness and observability. Figure 4 still applies, with the axes relabeled: on the horizontal axis is σ_ε, and on the vertical is $\sqrt{\sigma_\zeta^2 - \sigma_u^2}$.

With a normal distribution for ε, the optimal punishment length is infinite: $q^* = 0$. Such an outcome strains the imagination: presumably a new central banker or a new institution altogether would be put in place in finite time. It is very easy to modify the model here to deliver that result, by adding a strictly positive lower bound, $q^0 > 0$, on the return probability. The argument above proceeds exactly as before (cf. Figure 2), and the (unique) equilibrium has $q^* = q^0$. The reversion length is random, and it is straightforward to calculate its expected value as a function of q^0. Since the additional restriction operates on the money growth instrument, the result is to enlarge the region of parameter space where the exchange rate is the preferred instrument.

3. Robustness

Not all governments are as benevolent and clever as a Ramsey government. The possibility that the government is "bad," which may mean greedy, incompetent, or myopic, creates difficulties for a "good" (Ramsey) government. Some of the difficulties are unavoidable: a legacy of large outstanding debt, bad legislation, etc. can be difficult to undo. In addition, the behavior of the private sector will be predicated on a certain apprehension about the nature of the administration currently in power. In this section we will show that if a "good" government cannot easily distinguish itself from a "bad" one, this mistrust by the private sector makes its task more onerous. In such an environment a simple policy rule can be very useful, even if it cannot respond to shocks in the environment. In the model here, the fact that a rule reduces or eliminates the potential damage done by a "bad" government has a very useful effect on private behavior. This effect far outweighs the small additional gain that a "good" government could attain with discretion. As will be shown, even a moderate probability that the government is "bad" makes the rule worthwhile.

Suppose that there are two types of governments, *Ramsey* and "bad." Reputation equilibria are delicate, and there are countless ways for the other type of government to deviate from the Ramsey policy. Here we will assume that the "bad" type is myopic, setting current tax rates to maximize current-period utility. The Ramsey government behaves in the usual fashion, raising revenue in a way that maximizes the expected discounted utility of the representative household. For simplicity, we will assume that the government's type is i.i.d.

The environment is adopted from Fischer's (1980) paper. Each household receives an endowment of goods that can be invested or consumed directly. Invested goods earn a return but are also subject to taxation. The household can also use labor to produce goods. The government must finance an exogenous expenditure sequence. The tension is between the government's short-run temptation to use a (nondistorting) capital levy to finance current expenditures, and the adverse effect such a policy has on the incentive to invest. The expenditure sequence is stochastic, and for simplicity is taken to be i.i.d.

First we study a setting where policy is discretionary. If the government is known to be the Ramsey type and the discount factor is sufficiently close to one, then the standard reputation argument applies. In the setting here, the Ramsey government uses a carefully calculated capital tax to finance part of spending and to provide insurance against the high expenditure shock. The capital tax varies with the expenditure level, but its expected value is low enough so that investment is worthwhile.

If the type of government is uncertain, but the probability of the myopic type is not too high, a reputation equilibrium still exists. The policy of the Ramsey government is qualitatively similar to the previous case. The main difference is that the Ramsey government must offer a high enough expected return on capital during the periods when it is in office to compensate the household for the fact that capital earns a negative expected return when the myopic government is in power. The policy adopted by the Ramsey government becomes rather odd, and expected utility declines as the probability of a myopic government increases. The Ramsey government is willing to continue participating in this equilibrium because abandoning it means that households stop investing, which entails a substantial cost. (For sufficiently high probabilities reputation equilibria cease to exist, but here we will focus on probabilities that are below that threshold.)

We then consider what happens if, instead of allowing the government discretion in setting fiscal policy each period, the society adopts a policy rule placing an upper bound on the capital tax. If the probability of the Ramsey type is sufficiently close to one, this rule reduces welfare, since the insurance feature of a variable capital tax is lost. But if the probability of the myopic type is high enough, the rule is welfare-enhancing.

3.1 THE ENVIRONMENT

Each period the household receives an endowment of goods, ω, and an endowment of time. It can invest all or part of its goods endowment in a productive activity, and it can hide the rest. Let $\theta \in [0, 1]$ denote the fraction of the goods endowment that is invested. Investments earn a rate of return $r > 0$, but they can also be taxed. Hidden goods earn no return but cannot be taxed. Time spent working produces goods according to the linear technology $q = w\ell$, where $w > 0$ is an implicit wage rate and ℓ is labor supply.

Households value private consumption goods c and time worked ℓ according to a utility function that is additively separable and linear in labor supply:

$$U = E\left\{ \sum_{t=0}^{\infty} \beta^t [u(c(t)) - \ell(t)] \right\}.$$

Assume u is strictly increasing, strictly concave, and twice differentiable, and $0 < \beta < 1$. Assume $u'((1 + r)\omega) \gg w$, so that the household chooses to work even if it is consuming its entire endowment, with interest, and faces a positive tax on labor income.

Government expenditure is exogenous and stochastic. For simplicity assume it takes only two values, $g_1 = 0$ and $g_2 = g > 0$, and that the realizations are i.i.d. Let $\pi_1 = \pi$ and $\pi_2 = 1 - \pi$ denote the probabilities.

In each period the government levies flat-rate taxes $\tau_k \in [0, 1 + r]$, $\tau_\ell \in [0, 1]$ on capital and on labor income. The government cannot issue debt, so its budget must be balanced each period. Assume

$$r\omega < (1 - \pi)g, \tag{5}$$

so that the required revenue cannot be raised with a capital tax that leaves the household with a positive expected return on investment. For simplicity assume in addition that $g < (1 + r)\omega$, so that the required revenue *can* be raised with a confiscatory capital tax. Finally, assume that g is small enough so that it can be financed entirely with a labor tax when the household hides its good endowment.

3.2 RAMSEY GOVERNMENT

First consider an economy in which it is known for sure that the government is the Ramsey type. We are interested in settings where there is a reputation equilibrium of the usual form. The tax policy in that equilibrium is the one that the Ramsey government would employ if it could commit ex ante to fixed, state-contingent tax rates. For discount factors β that are sufficiently close to unity there an equilibrium of this form, supported by the threat of a reversion to the one-shot Nash equilibrium.

Suppose the government could precommit, and consider the problem of choosing the optimal tax policy subject to the constraints imposed by household behavior. In this stationary environment with i.i.d. expenditure shocks and no state variables, the solution is a stationary tax policy $\{(\tau_{\ell i}, \tau_{ki}), i = 1, 2\}$ that maximizes the household's expected utility per period, where subscripts $i = 1, 2$ denote the values of the tax rates, consumption, etc. in the two states.

Suppose that the household has invested all of its endowment, and consider its problem after the state i has been realized and the current tax rates $(\tau_{ki}, \tau_{\ell i})$ are known. Its problem is

$$\max_{c_i, \ell_i}[u(c_i) - \ell_i] \tag{6}$$

s.t.　$c_i = (1 + r - \tau_{ki})\omega + (1 - \tau_{\ell i})w\ell_i,$　$i = 1, 2.$　(7)

The equilibrium allocation must also satisfy the market-clearing condition for goods:

$$c_i + g_i = w\ell_i + (1 + r)\omega, \qquad i = 1, 2;$$　(8)

and the government's budget constraint (redundant, by Walras' law) must hold:

$$g_i = \tau_{ki}\omega + \tau_{\ell i}w\ell_i, \qquad i = 1, 2.$$

Finally, notice that the household's net income gain from investment in state i is $(r - \tau_{ki})\omega$. The household is willing to invest its endowment if and only if the associated change in expected utility is positive. Hence investment occurs if and only if the capital tax satisfies the rate of return constraint

$$\sum_i \pi_i \, u'(c_i)\omega(r - \tau_{ki}) \geq 0.$$　(9)

The Ramsey government's problem is

$$\max \sum_i \pi_i[u(c_i) - \ell_i]$$

subject to (8), (9), and the constraints imposed by household optimization. As shown in Appendix A, the solution $\{\theta^R, (c_i^R, \ell_i^R, \tau_{ki}^R, \tau_{\ell i}^R), i = 1, 2\}$, with $\theta^R = 1$, has the following features:

(i)　consumption is the same in the two states, $c_1^R = c_2^R$;
(ii)　the labor tax is the same in the two states, $\tau_{\ell 1}^R = \tau_{\ell 2}^R$;
(iii)　labor supply is higher by g in the second state, $\ell_2^R = \ell_1^R + g$;
(iv)　the expected capital tax is equal to the rate of return, $\sum_i \pi_i \tau_{ki}^R = r$;
(v)　capital is subsidized when spending is low and taxed when it is high, $\tau_{k_1}^R < 0 < \tau_{k_2}^R$.

Features (i)–(iii) follow from the assumption that utility is linear in labor supply. Given (i), result (iv) is an immediate consequence of the rate-of-return restriction in (9). Result (v) is an instance of the principle developed in Zhu (1992) and in Chari, Christiano, and Kehoe (1994): the capital tax in a stochastic setting can act as a perfect substitute for state-contingent debt of the type discussed in Lucas and Stokey (1983).

As in the monetary model of the previous section, the Ramsey policy can be sustained as the outcome in a reputation equilibrium in which the behavior of the government is disciplined by the threat of reversion to the repeated one-shot Nash equilibrium. In the latter equilibrium households have no incentive to invest. They hoard their goods endowment and all spending is financed with contemporaneous labor taxes. If spending is low the labor tax rate is zero, $\tau_{\ell 1}^N = 0$. If spending is high the labor tax $\tau_{\ell 2}^N > 0$ is set at the minimum level needed to raise the required revenue g. Any capital tax policy that violates (9) can be used, but no revenue is collected from it.

Notice that there are temptations to deviate in both states of the world. In the low-spending state there is a one-time gain from setting both tax rates to zero, and in the high-spending state there is a one-time gain from using a large capital levy. But for β sufficiently close to one the Ramsey government resists both temptations.

3.3 MIXED TYPES ($\lambda > 0$)

The equilibrium described above is valid for an economy in which it is known with certainty that the government in office is a Ramsey government. Suppose instead that the government's type is i.i.d., and let λ be the probability of the myopic type. Let mx and Rx denote values under myopic and Ramsey governments respectively in this mixed environment. We will look at equilibria in which households still have an incentive to invest in the mixed economy, so $\theta^x = 1$. If λ is not too large and β is sufficiently close to one, such equilibria exist.

The behavior of the myopic government is straightforward. In the low-spending state it sets both tax rates to zero, $\tau_{k_1}^{mx} = \tau_{\ell 1}^{mx} = 0$; and in the high-spending state it raises all of the required revenue from a capital tax, setting the labor tax to zero: $\tau_{k2}^{mx} = g/\omega$ and $\tau_{\ell 2}^{mx} = 0$. The household's problem is as in (6)–(7). Since the labor tax is the same in both states, it follows immediately that consumption is the same in both states: $c_1^{mx} = c_2^{mx} = c^{mx}$. The labor supplies in the two states are then determined by (8).

In a world with a positive (but small enough) probability of a myopic government, the Ramsey government must alter its strategy, since otherwise households will not be willing to invest. Conditional on the myopic type holding office, the capital tax is $\tau_{k2}^{mx} = g/\omega$ with probability $1 - \pi$ and zero otherwise. Hence a household faces an expected utility loss of

$$L \equiv u'(c^{mx}) \left\{ \left[(1 - \pi)\frac{g}{\omega} - r \right] \omega \right\} > 0$$

if it invests its entire endowment. The assumption in (5) implies that the term in braces is positive. The Ramsey type must offset this loss by offering an expected gain when it is in office.

In particular, the Ramsey type must raise the subsidy on capital in the low-spending state and/or cut the capital tax in the high-spending state so that, averaging over both types of government, the household faces a nonnegative expected rate of return. Thus, in the mixed economy with probability λ of a myopic government, the rate-of-return constraint for the Ramsey government is

$$\sum_i \pi_i u'(c_i^R)\omega(r - \tau_{ki}^R) \geq \frac{\lambda}{1 - \lambda}L. \tag{10}$$

For $\lambda = 0$ this inequality reduces to the one in (9), but for $\lambda > 0$ the right side is positive and increasing in λ.

The problem of the Ramsey government in the mixed economy is as before, with (10) in place of (9). As shown in Appendix B, for any fixed $\lambda > 0$ the solution $\{\theta^{Rx}, (c_i^{Rx}, \ell_i^{Rx}, \tau_{ki}^{Rx}, \tau_{\ell i}^{Rx}), i = 1, 2\}$ retains many of the qualitative features of the solution for $\lambda = 0$. Properties (i)–(iii) are unchanged: consumption and the labor tax are the same across the two states, and labor supply is higher by g in the second state. The analogue of property (iv) says that (10) holds with equality. Property (v) continues to hold if λ is not too large. In principle, however, the Ramsey type might subsidize capital in both states if λ is large enough.

Changes in the probability of a myopic administration affect the allocation under the Ramsey government as one would expect: consumption c^{Rx} is decreasing in λ; the labor tax τ_ℓ^{Rx} is increasing in λ; and both capital taxes τ_{ki}^{Rx} are decreasing in λ. That is, the subsidy on capital in the low-spending state is larger, and the tax on capital in the high-spending state is smaller. Expected utility, conditional on a Ramsey government being in office, is decreasing in λ.

As λ rises, the Ramsey government must increase the distorting labor tax to subsidize capital more heavily when spending is low and to finance a greater share of expenditure when spending is high. These costs are endured because there is a substantial gain to maintaining the incentives to invest.

3.4 A POLICY RULE

Alternatively, society could adopt a simple policy rule mandating a cap on the capital tax that is low enough to ensure that households have an incentive to invest. In our simple model the optimal cap is $\bar{\tau}_k = r/(1 - \pi)$. Both the Ramsey and myopic types use the same policy under the rule. In the low-spending state tax rates are zero, $\tau_{k1}^u = \tau_{\ell 1}^u = 0$. In the high-spending state the capital tax is set at the mandated maximum, $\tau_{k2}^u = \bar{\tau}_k$, and the labor tax $\tau_{\ell 2}^u > 0$ at the lowest rate consistent with budget balance. Expected utility under this policy rule is not as high as under the Ramsey policy, but the rule is robust against the blunders of the myopic government.

3.5 AN EXAMPLE

In this section we will look at a simple numerical example that illustrates an important point: the difference in expected utility under the reputation equilibrium compared with the policy rule is quite modest, even if the government is certain to be the Ramsey type. In addition, expected utility in the reputation equilibrium declines as the probability of the myopic type rises, and eventually the policy rule dominates.By contrast, the expected utility gain from using the rule rather than enduring the one-shot Nash outcome is very substantial. This result reflects the fact that the rule was deliberately constructed to exploit a large potential gain, ignoring small ones.

Utility is logarithmic, $u(c) = a \ln c$, and the parameter values are

$$a = 10, \quad w = 1, \quad \omega = 3, \quad r = 0.2, \quad g = 2, \quad \pi = \tfrac{1}{2}.$$

The discount factor β is assumed to be sufficiently close to one so that the reputation equilibrium exists.

Figure 5a–d displays the equilibrium outcomes as the probability of the myopic type increases from 0% to 70%. Obviously, nothing happens to the policies or outcomes under the myopic type or under the policy rule. What do change are the policies adopted by the Ramsey type and the weighted averages in the economy with mixed types.

Figure 5a displays the tax rates. Under the myopic type the average capital tax rate is 33% (an average of 67% and 0%), well above the 20% rate of return on capital. The labor tax is zero. Under the Ramsey type the average capital tax is 20% (an average of 51% and −11%) with $\lambda = 0$ and declines monotonically as λ rises. The labor tax is positive and increases with λ, offsetting the declining revenues from the capital tax. The reason for this pattern is clear: the Ramsey type adjusts its policy to maintain the incentive for households to invest. Under the policy rule the aver-

Figure 5 (a) TAX RATES; (b) CAPITAL-TAX REVENUE; (c) CONSUMPTION;
(d) EXPECTED UTILITY

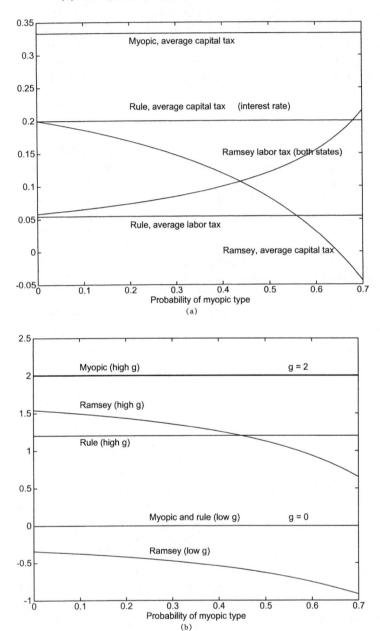

Figure 5 CONTINUED

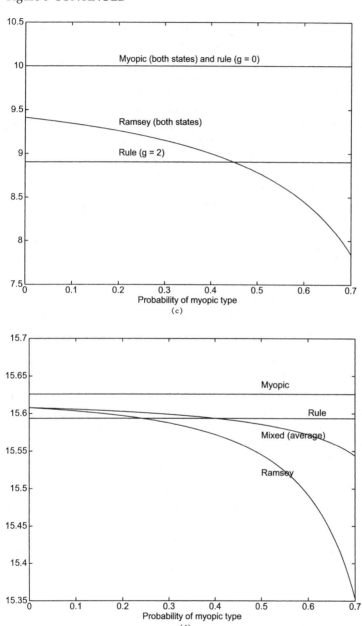

age capital tax is 20% (an average of 40% and 0%), and the average labor tax is a little over 5%.

Figure 5b displays revenue from the capital tax. Recall that government expenditure is 2 or 0. Under the myopic type revenue from the capital tax exactly covers spending: it is 2 or 0, depending on the state, and the labor tax is not used. Under the Ramsey type, if $\lambda = 0$ revenue from the capital tax is 1.55 or -0.35, depending on the state. As λ increases, both figures decline (the subsidy in the zero-spending state gets larger). Under the policy rule the revenue from the capital tax is $\bar{\tau}_k \omega = r\omega/(1 - \pi) = 1.2$ or 0, and the labor tax is used when spending is high.

Figure 5c displays consumption. Consumption is the same in both states under the myopic or Ramsey types, since each type sets the same labor tax in both states. Consumption falls rather sharply under the Ramsey government as λ rises. This change is a direct consequence of the rising labor tax. Under the policy rule consumption differs in the two states, since the labor tax varies.

Figure 5d displays expected utility under the myopic and Ramsey governments, as well as the weighted average, and under the policy rule. The rule delivers higher expected utility if $\lambda > 40\%$.

The figures for the one-shot Nash equilibrium are not displayed, since they are—literally—off the charts. Households do not invest, so there is no interest income and all revenue must be raised from the labor tax. When $g = 0$, labor supply is 7 and consumption is 10. When $g = 2$, the labor tax is 40%, labor supply is 5, and consumption is 10. The expected utility is 14.5. This dismal outcome deters the Ramsey type from abandoning the reputation equilibrium for reasonable β-values.

This simple model illustrates several points. The first is quantitative. A policy rule that is simple but well designed can capture much of the benefit available from commitment. Here the first-order effect comes from maintaining the incentive to invest, as can be seen by comparing expected utility under the Nash regime and under the policy rule. The simple rule cannot capture the further gains available from implicit insurance, but these are much smaller. Indeed, they vanish altogether if λ is large enough.

In addition, the behavior of the Ramsey government in this simple model suggests that the political-economy issues surrounding the reputational equilibrium cannot be neglected. Running for election on the Ramsey platform in this economy would be a difficult task indeed!

Finally, note that the damage a "bad" government can inflict is much larger if capital is long-lived. To keep the model here simple, capital was assumed to last for only one period. If capital is durable and expensive, "bad" government behavior may have much worse consequences.

4. Conclusion

To conclude it is useful to touch on some issues that the two formal models do not address. We begin with issues related to the monetary model.

As noted above, and as many authors have emphasized, models like the one analyzed here have a vast multiplicity of equilibria. We compared monetary instruments by looking at the best equilibrium within a certain class. But why should we suppose that the best equilibrium is likely to arise? In addressing this very practical question, it is useful to keep in mind that many of the equilibria in these games have similar outcome paths. In particular, there are many equilibria in which the bank plays the Ramsey strategy as long as its reputation is intact.

These equilibria differ in their description of how the bank loses its reputation, resulting in a reversion to a bad outcome, and in the precise description of the nature of the reversion. Here we assumed that one-shot Nash behavior prevailed during reversions and that the end of a reversion episode was linked to an observation of the signal, but neither feature is critical. For example, the most severe punishment could be used instead of one-shot Nash. And even if one-shot Nash is used, the reversions could be of fixed length, of completely random length, allow returns to the good state as a complicated function of current and past signals, etc. Indeed, the return probability could be interpreted as the (random) length of time required to reorganize the central bank or to install a new head of the bank in office. As an empirical matter it would be very difficult to distinguish sharply among these equilibria. They differ only in their descriptions of reversion behavior, and reversions are (necessarily) rare.

More importantly, the model's description of behavior during a reversion episode seems better taken with several grains of salt. During good times the central bank's behavior is stable and predictable. This is also roughly true in practice, and the model captures this behavior quite well. Reversions are not so precisely scripted, in reality or in the model. Choosing among reputation equilibria (on a theoretical level) and distinguishing among them (empirically) are equally difficult tasks. But they are also unimportant tasks, in the sense that the important aspect of behavior in the model is the robust feature shared by all the reputation equilibria, behavior during good times.

Having argued that choosing among reputation equilibria is not terribly important, there remains the issue of how reputations are established. Formal models that permit reputation equilibria always have a large multiplicity of other equilibria as well. Indeed, simply repeating the bad outcome is one possibility. As an empirical matter, countries with stable governments often manage to build and maintain reputations for good behavior in areas where it matters most: the public debt is honored; capital taxes are stable and not too high; intellectual-property rights are protected by patents, copyrights, and trademarks; and monetary policy is fairly stable. Reputations are central in explaining good outcomes in settings like these, where the policymaker has substantial discretion, but on a theoretical level little is understood about how reputations are built, how credibility is established.[11]

Since theory provides little or no guidance here, it may be more fruitful to view this as an empirical issue. Perhaps this is the role of the central banker (an individual) as opposed to the central bank (an institution). A successful central banker is one who can steer the economy toward a good equilibrium. Success requires that the central bank take the appropriate actions, but that is not enough. The central banker must convince the private sector that the bank will behave that way. Indeed, he (or she) must persuade the private sector that there is a commonly held belief that the bank will behave appropriately. Perhaps "leadership" is the name we give to the elusive qualities that enable some individuals to succeed at this task.

Initially establishing a reputation for good behavior is a critical task for a central banker. Adopting a more observable instrument for conducting policy, pegging an exchange rate rather than using the money growth rate, may ease the banker's task during the critical initial phase when he is attempting to establish a reputation for good behavior. Establishing a currency board is another way to accomplish the same task, in the sense that it acts as an easy-to-monitor instrument for conducting monetary policy.[12]

Of course, in the long run monetary and fiscal policy are linked through the government's budget constraint. Good monetary policy is simply infeasible without a conservative (balanced budget) fiscal policy. A government that runs substantial deficits, with no prospect of surpluses to retire the accumulating debt, will eventually fail in its efforts to float new bond issues. The problem is exacerbated if, as is typically the case, old debt must be rolled over as well. At some point the only feasible options are outright default, a large devaluation, or both. A government facing that situation typically finds the seignorage revenue from a large devaluation too attractive to resist, and monetary policy becomes the fiscal policy of last resort.[13]

11. See Faust and Svensson (2001) for an interesting exception.
12. Rogoff (1985) suggests an intriguing solution: simply appointing a central banker who places more weight on price stability.
13. See Zarazaga (1995) for a very interesting model in which episodic bouts of high inflation occur when decentralized fiscal policy is combined with centralized monetary policy.

The model analyzed here focuses on an issue that is critical for some central banks: those for which establishing and maintaining a reputation is a first priority. After that task has been largely accomplished, as it has been in the United States, in Japan, and elsewhere, other issues take center stage: which targets should be used, which monetary aggregates should be given the greatest attention, etc. These are important issues, but only after a reputation for good conduct has been fairly well established. If a bridge is in danger of collapsing, there is little point in repairing potholes. Only after the structural problems have been addressed is it useful to think about the quality of the road surface.

The model of fiscal policy analyzed above illustrates one danger from allowing too much discretion. The myopic government in the model can be thought of as representing administrations subject to a variety of short-run political pressures, arising from many possible sources. The model highlights the fact that a well-designed policy rule is one that pays attention to first-order effects (here, the incentive to invest), although it may neglect more subtle issues (here, the insurance available from a more subtle capital tax).

The model here has a representative household, but the same issue arises when there is heterogeneity. Differences among households create some divergence in views about fiscal policy, but if those differences are modest, there may still be a fair amount of common ground. There may be a set of policy rules that are advantageous to all, even if there is disagreement about the *optimum optimorum.*

The essence of good government is to design institutions that permit solution of the repeated moral-hazard problem. The goal of the models here has been to provide some insight into that problem, and how it affects decisions about policy regimes.

Appendix A

The set of simple two-state Markov equilibria for the money growth model is described in detail here. First the incentive compatibility (IC) constraints for the central bank are derived. Then the equilibria that minimize total expected discounted costs are characterized.

Suppose the economy is in the good state. Then households expect the central bank to permit money growth (net of real output growth) at the Ramsey rate, $\mu = \mu^g = 0$, so they set wages at $w^g = 0 + \alpha$. Households then observe the signal s and the actual inflation rate π. Households use a one-sided threshold to decide if the bank has deviated. If the signal lies below the threshold, $s \leq S^g$, they assume that the central bank has behaved as anticipated, and the state next period is good. Otherwise they assume the central bank has deviated, and the state next period is bad. In equilibrium the central bank sets $\mu = \mu^g = 0$, so $s \leq S^g$ if and only if $\varepsilon \leq S^g$.

When the economy is in the bad state, households expect the central bank to set money growth at the Nash rate, $\mu = \mu^b = \mu^N$, so they set wages at $w^b = \mu^N + \alpha$. They then observe s and π. Households use a two-sided test in the bad state, so the state next period is good if and only if the signal lies within the tolerance level set by the test, $s \in [\mu^N - \varepsilon^b, \mu^N + \varepsilon^b]$. Since the central bank sets money growth at the Nash rate μ^N, the signal s lies in the acceptable region if and only if $\varepsilon \in [-\varepsilon^b, \varepsilon^b]$.

In a two-state Markov equilibrium the expected discounted value of current and future losses from any period on depends only on the current state. Let c^g and c^b denote those expected values, and let

$$\Delta \equiv c^b - c^g$$

denote the difference between the two.

Fix $S^g \geq 0$, and suppose that the economy is in the good state. The Ramsey rate of money growth $\mu^g = 0$ is incentive-compatible for the central bank if and only if any other growth rate $\mu \neq 0$ leads to a (weakly) greater sum of current and future expected losses. If money grows at the rate μ, then the expected loss in the current period is $\Lambda(0, \mu)$. The state next period, and hence the payoffs from next period on, depend only on the signal s that is observed today. If money grows at the rate at μ and the signal s is observed, the error term is $\varepsilon = s - \mu$. Therefore, if S^g is the threshold for the accept region, the expected cost from next period on is

c^g if $\varepsilon \leq S^g - \mu$,

c^b if $\varepsilon > S^g - \mu$.

Hence the Ramsey growth rate $\mu = 0$ is incentive compatible for the central bank in the good state if and only if

$$\Lambda(0, \mu) + \beta\{F(S^g - \mu)c^g + [1 - F(S^g - \mu)]c^b\}$$
$$\geq \Lambda(0, 0) + \beta \{F(S^g - 0)c^g + [1 - F(S^g - 0)]c^b\}, \qquad \text{all } \mu.$$

Rearranging terms and using the definition of Δ, we can write this constraint as

$$\beta\Delta[F(S^g) - F(S^g - \mu)] \geq \Lambda(0, 0) - \Lambda(0, \mu)$$
$$= b\alpha\mu - \mu^2, \qquad \text{all } \mu. \tag{11}$$

The expression on the left side of (11) is zero at $\mu = 0$. Under Assumption 1 it is continuous and increasing in μ, convex for $\mu < S^g$, and concave for $\mu > S^g$. The expression on the right side is also zero at $\mu = 0$, and from (1) we see that it is increasing for $\mu < b\alpha$, decreasing for $\mu > b\alpha$, and everywhere concave. Hence (11) holds near $\mu = 0$ if and only if

$$\beta \Delta f(S^g) \geq b\alpha. \tag{12}$$

Condition (12) is the basic IC constraint that equilibria must satisfy. The interpretation is straightforward: $b\alpha$ is the marginal gain from increasing the expected inflation rate in the current period, $f(S^g)$ is the marginal increase in the probability of reversion to the bad state from that change, and $\beta \Delta$ is the discounted expected loss if a reversion occurs.

Similarly, the Nash rate of money growth, $\mu^b = \mu^N$, is incentive-compatible for the central bank in the bad state if and only if any other growth rate $\mu \neq \mu^N$ leads to (weakly) greater expected losses. Hence the required condition is

$$\beta \Delta \{[F(\varepsilon^b) - F(-\varepsilon^b)] - [F((\mu^N - \mu) + \varepsilon^b) - F((\mu^N - \mu) - \varepsilon^b)]\}$$
$$\geq \Lambda(\mu^N, \mu^N) - \Lambda(\mu^N, \mu), \quad \text{all } \mu.$$

Under Assumption 1 the left-hand side is strictly positive for all $\mu \neq \mu^N$, and it follows immediately from the definition of μ^N that the right-hand side is negative for all $\mu \neq \mu^N$. Hence any value $\varepsilon^b \geq 0$ satisfies the incentive constraint for the bad state.

For an equilibrium characterized by (S^g, ε^b), the probability of a reversion to the bad state (along the equilibrium outcome path) is $p = 1 - F(S^g)$, and the probability of a return to the good state is $q = F(\varepsilon^b) - F(-\varepsilon^b)$. Under Assumption 1 the relationship between the thresholds (S^g, ε^b) and the probabilities (p, q) is invertible, so we can formulate the problem in terms of the latter. Thus, the next step is to solve for Δ in terms of the probabilities (p, q).

Suppose (p, q) is an equilibrium pair. In equilibrium, the money growth rate in the good state is $\mu^g = 0$, and the probability of an accidental reversion is p. Hence the expected discounted value of current and future losses satisfies the recursive relation

$$c^g = \Lambda(0, 0) + \beta[c^g + p\Delta]. \tag{13}$$

Similarly, the money growth rate in the bad state is $\mu^b = \mu^N$, and $1 - q$ is the probability of remaining in the bad state. Hence c^b satisfies the recursive relation

$$c^b = \Lambda(\mu^N, \mu^N) + \beta[c^g + (1 - q)\Delta].$$

The difference between the two is

$$\Delta(p, q) = \frac{\delta}{1 - \beta(1 - p - q)}$$
$$= \delta\psi(p, q), \tag{14}$$

where $\delta = \Lambda(\mu^N, \mu^N) - \Lambda(0, 0)$.

Since $f(S^g) = \gamma(p)$, it then follows from (12) that the Ramsey rate of money growth is incentive-compatible in the good state for any $p, q \in [0,1]$ satisfying

$$\gamma(p)\beta\delta\psi(p, q) \geq b\alpha. \tag{15}$$

Since f is symmetric, so is γ. Hence if (15) holds for $\hat{p} \geq \frac{1}{2}$, it also holds for $p = 1 - \hat{p} \leq \frac{1}{2}$, and we can limit attention to p-values in the upper half of the distribution, $p \in (0, \frac{1}{2}]$.

Hence if the density $f(\varepsilon)$ satisfies Assumption 1, there exists a simple two-state Markov equilibrium for any pair $p \in (0, \frac{1}{2}]$ and $q \in [0, 1]$ satisfying (15). Since $\psi(p, q)$ is decreasing in q, for fixed p, if (15) holds anywhere, it holds for $q = 0$, establishing parts (a) and (b) of the proposition.

Substituting from (14) into (13), we find that expected cost per period in the (p, q) equilibrium is

$$(1 - \beta)c^g(p, q) = \Lambda(0, 0) + \beta p\delta\psi(p, q).$$

Hence expected costs are minimized if and only if (p, q) solves (3), establishing part (c) of the proposition.

Appendix B

Ramsey behavior for the tax model is characterized here. The cases $\lambda = 0$ and $\lambda > 0$ are similar and can be treated together.

It is convenient first to reformulate the problem as one of choosing the allocation $\{(c_i, \ell_i), i = 1, 2\}$ and the capital tax rates $\{\tau_{ki}, i = 1, 2\}$. To this end, note that the condition for the consumer's maximum is

$$(1 - \tau_{\ell i})wu'(c_i) - 1 = 0, \qquad i = 1, 2. \tag{16}$$

Multiply the budget constraint (7) by $u'(c_i)$ and substitute from (16) to get

$$u'(c_i)[c_i - (1 + r - \tau_{ki})\omega] - \ell_i = 0, \qquad i = 1, 2. \tag{17}$$

The constraints for the Ramsey government's problem are (8), (9) or (10), and (17). Let $\pi_i\mu_i$, ϕ, and $\pi_i\lambda_i$ be the multipliers for the three constraints. Then the conditions for a maximum are

$$0 = u_i' + \lambda_i\{u_i'' \cdot [c_i - (1 + r - \tau_{ki})\omega] + u_i'\} - \mu_i - \phi u_i''\omega[\tau_{ki} - r],$$

$$0 = -1 - \lambda_i + \mu_i w,$$

$$0 = (\lambda_i - \phi)u_i'\omega,$$

$i = 1, 2$. The last two equations imply

$$\lambda_i = \phi \text{ and } \mu_i = \frac{1 + \phi}{w}, \qquad i = 1, 2.$$

Then substituting into the first equation gives

$$(1 + \phi)\left(u_i' - \frac{1}{w}\right) + \phi(c_i - \omega)u_i'' = 0, \qquad i = 1, 2,$$

which suggests a solution with the same private consumption level in the two states, $c_1 = c_2 = c^R$. The remaining task is to find values for $(c^R, \{\ell_i^R, \tau_{ki}^R, i = 1, 2\})$ that satisfy the constraints, (8), (9) or (10), and (17).

Use the market-clearing condition (8) to write labor supply in the two states as

$$\ell_i^R = \frac{1}{w}[c^R - (1 + r)\omega + g_i], \qquad i = 1, 2. \tag{18}$$

Then use this fact and the budget constraint (17) to obtain

$$\tau_{ki}^R \omega u' = (1 - wu')\ell_i^R + g_i u', \qquad i = 1, 2. \tag{19}$$

The rate of return constraint (9) or (10) holds with equality.

Since consumption is the same in the two states, the rate of return constraint is

$$u'(c^{Rx})\omega\left(r - \sum_i \tau_{ki}^{Rx}\right) \geq \frac{\lambda}{1 - \lambda}L.$$

Notice that since consumption is different under the two types of government, expected returns must be weighted by marginal utilities as well as probabilities.

Hence

$$\omega u' \sum_i \pi_i \tau_{ki}^R = \omega u'r - \frac{\lambda}{1 - \lambda}L. \tag{20}$$

Taking the probability-weighted sum of the two equations in (19), substituting from (20), and using the fact that $\ell_2 = \ell_1 + g/w$, we obtain

$$r\omega u' - \Lambda = (1 - wu')\ell_1^R + \pi_2\frac{g}{w}.$$

Using (18), we find that c^R satisfies

$$r\omega u' - \Lambda = \left(\frac{1}{w} - u'\right)[c^R - (1 + r)\omega] + \pi_2\frac{g}{w}.$$

The labor supplies ℓ_1^R, ℓ_2^R can then be determined from (18), the capital tax rates from (19), and the labor tax—which is the same in both states—from (16).

REFERENCES

Atkeson, A., and P. J. Kehoe. (2001). The advantage of transparent instruments of monetary policy. Federal Reserve Bank of Minneapolis Staff Report 297.

Barro, R. J., and D. B. Gordon. (1983). Rules, discretion and reputation in a model of monetary policy. Journal of Monetary Economics 12:101–121.

Canzoneri, M. B. (1985). Monetary policy games and the role of private information. American Economic Review, 75:1056–1070.

Chari, V. V., L. J. Christiano, and P. J. Kehoe. (1994). Optimal fiscal policy in a real business cycle model. Journal of Political Economy 102:617–652.

————, and P. J. Kehoe. (1990). Sustainable plans. *Journal of Political Economy* 98: 783–802.

————, ————, and E. C. Prescott. (1989). Time consistency and policy. In *Modern Business Cycle Theory*, R. J. Barro (ed.). Harvard University Press.

Clarida, R., J. Gali, and M. Gertler. (1999). The science of monetary policy: A new Keynesian perspective. *Journal of Economic Literature* 37:1661–1707.

Cole, H., and L. Ohanian. (2001). New Deal policies and the persistence of the Great Depression. Federal Reserve Bank of Minneapolis.

Faust, J., and L. E. O. Svensson. (2001). Transparency and credibility: Monetary policy with unobserved goals. *International Economic Review* 42.

Fischer, S. (1980). Dynamics inconsistency, cooperation and the benevolent dissembling government. *Journal of Economic Dynamics and Control* 2:91–108.

Friedman, M. (1948). A monetary and fiscal framework for economic stability. *American Economic Review* 38:245–264. Reprinted in M. Friedman, *Essays in Positive Economics*, University of Chicago Press, 1953.

Goodfriend, M. (1986). Monetary mystique: Secrecy and central banking. *Journal of Monetary Economics* 17:63–92.

Green, E. J., and R. H. Porter. (1984). Noncooperative collusion under imperfect price information. *Econometrica* 52:87–100.

Ireland, P. N. (1997). Sustainable monetary policies. *Journal of Economic Dynamics and Control* 22:87–108.

————. (1999). Does the time-consistency problem explain the behavior of inflation in the United States? *Journal of Monetary Economics* 44:279–291.

Kydland, F. E., and E. C. Prescott. (1977). Rules rather than discretion: The inconsistency of optimal plans. *Journal of Political Economy* 85:473–491.

Lucas, R. E., and N. L. Stokey. (1983). Optimal fiscal and monetary policy in an economy without capital. *Journal of Monetary Economics* 12:55–93.

McCallum, B. T. (1999). Issues in the design of monetary policy rules. In *Handbook of Macroeconomics*, J. B. Taylor and M. Woodford (eds.). Elsevier.

Persson, T., and G. Tabellini. (1994). Introduction. In *Monetary and Fiscal Policy, Volume 1: Credibility*. Cambridge, MA: The MIT Press.

Phelan, C. (2001). Public trust and government betrayal. Federal Reserve Bank of Minneapolis Working Paper.

Poole, W. (1970). Optimal choice of monetary instruments in a simple stochastic macro model. *Quarterly Journal of Economics* 84:197–216.

————. (1985). The optimal degree of commitment to a monetary target. *Quarterly Journal of Economics* 100:1169–1190.

————. (1987). Reputational constraints on monetary policy. *Carnegie-Rochester Series on Public Policy* 26:141–182.

Rogoff, K. (1989). Reputation, coordination, and monetary policy. In *Modern Business Cycle Theory*, R. J. Barro (ed.). Harvard University Press, pp. 83–96.

Stokey, N. L. (1991). Credible public policy. *Journal of Economic Dynamics and Control* 15:627–656.

Zarazaga, C. E. J. M. (1995). Recurrent hyperinflations in a dynamic game with imperfect monitoring in the appropriation of seignorage. Working Paper, Federal Reserve Bank of Dallas.

Zhu, Xiaodong. (1992). Optimal fiscal policy in a stochastic growth model. *Journal of Economic Theory* 58:250–289.

Comment

PETER N. IRELAND
Boston College and NBER

1. Introduction

In this paper, Nancy Stokey presents two examples in which the time-consistency problem arises in a macroeconomic policymaking context. I consider these two examples to be extremely well chosen, for several reasons. First, each example deals with an important problem—the choice of a monetary policy instrument or the choice of a capital income tax rate—that is of considerable interest in and of itself. Second, each serves to introduce us to some powerful analytic techniques that recently have been developed by researchers working at the frontiers of economic science. The examples show us how far this branch of the literature has come, from a technical perspective, in the twenty-five years since the publication of Kydland and Prescott's (1977) original paper.

But, third and perhaps most important of all, I consider these two examples to be well chosen because each uses a model that shares its most basic features with all of the other models that have been developed in the literature that builds on Kydland and Prescott (1977). Thus, each of Nancy's models has implications for a wide range of issues that have already been studied extensively, and, by the same token, each remains silent on some important issues that have yet to be fully discussed, much less satisfactorily resolved, in the literature as it stands now.

In fact, because Nancy's models are so representative of others from this branch of the literature, I will be able to use one of them here in my discussion to provide answers of my own to two more basic and fundamental questions. First, what have we learned about the time-consistency problem in the twenty-five years since Kydland and Prescott (1977)? And second, what more might we hope to learn about the problem over the next twenty-five years?

2. The Model

My model is a simplified version of one of Nancy's: the model that she uses to study the trade-off between tightness and observability in the choice of a monetary policy instrument. My version of the model is simplified in that it eliminates the random and unobservable elements that play a key role in Nancy's analysis, but are less essential for my purposes. For the most part, I borrow my notation directly from Nancy's paper, although I make a few minor changes here and there, when they serve to make the results cleaner and easier to understand.

My model describes the behavior of a central bank, which chooses the rate of price inflation π, and a representative household, whose actions determine the rate of wage inflation w. As explained in more detail below, the representative household sets the rate of wage inflation based on its expectations of the central bank's choice of π. In this model, therefore, the variable w also serves as a convenient proxy for expected inflation.

The central bank's objectives are summarized by the single-period return or payoff function

$$R(\pi; w) = -\left(\frac{1}{2}\pi^2 + \frac{b}{2}(w - \pi + \alpha)^2\right),$$

where the parameters b and α are both nonnegative. The first term in this objective function captures the costs of inflation or, more precisely, penalizes deviations of the inflation rate π from the central bank's target of zero. To interpret the second term, consider the expectational Phillips curve

$$U = U^n - (\pi - w),$$

where U denotes the actual rate of unemployment, where U^n denotes the natural rate of unemployment, and where, since w measures expected inflation, $\pi - w$ serves as a measure of surprise inflation. Then

$$w - \pi + \alpha = U - (U^n - \alpha),$$

indicating that, according to the objective function R, the central bank sets a target $U^n - \alpha$ for the unemployment rate that lies *below* the natural rate. The parameter b measures the weight that the central bank places on achieving this goal for unemployment, relative to its goal for inflation.

The representative household in this model has a very simple objective: it wishes to set w as close as possible to the central bank's choice of π. The representative household has rational expectations, which here in the absence of shocks translates into perfect foresight. Thus, the household always accomplishes its goal by setting w exactly equal to π.

This condition, $w = \pi$, must always hold in equilibrium: it summarizes the implications of the household's optimizing behavior. What Kydland and Prescott's (1977) original paper teaches us is that macroeconomic outcomes depend critically on whether or not the central bank also views this equilibrium condition as a constraint that links its choice of π to the representative household's choice of w. To see this, let's consider the two basic cases.

CASE 1: COMMITMENT   In this first case, the central bank has the willingness and the ability to precommit to a choice for π at the beginning of the period, before the household embeds its expectations into a particular choice of w. Since the central bank moves first, it views the equilibrium condition $w = \pi$ as a constraint that links its choice of π to a subsequent setting for w. In this case, therefore, the central bank solves the constrained optimization problem

$$\max_{\pi} R(\pi; w) \quad \text{subject to} \quad w = \pi.$$

The first-order condition for this problem implies that the optimal inflation rate with commitment, denoted by π^c, equals zero:

$$\pi^c = 0.$$

When the central bank precommits to a choice for π, it recognizes that it is losing any ability it might otherwise have to surprise the representative household and thereby exploit the Phillips curve. Hence, in this case with commitment, the central bank abandons any idea of pushing unemployment below the natural rate, and instead focuses exclusively on achieving its goal of zero inflation.

CASE 2: NO COMMITMENT   In this second case, the central bank is either unwilling or unable to precommit, and effectively makes its choice of π after the representative household has embedded its expectations into a particular choice of w. Since the central bank moves second, it no longer perceives $w = \pi$ as a constraint. Instead, the central bank simply takes w as given, and solves the unconstrained optimization problem

$$\max_{\pi} R(\pi; w).$$

The first-order condition for this problem dictates that the central bank's optimal choice without commitment, denoted by π^{nc}, is given by

$$\pi^{nc} = \frac{b}{1 + b}(w + \alpha).$$

In equilibrium, however, the condition $w = \pi$ must still hold: in particular, the representative household perfectly anticipates the central bank's actions, and sets $w = \pi^{nc}$. Combining this equilibrium condition with the central bank's first-order condition reveals that in this case without commitment,

$$\pi^{nc} = b\alpha \geq 0.$$

Comparing the outcomes with and without commitment, $\pi^c = 0$ and $\pi^{nc} = b\alpha \geq 0$, serves to crystalize Kydland and Prescott's (1977) original message. The central bank that is either unwilling or unable to precommit to a choice of π finds itself tempted to exploit the expectational Phillips curve, in an effort to achieve its goal of pushing unemployment below the natural rate. The representative household has rational expectations, however, and understands that the central bank faces this temptation to inflate. The household, therefore, builds these inflationary expectations into its wage-setting decisions, so that unemployment remains at its natural rate. The central bank's efforts to exploit the Phillips curve lead only to a suboptimally high rate of inflation.

3. What Have We Learned since Kydland and Prescott (1977)?

But what else have we learned about the time-consistency problem in the twenty-five years since the publication of Kydland and Prescott's (1977) original paper? Comparing the outcomes $\pi^c = 0$ and $\pi^{nc} = b\alpha$ immediately reveals that in this simple version of Nancy's model, $b\alpha$ conveniently measures the inflationary bias that results when the central bank does not precommit to its choice for π. This expression, $b\alpha$, also suggests that there are at least two promising strategies that policymakers can use to minimize the inflationary bias, and thereby improve welfare.

One possibility involves setting the parameter α equal to zero, that is, instructing the central bank to stop targeting an unemployment rate that lies below the natural rate. McCallum (1995) argues passionately in favor of this solution to the central bank's time-consistency problem, and Blinder (1997) suggests that in practice, Federal Reserve officials have acted to minimize the importance of the time-consistency problem by behaving as if $\alpha = 0$. In fact, when $\alpha = 0$ in the simple model considered here, the time-consistency problem vanishes: outcomes with and without commitment coincide.

A second possibility involves setting the parameter b equal to zero, that is, instructing the central bank to stop caring so much about unemployment in the first place. This proposed solution to the time-consistency problem corresponds, of course, to Rogoff's (1985) suggestion that the appointment of a conservative central banker can lead to preferred outcomes in cases where monetary precommitment is impossible. And again, in the context of this simple model, outcomes with and without commitment coincide when $b = 0$.

Much of the recent literature that builds on Kydland and Prescott's (1977) original study focuses on the choice between these two solutions to the time-consistency problem for monetary policymaking. As noted above, both solutions work perfectly well in the context of the simple nonstochastic model used here. However, in more complicated models where random shocks give rise to a trade-off between the *variability* as well as the *levels* of inflation on one hand and unemployment on the other, Clarida, Gali, and Gertler (1999), Herrendorf and Lockwood (1997), and Svensson (1997) find that in addition to the *inflationary bias* that arises here, a *stabilization bias* also emerges in the absence of commitment: the discretionary central bank works too hard to stabilize unemployment, and not hard enough to stabilize inflation, in response to the shocks that hit the economy.

All three of these recent papers demonstrate that while the inflationary bias vanishes when $\alpha = 0$, so that the central bank's target for unemployment coincides with the natural rate, the stabilization bias remains. All three of these papers also suggest that the alternative solution of appointing a conservative central banker, with a lower value of b, can work to minimize both the inflationary bias and the stabilization bias, especially in cases where the conservative central banker is also offered an inflation contract of the kind first proposed by Walsh (1995). This, in my view, represents one of the most important lessons to have come out of the literature that builds on Kydland and Prescott (1977): that in situations where the time-consistency problem arises, it can be desirable to appoint policymakers whose preferences or incentives differ systematically from those of society as a whole.

In the U.S. economy, therefore, consider Federal Reserve Chairmen Volker and Greenspan, both of whom might reasonably be described as conservative in the Rogoffian sense of caring more about inflation, and less about unemployment, than the average American consumer or worker. It is certainly legitimate to ask whether, in a representative democracy like ours, it is really appropriate to give men like Volker and Greenspan power over such an important component of macroeconomic policy. The literature that builds on Kydland and Prescott (1977), however, provides us with a compelling response to this concern, by demonstrating that in situations like monetary policymaking, where the time-consistency problem may arise, it makes sense to appoint conservative central bankers—even when the ultimate goal is to maximize the welfare of the economy's representative household.

4. What More Can We Learn?

And what additional lessons might we hope to learn over the next twenty-five years? As a first step in answering this question, consider following Barro and Gordon (1983) and Ireland (1997) in allowing the monetary policymaking game described above to be repeated over an infinite horizon, where time periods are indexed by $t = 0, 1, 2, \ldots$. Suppose, as in Case 2 above, that the central bank does not precommit to its choice for inflation; but suppose, also, that the behavior of the representative household's expectations provides the central bank with an incentive to maintain a reputation for keeping inflation low.

More specifically, suppose that at the beginning of period $t = 0$, the representative household expects the central bank to choose an inflation rate $\pi_0 = \pi^{\text{rep}}$ for that period, where π^{rep} lies somewhere between $\pi^c = 0$ and $\pi^{\text{nc}} = b\alpha$. Suppose, in addition, that in each period $t = 1, 2, 3, \ldots$, the household continues to expect the central bank to choose $\pi_t = \pi^{\text{rep}}$ so long as it has always done so in the past. If, however, the central bank deviates during some period $t = 0, 1, 2, \ldots$, by choosing an inflation rate π_t that differs from π^{rep}, then the household's expectations permanently shift, so that the no-commitment choice $\pi^{\text{nc}} = b\alpha$ is expected forever after. Given the household's objective of setting w in line with expected inflation, these assumptions imply that for $t = 0$, $w_0 = \pi^{\text{rep}}$, while for all $t = 1, 2, 3, \ldots$,

$$
w_t = \begin{cases} \pi^{\text{rep}} & \text{if } \pi_s = \pi^{\text{rep}} \text{ for all } s = 0, 1, \ldots, t - 1, \\ \pi^{\text{nc}} = b\alpha, & \text{otherwise.} \end{cases}
$$

The question now becomes: given this behavior of private-sector expectations, will the central bank choose to maintain its reputation for selecting the lower inflation rate π^{rep}?

In the case where the central bank does maintain its reputation by choosing $\pi_t = \pi^{\text{rep}}$ for all $t = 0, 1, 2, \ldots$, its total discounted return over the infinite horizon is given by

$$
\frac{1}{(1 - \beta)} R(\pi^{\text{rep}}; \pi^{\text{rep}}),
$$

where β, the central bank's discount factor, lies between zero and one. In the alternative case, where the central bank deviates, it will always find it optimal to do so immediately, during period $t = 0$, by choosing π_0 to solve the problem

$$\max_{\pi} R(\pi; \pi^{\text{rep}}).$$

Hence, in this case, the central bank chooses $\pi_0 = \pi^{\text{dev}}$, where

$$\pi^{\text{dev}} = \frac{b}{1 + b}(\pi^{\text{rep}} + \alpha).$$

During each period thereafter, having lost its reputation, the best that the central bank can do is to select $\pi_t = \pi^{\text{nc}} = b\alpha$ for all $t = 1, 2, 3, \ldots$. Its total discounted return from deviating is therefore

$$R(\pi^{\text{dev}}; \pi^{\text{rep}}) + \frac{\beta}{1 - \beta}R(\pi^{\text{nc}}; \pi^{\text{nc}}).$$

It follows that the policy choice $\pi_t = \pi^{\text{rep}}$ for all $t = 0, 1, 2, \ldots$ is sustainable in this type of reputational equilibrium if and only if the incentive-compatibility constraint

$$R(\pi^{\text{rep}}; \pi^{\text{rep}}) \geq (1 - \beta)R(\pi^{\text{dev}}; \pi^{\text{rep}}) + \beta R(\pi^{\text{nc}}; \pi^{\text{nc}})$$

holds. Using the solutions $\pi^{\text{dev}} = [b/(1 + b)](\pi^{\text{rep}} + \alpha)$ and $\pi^{\text{nc}} = b\alpha$, this incentive constraint can be rewritten as

$$[\beta(2 + b) - 1](b\alpha)^2 + 2(1 - \beta)b\alpha\pi^{\text{rep}} - (\beta b + 1)(\pi^{\text{rep}})^2 \geq 0.$$

This last expression indicates that the zero-inflation policy that is optimal under commitment can be supported in a reputational equilibrium whenever $\beta \geq 1/(2 + b)$. And since b is nonnegative, this condition almost certainly holds: it is satisfied for any value of β exceeding $\frac{1}{2}$. Here, therefore, we have another lesson to have emerged from the literature since Kydland and Prescott (1977): a central bank that is sufficiently patient, and that is lucky enough to be endowed with a reputation for keeping inflation low, will find it optimal to maintain its reputation even if it lacks the ability to commit.

One can also show, however, that if $\beta \geq 1/(2 + b)$, so that the central bank's incentive constraint holds with $\pi^{\text{rep}} = 0$, then the incentive constraint also holds for *any* value of π^{rep} between $\pi^c = 0$ and $\pi^{\text{nc}} = b\alpha$. In this case, therefore, the model features multiple equilibria, supporting inflation rates that range all the way from zero to $b\alpha$. To see why this is a problem, consider a reputational equilibrium in which π^{rep} lies below $\pi^{nc} = b\alpha$, but closer to $\pi^{nc} = b\alpha$ than to $\pi^c = 0$. In such an equilibrium, the central bank benefits from maintaining its reputation: it achieves an outcome that improves upon the endless repetition of the one-shot outcome without commitment. At the same time, however, the central bank knows that even better equilibria exist, with even lower inflation rates. Yet the model provides absolutely no advice as to how the central bank might steer the economy towards these preferred, low-inflation equilibria.

Taylor (1982) suggests that a central bank ought to build credibility for a low-inflation policy by adopting that policy unilaterally and by demonstrating that it will stick with the policy, even if it imposes short-run costs on the economy. Taylor's pragmatic approach has considerable intuitive appeal, and may be a good strategy for any real-world central bank to follow. But it simply will not work in the context of the example considered here. In fact, the triggerlike behavior of the representative household's expectations that help support the reputational equilibria with π^{rep} $< \pi^{nc} = b\alpha$ dictates that expected inflation will actually jump *higher*, to $\pi^{nc} = b\alpha$, should the central bank deviate from π^{rep} by unexpectedly trying to disinflate.

How can a central bank establish a reputation for fighting inflation, or build credibility for a welfare-improving disinflationary program? In the literature that follows Kydland and Prescott (1977), work towards answering this question has only just begun. Significantly, providing answers to this question would seem to require departing in some way from the rational-expectations hypothesis, since, after all, the reputational equilibria in which inflation is stuck forever between $\pi^c = 0$ and $\pi^{nc} = b\alpha$ are bona fide rational-expectations equilibria. Cho and Matsui (1995) and Ireland (2000), for instance, both develop models of macroeconomic policymaking in which private agents are assumed to be boundedly rational. The objective of both of these papers is to identify restrictions on private-expectation formation that are weak enough to allow Taylor's (1982) pragmatic approach to work, but strong enough to prevent the policymaker from repeatedly fooling the boundedly rational agents. Still, much more work needs to be done along these lines: we have much to learn, over the next twenty-five years, about how governments can build credibility for the policies—like low inflation and low capital income tax rates—that we'd like them to pursue.

REFERENCES

Barro, R. J., and D. B. Gordon. (1983). Rules, discretion, and reputation in a model of monetary policy. *Journal of Monetary Economics* 12(July):101–121.

Blinder, A. S. (1997). Distinguished lecture on economics in government: What central bankers could learn from academics—and vice versa. *Journal of Economic Perspectives* 11(Spring):3–19.

Cho, I.-K., and A. Matsui. (1995). Induction and the Ramsey policy. *Journal of Economic Dynamics and Control* 19 (July–September):1113–1140.

Clarida, R., J. Gali, and M. Gertler. (1999). The science of monetary policy: A new Keynesian perspective. *Journal of Economic Literature* 37(December):1661–1707.

Herrendorf, B., and B. Lockwood. (1997). Rogoff's "conservative" central banker restored. *Journal of Money, Credit, and Banking* 29(November, Part 1):476–495.

Ireland, P. N. (1997). "Sustainable monetary policies." *Journal of Economic Dynamics and Control* 22(November):87–108.

———. (2000). Expectations, credibility, and time-consistent monetary policy. *Macroeconomic Dynamics* 4(December):448–466.

Kydland, F. E., and E. C. Prescott. (1977). Rules rather than discretion: The inconsistency of optimal plans. *Journal of Political Economy* 85(June):473–491.

McCallum, B. T. (1995). Two fallacies concerning central-bank independence. *American Economic Review* 85(May):207–211.

Rogoff, K. (1985). The optimal degree of commitment to an intermediate monetary target. *Quarterly Journal of Economics* 100(November):1169–1189.

Svensson, L. E. O. (1997). Optimal inflation targets, "conservative" central banks, and linear inflation contracts. *American Economic Review* 87(March):98–114.

Taylor, J. B. (1982). Establishing credibility: A rational expectations viewpoint. *American Economic Review* 72(May):81–85.

Walsh, C. E. (1995). Optimal contracts for central bankers. *American Economic Review* 85(March):150–167.

Comment[1]

LARS E. O. SVENSSON
Princeton University, NBER, and CEPR

Nancy Stokey's interesting and thought-provoking paper has two main parts. Section 2, "Reputation Building," discusses the choice of monetary-policy instruments by relying on Atkeson and Kehoe (2001). This discussion is in terms of a trade-off between observability and "tightness" (the correlation with the monetary-policy goal). Section 3, "Robustness," discusses the choice between discretion and commitment to a simple rule. This discussion is in terms of a trade-off between flexibility and myopia on the one hand and rigidity and farsightedness on the other.

I believe Section 2 is better described as concerned with the choice of an *intermediate target* for monetary policy rather than a monetary-policy *instrument*. The setting of the monetary-policy instrument (the Fed funds rate in the United States) is usually directly observable, whereas the rela-

1. I thank Annika Andreasson for secretarial and editorial assistance.

tion between the instrument setting and the monetary-policy goals is complex, making it difficult to infer the central bank's intentions from its instrument setting. Thus, I interpret Section 2 as a discussion of the pros and cons of either an exchange-rate target or a money-growth target as intermediate targets, when the final target (the goal) is inflation.

The choice of an intermediate target is a classic problem in the design of monetary policy. An ideal intermediate target is (1) highly correlated with the goal, (2) easier to control than the goal, and (3) easier to observe than the goal. The idea is that, if such an ideal intermediate target can be found, it may be better to aim for the intermediate target rather than to aim directly for the goal, and this way indirectly achieve the goal.

In current real-world monetary policy, the idea of intermediate targeting has largely been abandoned (except in a specific sense mentioned below). Instead, central banks nowadays aim directly for their goals, typically low inflation and (to some extent) stable output gaps, as in (flexible) inflation targeting. The main problem with inflation targeting is that the control of inflation (and the output gap) is very imperfect, due to the lags in, and different strengths of, the various channels in the transmission process from instrument adjustments to actual inflation and output. This makes it difficult to judge whether current policy settings are, and past policy settings were, appropriate. The best solution to this problem is to regard inflation and output-gap forecasts as intermediate targets.

Indeed, as discussed in Svensson (1997a), the inflation forecast is an ideal intermediate target variable when inflation is the final target variable. The inflation forecast is by definition the current variable that has the highest correlation with future inflation. It is easier to control than actual inflation, for instance, because it leaves out a number of unanticipated shocks that will later affect actual inflation. It is in principle easier to observe than actual inflation, since it is a variable currently available, whereas the corresponding actual inflation will only be observed some two years later (due to the lags) and then be contaminated by a number of intervening shocks. In particular, transparent inflation-targeting central banks *make* their inflation forecasts observable, by issuing detailed inflation reports where the forecast is presented and motivated. (Thus, arguably, the only ideal intermediate target variables are the forecasts of the final target variables.)

Section 3, "Robustness," discusses the trade-off between flexibility and an inflation bias on the one hand and rigidity and no inflation bias on the other. This is a well-known and classic issue. For instance, the purpose of a fixed exchange rate or a currency board in a country may be to avoid inflation bias by importing a less inflationary monetary policy from an anchor country. But this is a second-best solution, since monetary policy can then no longer be independent and respond to the specific shocks hitting the country.

In real-world monetary policy, however, it seems possible in many cases to get rid of any inflation bias *without* losing flexibility and stabilization. In order to discuss this, let us go back to the classic treatments in Kydland and Prescott (1977) and Barro and Gordon (1983a) of rules vs. discretion and the time-consistency problem. Although these issues in principle apply to a number of different policies, monetary policy provides the best examples, having arguably suffered the largest problems and benefited the most from their solutions.

The main result in the classic treatment was that discretion may result in an average inflation bias. The simplest way to illustrate this result is with the help of a simple Lucas-type Phillips curve,

$$y_t = \bar{y} + \alpha(\pi_t - E_{t-1}\pi_t) + \varepsilon_t,$$

where y_t is output in period t, $\bar{y}$ is potential output (the natural output level), α is a positive coefficient, π_t is inflation in period t, $E_{t-1}\pi_t$ denotes rational expectations of inflation in period t conditional on information available in period $t - 1$, and ε_t is a zero-mean i.i.d. shock. The central bank is assumed to control either inflation or output, and has a quadratic loss function,

$$L_t = (\pi_t - \pi^*)^2 + \lambda(y_t - \bar{y} - k)^2,$$

where π^* is an inflation target, λ is a positive weight, and k is a positive parameter. This formulation implies that the output target, $\bar{y} + k$, is larger than potential output, $\bar{y}$.

Discretionary optimization of the central bank implies the first-order condition

$$\pi_t - \pi^* + \lambda\alpha(y_t - \bar{y} - k) = 0.$$

Combining this condition and the Phillips curve gives the equilibrium outcome for inflation and output,

$$\pi_t = \pi^* + \lambda\alpha k - \frac{\lambda\alpha}{1 + \lambda\alpha^2}\varepsilon_t,$$

$$y_t = \bar{y} + \frac{1}{1 + \lambda\alpha^2}\varepsilon_t.$$

In particular, there is an average inflation bias, in that the unconditional mean of inflation exceeds the inflation target:

$$E[\pi_t] - \pi^* = \lambda \alpha k > 0.$$

Numerous solutions to the problem of average inflation bias under discretion have been suggested. One solution is a commitment to an optimal reaction function. In the absence of a commitment mechanism, this solution is not realistic. In particular, in any realistic problem, the optimal reaction function is quite complex and in practice unverifiable, making a commitment to it very difficult or impossible.

Another solution is by extension to non-Markov trigger-strategy equilibria, following Barro and Gordon (1983b). These have the inherent problem that follows from the folk theorem: there is no unique equilibrium. Furthermore, in the realistic situation with an atomistic private sector, there is no coordination mechanism by which a particular equilibrium could be achieved.[2] In addition, these equilibria are sometimes (and in Stokey's paper) referred to as having to do with "reputation." I think that is a (very common) misnomer. There is no uncertainty about the characteristics of the players in these settings. I think "reputation" is much more naturally associated with a situation of incomplete information, when the preferences of the central bank are not directly observable, as is the case in classic papers by Backus and Driffill (1985) and Cukierman and Meltzer (1986), and in the recent extension of the latter by Faust and Svensson (2001). In these papers, "reputation" is the private sector's best estimate of the preferences of the central bank.

A much-noted suggestion is McCallum's (1995) "just do it." This assumes that the central bank, in the absence of a commitment mechanism, just ignores the incentives to deviate from the socially optimal outcome that arises under discretion. I find this suggestion problematic because, to my knowledge, neither McCallum nor anyone else has presented a model where "just do it" is an equilibrium outcome. The best rationale for "just do it" that I am aware of is in Faust and Svensson (2001): There, increased transparency about the bank's actions makes the bank's "reputation" (the private sector's estimate of the bank's unobservable internal time-varying objectives) more sensitive to its actions. This increases the cost for the bank of deviating from its announced social objective and pursuing its internal objectives, and thus works as an implicit mechanism for commitment to the announced objective.

Many papers have fruitfully applied a principal–agent approach to the time-consistency problem. Here society (the principal) can assign loss functions to the central bank (the agent) that may differ from society's

---

2. Problems with trigger-strategy equilibria are further discussed in Ireland's comment preceding this one.

loss function, in order to improve the discretionary problem.[3] That is, it is assumed that it is possible to commit the central bank to a particular loss function, whereas the minimization of that loss function occurs under discretion. A well-known suggestion is Rogoff's (1985) "weight-conservative" central bank, where the central bank is assigned a relative weight λ on output stabilization that is less than that of society. This reduces average inflation and inflation variance, but increases output variance. This is often described as a necessary trade-off between inflation bias and "flexibility." However, this potential explanation of low inflation in some countries is rejected by the data: Countries with lower average inflation do not have higher output variability.

Another suggestion is an "inflation contract," by Walsh (1995) and Persson and Tabellini (1994), further discussed in Svensson (1997b), where lower inflation is assumed to be accompanied by an increased bonus to the central bank or its governor. This idea has never been tried in the real world (not even in New Zealand, counter to common misperceptions).

A third suggestion is an "output-conservative" central bank, meaning a loss function for the central bank where the output target is equal to potential output, $k = 0$. This eliminates the average inflation bias without increasing output variability and is hence consistent with the data. This explanation has been suggested by Blinder (1998) for the Fed. I believe this is the best single explanation for the apparent disappearance of average inflation bias in many countries. Indeed, I believe that the flexible inflation targeting currently applied in an increasing number of countries is consistent with central-bank loss functions where there is some modest weight on output-gap stability and the output target equals potential output. Thus, this solution to the inflation-bias problem need not imply any loss in flexibility. It is consistent with the insight that society had better find other policies than monetary policy (such as structural policies improving competition) to increase average and potential output.[4]

Issues of commitment and discretion have been discussed in a more general linear–quadratic model in early papers of Oudiz and Sachs (1985), Currie and Levine [collected in Currie and Levine (1993)], and Backus and Driffill (1986), with the model equations

$$\begin{bmatrix} X_{t+1} \\ E_t x_{t+1} \end{bmatrix} = A \begin{bmatrix} X_t \\ x_t \end{bmatrix} + Bi_t + \begin{bmatrix} \varepsilon_t + 1 \\ 0 \end{bmatrix}.$$

---

3. The possibility of improving the discretionary equilibrium by adjusting the parameters of the central-bank loss function was noted in Barro and Gordon (1983a, footnote 19).
4. Ireland, in his comment, interprets, McCallum's "just do it" as modifying the central-bank loss function by setting $k = 0$, but I can't find any support for that interpretation in McCallum (1995) (in McCallum's notation it would amount to setting $k = 1$).

Here, X_t is a vector of predetermined variables (one of these can be unity, in order to handle constants in a convenient way), x_t is as vector of forward-looking variables (jump variables, nonpredetermined variables), i_t is a vector of policy instruments, ε_t is a vector of zero-mean i.i.d. shocks, and A and B are matrices of appropriate dimension. The policymaker's intertemporal loss function in period t is

$$E_t(1 = \delta) \sum_{\tau=0}^{\infty} \delta^\tau L_{t+\tau},$$

where δ, $0 < \delta < 1$, is a discount factor, and the period loss function L_t is quadratic:

$$L_t = (Y_t - \hat{Y})'W(Y_t - \hat{Y}).$$

Here W is a positive semidefinite weight matrix, Y_t is a vector of target variables, and $\hat{Y}$ is a vector of corresponding target levels, which can be written

$$Y_t - \hat{Y} = C \begin{bmatrix} X_t \\ x_t \\ i_t \end{bmatrix},$$

where C is a matrix.

The optimal reaction function under *commitment* (the optimal "instrument rule") can be written

$$i_t = FX_t + \Phi\Xi_{t-1},$$

where F and Φ are matrices and Ξ_t is a vector of Lagrange multipliers for the equations for the forward-looking variables (the lower block of the model equations above), the equilibrium dynamics of which are given by

$$\Xi_t = SX_t + \Sigma\Xi_{t-1},$$

where S and Σ are matrices.

The equilibrium reaction function resulting from optimization under *discretion* can be written

$$i_t = \tilde{F}X_t,$$

where $\tilde{F}$ is a matrix. Compared to the optimal reaction function under commitment, there is generally *stabilization bias* [meaning that the matrix of response coefficients $\tilde{F}$ under discretion differs from the optimal response F under commitment, as discussed in Svensson (1997b), for instance] and *lack of history dependence* [$\Phi \equiv 0$, as discussed in Woodford (1999)]. Optimization under discretion thus results in a higher loss than under commitment.

Several solutions to the problem of how to improve the equilibrium under discretion have been suggested for this more general setting. One solution is a commitment to the optimal reaction function above. Unfortunately, in realistic problems the optimal reaction function is quite complex, making verification and other aspects of a commitment mechanism unrealistic.

A commitment to a *simple* (rather than optimal) instrument rule, such as a Taylor rule, has been suggested as a compromise. A simple instrument rule could be verifiable, and a commitment would in principle be feasible. No central bank has committed to a simple instrument rule, however, and prominent central bankers seem skeptical [see Svensson (2002) for further discussion].

One solution is a *commitment to continuity and predictability*, suggested by Svensson and Woodford (2002), who argue that such a commitment is to some extent consistent with both the rhetoric and the practice of current inflation targeting. It consists in internalizing the cost of deviating from previous expectations, and boils down to a modified period loss function of the form

$$L_t = (Y_t - \hat{Y})'W(Y_t - \hat{Y}) + \Xi_{t-1}(x_t - E_{t-1}x_t),$$

where Ξ_{t-1} is the vector of Lagrange multipliers from the previous decision period.

Another solution is a commitment to an *optimal targeting rule*, discussed in Svensson and Woodford (2002) and Svensson (2002), and consistent with previous work of Sims (1980), Rogoff (1985), Walsh (1995), and Svensson (1997a). An optimal targeting rule is an Euler condition, an optimal first-order condition for the target variables—essentially, the equality of the marginal rate of transformation between the target variables (given by the model equations) and the corresponding marginal rate of substitution (given by the loss function). One attraction of optimal targeting rules is that they are usually much simpler and more robust than the optimal reaction function, making a commitment to them more realistic. For instance, all additive shocks to the model equations vanish from the optimal targeting rule (but not from the optimal reaction function). In the simple Kydland–Prescott–Barro–Gordon model above, the optimal targeting rule is

$\pi_t - \pi^* + \lambda\alpha(y_t - \bar{y}) = 0.$

With lags in the transmission mechanism of monetary policy, the optimal targeting rule involves forecasts of the target variables rather than current values.

Another alternative is a commitment to a *simple targeting rule*, for instance, the simple rule emphasized by the Bank of England and Sweden's Riksbank that the two-year-ahead inflation forecast should be equal to the inflation target.

So what have we learnt about rules and discretion after twenty-five years? I believe the most important things we have learnt are:

The problem of average inflation bias seems to be gone. The single best explanation for its disappearance is probably *output-conservativeness* of central banks—that is, central banks, in addition to an explicit or implicit inflation target, have an explicit or implicit output target equal to (rather than exceeding) potential output. This also means that average inflation bias can be avoided without loss in flexibility or stabilization of the output gap.

Even if no average inflation bias occurs, discretion generally implies stabilization bias and lack of history dependence (although the quantitative importance of these two phenomena remains to be firmly established).

A principal–agent approach to central banking is useful. Commitment to objectives (loss functions) is probably more realistic and relevant than commitment to particular reaction functions (instrument rules).

Targeting rules may be more useful and realistic than instrument rules.

REFERENCES

Atkeson, A., and P. J. Kehoe. (2001). The advantage of transparent instruments of monetary policy. Federal Reserve Bank of Minneapolis Staff Report 297.
Backus, D., and J. Driffill. (1985). Rational expectations and policy credibility following a change in regime. *Review of Economic Studies* 52:211–222.
———, and ———. (1986). The consistency of optimal policy in stochastic rational expectations models. CEPR Discussion Paper No. 124.
Barro, R. J., and D. B. Gordon. (1983a). A positive theory of monetary policy in a natural-rate model. *Journal of Political Economy* 91:589–610.
———, and ———. (1983b). Rules, discretion and reputation in a model of monetary policy. *Journal of Monetary Economics* 12:101–121.
Blinder, A. S. (1998). *Central Banking in Theory and Practice: The 1996 Robbins Lectures*. Cambridge, MA: The MIT Press.
Cukierman, A., and A. H. Meltzer. (1986). A theory of ambiguity, credibility and inflation under discretion and asymmetric information. *Econometrica* 53:1099–1128.
Currie, D., and P. Levine. (1993). *Rules, Reputation and Macroeconomic Policy Coordination*. Cambridge: Cambridge University Press.

Faust, J., and L. E. O. Svensson. (2001). Transparency and credibility: Monetary policy with unobservable goals. *International Economic Review* 42:369–397.

Kydland, F. E., and E. C. Prescott. (1977). Rules rather than discretion: The inconsistency of optimal plans. *Journal of Political Economy* 85:473–491.

McCallum, B. (1995). Two fallacies concerning central-bank independence. *American Economic Review* 85, 207–211.

Oudiz, G., and J. Sachs. (1985). International policy coordination in dynamic macroeconomic models. In *International Economic Policy Coordination*, W. H. Buiter and R. C. Marston (eds.). Cambridge: Cambridge University Press.

Persson, T., and G. Tabellini. (1994). Designing institutions for monetary stability. *Carnegie-Rochester Conference Series on Public Policy* 39:53–84.

Rogoff, K. (1985). The optimal degree of commitment to a monetary target. *Quarterly Journal of Economics* 100:1169–1190.

Sims, C. A. (1980). Macroeconomics and reality. *Econometrica* 48:1–48.

Svensson, L. E. O. (1997a). Inflation forecast targeting: Implementing and monitoring inflation targets. *European Economic Review* 41:1111–1146.

———. (1997b). Optimal inflation targets, "conservative" central banks, and linear inflation contracts. *American Economic Review* 87:98–114.

———. (2002). What is wrong with Taylor rules? Using judgment in monetary policy through targeting rules. Princeton University, working paper.

———, and M. Woodford. (2002). Implementing optimal policy through inflation-forecast targeting. Princeton University, working paper.

Walsh, C. E. (1995). Optimal contracts for independent central bankers. *American Economic Review* 85:150–167.

Woodford, M. (1999). Optimal monetary policy inertia. Cambridge, MA: National Bureau of Economic Research. NBER Working Paper 7261.

Discussion

A theme taken up by several of the participants was the different possible interpretations of U.S. inflation history in the 1970s and 1990s. Greg Mankiw suggested as an alternative to Lars Svensson's interpretation that central bankers in the 1970s thought that the natural level of output was higher than it actually was, whereas in the 1990s, central bankers thought that the natural level of output was lower than it actually was. He added that such an alternative interpretation would be bad for the rules-vs.-discretion literature. It would imply that monetary policy in the 1990s was better than 30 years ago not because monetary policy was less discretionary in the 1990s than in the 1970s, but because central bankers were lucky in the shocks that hit the economy.

Robert Barsky proposed a variation on Mankiw's comment. Where Mankiw emphasized the importance of the Fed knowing or not knowing what was the natural level of output, Barsky suggested that an alternative explanation for recent U.S. inflation history is that the Fed learned the natural-rate hypothesis over time.

Bob Hall commented that when Alan Greenspan was asked why he tolerated unemployment below the natural rate in the 1990s, he replied that he had focused not on unemployment but on what was happening to prices. Hall's interpretation of this reply was that Greenspan's success relative to the central bankers of the 1970s can be attributed to a policy of price targeting, and not merely to good luck. Hall also maintained that, contrary to the teaching of Milton Friedman, the idea of an exogenous natural rate of unemployment is not a sensible one. On this point, Greg Mankiw responded that Friedman's idea was merely that the natural rate of unemployment was exogenous to monetary policy. Hall replied that there is strong evidence of hysteresis in the labor market and of monetary policy affecting the labor market, and hence exogeneity of the natural rate of unemployment to monetary policy is unlikely. Greg Mankiw desired clarification on the empirical evidence. He did not dispute that the natural rate of unemployment changes over time, but questioned Hall's certainty that monetary policy can affect the long-run level of unemployment.

Robert Barro suggested that Hall's interpretation of Alan Greenspan's approach is not accurate empirically, as there is clear evidence that the federal funds rate responds not only to inflation, but also to employment and other macroeconomic variables.

On the discussion of the natural-rate hypothesis, Lars Svensson maintained that potential output is a very useful concept both in theory and in practice. He allowed that, as it is an unobservable variable, the Fed can make mistakes in estimating it. His view, however, was that if the Fed had looked at Kalman-filter estimates of potential output in the 1970s, it would have realized that rising inflation meant a reduction in potential output.

Alberto Alesina contributed to the discussion on U.S. inflation history by saying that in looking for empirical evidence for or against the rules-vs.-discretion literature, it might be useful to look beyond the United States to the experience of other countries.

Alesina raised another issue of interest to several participants. He supported Stokey's view of reputation over that of the discussants. As evidence for the relevance of reputation in the real world, he cited the fact that major breakdowns in monetary rules and government default on debt are relatively rare in the developed world. He said this confirms the view that governments desire to maintain a reputation for repayment in order to be able to borrow again. He was of the opinion that multiplicity of reputational equilibria is not a crucial problem in the real world. He suggested that in the example of the Barro–Gordon model, the lowest possible level of inflation is an equilibrium that should be easy to coordinate on.

Nancy Stokey agreed that the dichotomy between rules and discretion can be overdrawn, and that reputation is important. She noted that while Argentina's currency board and peg to the dollar had implied a very strong rule for monetary policy, it was a rule the government had proved unable to maintain. On multiplicity of reputational equilibria, Stokey suggested that the role of the central bank is to be a cheerleader, selecting an equilibrium and persuading the private sector to behave accordingly. She added that empirical research into the means through which central banks do this would be useful.

Jonathan Parker drew attention to a little-known feature of many models with distortionary capital taxation. He explained that in these models, time-consistency problems can usually be eliminated by taxing capital a lot in the initial period. However, he noted that this result is a reversal of good and bad policy as economists usually see it, and that it is generally avoided by assuming that capitalism is better than socialism, or by focusing on stationary Markov-perfect equilibria. He commented that he would like to see a better foundation for the assumption that the government should not own all of capital, by adding to the model reasons why government is not good at running capital. He said that the interaction of this with time-consistency issues is an interesting direction for research over the next 25 years.

Alberto Alesina commented on the contention in Nancy Stokey's paper that while there might be many types of bad government, there is essentially only one type of good government. He proposed instead the view that there can be several types of good government, in particular in a nonrepresentative-agent world. For example, a "good" government representing the interests of capital will choose a different policy on capital and labor taxation from a "good" government representing the interests of labor.

Ken Rogoff questioned Lars Svensson's contention in his discussion that conservative central banks do not lead to higher output variability in practice. He suggested that Japan and Germany might be seen as counterexamples.

In conclusion, Nancy Stokey replied to Lars Svensson's comments on the observability issue in his discussion. She pointed out that in her simple model, the instrument is unobservable, but the target is observable. She commented that in a more realistic model, the observability problem would be whether central bankers are setting what they should be setting, a problem which would be made much more complex if they were trying to hit a moving target.

Aart Kraay and Jaume Ventura
THE WORLD BANK; AND MIT, CEPR, AND NBER

Current Accounts in the Long and the Short Run

1. Introduction

Countries are subject to transitory income shocks such as changes in the terms of trade, fluctuations in production, policy reforms, natural disasters, and many others. There is ample evidence that countries use their assets to buffer or smooth the effects of these shocks on consumption, raising savings when income is high and vice versa.[1] The main goal of this paper is to improve our understanding of the combination of assets that countries use for this purpose. In particular, we ask: How do countries allocate the marginal unit of savings between domestic and foreign assets? Or, equivalently, what are the effects of fluctuations in savings on domestic investment and the current account?[2]

The traditional view is that countries invest the marginal unit of savings in foreign assets. Underlying this view are the assumptions that investment risk is weak and diminishing returns are strong. The first assumption ensures that countries invest their savings only in those assets that offer the highest expected return. The second assumption implies that

We are grateful to Fabrizio Perri, Paul Scanlon, and the conference participants for their useful comments. The opinions expressed here are the authors', and do not necessarily reflect those of the World Bank, its executive directors, or the countries they represent.

1. For evidence on consumption smoothing, see Deaton (1992, pp. 133–134), who writes that "consumption is less volatile than income, it fluctuates less about its trend, the amplitude of its business cycle variation is less, and the variance of its growth rate is less than the variance of the growth rate of income."
2. Why do countries use assets to smooth consumption rather than simply buy insurance abroad? Implicit in this paragraph and basically in all that follows is the assumption that countries are unable or unwilling to sell their idiosyncratic risk. This assumption is a central tenet of the intertemporal approach to the current account (see Obstfeld and Rogoff, 1995), and it is widely thought to provide an accurate description of reality. The question of why this is so is one of the most intriguing puzzles in international finance. See Lewis (1999) for a survey of the literature on this topic.

investing any fraction of the marginal unit of savings in domestic capital would lower its expected return below that of foreign assets. Hence the marginal unit of savings is invested in foreign assets, justifying the *traditional rule* that fluctuations in savings lead to fluctuations in the current account of roughly the same magnitude. While theoretically coherent, this rule has consistently been rejected by the data. The top panel of Figure 1 shows pooled annual observations of the current account and savings for 21 OECD countries over the past 30 years. A regression of the current account on savings delivers a slope coefficient that is positive but much lower than one. This is nothing but the famous result of Feldstein and Horioka (1980) that fluctuations in savings lead to parallel fluctuations in investment, with only minor effects on the current account.

In an earlier paper, we proposed a new view: that countries invest the marginal unit of savings like the average one (Kraay and Ventura, 2000). This is what one should expect if, in contrast to the traditional view, investment risk is strong and diminishing returns are weak. The first assumption implies that countries are unwilling to change the composition of their portfolios, unless shocks have large effects on the distribution of asset returns. The second assumption ensures that the distribution of asset returns is unaffected by the way countries invest the marginal unit of savings. Hence, the marginal unit of savings is invested like the average one, leading to the *new rule* that fluctuations in savings lead to fluctuations in the current account that are equal to savings times the share of foreign assets in the country portfolio. This rule not only is theoretically coherent, but it also provides a surprisingly good description of the data. The bottom panel of Figure 1 shows that a simple regression of the current account on the interaction between savings and the share of foreign assets delivers a slope coefficient close to one and a zero intercept. Moreover, this interaction term by itself explains around 30 percent of the observed variation in the current account.[3]

Hidden in the bottom panel of Figure 1 is a vast difference between the predictive power of the new rule in the long and the short run. Figure 2 illustrates this point. In the top panel, we have plotted the average current account over a thirty-year period against the average of savings times the

3. Since foreign assets constitute a small fraction of observed country portfolios, this view implies that fluctuations in savings should mostly lead to parallel fluctuations in investment, and is therefore consistent with Feldstein and Horioka's finding. What we found most surprising about this view in our earlier paper is that it has sharply different implications for the current account response to an increase in savings in debtor and creditor countries. Since debtors by definition hold more than their wealth in domestic capital, they invest at home more than the increase in savings, resulting in a current account deficit. In contrast, creditor countries invest at home less than the increase in savings, resulting in a current account surplus.

Figure 1 THE TRADITIONAL RULE AND THE NEW RULE

Traditional Rule

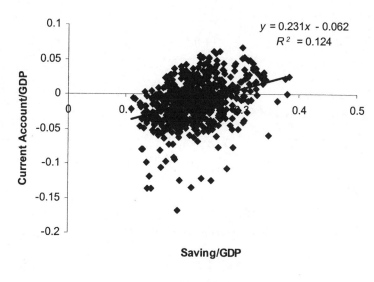

New Rule

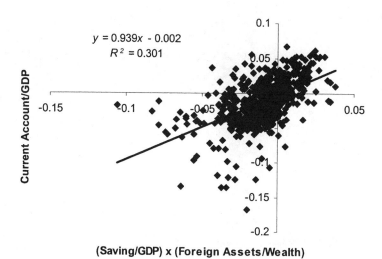

(Saving/GDP) x (Foreign Assets/Wealth)

Note: The top (bottom) panel plots the current account balance as a share of GDP against gross national saving (gross national saving interacted with the foreign asset position), pooling all available annual observations for an unbalanced panel of 21 OECD countries over the period 1966–1997.

Figure 2 PORTFOLIO GROWTH AND THE CURRENT ACCOUNT

Long Run

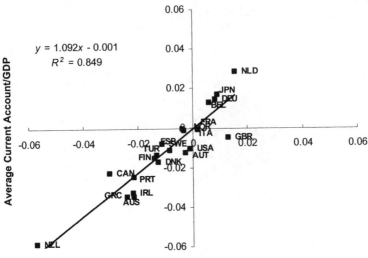

Average(Saving/GDP x Foreign Assets/Wealth)

Short Run

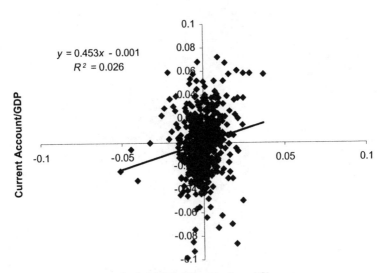

Saving/GDP x Foreign Asset Share

Notes: The top panel plots the period average of the current account as a share of GDP against the period average of gross national saving as a share of GDP interacted with the share of foreign assets in wealth for an unbalanced panel of 21 OECD countries over the period 1966–1997. The bottom panel plots the annual current account as a share of GDP against annual gross national saving as a share of GDP interacted with the annual foreign asset share, removing country means from both variables.

share of foreign assets during the same period. The new rule explains about 85 percent of the long-run or average cross-country differences in current accounts. In the bottom panel, we have plotted the (de-meaned) current account for each country and year against the (de-meaned) inter-action of savings and the initial share of foreign assets in wealth for the same country and year. The new rule explains essentially none of the year-to-year within-country differences in current accounts. The contrast between the two panels indicates a discrepancy between the long- and the short-run behavior of the current account.[4]

How do we reconcile the apparently haphazard behavior of the current account in the short run with its neat behavior in the long run? Is the short-run relationship between savings and the current account just noise, or are there clear patterns behind this cloud of points? The main contribu-tion of this paper, we think, is to provide clear answers to these questions. To do this, it is useful to start by pointing out that the new rule embodies the view that the current account primarily reflects *portfolio growth*, i.e. changes in the size of the country portfolio without systematic changes in its composition. The empirical success of the new rule in the top panel of Figure 2 simply reflects the observation that the composition of country portfolios has been remarkably stable in the long run. This is shown in Figure 3. If we want to understand why the new rule performs so poorly in the bottom panel of Figure 2, we must explain how and why in the short run increases in savings lead mostly to *portfolio rebalancing*, i.e. systematic changes in the composition of the country portfolio. If in addition we want to reconcile the two panels of Figure 2, we must go further and also explain why this short-run portfolio rebalancing is undone in the long run.

Our hypothesis is that this pattern is consistent with the view that ad-justment costs to investment are important. If this is the case, an increase in savings that raises investment reduces the expected return to capital and induces countries to rebalance their portfolios towards foreign assets. Under these conditions, the short-run current account surplus is larger than the one predicted by the new rule. Once savings return to normal, investment declines, adjustment costs disappear, and the country port-folio returns gradually to its original composition. Throughout this ad-justment process, the current account surplus is smaller than the one

---

Figure 3 PERSISTENCE OF COUNTRY PORTFOLIOS

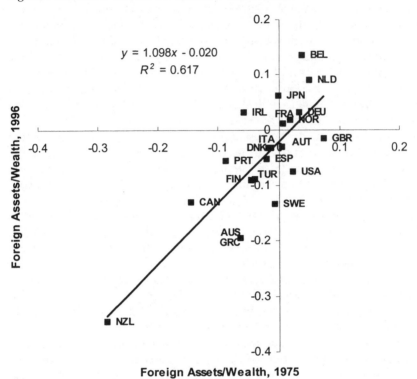

Foreign Assets/Wealth, 1975

Note: Throughout the paper, we use an unbalanced panel of 21 OECD countries over the period 1966–1997. Since we can construct a balanced panel of observations for this set of countries only over the period 1975–1996, we use 1975 here as the initial period.

predicted by the new rule. In the long run, the shock does not affect the composition of the country portfolio, and the new rule applies.

With this theoretical picture at hand, we go back to the data to search for patterns in the discrepancies between the observed current account and what the new rule would predict. When we do this, the picture that comes out from the data turns out to be clear and unambiguous: on impact, countries rebalance their portfolios towards foreign assets, and the new rule systematically underpredicts the short-run effects of increases in savings on the current account. In the years that follow, countries rebalance their portfolios back towards their original composition. During this period, the new rule systematically overpredicts the current account. We find that the whole adjustment process lasts about five years. Overall, the evidence is consistent with the view that adjustment costs to investment are important and, to avoid paying them, countries use foreign assets as a buffer stock to smooth fluctuations in investment.

The theory presented here can also reconcile two apparently contradictory observations about the relationship between the current account and investment. On the one hand, the long-run or cross-sectional correlation between investment and the current account is weak (Penati and Dooley, 1984; Tesar, 1991). On the other hand, the short-run or time-series correlation between investment and the current account is consistently negative (Glick and Rogoff, 1995). The theory presented here predicts that in the long run, portfolio rebalancing is small and the correlation between the current account and investment should be positive in creditor countries and negative in debtor ones. We show that the data are consistent with this prediction and that the weak cross-sectional correlation is the result of pooling data from debtor and creditor countries. The theory also predicts that in the short run portfolio rebalancing is important and this introduces a source of negative correlation between the current account and investment. This is true in all countries, regardless of whether they are debtors or creditors. We present a simple decomposition of the cross-sectional and time-series correlations between the current account and investment that illustrates this point.

The paper is organized as follows: Section 2 presents a stylized model that encapsulates the main elements of our portfolio-based theory of the current account. Section 3 uses the model to study how countries react to income shocks. Section 4 examines the empirical evidence and interprets it from the vantage point of the theory. Section 5 investigates the relationship between investment and the current account. Section 6 concludes.

2. An Intertemporal Model of the Current Account

In this section, we present a stylized model of how the current account responds to transitory income shocks. Since we stop short of modeling the world equilibrium and focus instead on a small open economy, these shocks should be interpreted as country-specific or idiosyncratic risk. Following the tradition of the intertemporal approach, we simply assume that countries are unable or unwilling to sell this risk in international markets. In particular, we adopt the starkest form of this view by assuming that the only asset that is traded internationally is a noncontingent bond.[5]

---

5. The intertemporal approach was developed by Sachs (1981, 1982), Obstfeld (1982), Dornbusch (1983), Svensson and Razin (1983), Persson and Svensson (1985), and Matsuyama (1987), among others. Obstfeld and Rogoff (1995) survey this research.

The model captures what we think are the essential elements of a port-folio-based theory of the current account. This theory is built around the concept of country portfolio and a simple decomposition of the current account that relies on this concept. By the country portfolio, we refer to the sum of all productive assets located within the country plus its net foreign asset position. The latter consist of the sum of all claims on domes-tic assets held by foreigners minus the sum of all claims on foreign assets held by domestic residents. In our simple model, the only productive asset located within the country is the stock of capital, and the net foreign asset position is simply the stock of noncontingent bonds owned by the country. By the *composition* of the country portfolio, we refer to the share of the net foreign asset position in it. To interpret the evolution of the current account it is useful to break it down into two pieces: changes in the size of the country portfolio, which we call *portfolio growth*; and changes in the composition of the country portfolio, or *portfolio rebalancing*.[6]

We study a small country populated by a continuum of identical con-sumers. There is a single good that can be used for consumption and investment. Consumers have access to two investment opportunities: for-eign loans and domestic capital. The interest rate on foreign loans is ρdt. To produce one unit of capital one unit of the single good is required. Since capital is reversible and does not depreciate, its price is equal to one and its return is equal to the flow of production minus operating costs. The flow of production generated by one unit of capital is $\pi dt + \sigma d\omega$, where π and σ are non-negative constants; and ω is a Wiener pro-cess, i.e., its changes are normally distributed with $E[d\omega] = 0$ and $E[d\omega^2] = dt$. That is, the flow of production is normally distributed with mean πdt and variance $\sigma^2 dt$. The operating costs αdt, are assumed to be propor-tional to the aggregate investment rate:

$$\alpha dt = \lambda \frac{dk}{k} \quad (\lambda \geq 0), \tag{1}$$

where k is the aggregate stock of capital at the beginning of the (infinites-imal) period. Since capital does not depreciate, this is also the stock of capital that was used in production in the previous period. Note that we are treating the relationship between operating costs and investment as a congestion effect or negative externality. One set of assumptions that justifies this relationship would be that investment requires a public input

---

6. Implicit in this decomposition is the assumption that asset price revaluations are small. This might be a poor assumption in some episodes. See Ventura (2001) for an example that shows this.

that costs λ per unit of investment and the government finances this input by raising a tax α on capital. There might be alternative and more compelling sets of assumptions that deliver this relationship. The reason we adopt it here is simply that it provides a tractable and effective way to capture the notion of adjustment costs to investment.[7]

The representative consumer values consumption sequences with these preferences:

$$E \int_0^\infty \ln (c) / e^{-\delta t} \, dt \qquad (\delta > 0). \tag{2}$$

Given our assumptions about the flow of production and the operating costs, the return to capital is $(\pi - \alpha)dt + \sigma d\omega$; and the representative consumer's budget constraint can be written as follows:

$$da = \{[(\pi - \alpha)(1 - x) + \rho x]a - c\}dt + (1 - x)a\sigma d\omega, \tag{3}$$

where c, a, and x denote consumption, wealth, and the share of foreign loans in the portfolio of the representative consumer. The budget constraint illustrates the standard risk–return trade-off underlying investment decisions. Each extra unit of wealth invested in domestic capital rather than foreign loans increases the expected return to wealth by $(\pi - \alpha - \rho)dt$, at the cost of raising the variance of this return by $\sigma^2 dt$. Finally, we assume that it is not possible to short-sell the capital stock, i.e., $x \leq 1$.

The representative consumer solves (2) subject to (3), taking the path of α as given. Solving this problem, we find the optimal consumption and portfolio decision[8]:

$$c = \delta a, \tag{4}$$

$$x = 1 - \max \left\{ \frac{\pi - \alpha - \rho}{\sigma^2}, 0 \right\}. \tag{5}$$

---

7. The q-theory postulates that investment raises the price of investment goods relative to consumption goods, leaving the productivity of capital constant. We instead postulate that investment lowers the productivity of capital, leaving the relative price of investment and consumption goods constant. It is likely that in real economies, both sorts of adjustment costs to investment are important. See Lucas (1967) for an early model that considers both types of adjustment costs; and Caballero (1999) and Dixit and Pyndick (1994) for two excellent expositions of existing models of adjustment costs of investment.

8. Merton (1971) solved this problem first. See also the appendix in Kraay and Ventura (2000).

When deciding their consumption, consumers behave as in the permanent-income theory of Friedman. Equation (4) shows that consumption is a fixed fraction of wealth and is independent of the expected return and volatility of available assets. When deciding their portfolio, consumers behave as in the mean–variance theory of Markowitz and Tobin. Equation (5) shows that the shares of each asset in the portfolio depend only on the mean and variance of the different assets and not on the level of wealth. The kink in the demand for foreign assets is the result of the short-sale constraint on domestic capital, i.e. $x \leq 1$.

In equilibrium, the demand and supply of capital must be equal, and this implies that

$$(1 - x)a = k + dk. \tag{6}$$

The left-hand side of equation (6) is the demand for capital. Since we have assumed that only domestic consumers hold domestic capital, this demand is equal to the share of their wealth that these consumers want to hold in domestic capital, times wealth. The right-hand side of equation (6) is the supply of capital, and consists of the capital stock at the beginning of the period plus the investment made during the (infinitesimal) period.

This completes the description of the model. There are two state variables (k and a) and one shock ($d\omega$). The new-rule model of our previous paper obtains as the limiting case in which $\lambda \to 0$. In this case, there are no adjustment costs to investment and the only state variable is the level of wealth. Assume that $\pi > \rho + \lambda(\rho - \delta)$. This parameter restriction ensures that the economy is productive enough so that the short-selling constraint on capital is never binding. Then, it is straightforward to use equations (1)–(6) to obtain the dynamics for the capital stock and wealth[9]:

$$\frac{dk}{k} = \lambda^{-1}\left(\pi - \rho - \sigma^2 \frac{k}{a}\right)dt, \tag{7}$$

$$\frac{da}{a} = \left[\sigma^2\left(\frac{k}{a}\right)^2 + \rho - \delta\right]dt + \frac{k}{a}\sigma\, d\omega. \tag{8}$$

Equations (7)–(8) provide the law of motion of the system from any given initial condition and sequence of shocks. Our next goal is to use this

---

9. To derive equations (7)–(8), remember that in the limit of continuous time $dkdt \approx 0$.

dynamical system to study how the current account responds to income shocks.

3. Portfolio Growth and Portfolio Rebalancing

To illustrate the model's implications, we analyze the behavior of savings, investment and the current account after a transitory income shock. To do this, it is useful first to establish some notation. Let S and CA be savings and the current account, each as a share of wealth, i.e., $S = da/a$ and $CA = d(xa)/a$. It follows that, along any particular sample path that we consider, the current account can be written as

$$CA = xS + dx. \tag{9}$$

Equation (9) shows that it is possible to interpret the current account as the sum of two terms. The first one measures the change in the stock of foreign assets that would keep constant the composition of the country portfolio, and this is what we refer to as *portfolio growth*. The second term measures the change in the composition of the country portfolio, and this is what we refer to as *portfolio rebalancing*.

To develop intuitions about the interplay between these two components of the current account, we present next a series of examples. In all of them, we assume the following sample path for the production shock:

$$d\omega = \begin{cases} 0, & t \in (-\infty, T_1), \\ \dfrac{\varepsilon}{\sigma}dt, & t \in [T_1, T_2) \quad (\varepsilon > 0), \\ 0, & t \in [T_2, \infty). \end{cases} \tag{10}$$

That is, the country experiences a sequence of unexpected production shocks equal to εdt times the capital stock for a finite period and zero afterwards. We refer to the period $[T_1, T_2)$ as the *shock period* and to $(-\infty, T_1)$ and $[T_2, \infty)$ as the *pre-* and *postshock periods*, respectively.

Figure 4 shows the behavior of the foreign asset position along this sample path. Regardless of the initial condition, during the preshock period the share of foreign assets converges towards

$$x^* = 1 + \frac{1}{2\lambda} - \sqrt{\left(\frac{1}{2\lambda}\right)^2 + \frac{\lambda^{-1}(\pi - \rho) - \rho + \delta}{\sigma^2}}.$$

Figure 4 THE SHARE OF FOREIGN ASSETS IN WEALTH

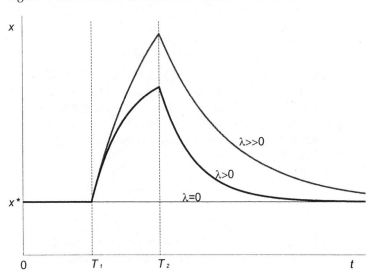

The simulation behind Figure 4 assumes that this value has been reached by $t = 0$. During the shock period the share of foreign assets increases steadily, albeit at a declining rate. The magnitude of this increase depends on λ. High values of λ imply that the effects of increased investment on operating costs are large and provide a strong inducement for investors to rebalance their portfolios towards foreign assests. During the postshock period, investment and operating costs decline. As a result, the share of foreign assets slowly returns to its preshock level. We next study the implications of this behavior of the share of foreign assets for the current account.

Consider first the case in which adjustment costs to investment are negligible, i.e, $\lambda \to 0$. Figure 4 shows that in this case the share of foreign assests is constant throughout. As a result, there is no portfolio rebalancing, i.e., $dx = 0$; and the current account is equal to portfolio growth, i.e., $CA = xS$. This is the new rule model that we analyzed in our previous paper, and its implications for a creditor and a debtor country are depicted in Figure 5. The top panel shows a creditor country, i.e. $x^* > 0$, while the bottom panel shows a debtor country, i.e. $x^* < 0$. Both countries raise their savings during the shock period as a result of the standard consumption-smoothing motive. Both countries also invest these marginal savings in domestic capital and foreign loans in the same proportions as their average portfolio. Since the foreign asset share is small in absolute value, we find that in both countries the increase in investment

Figure 5 PORTFOLIO GROWTH

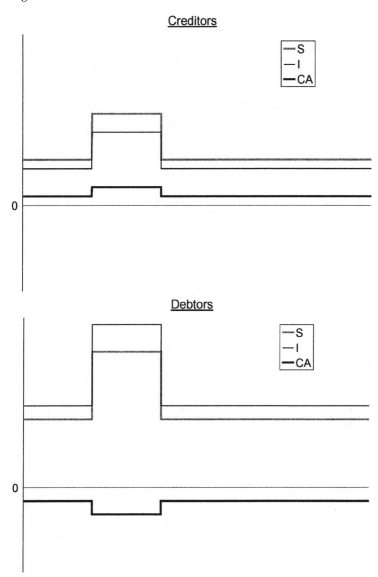

Notes: This figure shows saving (S), Investment (I), and the current account (CA), following a positive shock, in debtor and creditor countries, for the case λ = 0.

Figure 6 PORTFOLIO REBALANCING

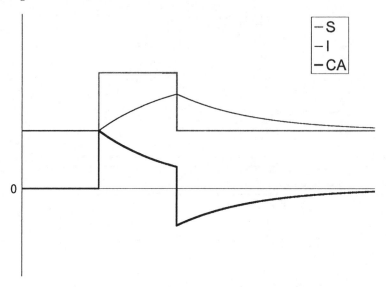

Notes: This figure shows saving (S), investment (I), and the current account (CA) following a positive shock, in a country with zero initial foreign assets, for the case $\lambda > 0$.

is of the same order of magnitude as the increase in saving. But it is not exactly the same, and this leads to different current account responses in debtor and creditor countries. In the creditor country, investment increases somewhat less than savings and the current account registers a surplus. In the debtor country, investment increases somewhat more than savings and the current account registers a deficit. This is the main result of our previous paper.

Consider next the case in which adjustment costs to investment are no longer negligible, i.e., $\lambda > 0$. Figure 6 shows the case of a country that is neither a debtor nor a creditor. By choosing the case $x^* = 0$, we know that in the absence of adjustment costs, the current account would be zero before, during, and after the shock. The country raises its savings during the shock period for the same consumption-smoothing motive as before. But adjustment costs now discourage large swings in investment, and this affects how these savings are distributed between domestic capital and foreign loans. During the shock period, the country uses most of its increase in savings to purchase foreign loans, while investment increases only gradually. Consumers rebalance their portfolios towards foreign assets, because the increase in investment raises operating costs and this lowers the expected return to domestic capital. The portfolio-rebalancing component of the current account is positive, and as a result the new rule underpredicts the current account surplus in the short run. In the postshock period investment falls slowly, but remains higher than normal for a while. Since productivity has returned to its preshock level, savings return to normal and the higher than normal investment is now financed by sale of foreign loans. Consumers rebalance their portfolios back towards their original composition, because the decline in investment lowers operating costs and this raises the expected return to domestic capital. The portfolio-rebalancing component of the current account is therefore negative, and as a result the new rule overpredicts the current account surplus in the medium run. As time passes, the country portfolio returns to its original composition and the new rule applies again in the long run.

This example clearly shows the role of foreign loans as a buffer stock to smooth the fluctuations in investment. Without access to foreign loans, countries would be forced not only to invest all of their savings at home but also to do so contemporaneously. Access to foreign loans permits countries to spread their domestic investment over time and, in this way, avoid paying high adjustment costs. To do this, countries temporarily place their savings in foreign loans and slowly convert them into domestic investment.

It is possible to design more complicated examples in which the current account exhibits richer dynamics. For instance, Figure 7 shows the case of positive adjustment costs in a creditor and a debtor country. One can interpret these examples as a combination of portfolio growth and portfolio rebalancing along the lines of the explanations of Figures 5 and 6. The theory developed here therefore equips us with a clear picture of the factors that determine how the current account reacts to increases in savings. The next step is to go back to actual data and attempt to interpret them from the vantage point of the theory.

4. The Process of Current Account Adjustment

In the introduction, we argued that in the long run most of the variation in current accounts in OECD countries is due to portfolio growth effects, while in the short run, current account fluctuations primarily reflect changes in the composition of country portfolios or portfolio rebalancing. We based this point on the observation that the simple interaction of a country's foreign asset share with its saving, averaged over the past thirty years, proved to be a very good predictor of the country's average current account. However, the same interaction using annual data proved to be

Figure 7 PORTFOLIO GROWTH AND PORTFOLIO REBALANCING

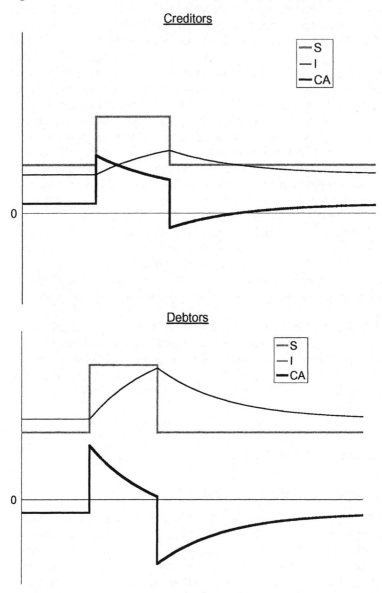

Notes: This figure shows saving (S), investment (I), and the current account (CA), following a positive shock, in debtor and creditor countries, for the case $\lambda > 0$.

a very poor predictor of year-to-year fluctuations in current accounts. This was shown in the two panels of Figure 2.[10]

The theory presented above has the potential to explain these observations. In the presence of adjustment costs to investment, the theory predicts that in the short run countries react to transitory income shocks by raising savings and rebalancing their portfolios towards foreign assets. If these costs are sufficiently strong, the theory can therefore explain why the short-run variation in the current account is dominated by portfolio rebalancing and not portfolio growth. The theory also predicts that in the aftermath of the shock countries gradually rebalance their portfolios back to their original composition. Therefore the theory can also explain why the long-run variation in the current account is dominated by portfolio growth and not portfolio rebalancing.

The theory also has very clear predictions for the patterns of portfolio rebalancing that we should observe in the data. The new-rule (portfolio-growth) component of the current account underpredicts the actual current account during the shock period as countries rebalance their portfolios towards foreign assets, whereas it overpredicts the current account after the shock as countries rebalance their portfolios back towards its original composition. In other words, a contemporaneous increase in savings should be associated with a positive portfolio-rebalancing component of the current account, whereas past increases in savings should be associated with negative values in the same component. Moreover, for the new rule to apply in the long run, these positive and negative components should be roughly of the same magnitude. In this section, we show that the data are consistent with these predictions.

We begin by decomposing observed current accounts into portfolio-growth and portfolio-rebalancing components. As in the theory, let x_{ct} denote the share of foreign assets in the portfolio of country c at the beginning of period t, and let S_{ct} and CA_{ct} denote gross national saving and the current account balance as a fraction of GDP during period t. We measure

10. Of course, one could argue that this discrepancy between the between-country and within-country results is simply due to much greater measurement error in the within-country variation in current accounts and portfolio growth than in the between-country variation. While measurement error is certainly present, we think it is clearly not the whole story. One way to see this is to notice that (1) measurement error in the RHS variable in our regression will bias the slope coefficient downward by a factor equal to the signal-to-noise ratio, and (2) measurement error in both the LHS and RHS variables will bias the R^2 by a factor equal to the product of the signal-to-noise ratios in the two variables. Since we observe a slope coefficient of one-half and an R^2 that falls from 0.85 in the between regression to 0.03 in the within regression, this implies a signal-to-noise ratio of only 0.55 in the RHS variable and 0.06 in the LHS variable. While there are clearly various measurement issues in our data, we find it implausible that the data are as noisy as this calculation would suggest.

the portfolio-growth component of the current account as $PG_{ct} \equiv x_{ct}S_{ct}$, i.e. the net purchases of foreign assets that would be observed during period t if a country were to distribute its saving between domestic and foreign assets in the same proportion as in its existing portfolio at the beginning of the period. We measure the portfolio-rebalancing component of the current account residually as the difference between the actual current account and the portfolio-growth component, i.e., $PR_{ct} \equiv CA_{ct} - x_{ct}S_{ct}$.

To implement this decomposition, we require data on current accounts, saving, and the share of foreign assets in country portfolios. We obtain annual data on current accounts in current U.S. dollars from the International Monetary Fund's *International Financial Statistics*. We measure gross national saving as the sum of the current account and gross domestic investment in current U.S. dollars, and express both as a fraction of GDP in current U.S. dollars, obtaining investment and GDP from the World Bank's world development indicators. We obtain data on the share of foreign assets in wealth from Kraay et al. (2000). We restrict attention to the set of 21 industrial countries for which at least 20 annual observations on this variable are available over the period 1966–1997 covered by this dataset.

With data on saving and the portfolio-rebalancing component of the current account in hand, we estimate a series of dynamic linear regressions of the form

$$PR_{ct} = \alpha_c + \sum_{v=1}^{p} \phi_{cv} \, PR_{c,t-v} + \sum_{v=0}^{q} \gamma_{cv} S_{c,t-v} + \beta_c' Z_{ct} + u_{ct}, \tag{11}$$

where PR_{ct} and S_{ct} are the portfolio-rebalancing components of the current account and saving as described above, Z_{ct} is a vector of control variables, and u_{ct} is a well-behaved error term. We then use the point estimates of the coefficients to retrieve the implied impulse response function of portfolio rebalancing in period $t + k$ to an increase in saving in period t, i.e. $\partial PR_{c,t+k}/\partial S_{ct}$. These impulse responses provide us with a picture of how countries change the composition of their portfolios following an increase in saving. The results of four such regressions are summarized in Table 1. The top panel of Table 1 reports the estimated coefficients, while the bottom panel reports the corresponding impulse response functions using the 21-country sample of annual observations. The estimated impulse response functions are also plotted in the four panels of Figure 8.

We begin by assuming that all of the slope coefficients are the same across countries. In our simplest specification, we also set $p = 0$ and intro-

Table 1 PORTFOLIO REBALANCING AND SAVING (ANNUAL DATA FOR 21 COUNTRIES)

	Regression 1		Regression 2		Regression 3		Regression 4	
	Coef.	S.E.	Coef.	S.E.	Coef.	S.E.	Mean Coef.	SD of Coefs.
Coefficient Estimates								
sy	0.598	0.096	0.504	0.080	0.746	0.079	0.691	0.286
sy(−1)	−0.281	0.133	−0.611	0.102	−0.824	0.104	−0.767	0.383
sy(−2)	−0.120	0.106	0.112	0.077	0.109	0.070	0.123	0.167
sy(−3)	−0.120	0.095	−0.043	0.073	0.040	0.067		
sy(−4)	−0.102	0.103	−0.031	0.065	−0.063	0.061		
sy(−5)	−0.060	0.078	0.020	0.058	0.019	0.057		
pr(−1)			0.754	0.056	0.845	0.057	0.837	0.216
pr(−2)			−0.114	0.069	−0.081	0.066	−0.152	0.186
pr(−3)			−0.031	0.049	−0.076	0.047		
dq					−0.375	0.050	−0.390	0.198
dpop					−0.684	0.188	−0.267	1.293
Country effects	Y		Y		Y			
Year effects	N		N		Y			
Impulse Responses								
t	0.598	0.096	0.504	0.054	0.746	0.059	0.691	0.286
t − 1	−0.281	0.133	−0.231	0.096	−0.193	0.095	−0.179	0.222
t − 2	−0.120	0.106	−0.119	0.058	−0.114	0.056	−0.111	0.142
t − 3	−0.120	0.095	−0.122	0.060	−0.098	0.054	−0.088	0.106
t − 4	−0.102	0.103	−0.102	0.042	−0.122	0.047	−0.059	0.076
t − 5	−0.060	0.078	−0.039	0.028	−0.068	0.040	−0.038	0.063
t − 6			−0.014	0.024	−0.040	0.037	−0.024	0.057
t − 7			−0.003	0.020	−0.019	0.035	−0.018	0.048
t − 8			0.000	0.016	−0.008	0.033	−0.014	0.041
t − 9			0.001	0.012	−0.002	0.030	−0.013	0.036
t − 10			0.001	0.009	0.001	0.027	−0.011	0.032

Note: This table reports the results of estimating equation (11) in the paper. The first three regressions assume slope coefficients are the same across countries. The last reports the mean and standard deviation across countries of country-by-country estimates. Standard errors for the impulse responses in regressions 2 and 3 are simulated using 500 draws from the estimated distribution of coefficients.

Figure 8 PORTFOLIO REBALANCING IN RESPONSE TO UNIT INCREASE IN SAVING
(ANNUAL DATA FOR 21 COUNTRIES)

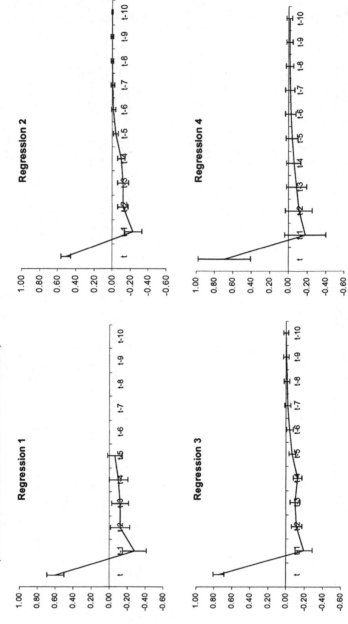

Notes: This figure reports the impulse response of the portfolio-rebalancing component of the current account to a one-year unit increase in saving implied by our estimates (11) under the four different specifications discussed in the text. The vertical bars denote one-standard-deviation intervals around the estimated coefficients.

duce $q = 5$ lags of saving.[11] The results of this specification are reported in the first regression of Table 1. In this case, the impulse response function simply consists of the estimated coefficients on current and lagged saving. We find a strong positive contemporaneous correlation between saving and the current account. The point estimate of 0.6 can be interpreted as the fraction of an increase in saving that, on impact, would be invested in foreign assets by a country with zero initial foreign assets. This fraction would be slightly higher (lower) in creditor (debtor) countries because of the portfolio-growth component. Since the latter measures the current account balance that would keep the composition of their portfolios constant following an increase in saving, it is by construction positive in creditor countries and negative in debtor ones.

The subsequent lags of saving all enter with negative coefficients that are decreasing in absolute value and, with the exception of the first lag, are not significantly different from zero. These coefficients can be interpreted as the fraction of the initial increase in saving that is reallocated back towards domestic assets in each of the subsequent five years. Interestingly, the sum of the coefficients on current and lagged saving is -0.09, which is insignificantly different from zero. This suggests that the initial shift toward foreign assets is largely undone in the next five years, with the bulk of the readjustment occurring in the first year following the increase in saving. This pattern is consistent with the predictions of the theory.

The rest of Table 1 reports a variety of robustness checks on this basic result. We begin by introducing lagged values of the portfolio-rebalancing component of the current account, and find that the first and second lags are strongly significant, while third (and higher) lags are not.[12] Although this slightly alters the point estimates of the coefficients on current and lagged saving, we find that the shape of the impulse response function is very similar to that reported in the first regression. The main difference

---

11. In unreported results, we find that fifth and higher lags of saving are insignificantly different from zero in most specifications, and adding higher lags has little effect on the point estimates of the coefficients on the first five lags.

12. We are assuming here that the time dimension of our panel is sufficiently large that we can obtain consistent estimates of the coefficients on the lagged dependent variable in the presence of fixed effects relying on large-T asymptotics. Remember also that saving is constructed as investment plus the current account, and the latter is highly correlated with the dependent variable in equation (11). To the extent that the portfolio-rebalancing component of the current account is measured with errors that are persistent over time, this could introduce a correlation between the residuals and current and lagged saving. In the specifications with lags of the dependent variable, we test for and do not reject the null of no serial dependence in the residuals, and so we can rule out this potential source of bias in our estimated impulse responses.

is that the initial shift toward foreign assets is slightly smaller than before, at 50% of the increase in saving.

In the next regression we augment the specification of the previous one with several additional control variables. To the extent that there are other shocks to returns that change the desired composition of country portfolios, and to the extent that these are correlated with saving, this will bias our results in directions which depend on the signs of these correlations. For example, if there are global shocks which raise saving and investment in all countries (such as changes in world interest rates), we will be underestimating the size of the initial shift toward foreign assets when saving increases. Similarly, if in countries and years in which saving is high, factors that increase the desired rate of investment (such as population or productivity growth) are also high, we may again be underestimating the shift toward foreign assets. To control for these factors, we introduce year dummies to capture global shocks, population growth, and Solow residuals as a proxy for productivity growth.[13] The third regression of Table 1 is this augmented specification. Population growth and Solow residuals enter significantly with the expected negative signs, and we find a larger shift toward foreign assets than before, with 75% of the initial increase in saving allocated toward foreign assets. However, the subsequent pattern of adjustment is the same as before, with the initial shift toward foreign assets being reversed in the next few years.

In the final regression, we relax the assumption that the slope coefficients in equation (11) are the same across countries, and instead estimate this equation separately for each country. Because of the fairly short time series available for each country, we adopt a more parsimonious lag structure, introducing only two lags of the dependent variable and of saving, as well as population growth and Solow residuals. We report the average and standard deviation across countries of the estimated coefficients in the last columns of Table 1.[14] Not surprisingly, we find that the country-by-country parameters are much less precisely estimated, and the dispersion across countries in the point estimates is large. Nevertheless, we find

---

13. We construct Solow residuals as the growth in GDP at constant prices less growth in employment times the period average share of labor in GDP, drawing the latter two variables from the OECD labor-force statistics and national accounts.

14. In the presence of parameter heterogeneity across countries, the pooled estimates reported in the previous two regressions will not deliver consistent estimates of the average (across countries) of these parameters when there is a lagged dependent variable (Pesaran and Smith, 1995). However, the average across countries of the estimated coefficients will provide a consistent estimate of the average response. We find results that are quantitatively quite similar across all specifications despite this potential source of bias in the estimates which impose parameter homogeneity across countries.

results that are qualitatively and quantitatively quite similar to those in the previous regressions. On average, the fraction of an increase in saving that is allocated to foreign assets is 0.7, and this initial shift toward foreign assets is quickly undone in subsequent periods.

One drawback of the annual data on which we have relied so far is that they are not informative about the intrayear dynamics of saving and the current account. For 12 of the countries in our sample, we were able to obtain quarterly observations on the current account, investment, and GDP beginning in 1980 or earlier from the *International Financial Statistics* and the OECD *Quarterly National Accounts*. For these countries, we linearly interpolate the annual data on the foreign asset share and use the result to construct quarterly portfolio growth and rebalancing components. We then re-estimate equation (11) using quarterly data, introducing eight lags of the portfolio-rebalancing component of the current account, and eight lags of saving. We do not have the quarterly data on population or employment growth required to introduce the same control variables as in the previous regressions with annual data (regressions 3 and 4 in Table 1). We therefore include only a set of period dummies and real GDP growth as controls.

As before, we summarize the results of these country-by-country regressions by computing the mean and standard deviation across countries of the estimated impulse responses. As shown in the top panel of Figure 9, we find that on impact, just over 60% of an increase in saving that lasts one quarter is invested abroad. Beginning immediately in the next quarter, this initial shift toward foreign assets begins to be reversed as countries run current account deficits. If we consider a shock to saving that lasts four quarters, the pattern that emerges is very similar to what we saw in the annual data. This is shown in the bottom panel of Figure 9. During the shock period, countries run positive but declining current account surpluses as they use foreign assets as a buffer stock to smooth investment. In subsequent years, countries run current account deficits in order to restore their original preshock portfolios.

To sum up, while portfolio growth explains much of the long-run variation in current accounts, portfolio rebalancing dominates in the short run. In all of our specifications, we find that the portfolio-rebalancing component of the current account follows a remarkably clear pattern. On impact, up to three-quarters of a shock to saving is invested abroad as countries use foreign assets as a buffer stock to smooth investment in the face of adjustment costs. In subsequent periods, the initial increase in saving produces current account deficits as countries shift their portfolios back to their original composition.

Figure 9 PORTFOLIO REBALANCING IN RESPONSE TO UNIT INCREASE
IN SAVING (QUARTERLY DATA FOR 12 COUNTRIES)

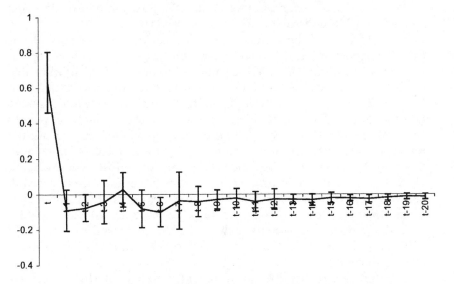

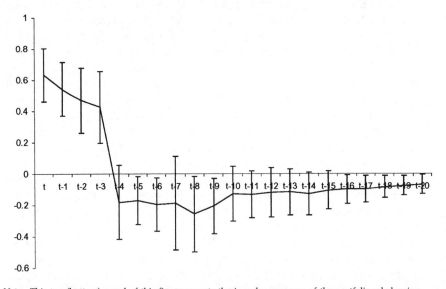

Notes: This top (bottom) panel of this figure reports the impulse response of the portfolio-rebalancing component of the current account to a one-quarter (four-quarter) unit increase in saving implied by our estimates (11), using quarterly data for 12 OECD countries. The vertical bars denote one-standard-deviation intervals around the estimated coefficients.

5. The Current Account and Investment

Over the past 20 years considerable empirical effort has been devoted to documenting the correlations between investment and the current account. Two stylized facts have emerged. First, cross-country correlations between investment and the current account are weak (Penati and Dooley, 1984; Tesar, 1991). Second, within countries the time-series correlation between investment and the current account is consistently negative (Glick and Rogoff, 1995). We document that these two stylized facts hold in our sample of countries in Figure 10. In the top panel we plot long-run averages of the current account as a fraction of GDP (on the vertical axis) against long-run investment rates (on the horizontal axis) for the 21 industrial countries in our sample. Across countries, we find a very weak negative correlation between the two, with a coefficient of -0.036. In the bottom panel, we plot the same two variables expressed as deviations from country means, pooling all available annual observations. Within countries, the correlation between investment and the current account is strongly negative, with a coefficient of -0.329.[15]

This difference between the correlations between the current account and investment in the long and in the short run is consistent with the view of the current account proposed in this paper. To see this, it is useful to write the current account and investment as follows:

$$CA_{ct} = x_{ct}S_{ct} + PR_{ct}, \tag{12}$$

$$I_{ct} = (1 - x_{ct})S_{ct} - PR_{ct}. \tag{13}$$

These equations decompose the current account and investment into their portfolio-growth and portfolio-rebalancing components. The key observation to explain the pattern of correlations between the current account and investment is that the long-run relationship between these variables is dominated by their portfolio-growth components, while the short-run relationship is dominated by the portfolio-rebalancing components. To make this statement precise, we decompose the coefficient of a regression of the current account on investment into the contributions of portfolio growth and portfolio rebalancing. Let β be this regression coefficient, and define

---

15. This is almost exactly the same as the average of country-by-country estimates reported in Glick and Rogoff (1995).

Figure 10 INVESTMENT AND THE CURRENT ACCOUNT

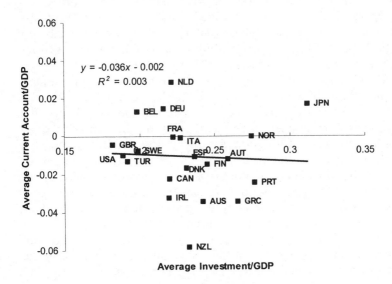

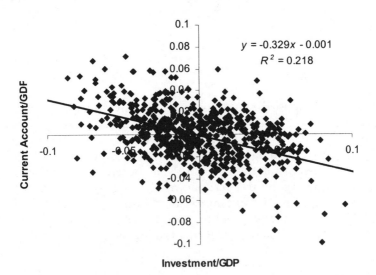

Notes: This figure plots the current account as a share of GDP against gross domestic investment as a share of GDP, using an unbalanced panel of 21 OECD countries over the period 1966–1997. The top panel plots period averages, and the bottom panel plots deviations from country means.

$$\beta^{PG} = \frac{Cov(xS, (1-x)I)}{Var(I)} \quad \text{and} \quad \beta^{PR} = \frac{Cov(CA, I)}{Var(I)} - \frac{Cov(xS, (1-x) \cdot I)}{Var(I)}.$$

Since $\beta = \beta^{PG} + \beta^{PR}$, we interpret β^{PG} and β^{PR} as the contributions of portfolio growth and portfolio rebalancing to the relationship between the current account and investment.

When we perform this decomposition on the between estimator in the top panel of Figure 10, we find that $\beta^{PG} = -0.041$ and $\beta^{PR} = 0.005$. Consistent with the theory, portfolio rebalancing plays no role in the long run, and the relationship between the current account and investment reflects only portfolio growth. Moreover, the theory predicts that the correlation between the current account and investment should be negative in debtor countries (where $x < 0$) and positive in creditor countries (where $x > 0$). The intuition is simple and follows immediately from the new rule: in debtor countries increases in saving generate even greater increases in investment, leading to current account deficits, while in creditor countries the increase in investment is less than that of saving, leading to current account surpluses. Since our sample of countries consists of a mixture of 15 debtor and 6 creditor countries, we should expect to find a negative but not especially strong correlation between investment and the current account in a cross section that pools all countries together. This is exactly what we found in the top panel of Figure 10. But when we divide our sample into debtors and creditors and compute the correlations separately in the two groups, we should find a negative correlation among debtors and a positive correlation among creditors. Figure 11 shows that this is the case. Of course, we have only a very small sample of creditors and debtors, and so these differences in slope should be taken with a grain of salt. Nevertheless, we note that they are consistent with the theory.

When we perform the same decomposition on the within estimator in the bottom panel of Figure 10, we find that $\beta^{PG} = -0.014$ and $\beta^{PR} = -0.315$. Consistent with the theory, portfolio rebalancing is important in the short run, and this introduces a source of negative correlation between the current account and investment. In the presence of adjustment costs, a shock to income in a given period triggers an adjustment process that lasts for many periods. In particular, a positive shock to income raises saving contemporaneously and is followed by several periods of portfolio rebalancing, as countries have higher than normal investment financed by current account deficits in order to restore their preshock portfolios. The opposite occurs when there is a negative shock. Thus positive shocks trigger a *ripple effect* of subsequent higher investment and lower current accounts, and vice versa for negative shocks. This effect is a source of negative correlation between investment and the current account within countries.

Figure 11 INVESTMENT AND THE CURRENT ACCOUNT IN THE LONG
RUN IN DEBTORS AND CREDITORS

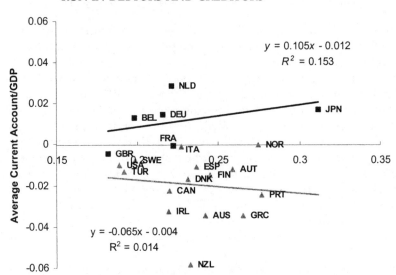

Notes: This figure plots the period average of the current account as a fraction of GDP against the period average of gross domestic investment as a fraction of GDP, using an unbalanced panel of 21 OECD countries over the period 1966–1997. The triangles (squares) correspond to countries with negative (positive) foreign assets averaged over the same period.

6. Concluding Remarks

By reconciling long- and short-run data, we further develop the view of the cyclical behavior of savings, investment, and the current account in industrial countries that we first proposed in Kraay and Ventura (2000). Faced with income shocks, countries smooth consumption by raising savings when income is high and vice versa. In the short run, countries invest most of their savings in foreign assets, only to rebalance their portfolios back to their original composition in the next four to five years. In the long run, country portfolios are remarkably stable, the new rule applies, and fluctuations in savings lead to fluctuations in the current account that are equal to savings times the share of foreign assets in the country portfolio. By using foreign assets as a buffer stock, countries smooth investment in order to save on adjustment costs.

An interesting implication of this view of international capital flows is that the stock of foreign assets and the current account are more volatile than consumption, investment, and the capital stock. But this does not mean that international capital flows are a factor that contributes to making macroeconomic aggregates more volatile or unstable. To the contrary, the view presented here suggests that the ability to purchase and sell foreign assets allows countries to smooth not only their consumption, but also their investment. Foreign assets and the current account absorb part of the volatility of these other macroeconomic aggregates.

Underlying the view proposed in this paper is the assumption that countries are unable or unwilling to use international financial markets to insure themselves against shocks. While few would question that this assumption is consistent with available evidence, it is certainly not consistent with existing theory. Until this inconsistency is resolved, we cannot claim a full understanding of international capital flows among industrial countries.

REFERENCES

Caballero, R. (1999). Aggregate investment. In *Handbook of Macroeconomics, Vol. 1B,* J. B. Taylor and M. Woodford (eds.). Amsterdam: Elsevier.

Deaton, A. (1992). *Understanding Consumption.* Oxford: Clarendon Press.

Dixit, A. K., and R. S. Pindyck. (1994). *Investment Under Uncertainty.* Princeton, NJ: Princeton University Press.

Dornbusch, R. (1983). Real interest rates, home goods, and optimal external borrowing. *Journal of Political Economy* 91:141–153.

Feldstein, M., and C. Horioka. (1980). Domestic savings and international capital flows. *Economic Journal* 90:314–329.

Glick, R., and K. Rogoff. (1995). Global versus country-specific productivity shocks and the current account. *Journal of Monetary Economics* 35:159–192.

Kraay, A., and J. Ventura. (2000). Current accounts in debtor and creditor countries. *Quarterly Journal of Economics* 95:1137–1166.

―――, N. Loayza, L. Servén, and ―――. (2000). Country portfolios. Cambridge, MA: National Bureau of Economic Research. NBER Working Paper 7795.

Lewis, K. (1999). Trying to explain home bias in equities and consumption. *Journal of Economic Literature* 37:571–608.

Lucas, R. E. (1967). Adjustment costs and the theory of supply. *Journal of Political Economy* 75:321–334.

Matsuyama, K. (1987). Current account dynamics in a finite horizon model. *Journal of International Economics* 23:299–313.

Merton, R. (1971). Optimum consumption and portfolio rules in a continuous-time model. *Journal of Economic Theory* 3:373–413.

Obstfeld, M. (1982). Aggregate spending and the terms of trade: Is there a Laursen–Metzler effect? *Quarterly Journal of Economics* 90:251–270.

―――, and K. Rogoff. (1995). The intertemporal approach to the current account. In *Handbook of International Economics,* vol. 3, G. Grossman and K. Rogoff (eds.). Amsterdam: Elsevier.

Penati, A., and M. Dooley. (1984). Current account imbalances and capital formation in industrial countries, 1949–81. *IMF Staff Papers* 31:1–24.

Persson, T., and L. Svensson. (1985). Current account dynamics and the terms of trade: Harberger–Laursen–Metzler two generations later. *Journal of Political Economy* 93:43–65.

Pesaran, H., and R. Smith. (1995). Estimating long-run relationships from dynamic heterogenous panels. *Journal of Econometrics* 68:79–113.

Sachs, J. (1981). The current account and macroeconomic adjustment in the 1970s. *Brookings Papers on Economic Activity* 1:201–268.

———. (1982). The current account in the macroeconomic adjustment process. *Scandinavian Journal of Economics* 84:147–159.

Svensson, L., and A. Razin. (1983). The terms of trade and the current account: The Harberger–Laursen–Metzler effect. *Journal of Political Economy* 91:97–125.

Tesar, L. (1991). Savings, investment and international capital flows. *Journal of International Economics* 31:55–78.

Ventura, J. (2001). A portfolio view of the U.S. current account deficits. Brookings Papers on Economic Activity.

Comment[1]

FABRIZIO PERRI
New York University, CEPR, and NBER

1. Introduction

This is a very interesting paper, and it contributes to our understanding of the determination of the current account in developed countries. In a previous paper [Kraay and Ventura (2000), henceforth KV] the authors developed a theory of the current account based on portfolio theory. They considered a world in which domestic residents can save in two assets: risky domestic capital and riskless foreign bonds. If the processes governing the returns to assets do not change much over time and if there are no other frictions, the optimal share of wealth in foreign bonds is kept to a constant level that depends only on the preference parameters and on the relative risk of domestic capital. This implies that when domestic consumers accumulate an additional unit of wealth, they invest it just like their existing portfolio. Since the current account is the change in the foreign asset position of a country, their theory implies that the current account should be roughly equal to the product of domestic saving (the increase in wealth) and the current share of foreign assets in the existing country portfolio. In the previous paper the authors argued that this theory explains very well the long-run evolution of the current account.

In this paper they instead show that even though in the long run the

1. I thank Aart Kraay and Jaume Ventura for kindly providing me their data set, and Alessandra Fogli for useful comments.

share of foreign assets in country portfolio is quite constant (consistently with their theory), in the short run there are significant deviations from the long-run share; in other words, short-run current account movements are not explained well by their theory. To reconcile this fact with their theory they modify their basic framework by introducing costs of adjusting domestic capital. These costs imply that in the short run countries are unwilling to change their domestic capital stock rapidly and thus shocks to their wealth will mostly affect their stock of foreign assets. Thus in the short run the share of foreign assets in their portfolio will be different from the long-run optimal constant level, but it will revert to that level in the long run. The authors call these deviations from the long-run share of foreign assets *portfolio rebalancing*.

Their theory implies that in response to a positive wealth shock we should on impact observe an increase in the current account and in domestic investment, but in subsequent periods a below average current account and above average investment. The authors identify wealth shocks in the data as shocks to saving, and they do find the response predicted by their theory, suggesting that portfolio rebalancing is indeed important in explaining the short-run behavior of the current account.

I believe that the authors, by bringing portfolio theory into international macroeconomics, have added an interesting dimension to the study of short-run current account dynamics. While the previous literature has stressed the role of the current account as the channel through which countries finance their investment to smooth their consumption (see for example Sachs, 1981), KV suggest another role: that of smoothing domestic investment growth to avoid adjustment costs.

In order to completely understand how an additional unit of saving is divided between domestic capital and foreign bonds, though, it is crucial to determine what is the cause of the increase in saving. If, for example, the increase in saving has been caused by a shock that has increased the return to domestic capital, such as a persistent productivity shock, then domestic consumers will want to invest all the additional saving, plus possibly foreign borrowing, in domestic capital; in this case increases in saving will be accompanied by current account deficits, as predicted by the standard intertemporal approach. If on the other hand the increase in saving does not change the relative return of the two assets, as for example in the case of a temporary productivity shock, then domestic consumers will want to invest it in both assets, and the increase in saving will be accompanied by current account surpluses, as described by KV.

I will first show that in the data both types of dynamics are present, suggesting the presence of two types of shocks; I will then present a simple intertemporal model of the current account that incorporates KV's

Table 1 MEDIAN CORRELATIONS,
21 COUNTRIES, 1966–1997

CA, Investment	CA, Saving	Investment, Saving
−0.40	0.29	0.78

All variables are ratios to GDP.

ideas and that can be used to assess the quantitative importance of the two types of shocks. The findings from the model are that both kinds of shocks and reactions are crucial to explain current account/investment dynamics.

The model can be also helpful to the reader in that it highlights the difference and similarities between the KV approach to the current account and the traditional intertemporal approach (see for example Backus, Kehoe, and Kydland, 1992, or Obstfeld and Rogoff, 1995).

2. What Are the Data Telling Us about Current Account/Investment Dynamics?

In this section I will extend in a simple way the data analysis of KV to further explore the relationship between investment, savings, and the current account.[2] Table 1 reports the median (across countries) correlations between these three variables.

Notice that even though investment and savings are quite strongly correlated, there is a large difference in the correlation between investment and current account (negative) and the correlation between current account and saving (positive). This observation suggests that the current account might respond differently depending on whether the underlying shock affects investment or affects saving. To further explore this idea it is useful to regress the current account-to-output ratio first on five lagged values of the saving-to-output ratio and then on five lagged values of the investment-to-output ratio.[3]

The estimated coefficients are then used to plot, in Figure 1, the current account responses to shocks in the saving-to-output ratio and the investment-to-output ratio. The top right panel depicts a temporary (exogenous) increase in saving, and the top left panel displays the responses of

2. The results presented in this section are based on the same data set used by KV.
3. The regressions also include country-specific fixed effects but no time dummies nor lagged values of the current account (as in KV's regression 1), and they are estimated using SUR. Results do not change significantly with the inclusion of time dummies or lagged values of the current account. The R^2 of the saving regression is 0.47, and that of the investment regression is 0.48.

Figure 1 CURRENT ACCOUNT RESPONSES TO A TEMPORARY 100-BASIS-
POINT INCREASE IN (a) SAVING / OUTPUT RATIO IMPULSE AND
(b) INVESTMENT / OUTPUT RATIO IMPULSE

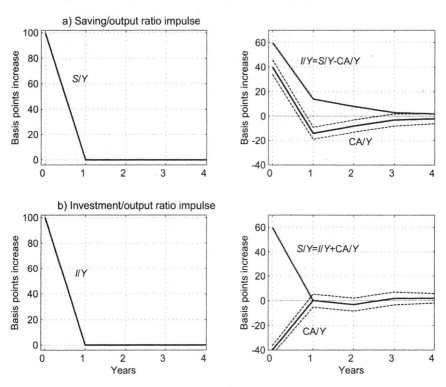

Note: The dashed lines are two-standard-error confidence bands.

the current account (estimated) and of investment (derived using the current account definition) to that increase. Similarly the bottom right panel depicts a temporary increase in investment, and the bottom left panel displays the responses of current account and saving.

The top two panels confirm KV's findings: in response to an increase in saving, countries increase both their current account position and their domestic investment position, but in subsequent periods they rebalance their portfolio by running current account deficits and further increasing domestic investment; the current account works as the buffer stock used to smooth out the increase in domestic investment. The fact that, on impact, both domestic investment and the current account increase suggests the importance of shocks to saving that do not change the relative returns between domestic and foreign assets.

The bottom two panels, on the other hand, show that when investment is treated as the independent variable the current account and investment on impact move in opposite directions. This suggests that countries are also hit by shocks that increase the return to domestic investment relative to foreign assets, and in response to these shocks they will increase investment, financing it using domestic savings as well as foreign borrowing.

Admittedly the results of these regressions are a bit difficult to interpret and have to be taken cautiously, as all variables involved are endogenously determined in response to some fundamental shocks. In the next section we will therefore present a simple model that slightly modifies the traditional intertemporal model of the current account to incorporate the insights of KV and that include two types of shocks. The model will show that dynamic relationships between current account, investment, and saving like the one depicted in Figure 1 arise as the optimal response to these two shocks.

3. A Small Open Economy Model

Consider an open economy, inhabited by a continuum of infinite-lived identical consumers, in which a homogenous good is produced and can be used for consumption or investment. Consumers can invest in domestic capital k_t or in a risk-free real bond b_t at the exogenously given world interest rate R. Time is discrete, and in each period consumers have a unit of time that they can allocate between labor (l_t) and leisure ($1 - l_t$) and get utility from consumption (c_t) and from leisure. They discount future utility at rate β and solve the following problem:

$$\max \sum_{t=0}^{\infty} \beta^t \frac{[c_t^\mu (1 - l_t)^{1-\mu}]^\sigma}{1 - \sigma}$$

s.t.

$$c_t + x_t + \psi(b_t - \bar{b})^2 + b_t \leq R b_{t-1} + w_t l_t,$$

$$k_t = (1 - \delta)k_{t-1} + x_t - \varphi\left(\frac{k_{t-1} - k_t}{k_{t-1}}\right)^2,$$

where σ is the parameter determining the intertemporal elasticity of substitution, x_t is the investment in domestic capital, w_t is the wage rate, δ is the depreciation rate of capital, and the parameter φ captures the intensity of the costs of adjusting the domestic stock of capital. Competitive firms rent domestic labor and capital to produce output y_t using a constant-return-to-scale technology, and the production process is subject to temporary (A_t^T) as well as persistent (A_t^P) productivity shocks[4] according to

$$y_t = A_t^P A_t^T k_{t-1}^\alpha l_t^{1-\alpha},$$

$$A_t^P = A_{t-1}^P + \varepsilon_t, \qquad A_t^T = \eta_t,$$

where α is the capital share in production and ε_t and η_t are normally distributed shocks with variances σ_ε^2, σ_η^2. For simplicity it is assumed that the permanent part of the shock process is a random walk, that the temporary part is i.i.d., and that the innovations to the shocks are uncorrelated.

The nonstandard element of the model is the term $\psi(b_t - \bar{b})^2$, which can be thought of as a convex bondholding cost and is a simple, even if crude, way of incorporating in this standard economy the insights of KV.

In a stochastic equilibrium of the KV model there is a unique long-run value of the foreign-bond position. This value is found by solving a portfolio problem, and it depends on the risk of domestic capital relative to foreign bonds and on the attitude of consumers toward risk. When shocks hit the economy, domestic households in the short run adjust the portfolio share of foreign bonds in order to reduce the capital adjustment costs. In the long run, though, mean–variance portfolio optimization makes the share of foreign bonds revert toward its long-run value (see Figure 4 of KV's paper).

When the economy presented here is solved using linear methods, the risk of the domestic capital (the variance of ε_t and η_t) has no effect on the portfolio decisions of domestic agents, and any average quantity of the foreign bond is consistent with a stochastic equilibrium. A consequence of this is that in a stochastic equilibrium the foreign-bond position is not mean-reverting and thus the dynamics discussed by KV are not present.

Introducing the bondholding cost is a simple trick that induces mean reversion in the foreign-asset position and thus allows the KV type of dynamics.[5] The long-run value around which foreign-asset position fluctuates and its degree of mean reversion are now exogenously determined by the parameters $\bar{b}$ and ψ.

To highlight the role of these bondholding costs, Figure 2 shows the impact of a temporary productivity shock on the current account (CA/Y), domestic investment (X/Y), saving (S/Y), and bond position (B/Y)

---

4. This specification allows a more flexible characterization of the persistence properties of productivity shocks. Both Baxter and Crucini (1995) and Glick and Rogoff (1995) have stressed the importance of the persistence of productivity in open economy models.
5. Heathcote and Perri (2002) also use this type of cost.

Figure 2 IMPULSE RESPONSES TO A TRANSITORY 1% PRODUCTIVITY
SHOCK

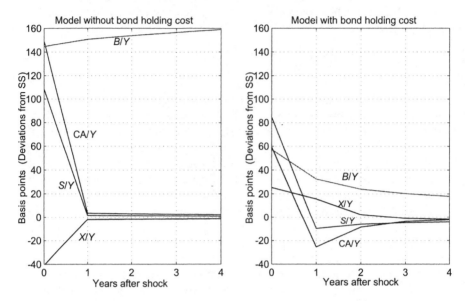

relative to output for an economy with $\bar{b} = 0$. The left panel displays the
response of the model with $\psi = 0$ (no cost), while the right panel displays
the response of an economy with positive ψ.

Temporary productivity shocks increase current output but do not affect the future productivity of capital, so in the model without costs agents
do not increase investment (X/Y falls) but save all the extra output in
foreign bonds (CA/Y rises). This is what KV call the "traditional rule."
Note that the bond position does not revert to its initial level. On the other
hand, in the model with the costs, domestic consumers do not want to
have a large change in their bond position, so they invest the additional
output in domestic capital as well as in foreign bonds. The presence of
adjustment cost on domestic investment is then the reason why on impact
households mostly invest in foreign bonds while in later periods they
reduce their foreign bond position, keeping investment in domestic capital high. Note also that now the foreign asset position exhibits mean reversion. Observe finally that the responses depicted in the right-hand panel
of Figure 2 are very similar to the one presented by KV in Figure 6, showing that this simple change modifies the standard intertemporal model of
the current account to establish the current account as a way of smoothing
investment.

Table 2   BENCHMARK PARAMETER
          VALUES

Preferences	$\beta = \dfrac{1}{R} = 0.96, \quad \mu = 0.3, \quad \sigma = 2$
Technology	$\alpha = 0.36, \quad \delta = 0.08$
Shocks	$\sigma_\varepsilon = 1\%, \quad \sigma_\eta = 0.5\%$
Costs	$\varphi = 0.8, \quad \psi = 0.13, \quad \bar{b} = 0$

The remainder of this discussion will address the quantitative importance of this role. First the choice of the model parameter values is discussed, and then numerical results are presented.

4. Parameter Values

The model is calibrated to annual data. Setting preference and technology parameters is a standard exercise (see for example Mendoza, 1991), and the values are reported in the first two rows of Table 2.

There are two nonstandard calibration issues. The first is the identification of the importance of temporary vs. permanent productivity shocks. This is a quite hard empirical problem that has a close parallel in the labor literature. Here I take a crude approach of estimation by simulation. I first normalize the value of σ_ε (the variance of persistent shocks) to 1% and set σ_η (the variance of the temporary shocks) so that, when a productivity process is simulated for 38 periods and current productivity is regressed on lagged productivity, a coefficient of 0.81 is obtained.[6] This procedure yields a value for σ_η of 0.5%.

The second issue is the determination of the parameters of the bondholding costs. The steady-state bond position $\bar{b}$ is set to 0, which roughly matches the foreign bondholdings in the cross section of countries in the KV dataset. To set the value of the intensity of the bondholding costs (ψ), one possibility is to match the volatility of investment or of the trade balance relative to output (as in Schmitt-Grohé and Uribe, 2002). The problem with that approach is that there are many combinations of ψ and φ (the adjustment costs on investments) that yield the same value for the

---

6. The value of 0.81 is obtained by regressing the multifactor productivity of the private business sector (from BLS) on the lagged multifactor productivity and on a linear time trend. The frequency of the series is annual, and the time period is 1960–1997. Note that for a quarterly frequency this value would imply a persistence of productivity of roughly 0.95.

Table 3   CORRELATIONS, DATA, AND MODELS

	CA, Investment	CA, Saving	Investment, Saving
Data	−0.40	0.29	0.78
Models			
Benchmark	−0.36	0.28	0.78
No bondholding costs	−0.78	0.63	−0.06
No transitory shocks	0.69	0.15	0.78
Large transitory shocks	0.02	0.61	0.78

All variables are ratios to GDP. Statistics from the model are average across 100 simulations, each of 38 periods.

target statistics, and unfortunately the results of the model are sensitive to the particular pair of ψ and φ chosen.

Note, though, from the impulse responses in Figure 2, that temporary productivity shocks always cause an increase in saving but, depending on the presence of the bondholding costs, cause either an increase or a decrease in investment; this implies that the correlation between savings and investment is highly sensitive to the size of the bondholding costs.[7] This observation suggests setting the bondholding cost to match the median correlation between investment and saving reported in Table 1 while setting the adjustment costs on investment to match a volatility of investment relative to output of 2.4.[8] This procedure yields values of $\psi = 0.13$ and $\varphi = 0.8$. The full set of benchmark parameters is reported in Table 2.

5. Results

In Table 3 the line labeled "Benchmark" reports the model's predicted current account/investment, current account/saving, and saving/investment correlations, using the benchmark parameter values. Although the model is calibrated to match only the investment/saving correlation, it does a good job in reproducing the other two correlations. Figure 3 reports the same current account responses presented in Figure 1, together with current account responses based on artificial data generated by the

7. One possible interpretation of the bondholding costs is the degree of international financial friction faced by the economy; with high bondholding costs countries international borrowing is costly and domestic saving is highly correlated with domestic investment; with low bondholding costs domestic saving and investment are not necessarily correlated.
8. This value is computed by taking the average of standard deviations of HP filtered annual real investment over HP filtered annual real GDP for the United States, Japan, Canada, and the European Union over the period 1966–1997. Data are from OECD quarterly national accounts.

Figure 3 DATA AND MODEL: CURRENT ACCOUNT RESPONSES TO
(a) SAVING/OUTPUT RATIO, (b) INVESTMENT/OUTPUT RATIO

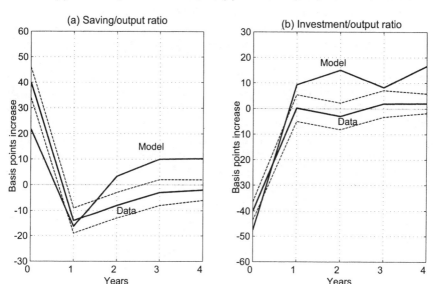

Note: The dashed lines are two-standard-error confidence bands.

model.[9] The figure suggests that the model is also able to capture quite well the entire dynamics of the current account in response to investment and saving fluctuations.

The remaining results presented in Table 3 establish that all elements of the model presented are indeed essential to understand the data.

The line labeled "No bondholding cost" reports the correlations predicted by a version of the model without the bondholding costs[10]; in this case in response to permanent productivity shocks agents borrow heavily to finance investment, leading to a counterfactually highly negative current account/investment correlation and to a counterfactually low saving/investment correlation. Also, in response to temporary productivity shocks, agents invest heavily in foreign bonds, leading to a counterfactually high correlation between savings and the current account.

The line labeled "No transitory shocks" shows that also the presence of transitory shocks is essential. The correlations reported there are from

9. The model-based impulse responses are computed by running on artificial data the same regression we run on the actual data.
10. In this parametrization of the model the adjustment cost on investment is set to a higher value so that the model still matches the relative volatility of investment.

a version of the model in which a single persistent productivity shock[11] is used and in which the parameters ψ and φ are chosen to match the same moments as in the benchmark case. Notice that in this case the model fails to reproduce the negative correlation between investment and the current account. The reason for this is that with a single persistent shock, investment tends to be very volatile relative to output, and quite large adjustment costs are required to match the relative volatility of investment in the data. When adjustment costs are large, agents do not undertake large investment in one period and hence do not need to run a current account deficit when they want to increase their investment.

Finally, the line labeled "Large temporary shocks" reports the results for a version of the model in which the predominant shocks are temporary productivity shocks[12] (like the shocks analyzed by KV). Notice that again the model cannot reproduce the negative correlation between investment and current account. When temporary shocks hit, on impact agents invest in domestic capital and in foreign bonds at the same time, and this induces positive correlation between the two variables; in the subsequent periods they rebalance their portfolio by keeping investment high and by running current account deficits, and this behavior induces a negative correlation between the variables. It turns out that quantitatively the two effects cancel, and that the overall correlation between investment and current account is close to 0 and not negative. This suggests that short-run current account dynamics cannot be understood using only the investment-smoothing argument.

6. Concluding Remarks

The previous literature has stressed the current account as a tool countries use to smooth consumption and finance their investment. This use seems particularly important when countries are hit by persistent productivity shocks. The important contribution of KV's paper is the suggestion of another role of the current account: in smoothing investment to reduce capital adjustment costs. This role seems important when countries are hit by temporary productivity shocks. The data and the simple model analyzed in these comments suggest that both shocks and thus both roles of the current account are at work and that both need to be considered

11. The persistence of this shock is set equal to the persistence of the composite shock in the original model.
12. In this case the variance of temporary shocks is set twice as large as that of permanent shocks, and the cost parameters are set to match the same moments. Obviously, in this case the persistence of the composite productivity does not match the data.

explicitly when trying to understand current account and investment dynamics.

REFERENCES

Backus, D., P. Kehoe, and F. Kydland. (1992). International real business cycles. *Journal of Political Economy* 100:745–775.
Baxter, M., and M. Crucini. (1995). Business cycles and the asset structure of foreign trade. *International Economic Review* 36:821–854.
Glick, R., and K. Rogoff. (1995). Global versus country-specific productivity shocks and the current account. *Journal of Monetary Economics* 35:159–192.
Heathcote, J., and F. Perri. (2002). Financial autarky and international business cycles. *Journal of Monetary Economics* 49:601–627.
Kraay, A., and J. Ventura. (2000). Current Account in debtor and creditor countries. *Quarterly Journal of Economics* 95:1137–1166.
Mendoza, E. (1991). Real business cycles in a small open economy. *The American Economic Review* 81:797–818.
Obstfeld, M., and K. Rogoff. (1995). The intertemporal approach to the current account. In *Handbook of International Economics*, G. Grossman and K. Rogoff (eds.). Amsterdam: Elsevier.
Sachs, J. (1981). The current account and macroeconomic adjustment in the 1970s. *Brookings Papers on Economic Activity* 1:201–268.
Schmitt-Grohé, S., and M. Uribe. (2002). Closing small open economy models. *Journal of International Economics*, forthcoming.

Comment

ERIC VAN WINCOOP
University of Virginia and NBER

1. Introduction

In terms of international capital mobility the world economy appears to be very closed and very integrated at the same time. During the East Asian financial crisis we saw enormous swings in net capital flows over a very short span of time, equal to 10% of GDP or more for some countries. During the same crisis net capital inflows to the United States almost doubled. Capital appears to rapidly reallocate across countries in response to perceived risk and expected returns. On the other hand, Feldstein and Horioka's (1980) finding that there is almost a one-to-one relationship between saving and investment rates in cross-section data remains true today, suggesting that almost all of national savings is invested at home and net capital flows remain relatively small. What could account for this seemingly paradoxical state of affairs?

The paper by Kraay and Ventura is a nice contribution that both documents this puzzle and sheds light on what may explain it. In my comments I will discuss both the evidence and theoretical explanations.

2. The Evidence: Short Run vs. Long Run

The starting point in developing their empirical evidence is the so-called *new rule*, which Kraay and Ventura documented in an earlier paper. The rule says that the change in the current account is equal to the change in national savings times the share of foreign assets in a country's portfolio. Since the share of foreign assets in the portfolio tends to be small due to home bias, this implies that most of a change in national saving is invested at home, consistent with Feldstein and Horioka's finding. The new rule appears to hold up very well in the long run, but not in the short run. The long run is captured by a cross-section relationship using the average over 30 years of saving and the current account as a percentage of GDP. The short-run relationship is found after subtracting from saving and the current account their long-run averages. In the long run the new rule holds almost perfectly, while in the short run it explains almost nothing of the relationship between the current account and saving.

The authors refer to the deviation from the new rule in the short run as the portfolio-rebalancing component of the current account: $CA_t - x_t S_t$, where x_t is the fraction of the portfolio invested abroad. In order to better understand what drives this deviation from the new rule, they regress $CA_t - x_t S_t$ on current and lagged saving rates, as well as several controls. The coefficient on current saving is large and positive, suggesting that about 60% to 70% of a change in savings is invested abroad (corresponding to a current account surplus). The coefficients on lagged savings are negative, though, with the sum of all coefficients close to zero. This suggests that for $x = 0$ a change in savings has little or no effect on the current account in the long run. It appears therefore that while initially most of a change in national savings is invested abroad, in the long run almost all of it is invested at home. Large swings in the current account are therefore possible in the short run, while the current account remains close to zero in the long-run.

The regressions on which the conclusions are based suffer from well-known endogeneity problems. Any time one regresses investment on saving or the current account on saving, it is questionable which affects which. The authors include some variables in the regression that can be expected to affect both saving and investment in the same direction, such as global shocks or population growth. That does not fully deal with the endogeneity problem, though. There may be exogenous shifts in investment that affect both saving and the current account and show up in the error term of a regression of $CA_t - x_t S_t$ on saving.

I have reason to believe though that the results will hold up to more careful empirical analysis. In Iwamoto and van Wincoop (2000) we compared the short- and long-run relationships between saving and investment rates by looking at correlations. This way one does not need to take a stand on the direction of causation. We captured the long run by looking at the cross-section relationship between saving and investment for OECD countries, and the short run by looking at the average time-series relationship for OECD countries. The results are summarized in Table 1.

In the raw data (using saving and investment rates as a share of GDP), the cross-section relationship is considerably stronger than the time-series relationship. In the second row we control for a variety of factors that might account for a positive relationship between saving and investment rates even when financial markets are perfectly integrated. For the cross-section data these are differences in growth rates, fiscal policy, and income levels across countries. For the time-series data they are global, business-cycle, and fiscal shocks. The correlations are based on the components of saving and investment rates that are orthogonal to these common factors. After controlling for common factors the cross-section correlation remains very high at 0.76. Since Feldstein and Horioka, a large literature has developed pointing to common factors as a potential explanation, so far none has convincingly held up for the cross-section evidence. The time-series correlation drops to a low 0.28 after controlling for common factors. It appears therefore that there is a strong long-term relationship between saving and investment that cannot be explained by common factors, while there is a very weak short-term relationship. This is in essence the same conclusion drawn by Kraay and Ventura.

The fact that the long-run cross-section relationship cannot be explained away easily by common factors suggests that Feldstein and Hori-

Table 1   CROSS-SECTION AND (AVERAGE) TIME-SERIES CORRELATION BETWEEN SAVING AND INVESTMENT FOR 15 OECD COUNTRIES

	Correlation	
	Cross section (1985–1990)	Time series (1975–1990)
Raw data	0.85	0.56
Controlling for common factors	0.76	0.28

oka, who interpreted the relationship as reflecting imperfect international capital mobility, were right after all. Data on saving and investment rates for regions within a country further confirm this. Iwamoto and van Wincoop (2000) show that for Japanese prefectures the cross-section correlation is close to zero. Other studies often obtain even substantially negative cross-section correlations for regions within a country. As pointed out, though, in van Wincoop (2000), the substantial negative correlations are a result of incorrect measurement of savings at the regional level. With a correct measurement of saving the correlations are close to zero. This evidence suggests that borders across regions within a country are much less of a barrier to capital flows than international borders. It remains to be explained, though, why the short-term (time-series) relationship is so much weaker than the long-term cross-section relationship between national saving and investment rates.

3. The Theory: Why Is the Savings–Investment Relationship Much Weaker in the Short Run?

The answer suggested by Kraay and Ventura is adjustment costs of investment. When there are substantial short-term adjustment costs, one may expect that in the short run most of an increase in saving is invested abroad. In the long run adjustment costs play no role and it is again the case that a rise in saving leads to a rise in domestic investment of similar magnitude. The paper illustrates this story in the context of a simple portfolio-choice model, in which agents can invest in domestic capital and foreign bonds. A critical assumption is that domestic capital can only be held by domestic agents. This is an exogenous home-bias assumption, which leads to the close relationship between saving and investment in the long run.

The paper only considers the impact of a temporary productivity shock. Although this can be used to illustrate the portfolio-rebalancing effect that leads to the deviation from the new rule in the short run (and therefore a weak short-run S–I relationship), the example tells us little about the long run. One could alternatively consider a permanent increase in saving, for example through a drop in the time discount rate. It will again be the case that in the short run most of the rise in saving is invested abroad due to the adjustment costs associated with domestic investment. In the long run the new rule will hold again, so that most of the rise in saving is invested at home.

The new rule can actually be expected to hold in the long run almost irrespective of particular modeling assumptions one makes. As long as one makes one of many possible assumptions to assure that there is a steady-state level of foreign bondholdings, the new rule applies. This can be seen as follows. With b and k respectively foreign-bond holdings and the capital stock, and g the steady-state growth rate, we have in steady state $S = db + dk = g(b + k)$ and $I = gk$. It follows that $CA = S - I = gb = xS$, where $x = b/(b + k)$ is the share of the portfolio invested abroad. The new rule becomes more than a simple accounting identity, though, when it is interpreted as saying that the current account is equal to saving times a *constant x*. In Kraay and Ventura (2000), the authors find that the fraction of the portfolio invested abroad indeed does not fluctuate a lot, although it fluctuates substantially more over a 10-year period than over a 1-year period. This appears to be inconsistent with the proposed theory, in which there is only portfolio rebalancing in the short run and not in the long run. In the theory expected returns are constant in the long run due to the constant-returns-to-scale production function, while in the short run expected returns can change due to adjustment costs.

Instead of temporary changes in x, as in the proposed theory, consider a case in which there are small permanent changes in the fraction invested abroad. The following example illustrates that this can have a much bigger impact on the current account in the short run than in the long run. Consider a shock that leads to a permanent increase in x from 0 to 0.01 and a permanent rise in savings from 10% to 15% of GDP. Since $CA = xS$ in the long run, it is easily checked that investment will rise by 4.85% of GDP in the long run, almost exactly the same as the rise in saving. The current account will rise by only 0.15% of GDP. So saving and investment move closely together in the long run, and applying the new rule when holding x at zero gives a reasonably close prediction (of zero) of the change in the current account. If the capital–output ratio is 3 (about average), b/y will immediately rise by 0.03, so that there will be an immediate current account surplus of 3% of GDP. In the short run therefore most of the increase in saving (60% of it) is invested abroad.

This example suggests that a model where shocks lead to small but permanent portfolio rebalancing can account for the evidence. One therefore does not need constant returns to scale in the long run. To capture the evidence best, a model should have the following features: (i) x is small, (ii) changes in x are relatively small, (iii) long-run changes in x are at least as big as short-run changes. In order to capture (i) endogenously, one can introduce features such as information asymmetries or contract enforcement problems. My guess is that such a model naturally also leads to (ii): the source of the home bias is likely also to make the fraction invested abroad relatively insensitive to expected returns. Finally, (iii) is easily captured as long as we avoid constant returns to scale in the long run and very large short-run adjustment costs.

4. To Conclude

The evidence that Kraay and Ventura have presented is intriguing. It suggests that the current account is an important buffer for shocks in the short run, but is relatively little affected by shocks in the long run. In other words, saving and investment are closely tied in the long run, but not the short run. The evidence begs for a theory. In my view models that endogenously introduced home bias are likely to be most fruitful for understanding these stylized facts. Along this line it would also be interesting to explore the implications of Obstfeld and Rogoff (2000), who have suggested trade costs as the source of all major puzzles in international macroeconomics, including the portfolio-home-bias and Feldstein–Horioka puzzles.

REFERENCES

Feldstein, M., and C. Horioka. (1980). Domestic savings and international capital flows. *Economic Journal* 90:314–329.
Iwamoto, Y., and E. van Wincoop. (2000). Do borders matter? Evidence from Japanese regional net capital flows. *International Economic Review* 41(1):241–269.
Kraay, A., and J. Ventura. (2000). Current accounts in debtor and creditor countries. *Quarterly Journal of Economics* 95:1137–1166.
Obstfeld, M., and K. Rogoff. (2000). The six major puzzles in international macroeconomics: Is there a common cause? In *NBER Macroeconomics Annual 2000*, B. S. Bernanke and K. Rogoff (eds.). Cambridge, MA: The MIT Press.
van Wincoop, E. (2000). Intranational versus international saving–investment comovements. In *Intranational Macroeconomics*, G. Hess and E. van Wincoop (eds.). Cambridge University Press, pp. 11–36.

Discussion

An issue that concerned a number of participants was the assumption that claims on capital could not be traded internationally. Robert Barro noted that if claims on capital can be traded internationally, gross rather than net foreign assets are what matter. In particular, he noted that there is always a positive relationship between savings shocks and the current account, but the magnitude of the effect depends on the percentage of the capital stock that is domestically owned.

On this point, Gian-Maria Milesi-Ferretti noted that the size of portfolio diversification has changed a lot over the authors' sample period. As an example, he said that for the United Kingdom, while foreign assets plus foreign liabilities were 40% of GDP in 1966, in 2002 they were 320% of GDP. He pointed out that this is a much more significant change than the change in net positions over the same period. As a result, he agreed with Barro in finding the authors' bond-type modeling strategy puzzling.

The treatment of shocks in the paper and resulting endogeneity concerns raised interest among the participants. Pierre-Olivier Gourinchas noted that the literature on the intertemporal approach to the current account suggests paying special attention to the distinction between transitory and permanent shocks. He felt that while Kraay and Ventura had dealt with this issue in the model, they had not paid it sufficient attention in the empirical part of the paper. He suggested that if the issue were addressed, it would affect the estimated impulse responses. Echoing the discussants, he also said he would have liked to see the authors consider other types of shocks in addition to productivity shocks; for example, shocks to government spending. He wondered whether, in the data, it would be possible to identify different kinds of responses to different shocks.

Alan Stockman also wondered whether different shocks might explain the short- and long-run behavior of the current account. He noted that this fact might be masked if shocks are not well identified. He also pointed out that among developed countries, there are lots of highly correlated shocks. He saw this as a problem for the paper, although there might be predictions about the differential behavior of countries that are more or less synchronized with the international business cycle.

Charles Engel questioned the contention that all of the explanations of the Feldstein–Horioka puzzle are unsatisfactory. He noted that he had always found the budget-constraint explanation convincing, as budget constraints imply a long-run relationship between savings and investment while leaving a great deal of flexibility in explaining the short-run relationship between them. He also pointed out that when there is a budget constraint, it is unlikely that there are instruments for saving that are uncorrelated with investment.

Also on the issue of endogeneity, Mark Gertler suggested that with quarterly data, the portfolio-rebalancing and savings variables could be embedded in a VAR, and their joint responses to standard identified shocks such as money shocks and productivity shocks could be examined. Bob Hall suggested that looking at cross-covariances in a general-equilibrium framework would be an attractive way of sidestepping the identification issues raised by the authors' regressions.

The authors' assumptions about adjustment costs were commented upon by several participants. Pierre-Olivier Gourinchas was worried that the results were not robust to adjustment-cost assumptions. He was concerned particularly by the fact that, as a result of the particular assumptions, investment doesn't jump in response to productivity shocks in the model.

Mark Gertler made some suggestions on how to explain the slow adjustment of investment without appealing to huge adjustment costs. In addition to the financial-market frictions discussed by Fabrizio Perri, he

mentioned planning lags. He cited evidence documented by Owen La-
mont that large corporations make investment decisions one year in advance, and that up to 90% of investment is committed in advance.

Gian-Maria Milesi-Ferretti argued that, in contrast to the maintained
hypothesis of the paper, the share of net foreign assets in wealth is not
empirically stable. As evidence, he referred to the authors' paper on country portfolios, which he said suggested that net foreign asset positions are
nonstationary and that countries' positions as creditors and debtors
change over time.

In response to the discussants and other participants, Jaume Ventura
defended the authors' assumption of limited international risk sharing.
He remarked that the intertemporal approach to the current account is
successful precisely because of the home bias in portfolios it generates.
He noted that recent research by Fabrizio Perri and Pat Kehoe explores
how frictions such as lack of trust and the inability to write contracts
might generate the budget constraint that the intertemporal approach to
the current account takes as given. On Milesi-Ferretti's point on the stability of country portfolios, he acknowledged that country portfolios are not
always stable. In particular, he remarked that the debt crisis in developing
countries in the 1980s resulted in very unstable portfolios in those countries. He noted that the intertemporal theory of the current account does
not work particularly well for developing countries. The budget constraint is on the one hand too tight, in that it does not allow for risk sharing, but on the other hand too loose, in that it allows countries to consume
a lot in any given period, without regard for future willingness to pay.
However, he maintained that the budget constraint is approximately correct for developed countries. On the issue of endogeneity and shocks, Ventura explained that the authors found their story with transitory shocks
to income and consequent oscillations in savings more relevant than a
story with permanent shocks to productivity, because they felt it did a
better job of explaining the long-run as well as the short-run evidence.

Aart Kraay made a further comment on Milesi-Ferretti's point about
the stability of country portfolios. He responded that the fact that not all
developed-country portfolios are completely stable merely amounts to
saying that the R^2 is not equal to one. On the issue of endogeneity, he
pointed out that it is very difficult to find convincing instruments for savings. However, he felt that the most important thing to worry about is
the possibility that there are omitted variables driving savings and investment in such a way as to give exactly the results in the paper. He said
that the Feldstein–Horioka literature had searched for such variables, but
had not had great success in explaining the cross section, and in any case
these variables were controlled for in the empirical work.

J. Bradford DeLong
UNIVERSITY OF CALIFORNIA AT BERKELEY AND NBER

Productivity Growth in the 2000s

1. Introduction

In the early 1970s, U.S. productivity growth fell off a cliff. Measured output per person-hour had averaged a growth rate of 2.8% per year from 1947 to 1973. It averaged a growth rate of only 1.3% per year from 1973 to 1995. In the second half of the 1990s American productivity growth resumed its pre-1973 pace. Between 1995 and the third quarter of 2002, U.S. measured nonfarm-business output per person-hour worked appeared to grow at an annual rate of 2.8% per year.

Nearly all observers agree on the causes of the productivity speedup of 1995–2002. It is the result of the extraordinary wave of technological innovation in computer and communications equipment. Assume that this near-consensus is correct: that the productivity growth speedup in the second half of the 1990s was the result of the technological revolutions in data processing and data communications. What, then, will the future hold? Will the decade of the 2000s see labor productivity growth more like the fast growth seen in the late 1990s? Or more like the slow growth of the 1980s?

In my view, the way to bet is that the next ten years or so will see labor productivity growth as fast as or faster than the U.S. economy has seen since 1995. The answer to the question, "What can we expect from productivity growth in America over the next 10 to 20 years?" is "We can expect very good things."

The case for this point of view follows almost immediately from simple growth accounting and growth theory. The main argument of this paper

I would like to thank the University of California at Berkeley for financial support, and Martin Baily, Susanto Basu, Tim Bresnehan, Nick Crafts, Paul David, Roger Ferguson, John Fernald, Michael Froomkin, Mark Gertler, Robert Gordon, Ned Gramlich, Christopher Gust, Robert Hall, Chad Jones, Boyan Jovanovic, Jaime Marquez, Ken Rogoff, Paul Romer, Suzanne Scotchmer, Andrei Shleifer, Dan Sichel, Larry Summers, Manuel Trajtenberg, Hal Varian, Robert Waldmann, and Gavin Wright for helpful discussions and comments.

begins, after a brief review of the recent history and recent assessments of the cases of changes in productivity growth, by considering the simplest possible growth-theory model that has traction on the major issues. In the near-consensus analysis, increased total factor productivity (TFP) in the information technology (IT) capital-goods-producing sector, coupled with extraordinary real capital deepening as the quantity of real investment in IT capital bought by a dollar of nominal savings grows, has driven the productivity growth acceleration of the later 1990s. The extraordinary pace of invention and innovation in the IT sector has generated real price declines of between 10% and 20% per year in information processing and communications equipment for nearly forty years so far. These extraordinary cost declines have made a unit of real investment in computer or communications equipment absurdly cheap, and hence made the quantity of real investment and thus capital deepening in IT capital absurdly large.[1]

In the 1990s the expanding role and influence of these leading sectors became macroeconomically significant. In a standard growth-accounting framework, the later 1990s saw rapid labor productivity growth because of (1) rapid technological progress in the leading sectors, (2) a healthy share of expenditure on the products of these leading sectors, raising the real IT capital–output ratio, and (3) continued utility of IT capital in production. Continued declines in the prices of IT capital mean that a constant nominal flow of savings channeled to such investments brings more and more real investment. The social return to IT investment would have to suddenly drop to nearly zero, the share of nominal investment spending devoted to IT capital would have to collapse, or technological progress in IT would have to slow drastically, for labor productivity growth in the next decade to reverse itself and return to its late 1970s or 1980s levels. Yet there are no technological reasons for the pace of productivity increase in our economy's leading sectors to decline over the next decade or so. Thus if nominal shares of expenditure on IT capital and of income attributable to existing IT capital remain constant, we can expect the next decade or more to be like the past since 1995. That is the lesson that growth-theory finger exercises have to teach us.

Second, there are four unknown cards in the hole—four reasons to think that the future is likely to be brighter than the simplest models suggest. First, the elasticity of demand for IT goods is likely to remain high. A high elasticity of demand for IT technology goods means that as prices fall, expenditure shares will not remain constant but will rise, boosting

1. It may indeed be the case that a unit of real investment in computer or communications equipment "earned the same rate of return" as any other unit of real investment, as Robert Gordon (2002) puts it. But the extraordinary cheapness of the real unit of capital contributed a major component to the acceleration of labor productivity growth.

growth. Second, the long-time trend shows the share of national income attributable to the returns on the existing IT capital stock rising as well. It would be surprising if this forty-year trend suddenly stopped today. A rising share of national income attributable to existing IT capital would boost growth as well.

Third, Basu, Fernald, and Shapiro (2002) take adjustment costs in investment seriously, and conclude that late-1990s growth undershot trend growth by about 0.5 percentage points per year. Fourth, Paul David (1991) has argued for decades that general-purpose technologies boost labor productivity in two stages: (1) first, capital deepening; (2) second, social learning about how to use new technologies efficiently, a process that drives rapid TFP growth for an extensive period of time but that cannot begin until diffusion is nearly complete. If the pattern he believes holds turns out to hold for IT we can expect to see rapid TFP growth in IT-using industries emerge at some point as an additional growth-promoting factor.

Now it is not likely that all of these hole cards will turn out to be valuable face cards. But it is highly unlikely that none of them will be winners. Thus standard growth-accounting analyses predict a future like the recent past to be a lower bound to reasonable forecasts of future productivity growth.

Is there any reason to be pessimistic? I can think of only one possible hole card on the pessimistic side—a fear of large-scale governmental failure in setting forth the institutional framework to support information-age markets. If governments fail to properly structure the micro marketplace to encourage the growth of high-productivity IT-based industries and practices, then and only then will optimistic macro conclusions be cast into doubt.

2. The Pattern of Growth in the Later 1990s

2.1 ASSESSMENTS OF THE RECENT PRODUCTIVITY GROWTH SPEEDUP

In the early 1970s, U.S. productivity growth fell off a cliff. Measured output per person-hour worked in nonfarm business had averaged a growth rate of 2.84% per year from 1947 to 1973. It averaged a growth rate of only 1.34% per year from 1973 to 1995.[2] The productivity slowdown meant

---

2. The deceleration in the growth rate of total real GDP was somewhat smaller: the social changes that brought more women into the paid labor force in enormous numbers cushioned the effect of this productivity slowdown on the growth rate of measured total real GDP, if not its effect on Americans' material welfare.

that, according to official statistics, Americans in 1995 were only 70% as productive as their predecessors back in the early 1970s would have expected them to be. The productivity slowdown gave rise to an age of diminished expectations that had powerful although still debated effects on American politics and society.[3]

In the second half of the 1990s American productivity stood up, picked up its mat, and walked. It resumed its pre-1973 pace. Between 1995 and the third quarter of 2002, U.S. measured nonfarm-business output per person-hour worked appeared to grow at an annual rate of 2.79% per year.[4]

Noneconomists tended to attribute a large chunk of fast late-1990s growth to "cyclical" factors.[5] Economists, however, have had a much harder time attributing more than a few tenths of a percentage point per year of late-1990s growth to the business cycle.[6] The standard indicators of high cyclically-driven productivity were absent. Moreover, as Susanto Basu, John Fernald, and Matthew Shapiro have argued, there are stronger reasons for thinking that the adjustment costs associated with moving to a more IT-capital-intensive growth path led actual growth to understate trend growth than for thinking that cyclical factors led actual growth to overstate trend growth in the second half of the 1990s.[7] And the extremely rapid runup of stock prices indicated that at least the marginal investor

3. See Krugman (1994) for one interpretation of how the productivity slowdown made a significant difference.
4. Figuring out what the growth rate of real output has been since 1994 poses unusual challenges. The most important of these is the discrepancy between national product and national income. In 1994 the statistical discrepancy between the two—the amount you had to add to national product in order to get to national income after making all of the conceptual and definitional adjustments—was +$59 billion. By 2000 this statistical discrepancy was −$130 billion. National income grew by an extra $190 billion relative to national product between 1994 and 2000, not because of conceptual definitions but because of errors and omissions (or, rather, inconsistent and changing patterns of errors and omissions). By now this shift in the statistical discrepancy adds up to an amount equal to 3.5% of national product. Take national product as your guide to the growth of the American economy, and you conclude that measured real labor productivity growth from 1995 to 2002 was 2.63% per year. Take national income as your guide and you conclude that it was 2.95% per year. Split the difference—as Martin Baily (2002) recommends—and you conclude that it was 2.77% per year. I am agnostic as to which of the two measures of the economy's size is going awry, and so I follow Baily and split the difference. Note that this divergence between product- and income-side measures of economic output is very recent. Between 1959 and 1973, product grew faster than income by an average of only 0.04% per year. Between 1973 and 1995, income grew faster than product by an average of 0.02% per year. The sustained growth discrepancy between 1995 and 2002 of 0.35% per year is extremely unusual.
5. See, for example, Kosterlitz (2002).
6. See Gordon (2002) and Gordon (2000a, 2000b).
7. See Basu, Fernald, and Shapiro (2001).

in equities anticipated that the acceleration of economic growth that started in the mid-1990s would last for decades or longer.[8]

The causes of the productivity slowdown of 1973–1995 or so remain disappointingly mysterious. Baily (2002) calls the growth-accounting literature on the slowdown "large but inconclusive." No single factor provides a convincing and coherent explanation, and the residual position that a large number of growth-retarding factors suddenly happened to hit at once is but the least unlikely of the residual explanations.[9]

By contrast, nearly all agree on the causes of the productivity speedup of 1995–2001: it is the result of the extraordinary wave of technological innovation in computer and communications equipment. Even though the failure of economists to reach consensus in their explanations of the productivity slowdown has to leave one wary of the reliability of the consensus about the causes of the productivity speedup, the depth and range of this near-consensus is remarkable.

Robert Gordon (2002) writes that cyclical factors account for "0.40" percentage points of the growth acceleration, and that the rest is fully accounted for by IT—an "0.30 [percentage] point acceleration [from] MFP growth in computer and computer-related semiconductor manufacturing" and a "capital-deepening effect of faster growth in computer capital . . . [that] in the aggregate economy accounts [for] 0.60 percentage points of the acceleration."

Kevin Stiroh (2001) writes that "all of the direct contribution to the post-1995 productivity acceleration can be traced to the industries that either produce [IT capital goods] or use [them] most intensively, with no net contribution from other industries . . . relatively isolated from the [IT] revolution."

Oliner and Sichel (2000) write that "the rapid capital deepening related to information technology capital accounted for nearly half of this increase" in labor productivity growth, with a powerful "additional growth contribution . . . com[ing] through efficiency improvement in the *production* of computing equipment." Jorgenson, Ho, and Stiroh (2001) reach the same conclusions about the importance of IT capital deepening and increased efficiency in the production of computing and communications

---

8. See Greenwood and Jovanovic (1999).

9. See Fischer (1988), Griliches (1988), Jorgenson (1988), and Gordon (2000b, 2002). Jorgenson (1988) convincingly demonstrates that the oil price shocks can plausibly account for slow growth in potential output in the 1970s, but why does potential output growth remain slow after 1986 after real oil prices have fallen again? Griliches (1988) finds that an explanation in terms of a slowdown in innovation is unattractive, but Gordon (2000b, 2002) finds such an explanation attractive.

equipment as major drivers of the productivity growth acceleration, and they go on to forecast that labor productivity growth will be as high in the next decade as it has been in the past half decade.[10]

The only major empirical study taking a stand against this explanation is that of the McKinsey Global Institute (2001), which presents a regression of the growth in value added per worker and the increase in computer capital by industry. When industry observations are counted equally, it finds next to no correlation between computer capital and labor productivity. When industries are weighted by employment, it finds a statistically significant and substantively important connection. It is unclear why the McKinsey Global Institute prefers its unweighted regressions to its weighted ones.

In its case studies the McKinsey Global Institute attributes rapid growth in productivity in the retail distribution sector to managerial innovations on the part of Wal-Mart, coupled with competitive pressure exerted by Wal-Mart on the rest of the sector. However, Wal-Mart's founders and executives have long attributed much of their competitive success to the skillful and intensive use of IT. For example, Sam Walton (1992) wrote in his autobiography (quoted in Cohen, DeLong, and Zysman, 2000) about how "information sharing [was] a new source of power . . . [W]e believed in showing a store manager every single number relating to his store, and eventually we began sharing those numbers with the department heads in our stores. . . . That's why we've spent hundreds of millions of dollars on computers and satellites—to spread all the little details around the company as fast as possible. But they were worth the cost. It's only because of information technology that our store managers have a really clear sense of what they're doing most of the time. . . ."

One of the few prominent economists who appear to expect slow productivity growth over the medium turn is Joseph Stiglitz. As Stiglitz is quoted by Kosterlitz (2002): "The fact that things have stabilized does not mean they've recovered. When people say things are not so bleak, they mean that the economy is not in free fall, not in a negative spiral." Kosterlitz goes on to write, "The recovery, [Stiglitz] says, might not be as snappy as the conventional models used by the forecasters suggest. 'Most downturns have been inventory recessions. They tend to be short-lived; as companies deplete their inventories, things improve. This is different. It's not just an inventory downturn, but also a case of overcapacity in areas where there was lots of investing—IT, telecom. . . . These represent a significant

---

10. However, Jorgenson, Ho, and Stiroh expect total real GDP growth to slow because of slower growth in hours worked—they forecast 1.1% per year growth in hours over the next decade, compared to 2.3% per year from 1995 to 2000.

share of investment in the late 1990s,' said Stiglitz. Things won't improve until industry gets rid of excess equipment and employees, he says. 'The real restructuring takes time.'"

Such arguments that recessions are the result of "overinvestment" which must inevitably lead to a period of slow growth during which the overhang of excess capital is "liquidated" have often been made in economics (see DeLong, 1991). But it appears, to me at least, hard to sustain a claim that we are in such a situation today. With the prices of IT goods falling as rapidly as they are, surely real capital-output ratios in IT sectors are below their long-run values. In such a case, it makes no sense to claim that there is a capital overhang to be "liquidated": such a claim requires that the ratio of the real stock of IT capital to output be above its long-run level. Investment in the near future in many IT sectors may be low, but low investment seems much more likely to be attributable to low demand or to failures of appropriability of the products of investment than to too much capital.

2.2 INFORMATION TECHNOLOGY AND POST-W.W. II ECONOMIC GROWTH

Compare our use of IT today with our predecessors' use of IT half a century ago.[11] The decade of the 1950s saw electronic computers largely replace mechanical and electromechanical calculators and sorters as the world's automated calculating devices. By the end of the 1950s there were roughly 2000 installed computers in the world: machines like Remington Rand UNIVACs, IBM 702s, or DEC PDP-1s. The processing power of these machines averaged perhaps 10,000 machine instructions per second.

Today, talking rough orders of magnitude only, there are perhaps 300 million active computers in the world with processing power averaging several hundred million instructions per second. Two thousand computers times 10,000 instructions per second is 20 million. Three hundred million computers times, say, 300 million instructions per second is 90 quadrillion—a 4-billion-fold increase in the world's raw automated computational power in forty years, an average annual rate of growth of 56%.

Such a sustained rate of productivity improvement at such a pace is unprecedented in our history. Moreover, there is every reason to believe that this pace of productivity growth in the leading sectors will continue for decades. More than a generation ago Intel Corporation's co-founder Gordon Moore noticed what has come to be called Moore's law—that improvements in semiconductor fabrication allow manufacturers to dou-

---

11. For an extended version of this part of the argument, see Cohen, DeLong, and Zysman (2000).

ble the density of transistors on a chip every eighteen months. The scale of investment needed to make Moore's law hold (Figure 1) has grown exponentially along with the density of transistors and circuits, but the law has continued to hold, and engineers see no immediate barriers that will bring the process of improvement to a halt anytime soon.

2.2.1 Investment Spending As the computer revolution proceeded, nominal spending on IT capital rose (Figure 2) from about 1% of GDP in 1960 to about 2% of GDP by 1980 to about 3% of GDP by 1990 to between 5% and 6% of GDP by 2000. All throughout this time, Moore's law meant that the real price of IT capital was falling as well. As the nominal spending share of GDP spent on IT capital grew at a rate of 5% per year, the measured price of information-processing equipment plus software fell steadily at a pace between 5% and 10% per year.

At chain-weighted real values constructed using 1996 as a base year, real investment in IT equipment and software was equal to 1.7% of real GDP in 1987 (although it is important to remember that this does not mean that real investment in IT equipment plus software was a 1.7% share

Figure 1 REAL INVESTMENT IN INFORMATION TECHNOLOGY
EQUIPMENT AND SOFTWARE, AND REAL GDP

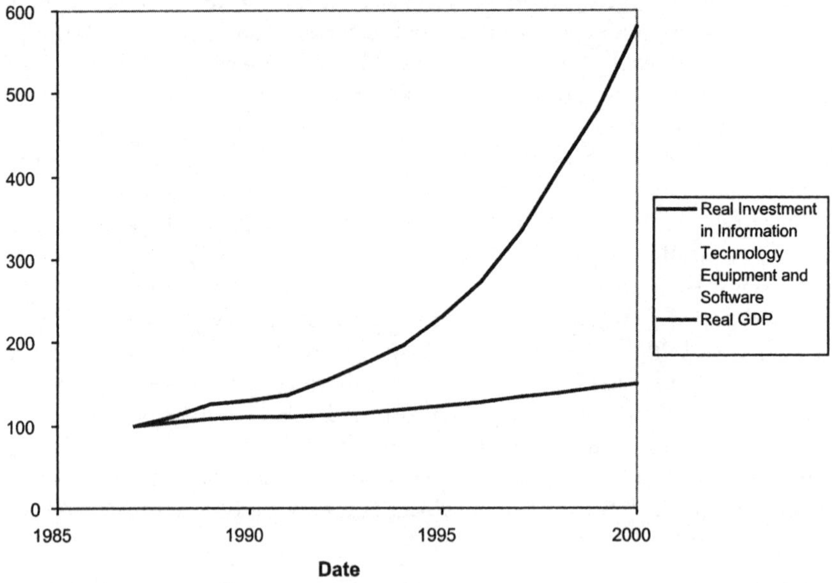

Source: National Income and Product Accounts.

Figure 2 NOMINAL SPENDING ON INFORMATION TECHNOLOGY
EQUIPMENT PLUS SOFTWARE AS A SHARE OF NOMINAL GDP

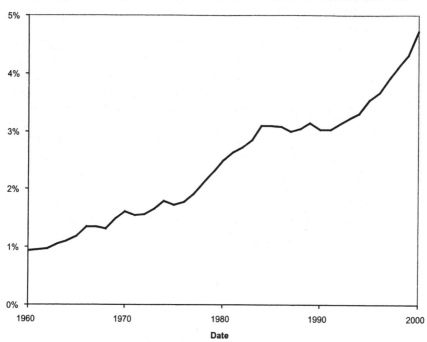

Date

of GDP; in the world of chain-weighted statistics, real components do not sum to their aggregate). By 2000 it was equal to 6.8% of real GDP.[12] The steep rise in real investment in information-processing equipment (and software) drove a steep rise in total real investment in equipment: by and large, the boom in real investment in information-processing equipment driven by rapid technological progress and the associated price declines was an addition to, not a shift in, the composition of overall real equipment investment.

2.2.2 Macro Consequences A naive back-of-the-envelope calculation would suggest that this sharp rise in equipment investment was of sufficient magnitude to drive substantial productivity acceleration: at a total social rate of return to investment of 15% per year, a 6-percentage-point rise in the investment share would be predicted to boost the rate of growth of real gross product by at least about 1 percentage point per year. And

12. For an excellent overview of what forms of addition and comparison are or are not legitimate using real chain-weighted values, see Whelan (2000a).

that is the same order of magnitude as the 1.0- to 1.6-percentage-point acceleration in annual labor productivity growth rates seen in the second half of the 1990s.

The acceleration in the growth rate of labor productivity (Figure 3) and of real GDP in the second half of the 1990s effectively wiped out all the effects of the post-1973 productivity slowdown. The U.S. economy in the second half of the 1990s was, according to official statistics and measurements, performing as well in terms of economic growth as it had routinely performed in the first post-W.W. II generation. It is a marker of how much expectations had been changed by the 1973–1995 period of slow growth that 1995–2001 growth was viewed as extraordinary and remarkable.

Nevertheless, the acceleration of growth in the second half of the 1990s was large enough to leave a large mark on the economy even in the relatively short time it has been in effect. Real output per person-hour worked in the nonfarm business sector today is 10% higher than one would have predicted back in 1995 by extrapolating the 1973–1995 trend. That such a large increase in the average level of productivity can be accumulated

Figure 3 LOG LABOR PRODUCTIVITY IN NONFARM BUSINESS

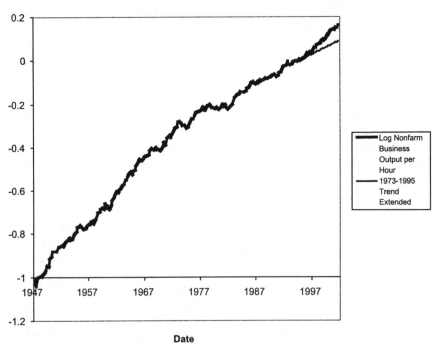

Source: National Income and Product Accounts.

Figure 4 UNEMPLOYMENT AND THE CHANGE IN INFLATION

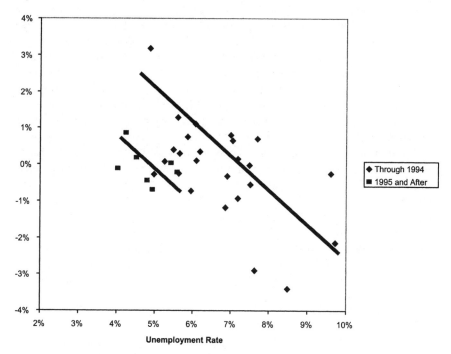

Source: Bureau of Labor Statistics, Bureau of Economic Analysis.

over a mere seven years just by getting back to what seemed "normal" before 1973 is an index of the size and importance of the 1973–1995 productivity slowdown.

2.2.3 Cyclical Factors   Alongside the burst of growth in output per person-hour worked came significantly better labor-market performance (Figure 4). The unemployment rate consistent with stable inflation, which had been somewhere between 6% and 7% of the labor force from the early 1980s into the early 1990s, suddenly fell to 5% or even lower in the late 1990s. All estimates of nonaccelerating-inflation rates of unemployment (NAIRUs) are hazardous and uncertain,[13] but long before 2001 the chance that the inflation–unemployment process was a series of random draws from the same urn after as before 1995 was negligible.

This large downward shift in the NAIRU posed significant problems for anyone wishing to estimate the growth of the economy's productive

13. See Staiger, Stock, and Watson (1997).

potential over the 1990s. Was this fall in the NAIRU a permanent shift that raised the economy's level of potential output? Was it a transitory result of good news on the supply-shock front—falling rates of increase in medical costs, falling oil prices, falling other import prices, and so forth—that would soon be reversed? If the fall in the NAIRU was permanent, then presumably it produced a once-and-for-all jump in the level of potential output, not an acceleration of the growth rate of potential output. But how large a once-and-for-all jump? Okun's law would suggest that a 2-percentage-point decline in the unemployment rate would be associated with a 5% increase in output.

Production-funtion-based analyses, however, would suggest that a 2-percentage-point decline in the unemployment rate would be associated with a roughly 1.5% increase in output. One must take account of the effect of falling unemployment on the labor force and the differential impact of the change in unemployment on the skilled and the educated.

However, none of the other available cyclical indicators suggest that the late-1990s economy was an unusually high-pressure economy. The average workweek (Figure 5) was no higher in 2000, when the unemployment rate approached 4% than it had been in 1993, when the unemployment rate fluctuated between 6% and 7%.

Capacity utilization (Figure 6) was lower during the late 1990s than it had been during the late 1980s, when unemployment had been 1.5 percentage points higher.[14] Low and not rising inflation, a relatively short workweek, and relatively low capacity utilization—these all suggested that the fall in the unemployment rate in the late 1990s was not associated with the kind of high-pressure economy assumed by Okun's law.

3. A Simple Model

Given that the acceleration in productivity growth in the second half of the 1990s was primarily driven by the revolution in IT, what conclusions can be drawn about the likely pace of productivity growth in the future? The first step in answering this question is to write down a simple model that has at least some traction on the major issues. The second step is then to use that model to analyze future productivity growth. And the third step is to step back from the model, and to consider the importance of the factors that the model leaves out.

The simple model will be one in which there is (1) an ongoing technological revolution in the production of data-processing and data-commu-

---

14. One reason, however, for the low measured capacity utilization in the late 1990s was the belief that high levels of investment were expanding capacity at a furious rate.

Figure 5 AVERAGE BUSINESS WORKWEEK

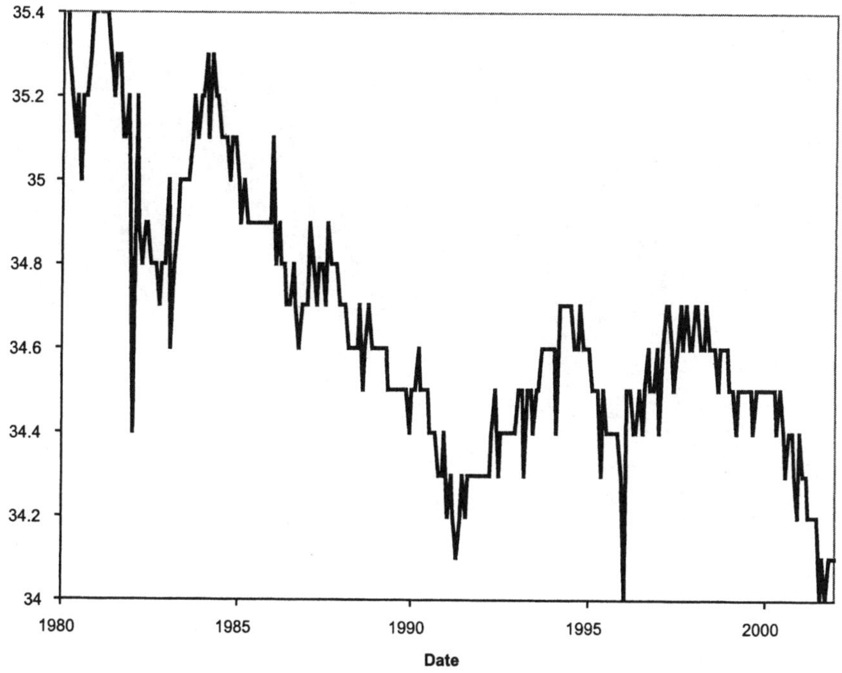

Source: Bureau of Labor Statistics.

nications capital, which is (2) an important input into production. The analysis of the model will largely turn on whether there is reason to antici- pate that the pace of technological progress in IT is going to slow, that the share of GDP spent on IT investment is going to decline, or that the share of national product attributable to returns earned on the existing IT capital stock is going to fall. Yet if none of the three of these happens, then this growth-theory finger exercise predicts that we can expect the medium-run future to be as bright for measured productivity growth as the recent past has been.

The third stage consists of analyzing the four hole cards—four reasons to think that the future is likely to be brighter than the simplest possible model suggests. First, the elasticity of demand for IT is likely to remain high—which means that as prices fall, expenditure shares will not remain constant but will rise, boosting growth. Second, the long-time trend shows the income share attributable to IT capital rising: it would be surprising if this forty-year trend suddenly stopped today, and rising income shares of IT boost growth as well. Third, Basu, Fernald, and Shapiro take adjust-

Figure 6 CAPACITY UTILIZATION (%)

Source: Federal Reserve.

ment costs in investment seriously, and conclude that late-1990s growth undershot trend growth by about 0.5 percentage points per year. Fourth, Paul David has argued for decades that general-purpose technologies boost labor productivity in two stages: (1) first, capital deepening; (2) second, social learning about how to use new technologies efficiently, a process that drives rapid TFP growth for an extensive period of time but that cannot begin until diffusion is nearly complete.

Surely not all of these will turn out to be valuable face cards. But I think it highly unlikely that none of them will win any hands. And I think they are likely to outweigh the only possible hole card on the pessimistic side that I can think of—large-scale governmental failure in setting forth the institutional framework to support information-age markets.

3.1 BASIC THEORY

Suppose that the economy produces two types of output—regular goods, which we will denote by a superscript r, and IT capital, which we will denote by an i. At each moment in time there is a set cost price p_t^i at which output in the form of regular goods can be transformed into IT capital and vice versa.

Let the economy produce two types of output—regular goods, which we will denote by an r, and IT capital, which we will denote by an i. And let at each moment in time the relative price of IT goods be a constant p_t^i, at which output in the form of regular goods can be traded off into IT capital and vice versa. Thus

$$Y_t = Y_t^r + p_t^i Y_t^i. \tag{1}$$

With regular goods serving as numeraire, the total output Y_t is equal to the output Y_t^r of regular goods plus $p_t^i Y_t^i$, the output of IT capital multiplied by its current cost price.

The total output Y_t is itself determined by a standard production function:

$$Y_t = F(A_t, K_t^r, K_t^i, L_t), \tag{2}$$

where A_t is the exogenous level of TFP, K_t^r is the stock of *normal* (non-IT) capital, K_t^i is the stock of IT capital, and L_t is the labor force.

Suppose further that because of ongoing technological revolutions the cost price of IT is declining at a constant proportional rate π. Now note that Y_t is not a measure of real output—real output will grow faster than Y_t as p_t^i falls, because the ability to make IT goods more cheaply is a source of productivity growth as well. I will use Y_t^* to stand for a chain-weighted measure of real output so that we capture this additional source of growth.

Then in this framework the proportional rate of growth of real chain-weighted real output Y^* will be

$$\frac{d \ln Y_t^*}{dt} = \frac{\partial F}{\partial A} \frac{A}{Y} \frac{d \ln A_t}{dt} + \frac{\partial F}{\partial K^r} \frac{K_t^r}{Y} \frac{d \ln K_t^r}{dt}$$

$$+ \frac{\partial F}{\partial K^i} \frac{K_t^i}{Y} \frac{d \ln K_t^i}{dt} + \frac{\partial F}{\partial L} \frac{L}{Y} \frac{d \ln L_t}{dt} + X_t^i \pi. \tag{3}$$

The rate of growth of real output will be equal to contributions from labor, normal capital, IT capital, and TFP in the production of regular output, plus an extra term equal to the share of total expenditure on IT capital X_t^i times the rate π at which the cost price of IT goods is declining.

Under the assumptions of constant returns to scale and competition, $(\partial F / \partial K)(K/Y)$ and like terms are simply the shares of national income appropriated by each of the three factors of production. So let us use s_i, s_r, and s_L as a shorthand for those terms, and also normalize the TFP term A, and thus rewrite (3) as

$$\frac{d \ln Y_t^*}{dt} = \frac{d \ln A_t}{dt} + s_r \frac{d \ln K_t^r}{dt} + s_i \frac{d \ln K_t^i}{dt} + s_L \frac{d \ln L_t}{dt} + X_t^i \pi. \tag{4}$$

If we assume a constant proportional growth rate n for the labor force, a constant growth rate a for TFP in the production of normal output Y, and constant shares of nominal expenditure X^r and X^i on normal and IT gross investment, then (4) becomes

$$\frac{d \ln Y_t^*}{dt} = a + s_L n + s_r \left(\frac{X^r Y}{K^r} - \delta^r \right) + s_i \left(\frac{X^i Y}{p_t^i K^i} - \delta^i \right) + X^i \pi. \tag{5}$$

And if we are willing to impose constant returns to scale in the three factors of labor, normal capital, and IT capital, then we can rewrite (5) with the rate of growth of labor productivity on the left-hand side as

$$\frac{d \ln(Y_t^*/L_t)}{dt} = a + s_r \left(\frac{X^r Y}{K^r} - (\delta^r + n) \right) + s_i \left(\frac{X^i Y}{p_t^i K^i} - (\delta^i + n) \right) + X^i \pi. \tag{6}$$

3.2 IMPLICATIONS OF BASIC THEORY

The first two terms on the right-hand side are very standard: the TFP growth a, and the contribution from the deepening of the ratio of normal capital per worker:

$$s_r \left(\frac{X^r Y}{K^r} - (\delta^r + n) \right), \tag{7}$$

equal to the normal *capital share* s_r times the net proportional rate of growth of the normal capital stock—its expenditure share X^r divided by the capital–output ratio K^r/Y, minus the labor-force growth rate n plus the depreciation rate δ^r.

But there are the two extra terms. The second term,

$$X^i \pi, \tag{8}$$

is what Oliner and Sichel refer to as the "additional growth contribution ... com[ing] through efficiency improvement in the *production* of computing equipment." Even if the level of potential normal output were to remain constant, the fact that the economy is able to make IT capital more and more cheaply in terms of normal goods is a genuine improvement in productivity.

The first term,

$$s_i\left(\frac{(X^i/P_i^i)Y}{K^i} - (\delta^i + n)\right),$$

(9)

is the contribution to the production of normal output from the net increase in IT capital stock per worker. However the numerator is not the nominal share of GDP expended on IT capital X^i, but the real share X^i/p_t^i. And—because the cost price of IT capital is falling at the rate π—a constant nominal expenditure share means that the real expenditure share relevant for the contribution of IT capital to output growth is growing at a proportional rate π. It is no surprise at all that as long as the nominal expenditure share on IT capital remains constant and the technological revolution is ongoing, the economy exhibits a steadily rising real gross investment expenditure share X^i/p_t^i, and a steadily rising ratio of real IT capital to normal output.[15]

This is in fact what happened in the original industrial revolution: as the dynamic modern sector grew to encompass the bulk of the economy, overall productivity growth accelerated.[16] The heroic age of double-digit annual productivity increase within the steam-power and textile-spinning sectors of the economy ended before the nineteenth century was a quarter over. Yet the major contribution of steam power and textile machinery to British aggregate economic growth took place in the middle half of the nineteenth century. Thus historians of the British industrial revolution like Landes (1969) focus on the late eighteenth century, while macroeconomists and sociologists focus on the mid-nineteenth century: the lag in time between the major innovations and fastest proportional growth of the leading sector on the one hand, and its major influence on aggregates on the other, is likely to be substantial.

If we follow Whelan (2001) and define as auxiliary variables the nomi-

---

15. There are some subtleties about what is the right way to measure output and how to define a "steady state" in models like this. Exactly what is the most useful way is insightfully explored by Whelan (2001).
16. See Crafts (1985).

nal regular capital–output ratio κ_t^r and the nominal current-dollar-value IT capital–output ratio κ_t^i by

$$\kappa_t^r = \frac{K_t^r}{Y_t}, \tag{10}$$

$$\kappa_t^i = \frac{p_t^i K_t^i}{Y_t}, \tag{11}$$

then we can construct a pseudo-steady-state path for this economy. In the equation for the proportional rate of change of regular output Y,

$$\frac{d \ln(Y_t/L_t)}{dt} = a + s_r\left(\frac{X^r Y_t}{K_t^r} - (\delta^r + n)\right) + s_i\left(\frac{X^i Y_t}{p_t^i K_t^i} - (\delta^i + n)\right), \tag{12}$$

we can substitute in these auxiliary nominal capital–output ratios:

$$\frac{d \ln(Y_t/L_t)}{dt} = a + s_r\left(\frac{X^r}{\kappa_t^r} - (\delta^r + n)\right) + s_i\left(\frac{X^i}{\kappa_t^i} - (\delta^i + n)\right), \tag{13}$$

and then derive rates of change of these ratios:

$$\frac{d\kappa_t^r}{dt} = (1 - s_r)X^r - [a + (1 - s_r)(\delta^r + n) - s_i(\delta^i + n)]\kappa_t^r - s_i X^i\left(\frac{\kappa_t^r}{\kappa_t^i}\right), \tag{14}$$

$$\frac{d\kappa_t^i}{dt} = (1 - s_i)X^i - [a + \pi + (1 - s_i)(\delta^i + n) - s_r(\delta^r + n)]\kappa_t^i - s_r X^r\left(\frac{\kappa_t^i}{\kappa_t^r}\right). \tag{15}$$

We also substitute the nominal capital–output ratios into the production function:

$$\frac{Y_t}{L_t} = A_t\left(\frac{K_t^r}{L_t}\right)^{s_r}\left(\frac{K_t^i}{L_t}\right)^{s_i}, \tag{16}$$

to obtain

$$\frac{Y_t}{L_t} = A_t^{1/(1-s_r-s_i)}(\kappa_t^r)^{s_r/(1-s_r-s_i)}(\kappa_t^i)^{s_i/(1-s_r-s_i)}(p_t^i)^{-s_i/(1-s_r-s_i)}. \tag{17}$$

The dynamics of output per worker in the economy can then be analyzed in terms of the (constant) proportional increase in the TFP A, the (constant) proportional decrease in the real cost price of IT goods, and the dynamic evolution of the nominal capital–output ratios:

$$\frac{d \ln(Y_t/L_t)}{dt} = \frac{a}{1 - s_r - s_i} + \frac{s_i \pi}{1 - s_r - s_i}$$

$$+ \frac{s_r}{1 - s_r - s_i} \frac{d \ln \kappa_t^r}{dt} + \frac{s_i}{1 - s_r - s_i} \frac{d \ln \kappa_t^i}{dt}. \qquad (18)$$

From (14), (15), and (18), we can calculate the behavior of the economy in its long-run pseudo-steady state. We can see that the proportional growth rate of Y/L will be

$$\frac{d \ln(Y_t/L_t)}{dt} = \frac{a}{1 - s_r - s_i} + \frac{\pi s_i}{1 - s_r - s_i} \qquad (19)$$

and the long-run growth rate of real output per worker will be

$$\frac{d \ln(Y_t^*/L_t)}{dt} = \frac{a}{1 - s_r - s_i} + \frac{\pi s_i}{1 - s_r - s_i} + X^i \pi, \qquad (20)$$

which is the sum of three terms: a term capturing the effect of background TFP growth a on the economy, a term capturing the effect of ongoing capital deepening made possible by falling IT capital prices, and a term capturing the direct effect of improvements in efficiency in the production of IT goods.

How to calibrate this simple theoretical result (20) to the American economy? Over the years since 1995, X^i—the share of expenditure on IT and related forms of capital—has averaged some 6% of GDP. According to Oliner and Sichel (2000), s_i—the share of income attributable to IT capital—has averaged 7% of GDP. Assuming an income share for other kinds of capital of 33%, then at a 10%-per-year decline in the real prices of IT goods the last two terms—the acceleration terms—of equation (20) amount to a productivity-growth boost of 1.8% per year. This is a larger boost to growth than was in fact seen in the acceleration in the later 1990s. Thus this growth accounting exercise certainly does not suggest that productivity growth in the next decade will be lower than in the recent past, as long as Moore's law continues to hold and the prices of IT goods continue to decline rapidly.

However, there is no special reason to think that such a steady-state analysis is the best we can do. The steady state assumes constant nominal investment shares in IT capital, a constant rate of real price decrease in this technologically explosive leading sector, and a constant share parameter s_i. Yet all the evidence we have suggests that all three of these variables move, and move radically, in a decade or less. The American economy began the 1980s very far away from its pseudo-steady state: back then the GDP share of nominal spending on IT investment was only 40% of its current value, and likewise for the share of national income attributable to the IT capital stock.

Thus the potential importance of the first hole card: economies that are approaching their steady-state growth paths from below grow faster than in steady state. With two kinds of capital goods depreciating at different

Figure 7 SAMPLE SIMULATIONS: SPEED OF CONVERGENCE TO THE
PSEUDO-STEADY-STATE GROWTH PATH

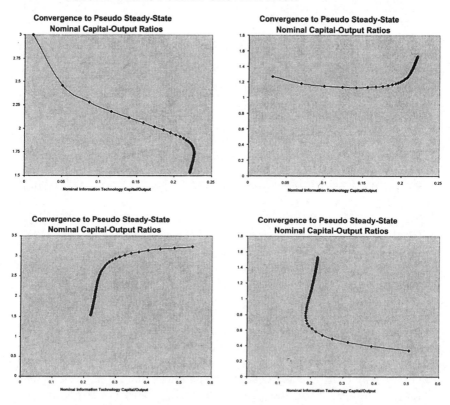

Parameters: $a = 0.01$, $n = 0.01$, $X^i = 0.06$, $X^r = 0.14$, $s_i = 0.1$, $s_r = 0.5$, $\delta^i = 0.1$, $\delta^r = 0.3$, $\pi = 0.1$.

rates, the simple model has no theoretically tractable dynamics. However, simulations (Figure 7) suggest that it is overwhelmingly likely that in such a case the nominal capital–output ratio for the most rapidly depreciating kind of capital converges fairly rapidly—within two decades—to a value near its steady-state value.

This suggests that any additional contribution to growth from convergence dynamics will be confined to the next decade or so.

4. A Demand-Side Model

4.1 A MODEL OF CHANGING DEMAND SHARES

However, this leaves unexamined the question of why the income and expenditure shares of IT capital have been rising so rapidly over the past several decades. In order to even grapple with these questions, we have to look on the demand-for-IT side. What determines whether the demand for IT capital and thus for investment grows more rapidly or less rapidly than output as a whole?

An alternative approach is to simplify the production side of the model radically, and instead focus on the implications of changing prices of IT goods for demand. If the TFP in the rest of the economy is growing at a rate π_R, and if the TFP in the leading industries and sectors is growing at a faster rate π_L, then the TFP growth in the economy as a whole will be equal to

$$\pi = \sigma\pi_L + (1 - \sigma)\pi_R, \tag{21}$$

where σ is the share of total expenditure on the goods produced by the economy's fast-growing technologically dynamic leading sectors.

As the process of innovation and technological revolution in the leading sectors proceeds, we would not expect the leading sector share σ of total expenditure to remain constant. If the goods produced by the leading sector have a high (or low) price elasticity of demand, the falls over time in their relative prices will boost (or reduce) the share of total expenditure σ: only if the price elasticity of demand, ε_P, is one will the fall in the relative price of leading-sector products produced by the technological revolutions leave the leading-sector share unchanged.[17]

---

17. The demand share will also depend on the income elasticity of demand. If the goods produced by the leading sectors are superior (or inferior) goods, the share σ will rise (or fall) as economic growth continues: only if the income elasticity of demand, ε_I, for its products is one will changes in the overall level of prosperity leave the leading sector share unchanged. But I will not model this effect here.

Moreover, the leading-sector share of total expenditure σ matters only as long as the leading sector remains technologically dynamic. Once the heroic phase of invention and innovation comes to an end and the rate of TFP growth returns to the economy's normal background level π_R, the rate of productivity growth in the economy as a whole will return to that same level π_R and the leading-sector share of expenditure σ will no longer be relevant.

Thus four pieces of information are necessary to assess the aggregate economic impact of an explosion of invention and innovation in a leading sector:

The initial share of expenditure on the leading sector's products, σ_0.
The magnitude of the relative pace of cost reduction, $\pi_L - \pi_R$, during the leading sector's heroic age of invention and innovation.
The duration of the leading sector's heroic age of invention and innovation.
The price elasticity of demand, ε_P, for the leading sector's products.

To gain a sense of the importance of these factors, let's consider a few simulations with sample parameter values. For simplicity's sake, set the initial share of expenditure on the leading sector's products, σ_0, equal to 0.02; set the income elasticity of demand for the leading sector's products, ε_I, equal to 1.0; set the heroic age of invention and innovation to a period 40 years long; and set the background level of TFP growth, π_R, to 0.01 per year. Consider three values for the price elasticity of demand, ε_P: 0.5, 2.0, and 4.0. And consider two values for the wedge in the annual rate of technological progress between the leading sector and the rest: 0.03 and 0.05.

With a price elasticity of demand of 0.5, the expenditure share of the leading sectors declines from its original value of 2% as technology advances and the prices of leading-sector goods fall. With a productivity wedge of 5% per year, the initial rate of growth of economy-wide productivity growth is 1.1% per year—1% from the background growth of the rest of the economy, and an extra 0.1% from the faster productivity growth in the one-fiftieth of the economy that is the leading sector. By the twelfth year the expenditure share on leading-sector products has fallen below 1.5%. By the twenty-eighth year it has fallen below 1.0%. By the fortieth year it has fallen to 0.7%.

The low initial and declining share of the leading sector in total expenditure means that 40 years of 6%-per-year productivity growth in the leading sector has only a very limited impact on the total economy. After 40 years, the total productivity in the economy as a whole is only 2.54% higher than if the leading sector had not existed at all. Rapid productivity growth in the leading sector has next to no effect on productivity growth in the economy as a whole, because the salience of the leading sector falls, and the salience of other sectors resistant to productivity improvement rises, as technology advances. This is Baumol and Bowen's (1966) "cost disease" scenario: innovations become less and less important because the innovation-resistant share of the economy rises over time. Indeed, as time passes the rate of aggregate growth converges to the rate of growth in the productivity-resistant rest of the economy.

By contrast, with a price elasticity of 4 the expenditure share of the leading sectors grows rapidly from its original value of 2%. With a pro-ductivity-growth wedge of 5% per year, the leading-sector share of spend-ing surpasses 10% by year 12 and 30% by year 20, and reaches 89% by year 40. As the spending share of the leading sectors rises, aggregate pro-ductivity growth rises too: from 1.1% per year at the start to 1.4% per year by year 10, 2.4% per year by year 20, 4.2% per year by year 30, and 5.4% per year by year 40. The impact on the aggregate economy is enor-mous: the TFP after 40 years is 113% higher than it would have been had the leading sector never existed.

There is only one reason for the sharp difference in the effects of innova-tion in the leading sector: the different price elasticities of demand for leading-sector products in the two scenarios. The initial shares of leading-sector products in demand, the rate of technology improvement in the leading sector, and the duration of the technology boom are all the same. But when the demand for leading-sector products is price-elastic, each advance in technology and reduction in the leading sector's costs raises the salience of the leading sector in the economy and thus brings the pro-portional rate of growth of the aggregate economy closer to the rate of growth in the leading sector itself. By the end of the 40-year period of these simulations, the scenario with the price elasticity of 4 has seen the leading sectors practically take over the economy, and dominate demand. This is the "true economic revolution" scenario: not only does productiv-ity growth accelerate substantially and material welfare increase, but the structure of the economy is transformed as the bulk of the labor force shifts into producing leading-sector products and the bulk of final de-mand shifts into consuming leading-sector products.

What determines whether demand for a leading sector's products is price-inelastic (in which case we are in Baumol and Bowen's "cost dis-ease" scenario in which technological progress in the leading sector barely affects the aggregate economy at all) or price-elastic (in which case we are in the "economic revolution" scenario, and everything is trans-formed)? What determines the income and price elasticities of demand for the high-tech goods that are the products of our current leading sectors?

4.2 HOW USEFUL WILL COMPUTERS BE?

What factors determine what the ultimate impact of these technologies will be? What is there that could interrupt a bright forecast for productivity growth over the next decade? There are three possibilities: The first is the end of the era of technological revolution—the end of the era of declining prices of IT capital. The second is a steep fall in the share of total nominal expenditure devoted to IT capital. And the third is a steep fall in the social marginal product of investment in IT—or, rather, a fall in the product of the social return on investment and the capital–output ratio. The important thing to focus on in forecasting is that none of these have happened: In 1991–1995 semiconductor production was 0.5% of nonfarm business output; in 1996–2000 it averaged 0.9%. Nominal spending on IT capital rose from about 1% of GDP in 1960 to about 2% by 1980 to about 3% by 1990 to between 5% and 6% by 2000. Computer and semiconductor prices declined at 15–20% per year from 1991 to 1995 and at 25–35% per year from 1996 to 2000.

However, whether nominal expenditure shares will continue to rise in the end hinges on how useful data processing and data communication products turn out to be. What will be the elasticity of demand for high-technology goods as their prices continue to drop? The greater is the number of different uses found for high-tech products as their prices decline, the larger will be the income and price elasticities of demand—and thus the stronger will be the forces pushing the expenditure share up, not down, as technological advance continues. All of the history of the electronics sector suggests that these elasticities are high, nor low. Each successive generation of falling prices appears to produce new uses for computers and communications equipment at an astonishing rate.

The first, very expensive computers were seen as good at performing complicated and lengthy sets of arithmetic operations. The first leading-edge applications of large-scale electronic computing power were military: the burst of innovation during World War II that produced the first one-of-a-kind hand-tooled electronic computers was totally funded by the war effort. The coming of the Korean War won IBM its first contract to actually deliver a computer: the million-dollar Defense Calculator. The military demand in the 1950s and the 1960s by projects such as Whirlwind and SAGE (Semi-Automatic Ground Environment)—a strategic air defense system—both filled the assembly lines of computer manufacturers and trained the generation of engineers that designed and built them.

The first leading-edge civilian economic applications of large—for the time (the 1950s)—amounts of computer power came from government agencies like the Census and from industries like insurance and finance, which performed lengthy sets of calculations as they processed large amounts of paper. The first UNIVAC computer was bought by the Census Bureau. The second and third orders came from A.C. Nielson Market Research and the Prudential Insurance Company. This second, slightly cheaper generation of computers was used not to make sophisticated calculations, but to make the extremely simple calculations needed by the Census and by the human-resource departments of large corporations. The Census Bureau used computers to replace their electromechanical tabulating machines. Businesses used computers to do the payroll, report-generating, and record-analyzing tasks that their own electromechanical calculators had previously performed.

The still next generation of computers—exemplified by the IBM 360 series—were used to stuff data into and pull data out of databases in real time—airline reservation processing systems, insurance systems, inventory control. It became clear that the computer was good for much more than performing repetitive calculations at high speed. The computer was much more than a calculator, however large and however fast. It was also an organizer. American Airlines used computers to create its SABRE automated reservations system, which cost as much as a dozen airplanes. The insurance industry automated its back-office sorting and classifying.

Subsequent uses have included computer-aided product design, applied to everything from airplanes designed without wind tunnels to pharmaceuticals designed at the molecular level for particular applications. In this area and in other applications, the major function of the computer is not as a calculator, a tabulator, or a database manager, but as a what-if machine. The computer creates models of what would happen if the airplane, the molecule, the business, or the document were to be built up in a particular way. It thus enables an amount and a degree of experimentation in the virtual world that would be prohibitively expensive in resources and time in the real world.

The value of this use as a what-if machine took most computer scientists and computer manufacturers by surprise. None of the engineers designing software for the IBM 360 series, none of the parents of Berkeley UNIX, nobody before Dan Bricklin programmed Visicalc had any idea of the utility of a spreadsheet program. Yet the invention of the spreadsheet marked the spread of computers into the office as a what-if machine. Indeed, the computerization of Americas white-collar offices in the 1980s was largely driven by the spreadsheet program's utility—first Visicalc, then Lotus 1-2-3, and finally Microsoft Excel.

For one example of the importance of a computer as a what-if machine, consider that today's complex designs for new semiconductors would be simply impossible without automated design tools. The process has come full circle. Progress in computing depends upon Moore's law; and the progress in semiconductors that makes possible the continued march of Moore's law depends upon progress in computers and software.

As increasing computer power has enabled their use in real-time control, the domain has expanded further as lead users have figured out new applications. Production and distribution processes have been and are being transformed. Moreover, it is not just robotic auto painting or assembly that have become possible, but scanner-based retail quick-turn supply chains and robot-guided hip surgery as well.

In the most recent years the evolution of the computer and its uses has continued. It has branched along two quite different paths. First, computers have burrowed inside conventional products as they have become embedded systems. Second, computers have connected outside to create what we call the World Wide Web: a distributed global database of information all accessible through the single global network. Paralleling the revolution in data-processing capacity has been a similar revolution in data communications capacity. There is no sign that the domain of potential uses has been exhausted.

One would have to be pessimistic indeed to forecast that all these trends are about to come to an end. One way to put it is that modern semiconductor-based electronics technologies fit Bresnahan and Trajtenberg's (1995) definition of a *general-purpose technology*—one useful not just for one narrow class but for an extremely wide variety of production processes, one for which each decline in price appears to bring forth new uses, one that can spark off a long-lasting major economic transformation. There is room for computerization to grow on the intensive margin, as computer use saturates potential markets like office work and email. But there is also room to grow on the extensive margin, as microprocessors are used for tasks (like controlling hotel-room doors or changing the burn mix of a household furnace) that few, two decades ago, would have thought of.

5. Additional Considerations

Moreover, the analysis so far has left out a substantial number of important considerations.

5.1 PREVIOUS INDUSTRIAL REVOLUTIONS

The first of these is that previous industrial revolutions driven by general-purpose technologies have seen an initial wave of adoption followed by rapid TFP growth in industries that use these new technologies as businesses and workers learn by using. So far this has not been true of our current wave of growth. As Robert Gordon (2002) has pointed out at every opportunity, there has been little if any acceleration of TFP growth outside of the making of high-tech equipment itself: the boosts to labor productivity look very much like what one would expect from capital deepening alone, not what one would expect from the fact that the new forms of capital allow more efficient organizations.

Paul David (1991) at least has argued that a very large chunk of the long-run impact of technological revolutions does emerge only when people have a chance to thoroughly learn the characteristics of the new technology and to reconfigure economic activity to take advantage of it. In David's view, it took nearly half a century before the American economy had acquired enough experience with electric motors to begin to use them to their full potential. By his reckoning, we today are only halfway through the process of economic learning needed for us to even begin to envision what computers will be truly useful for.

Moreover, as Crafts (2002) argues, the striking thing is not that there was a "Solow paradox" of slow productivity growth associated with computerization, but that people did not expect the economic impact to start slow and gather force over time. As he writes, "in the early phases of general purpose technologies their impact on growth is modest." It has to be modest: "the new varieties of capital have only a small weight relative to the economy as a whole." But if they are truly general-purpose technologies, their weight will grow.

Susanto Basu's comment on this paper suggests that we are finally beginning to see Paul David's point begin to have force. As time passes, it looks like a larger and larger share of the TFP growth acceleration is coming in industries outside of the high-tech sector—in industries that are learning how to use IT products to boost their own efficiency of operations.

5.2 ADJUSTMENT COSTS

Basu, Fernald, and Shapiro (2001) estimate that because of adjustment costs productivity growth in the second half of the 1990s *undershot* the long-run technology trend by half a percentage point per year or more. Our standard models tell us that investment is more or less stable over time because adjustment costs are substantial: to invest 10% of national product in equipment this year and 2% the next is much worse than investing a steady 6% in equipment. But the 1990s saw sudden, unprecedented, large shifts in real investment shares. If our standard explanations of why investment does not swing more wildly are correct, then the penalties enforced by adjustment costs on American economic growth in the late 1990s must have been relatively large.

As Martin Baily (2002) has observed, there is independent evidence for these adjustment costs: "microeconomic analyses of plants and firms find substantial adjustment costs to investment and lags between investment and productivity." Thus it is highly naive to follow "the growth accounting approach," and to assume that "increases in capital intensity have an impact on productivity in the same year" or even the same five-year period in which they occur.

5.3 ECONOMIC GOVERNANCE

There is, however, the one remaining hole card: the pessimistic one. The government's role in a market economy is to provide the underlying definitions of property rights, mechanisms of rights enforcement, and corrections of externalities so that the price signals sent by the market to firms correspond to economic efficiency and social values. As the structure of the economy changes, surely the proper government-provided institutional underpinnings must change too. But is government able to fulfill this market-structuring task?

The macroeconomist tends to foresee a future of falling high-tech prices, rising expenditure shares, rapidly growing capital–output ratios, and fast labor productivity growth. Yet as one looks at IT, one cannot help but be struck by the fact that the most far-reaching and important consequences may well be microeconomic. Issues of the benefits from the extent of the market, of price discrimination and the distribution of economic well-being, of monopoly, and of the interaction of intellectual property with scientific communication and research are all very important and very complicated. And if governments fail to properly structure the micro marketplace, then optimistic macro conclusions will be immediately cast into doubt.

It is obvious that the creation of knowledge is a cumulative enterprise: Isaac Newton said that the only reason he was able to see farther than others was that he stood on the shoulders of giants. Whenever we consider the importance of property rights over ideas in giving companies incentives to fund research and development, we need to also consider the importance of free information exchange and use in giving researchers the power to do their jobs effectively. Can governments construct intellectual-property systems that will both enhance information exchange and provide sufficient monetary incentives? It is an open question.

One possible solution may be price discrimination. In the past, price discrimination—charging one price to one consumer and a different price for essentially the same good to another consumer—has been seen as a way for monopolies to further increase their monopoly profits. In the information age the background assumption may be different. We may come to see price discrimination as an essential mechanism for attaining economic efficiency and social welfare.

Third, if we call the economy of the past two centuries primarily *Smithian*, the economy of the future is likely to be primarily *Schumpeterian*. In a Smithian economy, the decentralized market does a magnificent job (if the initial distribution of wealth is satisfactory) at producing economic welfare. Since goods are *rival*—my sleeping in this hotel bed tonight keeps you from doing so—one person's use or consumption imposes a social cost: since good economic systems align the incentives facing individuals with the effects of their actions on social welfare, it makes sense to distribute goods by charging prices equal to marginal social cost. Since goods are *excludable*—we have social institutions to enforce property rights, in the case of my hotel room the management, the police, and the courts— it is easy to decentralize decision making and control, pushing responsibility for allocation away from the center and to the more entrepreneurial periphery where information about the situation on the ground is likely to be much better.

In a Schumpeterian economy, the decentralized market does a much less good job. Goods are produced under conditions of substantial increasing returns to scale. This means that competitive equilibrium is not a likely outcome: the canonical situation is more likely to be one of natural monopoly. But natural monopoly does not meet the most basic condition for economic efficiency: that price equals marginal cost. However, prices cannot be *forced* to be equal to marginal cost, because then the fixed setup costs are not covered. Relying on government subsidies to cover fixed setup costs raises problems of its own: it destroys the entrepreneurial energy of the market and replaces it with the group-think and red-tape defects of admininstrative bureaucracy. Moreover, in a Schumpeterian economy it is innovation that is the principal source of wealth—and temporary monopoly power and profits are the reward needed to spur private enterprise to engage in such innovation. The right way to think about this complex set of issues is not clear. The competitive paradigm cannot be fully appropriate. But it is not clear what is.

Consider, for example, the U.S. Gilded Age toward the end of the nineteenth century. The Gilded Age saw the coming of mass production, the large corporation, the continent-wide market, and electric power to the United States. You needed more than the improvements in production technology that made possible the large-scale factory in order to arrive at the large industrial organization and the high-productivity, mass-production economy. From our viewpoint today we can look back and say that in the United States this economic transformation rested on five things:

Limited liability.
The stock market.
Investment banking.
The continent-wide market.
The existence of an antitrust policy.

Legal and institutional changes—limited liability, the stock market, and an investment banking industry—were needed to assemble the capital to build factories on the scale needed to serve a continental market. Without limited liability, individual investors would have been unwilling to risk potentially unlimited losses from the actions of managers they did not know and could not control. Without the stock and bond markets, investors would have been less willing to invest in large corporations because of the resulting loss of liquidity. Without investment banking, investors' problem of sorting worthwhile enterprises from others would have been much more difficult.

Moreover, political changes—the rise of antitrust—were needed for two reasons. The first was to try to make sure that the enormous economies of scale within the grasp of the large corporation were not achieved at the price of replacing competition by monopoly. The second was the political function of reassuring voters that the growing large corporations would be the economy's servants rather than the voters' masters.

Last, institutional changes were needed to make sure that the new corporations could serve a continental market. For example, think of Swift Meatpacking. Swift's business was based on a very good idea: mass-slaughter the beef in Chicago, ship it dressed to Boston, and undercut local small-scale Boston-area slaughterhouses by a third at the butcher shop. This was a very good business plan. It promised to produce large profits for entrepreneurs and investors and a much better diet at lower cost for consumers. But what if the Massachusetts legislature were to require for reasons of health and safety that all meat sold in Massachusetts be inspected live and on the hoof by a Massachusetts meat inspector in Massachusetts immediately before slaughter?

Without the right system of governance—in this case U.S. federal preemption of state health and safety regulation affecting interstate commerce—you wouldn't have had America's Chicago meatpacking industry (or Upton Sinclair's *The Jungle*). That piece of late-nineteenth century industrialization wouldn't have fallen into place.

Because American institutions changed to support, nurture, and manage the coming of mass production and the large-scale business enterprise chronicled by Alfred Chandler—and because European institutions by and large did not—it was America that was on the cutting edge at the start of the twentieth century. It was America that was "the furnace where the future was being forged," as Leon Trotsky once said.

What changes in the government-constructed underpinnings of the market economy are needed for it to flourish as the economic changes produced by computers take hold? Optimistic views of future macro productivity growth assume that government will—somehow—get these important micro questions right.

6. Conclusion

The main argument of this paper has been that standard growth models predict a bright future. Increased TFP in the IT capital-goods-producing sector, coupled with extraordinary real capital deepening as the quantity of real investment in IT capital bought by a dollar of nominal savings grows, has driven the productivity growth acceleration of the later 1990s, and promise to drive equal or faster growth in the next decade. The extraordinary pace of invention and innovation in the IT sector has generated real price declines of between 10% and 20% per year in information processing and communications equipment for nearly forty years so far. These extraordinary cost declines have made a unit of real investment in computer or communications equipment absurdly cheap, and hence made the quantity of real investment and thus capital deepening in IT capital absurdly large.

Continued declines in the prices of IT capital mean that a constant nominal flow of savings channeled to such investments brings more and more real investment. The social return to IT investment would have to drop suddenly to nearly zero, the share of nominal investment spending devoted to IT capital would have to collapse, or technological progress in IT would have to slow drastically, for labor productivity growth in the next decade to reverse itself and return to its late 1970s or 1980s levels. Yet there are no technological reasons for the pace of productivity increase in our economy's leading sectors to decline over the next decade or so.

Moreover, the future may well be brighter than the simplest models suggest. First, elasticity of demand for IT goods is likely to remain high. A high elasticity of demand for IT goods means that as prices fall, expenditure shares will not remain constant but will rise, boosting growth. Second, the long-time trend shows the share of national income attributable to the returns on the existing IT capital stock rising as well. This rise should boost growth as well. Third, Basu, Fernald, and Shapiro (2001) take adjustment costs in investment seriously, and conclude that late-1990s growth undershot trend growth by about 0.5 percentage points per year. Fourth, David (1991) has argued for decades that general-purpose technologies boost labor productivity in successive stages, with the largest boost coming after the technology has diffused throughout the economy.

Is there any reason to be pessimistic? Only a fear of large-scale governmental failure in setting forth the institutional framework to support information-age markets could lead to a pessimistic forecast of future growth.

REFERENCES

Baily, M. (2002). The new economy: Post-mortem or second wind? *Journal of Economic Perspectives,* 16(2) (Spring):3–22.
Basu, S., J. Fernald, and M. Shapiro. (2001). Productivity growth in the 1990s: Technology, utilization, or adjustment? Cambridge, MA: National Bureau of Economic Research. NBER Working Paper 8359.
Baumol, W., and W. Bowen. (1966). Performing Arts: The Economic Dilemma. New York: Twentieth Century Fund.
Bresnahan, T., and M. Trajtenberg. (1995). General purpose technologies: "Engines of growth"? *Journal of Econometrics* 65:83–108.
Cohen, S., J. B. DeLong, and J. Zysman. (2000). Tools for thought: What is new and important about the e-conomy. Berkeley: BRIE. Working Paper 138.
Crafts, N. F. R. (1985). *British Economic Growth during the Industrial Revolution.* Oxford: Oxford University Press.
———. (2000). The Solow productivity paradox in historical perspective. London: London School of Economics. Mimeo.
David, P. (1991). Computer and dynamo: The modern productivity paradox in a not-too-distant mirror. In *Technology and Productivity: The Challenge for Economic Policy.* Paris: OECD.
DeLong, J. B. (1991). Liquidation cycles and the Great Depression. Cambridge, MA: Harvard University. Mimeo.
Fischer, S. (1988). Symposium on the slowdown in productivity growth. *Journal of Economic Perspectives* 2(4, Fall):3–7.
Gordon, R. (2000a). Does the "new economy" measure up to the great inventions of the past? *Journal of Economic Perspectives* 14(4):49–74.
———. (2000b). Interpreting the "one big wave" in U.S. long term productivity growth. Cambridge, MA: National Bureau of Economic Research. NBER Working Paper 7752.
———. (2002). Technology and economic performance in the American economy. Cambridge, MA: National Bureau of Economic Research. NBER Working Paper 8771.
Greenwood, J., and B. Jovanovic. (1999). The information technology revolution and the stock market. *American Economic Review* 89(2, May):116–122.
Griliches, Z. (1988). Productivity puzzles and R & D: Another nonexplanation. *Journal of Economic Perspectives* 2(4, Fall):9–21.
Jorgenson, D. (1988). Productivity and postwar U.S. economic growth. *Journal of Economic Perspectives* 2(4, Fall):23–41.
———, M. Ho, and K. Stiroh. (2001). Projecting productivity growth: Lessons from the U.S. growth resurgence. Cambridge, MA: Harvard University. Mimeo.
Kosterlitz, J. (2002). What went wrong? *National Journal,* January 4.

Krugman, P. (1994). *The Age of Diminished Expectations*, 4th ed. Cambridge, MA: The MIT Press.
Landes, D. (1969). *The Unbound Prometheus*. Cambridge: Cambridge University Press.
McKinsey Global Institute. (2001). *U.S. Productivity Growth, 1995–2000*. Washington: McKinsey.
Oliner, S., and D. Sichel. (2000). The Resurgence of Growth in the Late 1990s: Is Information Technology the Story? *Journal of Economic Perspectives* 14(4):3–22.
Staiger, D., J. H. Stock, and M. W. Watson. (1997). The NAIRU, unemployment and monetary policy. *Journal of Economic Perspectives* 11(1, Winter):33–49.
Stiroh, K. (2001). Information technology and the U.S. productivity revival: What do the industry data say? New York: Federal Reserve Board of New York. Working Paper 115.
Walton, S. (1992). *Made in America: My Story*. New York: Bantam Books.
Whelan, K. (2000a). A guide to the use of chain-aggregated NIPA data. Washington: Federal Reserve Board. Mimeo.
———. (2001). A two sector approach to modeling NIPA data. Washington: Federal Reserve Board. Mimeo.

Comment

SUSANTO BASU
University of Michigan and NBER

Economists are not particularly good at understanding large, one-time structural changes. We are not notably successful at working in real time. And despite much effort, especially over the past 20 years, we still have no generally accepted understanding of the underlying sources of technical change. Any single paper that tries to tackle all three problems at once is both incredibly ambitious, and almost surely destined to failure. Thus, it is not surprising that DeLong's paper does not succeed in explaining the enormously important and extremely puzzling behavior of productivity growth in the United State since the mid-1990s—no single paper could be expected to do so. But it illuminates and elucidates most of the important issues that need to be addressed if we are to succeed as a profession in explaining this very important puzzle. In keeping with the spirit of the paper, my comment tries to put on the table one more fact that needs to be explained if we are to have a tolerably complete understanding of the recent productivity acceleration.

Before doing so, however, I want to shift the discussion from labor productivity, which is the focus of DeLong's paper, to technical change (which, under standard conditions, is equivalent to total factor productivity). The reason is twofold. First, a focus on labor productivity conflates impulses and propagation mechanisms, and gives the somewhat mis-leading impression that we understand the sources of productivity growth better than we actually do. DeLong's paper actually takes the rate of technical change and its recent acceleration as given, and combines these with various standard models of investment. But the fact that we understand how falling capital-goods prices can induce capital accumula-tion does not mean that we truly understand the reasons for higher labor or total factor productivity growth in the United States. Second, focusing on technical change helps put an important fact into sharper focus.[1]

To understand the claims I make below, it's necessary to do a bit of growth accounting. Assume that the economy comprises just two sectors, one producing information technology (IT)—here identified with the pro-duction of computers, semiconductors, and telecommunications equip-ment—and the other producing everything else (called NT, for non-IT). Furthermore, assume that production in each sector can be represented using a production function for gross output (Q), using capital (K), labor (L), intermediate inputs (M), technology (T), and gross investment (I):

$$Q_j = F(K_j, L_j, M_j, T_j, I_j), \qquad j = \text{IT, NT.} \tag{1}$$

The only variable that is not completely standard is investment. Its pres-ence is meant to capture the costs of adjusting the capital stock, here taken to be internal (output-reducing) rather than external, as is often assumed. One should think of these "costs" in a very broad sense as including com-plementary (but otherwise unmeasured) investments. Thus, rather than workers and machines being idled as new capital is installed, perhaps machines are idled and workers sent to be retrained on the new equip-ment. Furthermore, the retraining—both formal and on the job—can last far longer and be much more costly than a quick office or factory shutdown.[2]

Letting lowercase letters represent natural logs of their uppercase coun-terparts, letting starred variables be their steady-state values, and approx-imating time derivatives by finite differences, equation (1) implies that the unobserved technical change in each sector can be approximated as[3]

---

1. Sometimes the use of labor productivity is justified by claiming that it gives a way to take account of unmeasured output in the household sector. But Basu and Fernald (2001) argue that total factor productivity is in fact a superior welfare measure as well: by sub-tracting the change in labor input from output growth, the TFP calculation implicitly values home production at its marginal opportunity cost in forgone market wages.
2. In principle, one can add costs of adjusting all the inputs, especially labor. However, empirically the costs of adjusting capital seem much larger, and the object of the exercise is to understand the late 1990s, which were characterized by extremely high rates of capital investment.
3. See Basu, Fernald, and Shapiro (2001) for a derivation.

$$\Delta t_j = \Delta q_j - \mu_j(S_j^K \, \Delta k_j + s_j^L \, \Delta l_j + s_j^M \, \Delta m_j) - \frac{F_5^* I^*}{Q^*} \, \Delta i_j, \tag{2}$$

where the s_j terms are the shares of input costs in the total revenue of sector j, and μ_j is the ratio of price to marginal cost in that sector.

From the discussion above, we expect that $F_5 < 0$. Hence, the last term in equation (2) is actually positive as long as investment is growing. The intuition is that the process of installing capital is in fact an output of the firm, although it is not recorded as such because it is not a market good. If the firm installs capital instead of producing market output then measured output falls, but total output does not fall as much and may actually rise. The last term in equation (2) adds back this unmeasured output growth, which means that in times of high investment *growth* technology is actually rising faster than the usual calculation would lead us to believe.[4]

One can aggregate technical change in the two sectors to get a measure of overall technology growth using Domar (1961) aggregation, extended to allow for imperfect competition:

$$\Delta t = \sum_{j=\mathrm{IT,NT}} \frac{P_j Y_j}{P_{\mathrm{IT}} Y_{\mathrm{IT}} + P_{\mathrm{NT}} Y_{\mathrm{NT}}} \frac{\Delta t_j}{1 - \mu_j s_j^{M'}} \cdot \tag{3}$$

where $P_j Y_j$ is the total revenue in sector j.

Basu, Fernald, and Shapiro (2001) implement this framework, with additional controls for variable factor utilization. Using their industry-level results (not reported in their paper), one can compute time series of technical change for the aggregate and the contributions of IT and NT to that aggregate change. Following the recent convention (e.g., Stiroh, forthcoming), I take the IT-producing industries to be SIC 35 and 36. Table 1 shows the means of these series for various sample periods.

Lines 2 and 3 show the results for the first and second halves of the 1990s. In both subperiods IT has an importance disproportionate to its size (about 5.5% of the economy). However, since the IT-producing sectors are such a small share of the economy, most of the growth in technical change for the economy as a whole is driven by technical change in the non-IT-producing sectors. Subtracting line 2 from line 3 gives the results for the late 1990s acceleration on line 4. The surprising result is that of the 1.9-percentage-point acceleration in technical change, only 0.3 percentage points came from IT. The acceleration of technical change in the economy

---

4. This idea is similar to the "1974" hypothesis of Yorukoglu and Greenwood (1997). In terms of implementation, the main difference is their suggestion that the costs of adjustment may last for many years, so one should have a number of lags of investment as well as current investment in equations (1) and (2).

Table 1   TECHNICAL CHANGE BY INDUSTRY GROUP AND SUBPERIOD

Subperiod	Total	From IT	From NT
		Δt	
1987–1999	2.0	0.5	1.5
1990–1995	1.2	0.3	0.9
1995–1999	3.1	0.7	2.4
Late 1990s acceleration	1.9	0.3	1.6

in the second half of the 1990s was due to something other than faster technical change in the sectors producing computers and telecommunications equipment.

This result, seemingly intuitive, is actually quite difficult to reconcile with the usual formalization of production. DeLong cites Stiroh (forthcoming) as saying that some of the labor productivity gains in the economy come from IT-using sectors. But the same should not be true of total factor productivity. According to the usual model of production—e.g., the production function for NT in equation (1)—more or better inputs are movements *along* the production function, not shifts *of* the production function. As the usual dictum has it, "cheaper inputs don't shift production functions."

There are at least four stories that might explain this observation. Two attribute it to mismeasurement, and two to actual technical change. The first mismeasurement story is that IT capital quality is growing faster than measured in the statistics, so there is effectively more IT investment than is actually measured, with the unmeasured investment wrongly showing up as faster technical change. This story seems unlikely, because a number of papers by Erik Brynjolfsson and his coauthors (e.g., Brynjolfsson, Hitt, and Yang, 2000) show that the increased investment raises productivity five or more years after the investment is made, not immediately as one would expect with straightforward mismeasurement. The second story is actually the preferred explanation of Brynjolfsson, Hitt, and Yang (2000) for their results. They attribute the increases in productivity and stock market valuation after IT investment to unmeasured complementary investments—for example, training, learning-by-doing, and general research on using IT effectively. Here the question is whether these unmeasured investments are nonrival. If they are, at least in part—and many of them sound like some form of knowledge—then they do constitute technical change in the sense that other firms can boost production without incurring similar resource costs. Of course innovations may take some time to spread to other firms—this temporary competitive advantage is presumably why the private investment is worthwhile—but slow diffusion of technology is actually a reason to be hopeful, for it indicates that many of the social returns to these complementary investments may lie ahead.

The two interpretations of the Table 1 results as denoting actual technological change are quite similar to the nonrival complementary investment story. The first takes seriously the idea of computers and telecommunications as a new general-purpose technology (GPT) (see Helpman and Trajtenberg, 1998). As these models assume and economic history shows clearly, a GPT needs to be combined with various specific innovations in order to yield large production efficiencies. These innovations often require substantial time, and secondary innovations of their own, to change the structure of production. The second interpretation— really a special case of the GPT story—is that there is capital-biased (Solow-neutral) technical change. In principle the derivative of equation (1) with respect to T may depend on all the other variables, including K. Jorgenson (1988) has used the idea of energy-biased technical change to explain the productivity slowdown that started in the late 1960s or early 1970s. One problem with this story has always been the absence of a major speedup in productivity growth following the collapse of oil prices in the mid-1980s. A simpler, unified explanation is the hypothesis of directed technical change: the idea that innovation is directed towards economizing on expensive inputs while being profligate with cheap ones. In the 1950s and 1960s the cheap input was oil; in the 1990s it was IT hardware. But in any given subperiod, directed technological change may be indistinguishable from factor-biased technical progress. It is in this sense that the second explanation is a special case of the first.

Thus, my intuition is that the key to understanding the productivity acceleration of the 1990s is making progress on modeling the process of directed technological change in the presence of a new GPT and, especially, confronting the models with detailed industry- and firm-level data. There are now some excellent overviews on how one might go about these difficult tasks—see, especially, Bresnahan (2001). But it is fair to say that these appealing stories have not had many empirical successes. If the stories are right, then technical change in the non-IT sectors have been driven by technical progress in IT, which has led to ever-falling prices for IT equipment. I tried to estimate the reduced-form model, correlating the industry residuals in the non-IT sector on lagged technical change in IT using the industry-level data used to construct Table 1. I found no evidence of a strong or stable relationship between the two. One can come up with many reasons why this relatively aggregative approach might not be successful. But the failure is disappointing nonetheless, because it means that there is little direct evidence for some of the most appealing economic models that might explain the major acceleration in productivity in the mid-1990s. Despite DeLong's nice paper, this area still abounds with questions awaiting answers.

REFERENCES

Basu, S., and J. G. Fernald. (2001). Aggregate productivity and aggregate technology. *European Economic Review* 46(6):963–991.
Basu, S., J. G. Fernald, and M. D. Shapiro. (2001). Productivity growth in the 1990s: Technology, utilization, or adjustment? *Carnegie-Rochester Conference Series on Public Policy* 55(1, December):117–165.
Bresnahan, T. (2001). The mechanisms of information technology's contribution to economic growth. Manuscript.
Brynjolfsson, E., L. M. Hitt, and S. Yang. (2000). Intangible assets: How the interaction of computers and organizational structure affects stock market valuations. MIT, working paper.
Domar, E. D. (1961). On the measurement of technical change. *Economic Journal* 71(December):710–729.
Helpman, E., and M. Trajtenberg. (1998). Diffusion of general purpose technologies. In *General Purpose Technologies and Economic Growth*, E. Helpman (ed.). Cambridge, MA: The MIT Press.
Jorgenson, D. W. (1988). Productivity and postwar U.S. economic growth. *Journal of Economic Perspectives* 2(4, Fall):23–41.
Stiroh, K. J. (forthcoming). Information technology and the U.S. productivity revival: What do the industry data say? *American Economic Review*.
Yorukoglu, M., and J. Greenwood. (1997). 1974. *Carnegie-Rochester Conference Series on Public Policy* 46(June):49–95.

Comment

BOYAN JOVANOVIC
New York University

1. Introduction

Bradford DeLong offers us an entertaining, well-written, and balanced introduction to the "new economy." We all hope, of course, that in the next decade or two we will see the economy return to the high growth rates that it experienced in the late 1990s. As consumers and workers, we hope that the productivity slowdown of the 1970s was a symptom of an investment episode that will pay off in the near future in the form of cheaper new products and higher wages for our labor services. And as a growth theorist, I root for the new economy because Schumpeter-style creative destruction is, to me, much more exciting to think about than an economy in a steady forward creep.

Brad's assessment is balanced: On the one hand, the productivity slowdown of the 1970s is still unexplained, and it is not at all clear that the slowdown represented a conscious sacrifice of output in return for expected future growth. On the other hand, Brad says that the rapid productivity growth of the late 1990s will probably persist for some time because

1. producers will rely even more on IT capital than they do at present (Section 4), and
2. Moore's Law will probably continue to hold for a decade or longer (Sections 2 and 4).

I agree with almost everything that Brad says in this paper, and I shall merely expand on these two specific points.

2. The Growing Share of IT Capital

As Brad observes in Section 5 of his paper, the GPTs of the past should provide us with a clue about what will happen in the coming decades. Let us take a look at the electrification of the United States after 1890. Warren Devine (1983) shows that electricity made its impact on industry in two waves. The first wave did not use electricity to its fullest extent. It simply used electricity to drive the main shaft to which machinery was attached by belts. Only after 1910, when individual drive was introduced with each machine itself plugged into an electric socket, were the full benefits achieved.

Figure 1 plots the isoquants of two technologies. The first technology, *shafts*, was intensive in nonelectrical equipment; it relied on electricity only to power the main drive to which old machinery was attached exactly as it had been when the main drive was powered by a steam engine. As a source of energy per se, electricity was cheaper than steam, but the shafts technology attained only a fraction of the cost savings that electrification had to offer. To get the full potential, one had to use electrical equipment plugged into sockets. This *wires* technology allowed more freedom in the type of building used and in the layout of the equipment, and it avoided the noise, dirt, and clutter of a factory where the conduits of power were belts linking the machinery to the heavily greased shafts.

Assume that each technology is Leontieff and yields constant returns to scale. Initially electrical equipment is expensive. Let the initial isocost line be P_1-P_1. We choose the initial date so that shafts and wires are equally affordable, and points A and A^* both yield a level of output equal to Y. Since returns are constant, this indifference must hold at any budget line parallel to P_1-P_1.

Over time, the budget line twists anticlockwise to, e.g., P_1-P_2. There, more output can be produced at point C with wires than at point B with shafts (i.e., $Y_3 < Y_2$). Figure 2 leaves out the switching costs that held

Figure 1 THE SWITCH FROM SHAFTS TO WIRES

Other Capital

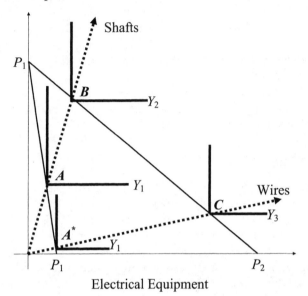

Electrical Equipment

firms from using wires until the 1910–1930 period. As old and new factories were wired, productivity rose sharply.

Now fast-forward to the early 1970s when the U.S. economy began converting from the mainframe to the microcomputer. For "shafts" read "mainframe" and for "wires" read "PC," and the same story applies. The productivity growth of the late 1990s is, by most accounts, the result of this switch.

What does this say about today? Businesses shifted from shafts to wires between 1910 and 1930. They shifted from mainframes to personal computers after 1970. Each wave was followed by an episode of high productivity growth, and we hope that we are—or that we shall soon again be—in the middle of one such growth episode.

3. Computers vs. Electricity and Internal Combustion Engines

Moore's law translates into a rapid rate of price decline for computers and related equipment. Let us compare the price index for computers

Figure 2 PRICES AND CUMULATIVE QUANTITIES OF NEW-ECONOMY
PRODUCTS

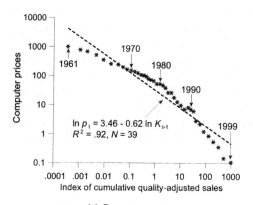

(a) Computer systems

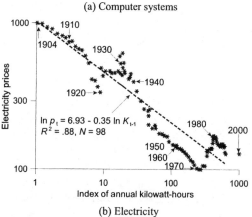

(b) Electricity

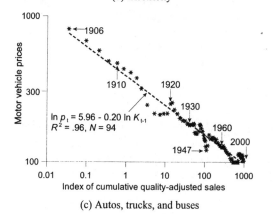

(c) Autos, trucks, and buses

with those of electricity and the internal combustion engine at a comparable stage in their development.

Gordon Moore stated his law in terms of time, but this does not tell
us why computer prices fell. One hypothesis is that computer producers
become more efficient as they sell more and more computers. Other GPTs
also improved as they were applied. Management scientists often measure the application of a technology by the cumulative sales of its output. Let us therefore restate Moore's law in terms of cumulative-output
growth instead of in terms of the passage of time.

Let p denote the price of a product. As the cost of producing it declines,
so does its price, and all this is caused by the rise in the cumulative output,
K, of all producers combined:

$$p = \left(\frac{K}{B}\right)^{-\beta},\tag{1}$$

where B is a constant. In logarithmic form, (1) reads

$$\ln p_t = \beta_0 - \beta \ln K_{t-1},\tag{2}$$

where $\beta_0 = -\beta \ln B$. Jovanovic and Rousseau (2002) estimate this equation
for three GPTs: computers, electricity, and the internal combustion engine. Figure 2 presents pairwise combinations of $\ln p_t$ and $\ln K_{t-1}$ on an
annual basis for each technology and plots a regression line through the
points. The regression estimates are reported in Figure 2 itself.

The computer, displayed in panel (a), shows much the fastest decline
in p, and the effect seems to be accelerating.[1] Panels (b) and (c)—electricity
and cars—show a lower decline and no acceleration. Even if Moore's law
were to slow to a quarter of its current pace, it still would dwarf the
typical price decline in the other two GPTs. In fact, experts such as Meindl,
Chen, and Davis (2001) tell us that Moore's law will hold at its current
pace for at least another 20 years.

4. Conclusion

Moore's law is unique: Capital goods have never declined in price as fast
as they are declining at present. On these grounds alone, productivity
growth should for a while be well above its twentieth-century average.

Moreover, the use of IT involves a network externality in a way that

---

1. A description of how the price series were constructed is in Jovanovic and Rousseau
(2002)—note 3 in the published version or note 2 in the NBER version.

neither electricity nor internal combustion did. This is apparent in the rising value of the Internet as more and more businesses get online. In spite of their low cost, computers and information systems have spread in full force only in a few rich countries. As people elsewhere join the network, they too will enjoy some of the gains that we saw in the United States in the 1990s, and the network effect will then lead to higher growth globally.

REFERENCES

Devine, W., Jr. (1983). From shafts to wires: Historical perspective on electrification. *Journal of Economic History* 43(2):347–372.
Jovanovic, B., and P. L. Rousseau. (2002). Moore's law and learning by doing. *Review of Economic Dynamics* 5(2, April):346–375. NBER Working Paper 8762. Cambridge, MA: National Bureau of Economic Research.
Meindl, J. D., Q. Chen, and J. A. Davis. (2001). Limits on silicon nanoelectronics for terascale integration. *Science* 293:2044–2049.

Discussion

Bob Gordon emphasized that even if Moore's law continues to hold, it is not certain what will happen to real computer investment, as this depends on the elasticity of demand for computing power. Gordon speculated that the key question is what "killer applications" on the demand side will be able to soak up the increase in computing power made possible by Moore's law and the fall in computer prices. He commented that the question of the extent to which productivity growth is driven by the old economy vs. the new economy is an interesting one, and remarked that several old-economy sectors such as landscaping are expanding in importance.

Brad DeLong remarked that the interaction of public policy, intellectual-property rights, and the development of new applications for computing power is a very interesting theme. He expressed surprise that the pricing and limitation of access to intellectual property is proceeding so slowly, especially considering the fact that some firms such as AOL–Time Warner are at one and the same time facilitating access and fighting to restrict access. However, Bob Hall disagreed with what he referred to as DeLong's pessimism on how the economy handles Schumpeterian goods. He remarked that while pessimism might be justified in theory, in practice the market for software functions quite successfully without government intervention.

Bob Hall commented further that, contrary to the assumption of the literature, there are two general-purpose technologies present rather than just one. He differentiated between the computer and the database as two distinct general-purpose technologies. He remarked that the success of companies such as WalMart, Dell, Southwest, and Ebay is built on the ability to keep track of huge amounts of data rather than on the computer as such. On Gordon's point with respect to new-economy- vs. old-economy-driven productivity growth, he was of the opinion that most sectors have not yet even begun to harness the power of modern IT. As an example, he compared WalMart with Kmart.

DeLong drew Hall's attention to the finding in the recent McKinsey U.S. productivity study that a large share of productivity growth at the micro level is due not to IT, but to competitive pressure from WalMart on the retail sector. He asked Hall how it is possible that this competitive pressure is not related to WalMart's use of IT. Hall responded that WalMart's success arises not just from its use of IT in the realm of logistics, but also from its success in human-resource management. Bob Gordon added that the advantage of Southwest Airlines over companies such as United lies in its employee relations rather than in its use of technology.

Mark Gertler asked DeLong to speculate further on the source of the productivity slowdown of the 1970s. He suggested a connection between low-frequency movements in unemployment and labor productivity as a starting point. DeLong replied that he saw the causality going from labor productivity to unemployment. He found plausible a story that linked low productivity growth to high unemployment through workers' expectations of wage growth that failed to keep in step with productivity.

Justin Wolfers invited Brad DeLong to speculate on the impact of IT on the progress of economic science. DeLong and Gordon both responded by referring to Griliches's comment that cheap computers meant too many regressions and too little thought put into specification. However, Bob Gordon remarked that the work of Stock and Watson would not be possible without the advances in computing power that have taken place.

Summing up, Brad DeLong agreed with Susanto Basu's discussion that it is embarrassing not to be able to say much about multifactor productivity growth. However, he commented that the danger in focusing on TFP growth is that capital deepening might be ignored. Looking forward, he speculated that a substantial amount of labor productivity growth will come about through capital deepening as a result of Moore's law and the falling price of IT. He also suggested that capital deepening might be responsible for the recent phenomenon of falling labor inputs at the same time as very little fall in real GDP. On the question of TFP growth outside the IT sector, he suggested that the computer is not merely a case of an input whose price is falling, but of an entirely new kind of input of the kind referred to by stories of the general-purpose-technology type. He agreed with both discussants that it makes sense to try to model multifactor productivity as generated by some form of human action. However, he noted that the importance of multifactor productivity suggests that if it were generated by some particular activity, economists would already have an idea of what that activity is, and how to encourage it.

James H. Stock and Mark W. Watson

DEPARTMENT OF ECONOMICS AND THE
KENNEDY SCHOOL OF GOVERNMENT, HARVARD UNIVERSITY,
AND NBER; AND
DEPARTMENT OF ECONOMICS AND THE WOODROW WILSON SCHOOL,
PRINCETON UNIVERSITY,
AND NBER

Has the Business Cycle Changed and Why?

1. Introduction

The U.S. economy has entered a period of moderated volatility, or quiescence. The long expansion of the 1990s, the mild 2001 recession, and the current moderate recovery reflect a trend over the past two decades towards moderation of the business cycle and, more generally, reduced volatility in the growth rate of GDP.

This reduction in volatility is evident in the plot of the four-quarter growth rate of real GDP in Figure 1. As is summarized in Table 1, during the 1960s the standard deviation of GDP growth was approximately 2.0 percentage points. It rose to 2.7 percentage points in the 1970s and was 2.6 percentage points in the 1980s. But during the 1990s, the standard deviation of four-quarter GDP growth was only 1.5 percentage points.

This moderation in volatility was noticed early on by those whose daily job it is to track the U.S. economy: the earliest analysis of this volatility reduction that we are aware of is an unpublished internal memorandum at the Board of Governors of the Federal Reserve System written by two staff economists (Gilchrist and Kashyap, 1990). The first published articles to identify this moderation in volatility were by Kim and Nelson (1999) and McConnell and Perez-Quiros (2000), who independently concluded

This research was funded in part by NSF grant SBR-9730489. We thank Shaghil Ahmed, Susanto Basu, Ben Bernanke, Jean Boivin, John Fernald, Jordi Gali, Robert Hall, Robert Hodrik, Robert King, Lou Maccini, Athanasios Orphanides, Pierre Perron, Jeremy Piger, Glenn Rudebusch, Beth Anne Wilson, and the editors for helpful discussions and suggestions.

Figure 1 ANNUAL GROWTH RATES OF GDP

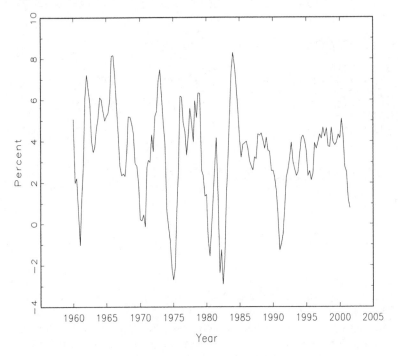

Table 1   SUMMARY STATISTICS FOR FOUR-QUARTER
         GROWTH IN REAL GDP, 1960–2001

Sample period	Mean (%)	Standard deviation (%)
1960–2001	3.3	2.3
1960–1969	4.3	2.0
1970–1979	3.2	2.7
1980–1989	2.9	2.6
1990–2001	3.0	1.5

Notes: Summary statistics are shown for $100 \times \ln(GDP_t / GDP_{t-4})$, where GDP_t is the quarterly value of real GDP.

that there was a sharp decline, or break, in the volatility of U.S. GDP growth in the first quarter of 1984. The moderation was also documented by Simon (2000). These papers have stimulated a substantial recent literature, much of it yet unpublished, that characterizes this decline in volatility and searches for its cause.[1]

1. See Ahmed, Levin, and Wilson (2002), Basistha and Startz (2001), Blanchard and Simon (2001), Boivin and Giannoni (2002a, 2002b), Chauvet and Potter (2001), Feroli (2002), Go-

This article has two objectives. The first is to provide a comprehensive characterization of the decline in volatility using a large number of U.S. economic time series and a variety of methods designed to describe time-varying time-series processes. In so doing, we review the literature on the moderation and attempt to resolve some of its disagreements and discrepancies. This analysis is presented in Sections 2, 3, and 4. Our empirical analysis and review of the literature leads us to five conclusions:

1. The decline in volatility has occurred broadly across the U.S. economy: since the mid-1980s, measures of employment growth, consumption growth, and sectoral output typically have had standard deviations 60% to 70% of their values during the 1970s and early 1980s. Fluctuations in wage and price inflation have also moderated considerably.
2. For variables that measure real economic activity, the moderation generally is associated with reductions in the conditional variance in time-series models, not with changes in the conditional mean; in the language of autoregressions, the variance reduction is attributable to a smaller error variance, not to changes in the autoregressive coefficients. This conclusion is consistent with the findings of Ahmed, Levin, and Wilson (2002), Blanchard and Simon (2001), Pagan (2000), and Sensier and van Dijk (2001).
3. An important unresolved question in the literature is whether the moderation was a sharp break in the mid-1980s, as initially suggested by Kim and Nelson (1999) and McConnell and Perez-Quiros (2000), or part of an ongoing trend, as suggested by Blanchard and Simon (2001). In our view the evidence better supports the break than the trend characterization; this is particularly true for interest-sensitive sectors of the economy such as consumer durables and residential investment.
4. Both univariate and multivariate estimates of the break date center on 1984. When we analyze 168 series for breaks in their conditional variance, approximately 40% have significant breaks in their conditional variance in 1983–1985. Our 67% confidence interval for the break date in the conditional variance of four-quarter GDP growth (given past values of GDP growth) is 1982:4 to 1985:3, consistent with Kim and Nelson's (1999) and McConnell and Perez-Quiros's (2000) estimate of 1984:1.
5. This moderation could come from two nonexclusive sources: smaller unforecastable disturbances (*impulses*) or changes in how those distur-

lub (2000), Herrera and Pesavento (2002), Kahn, McConnel, and Perez-Quiros (2001), Kim, Nelson, and Piger (2001), Pagan (2000), Primiceri (2002), Ramey and Vine (2001), Sensier and van Dijk (2001), Simon (2001), Sims and Zha (2002), and Warnock and Warnock (2001). These papers are discussed below in the context of their particular contribution.

bances propagate through the economy (*propagation*). Although the propagation mechanism (as captured by VAR lag coefficients) appears to have changed over the past four decades, these changes do not account for the magnitude of the observed reduction in volatility. Rather, the observed reduction is associated with a reduction in the magnitude of VAR forecast errors, a finding consistent with the multivariate analyses of Ahmed, Levin, and Wilson (2002), Boivin and Giannoni (2002a, 2002b), Primiceri (2002), Simon (2001), and Sims and Zha (2002), although partially at odds with Cogley and Sargent (2002).

The second objective of this article is to provide new evidence on the quantitative importance of various explanations for this "great moderation." These explanations fall into three categories. The first category is changes in the structure of the economy. Candidate structural changes include the shift in output from goods to services (Burns, 1960; Moore and Zarnowitz 1986), information-technology-led improvements in inventory management (McConnell and Perez-Quiros, 2000; Kahn, McConnel, and Perez-Quiros, 2001, 2002), and innovations in financial markets that facilitate intertemporal smoothing of consumption and investment (Blanchard and Simon, 2001). The second category is improved policy, in particular improved monetary policy (e.g., Taylor, 1999b; Cogley and Sargent, 2001), and the third category is good luck, that is, reductions in the variance of exogenous structural shocks.

We address these explanations in Section 5. In brief, we conclude that structural shifts, such as changes in inventory management and financial markets, fail to explain the timing and magnitude of the moderation documented in Sections 2–4. Changes in U.S. monetary policy seem to account for some of the moderation, but most of the moderation seems to be attributable to reductions in the volatility of structural shocks. Altogether, we estimate that the moderation in volatility is attributable to a combination of improved policy (10–25%), identifiable good luck in the form of productivity and commodity price shocks (20–30%), and other, unknown forms of good luck that manifest themselves as smaller reduced-form forecast errors (40–60%); as discussed in Section 5, these percentages have many caveats.

2. Reductions in Volatility throughout the Economy

This section documents the widespread reduction in volatility in the 1990s and provides some nonparametric estimates of this reduction for 22 major economic time series. We begin with a brief discussion of the data.

2.1 DATA AND TRANSFORMATIONS

In all, we consider data on 168 quarterly macroeconomic time series from 1959:1 to 2001:3. The U.S. data represent a wide range of macroeconomic activity and are usefully grouped into six categories: (1) NIPA decompositions of real GDP, (2) money, credit, interest rates, and stock prices, (3) housing, (4) industrial production, (5) inventories, orders, and sales, (6) employment. In addition, we consider industrial production for five other OECD countries. Seasonally adjusted series were used when available.

Most of our analysis uses these quarterly data, transformed to eliminate trends and obvious nonstationarity. Specifically, most real variables were transformed to growth rates (at an annual rate), prices and wages were transformed to changes in inflation rates (at an annual rate), and interest rates were transformed to first differences. For some applications (such as the data description in Section 2.2) we use annual growth rates or annual differences of the quarterly data. For variable transformed to growth rates, say X_t, this means that the summary statistics are reported for the series $100 \times \ln(X_t/X_{t-4})$. For prices and wages, the corresponding transformation is $100 \times [\ln(X_t/X_{t-1}) - \ln(X_{t-4}/X_{t-5})]$, and for interest rates the transformation is $X_t - X_{t-4}$. Definitions and specific transformations used for each series are listed in Appendix B.

2.2 HISTORICAL VOLATILITY OF MAJOR ECONOMIC TIME SERIES

2.2.1 Volatility by Decade   Table 2 reports the sample standard deviation of 22 leading macroeconomic time series by decade (2000 and 2001 are included in the 1990s). Each decade's standard deviation is presented relative to the full-sample standard deviation, so a value less than one indicates a period of relatively low volatility. All series were less volatile in the 1990s than over the full sample, and all but one series (consumption of nondurables) were less volatile in the 1990s than in the 1980s. On the demand side, the 1990 relative standard deviations ranged from 0.65 (government spending and residential investment) to 0.89 (nonresidential investment). On the production side, the standard deviations during the 1990s, relative to the full sample, range from 0.65 (durable goods production) to 0.87 (services). Comparable volatility reductions are found when standard deviations are compared before and after the 1984:I break date of Kim and Nelson (1999) and McConnell and Perez-Quiros (2000) (Table 2, final column).

This decline in volatility is reflected in other series as well. For example, the relative standard deviation of annual growth of nonagricultural em-

Table 2 STANDARD DEVIATIONS, BY DECADE, OF ANNUAL GROWTH RATES OR CHANGES OF 22 MACROECONOMIC TIME SERIES

Series	Standard deviation 1960–2001 (%)	Standard deviation, relative to 1960–2001				Standard deviation 1984–2001, relative to 1960–1983
		1960–1969	1970–1979	1980–1989	1990–2001	
GDP	2.3	0.98	1.18	1.14	0.67	0.59
Consumption	1.9	0.97	1.17	1.07	0.78	0.62
Consumption—durables	6.6	0.87	1.18	1.13	0.79	0.71
Consumption—nondurables	1.8	1.06	1.22	0.81	0.87	0.66
Consumption—services	1.2	1.07	0.84	1.20	0.88	0.73
Investment (total)	10.4	0.82	1.15	1.22	0.77	0.78
Fixed investment—total	6.7	0.77	1.29	1.04	0.84	0.75
Nonresidential	6.7	0.87	1.17	1.06	0.89	0.87
Residential	13.4	0.78	1.25	1.23	0.65	0.52
Δ(inventory investment)/GDP, × 100	0.6	1.12	0.92	1.22	0.71	0.80
Exports	6.4	1.07	1.13	1.12	0.66	0.60
Imports	7.2	0.87	1.24	1.14	0.70	0.71
Government spending	2.5	1.40	1.00	0.85	0.65	0.69
Production						
Goods (total)	3.6	0.97	1.13	1.13	0.76	0.70
Nondurable goods	7.3	1.00	1.14	1.16	0.68	0.63
Durable goods	2.5	0.92	1.16	1.22	0.65	0.61
Services	1.1	1.41	0.52	1.01	0.87	0.73
Structures	6.2	0.73	1.33	1.11	0.73	0.67
Nonagricultural employment	1.7	0.94	1.21	1.09	0.73	0.62
Price inflation (GDP deflator)	0.4	0.69	1.51	1.06	0.50	0.48
90-day T-bill rate	1.7	0.51	1.10	1.43	0.75	0.71
10-year T-bond rate	1.2	0.43	0.65	1.67	0.82	1.13

Notes: NIPA series are annual growth rates, except for the change in inventory investment, which is the annual difference of the quarterly change in inventories as a fraction of GDP. Inflation is the four-quarter change in the annual inflation rate, and interest rates are in four-quarter changes.

ployment in the 1990s was 0.73. The 1990s were also a period of quiescence for inflation: changes in annual price inflation, measured by the GDP deflator, has a relative standard deviation of 0.50. As noted by Kim, Nelson, and Piger (2001), Watson (1999), and Basistha and Startz (2001), the situation for interest rates is somewhat more complex. Although the variance of interest rates decreased across the term structure, the decrease was more marked at the short than at the long end, that is, the relative volatility of long rates increased.

2.2.2 Estimates of Time-Varying Standard Deviations Figure 2 provides graphical evidence on the decline in volatility for the 22 time series in Table 2. The light line in Figure 2 is a "raw" estimate of the volatility of the series, the absolute value of the deviation of each series (transformed as in Table 2) from its mean. To provide a guide to the numerical importance of the change in the standard deviation, the NIPA series are weighted by their average nominal share in GDP from 1960 to 2001 (the weights are indicated in the figure labels).[2] For example, for consumption, the light line is the absolute value of the demeaned four-quarter growth in consumption, weighted by the average share of consumption, 0.64. The solid, smoother line is a two-sided estimate of the instantaneous time-varying standard deviation of the series, based on a fourth-order autoregression [AR(4)] with time-varying parameters and stochastic volatility. This model and associated non-Gaussian smoother are conceptually similar (but different in details) to the multivariate approach in Cogley and Sargent (2002) and are discussed further in Appendix A.

The results in Figure 2 present a varied picture of the decline in volatility. For some series—GDP, total goods production, durable-goods consumption and production, total investment, residential investment, construction output, and imports—volatility declines sharply in the mid-1980s. A closer look at the components of investment shows that the overall decline in its volatility is associated with a sharp decline in residential investment in the mid-1980s. For some series, such as consumption of nondurables and government consumption, volatility is essentially unchanged over the sample. The volatility of employment growth seems to

2. Specifically, let $\Delta_4 \ln \text{GDP}_t = \ln(\text{GDP}_t / \text{GDP}_{t-4})$ be the four-quarter growth rate of GDP, and let X_{jt} denote the level of the jth of n components of GDP, where imports have a negative sign and where X_{nt} is the quarterly change in inventory investment. Then $\Delta_4 \ln \text{GDP}_t \approx S_{1t} \Delta_4 \ln X_{1t} + \cdots + S_{n-1,t} \Delta_4 \ln X_{n-1,t} + (\Delta_4 X_{nt})/\text{GDP}_t$, where S_{jt} is the GDP share of the jth component at date t. The first $n - 1$ terms are the share-weighted growth rates of the components, other than inventories, and the final term is the four-quarter difference of the quarterly change in inventories, relative to GDP. If the terms in the expression for $\Delta_4 \ln \text{GDP}_t$ were uncorrelated (they are not), then the sum of their variances would equal the variance of $\Delta_4 \ln \text{GDP}_t$.

Figure 2 TIME-VARYING STANDARD DEVIATIONS

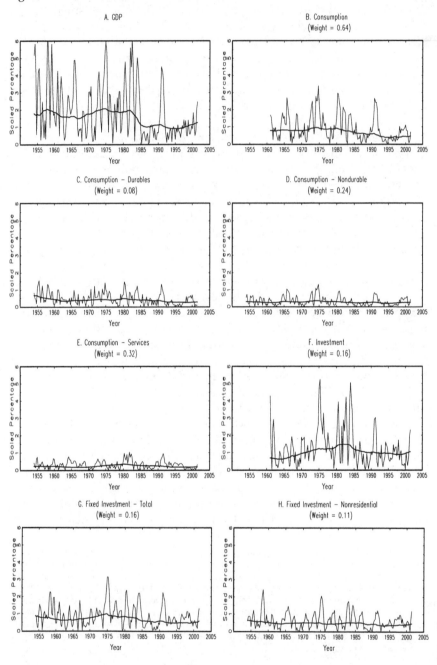

Figure 2 CONTINUED

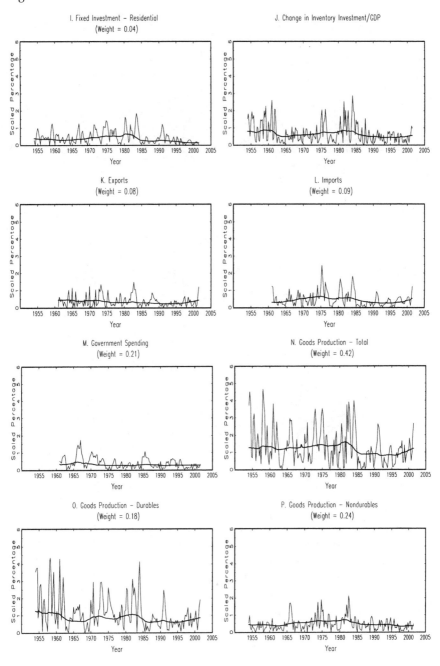

Figure 2 CONTINUED

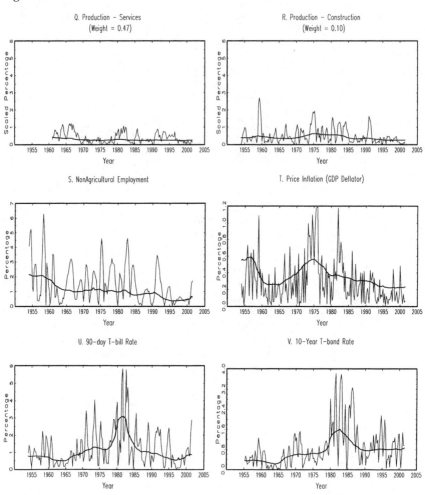

have declined in steps, first falling from the 1950s to the 1960s, then falling again in the early 1980s and the early 1990s. The volatility of changes in short-term interest rates fell sharply in the mid-1980s, then continued to fall, whereas long-term rates remain as volatile as they were in the 1970s.

2.2.3 Results for Other Series The decline in volatility seen for the 22 series in Table 2 is typical of other macroeconomic time series. Across the 168 series listed in Appendix B (including the 22 in Table 2), the median relative standard deviation in the 1990s is 0.73, and 78% of the series had a relative standard deviation less than 0.85 in the 1990s. For example, the relative standard deviation of the overall index of industrial production in the 1990s was 0.63; this reduction is also found in the various industrial production sectors, with sectoral relative standard deviations ranging from 0.59 (consumer goods) to 0.77 (utilities). Orders and inventories showed a similar decline in volatility; the average relative standard deviation was 0.68 for these series in the 1990s. As discussed in more detail by Warnock and Warnock (2001), the standard deviation of employment also fell in most sectors (the exceptions being contract construction, FIRE, services, and wholesale and retail trade, where the relative standard deviations are close to one). Although broad measures of inflation show marked declines in volatility, some producer prices showed little decrease or an increase in volatility, and the overall index of producer prices has a relative standard deviation close to one.

Finally, as discussed in Blanchard and Simon (2001) and Simon (2001), the decrease in volatility is not unique to the United States. The relative standard deviation of industrial production indexes for several other developed countries were low in the 1990s. However, some countries (France, Japan, and Germany) also experienced low variability in the 1980s and experienced somewhat more variability in the 1990s.

2.2.4 Implications for Recessions and Expansions   Because recessions are defined as periods of absolute decline in economic activity, reduced volatility with the same mean growth rate implies fewer and shorter recessions. As discussed further by Kim and Nelson (1999), Blanchard and Simon (2001), Chauvet and Potter (2001), and Pagan (2000), this suggests that the decrease in the variance of GDP has played a major role in the increased length of business-cycle expansions over the past two decades.

2.3 SUMMARY

The moderation in volatility in the 1990s is widespread (but not universal) and appears in both nominal and real series. When the NIPA series are weighted by their shares in GDP, the decline in volatility is most pronounced for residential investment, output of durable goods, and output of structures. The decline in volatility appears both in measures of real economic activity and in broad measures of wage and price inflation. For the series with the largest declines in volatility, volatility seems to have fallen sharply in the mid-1980s, but to draw this conclusion with confidence we need to apply some statistical tests to distinguish distinct breaks from steady trend declines in volatility, a task taken up in the next section.

3. Dating the Great Moderation

The evidence in Section 2 points toward a widespread decline in volatility throughout the economy. In this section, we consider whether this decline is associated with a single distinct break in the volatility of these series and, if so, when the break occurred. We study the issue of a break in the variance, first using univariate methods, and then using multivariate methods. We begin by examining univariate evidence on whether the change in the variance is associated with changes in the conditional mean of the univariate time-series process or changes in the conditional variance.

3.1 CHANGES IN MEAN VS. CHANGES IN VARIANCE: UNIVARIATE EVIDENCE

The changes in the variance evident in Figure 2 could arise from changes in the autoregressive coefficients (that is, changes in the conditional mean of the process, given its past values), changes in the innovation variance (that is, changes in the conditional variance), or both. Said differently, the change in the variance of a series can be associated with changes in its spectral shape, changes in the level of its spectrum, or both. Research on this issue has generally concluded that the changes in variance are associated with changes in conditional variances. This conclusion was reached by Blanchard and Simon (2001) for GDP and by Sensier and van Dijk (2001) using autoregressive models, and by Ahmed, Levin, and Wilson (2002) using spectral methods. Kim and Nelson (1999) suggest that both the conditional mean and conditional variance of GDP changed, although Pagan (2000) argues that the changes in the conditional mean function are quantitatively minor. Cogley and Sargent (2002) focus on the inflation process and conclude that although most of the reduction in volatility is associated with reductions in the innovation variance, some seems to be associated with changes in the conditional mean.[3]

3.1.1 Tests for Time-Varying Means and Variances We take a closer look at the issue of conditional means vs. conditional variances using a battery of break tests, applied to time-varying autoregressive models of the 168 series listed in Appendix B. The tests look for changes in the coefficients in the AR model

---

3. Cogley and Sargent (2001, 2002) are especially interested in whether there has been a change in the persistence of inflation. The evidence on this issue seems, however, to be sensitive to the statistical method used: Pivetta and Reis (2001) estimate the largest root in the inflation process to have stably remained near one from 1960 to 2000. Because our focus is volatility, not persistence, we do not pursue this interesting issue further.

$$y_t = \alpha_t + \phi_t(L)y_{t-1} + \varepsilon_t, \tag{1}$$

where

$$\alpha_t + \phi_t(L) = \begin{cases} \alpha_1 + \phi_1(L), & t \le \kappa, \\ \alpha_2 + \phi_2(L), & t > \kappa, \end{cases} \quad \text{and} \quad \text{Var}(\varepsilon_t) = \begin{cases} \sigma_1^2, & t \le \tau, \\ \sigma_2^2, & t > \tau, \end{cases}$$

where $\phi_1(L)$ and $\phi_2(L)$ are lag polynomials and κ and τ are break dates in, respectively, the conditional mean and the conditional variance. This formulation allows for the conditional mean and the conditional variance each to break (or not) at potentially different dates.

We use the formulation (1) to test for changes in the AR parameters. First, the heteroscedasticity-robust Quandt (1960) likelihood ratio (QLR) statistic [also referred to as the sup–Wald statistic; see Andrews (1993)] is used to test for a break in the conditional mean. Throughout, QLR statistics are computed for all potential break dates in the central 70% of the sample. We test for a break in the variance at an unknown date τ by computing the QLR statistic for a break in the mean of the absolute value of the residuals from the estimated autoregression (1), where the autoregression allows for a break in the AR parameters at the estimated break date $\hat{\kappa}$ (see Appendix A). Although the QLR statistic is developed for the single-break model, this test has power against other forms of time variation such as drifting parameters (Stock and Watson, 1998): rejection of the no-break null by the QLR statistic is evidence of time variation, which may or may not be of the single-break form in (1).

3.1.2 Estimated Break Dates and Confidence Intervals In addition to testing for time-varying AR parameters, in the event that the QLR statistic rejects at the 5% level we report OLS estimates of the break dates $\hat{\kappa}$ (AR coefficients) and $\hat{\tau}$ (innovation variance), and 67% confidence intervals computed following Bai (1997).[4]

3.1.3 Results Results for the 22 series are summarized in Table 3. For GDP, the QLR statistic fails to reject the null hypothesis of no break in the coefficients of the conditional mean. In contrast, the null hypothesis of no break in the conditional variance is rejected at the 1% significance level. The break date is estimated to be 1983:2, which is consistent with estimated break dates reported by McConnell and Perez-Quintos (2001)

---

4. The break estimator has a non-normal, heavy-tailed distribution, so 95% intervals computed using Bai's (1997) method are so wide as to be uninformative. We therefore deviate from convention and report 67% confidence intervals.

Table 3   TESTS FOR CHANGES IN AUTOREGRESSIVE PARAMETERS

	Conditional mean			Conditional variance					
				Break only			Trend and break		
							p-Value		
Series	p-Value	Break date	67% Confidence interval	p-Value	Break date	67% Confidence interval	Trend	Break	Break date
GDP	0.98			0.00	1983:2	1982:4–1985:3	0.63	0.00	1983:2
Consumption	0.55			0.00	1992:1	1991:3–1994:1	0.00	0.11	
Consumption—durables	0.04	1987:3		0.00	1987:3	1987:2–1990:2	0.68	0.03	1987:3
Consumption—nondurables	0.00	1991:4	1991:2–1992:2	0.08			0.96	0.80	
Consumption—services	0.00	1969:4	1969:2–1970:2	0.18			0.03	0.00	1971:3
Investment (total)	0.05			0.13			0.06	0.25	
Fixed investment—total	0.69			0.01	1983:3	1983:1–1986:4	0.65	0.07	
Nonresidential	0.47			0.70			0.69	0.60	
Residential	0.10			0.00	1983:2	1983:1–1985:2	0.08	0.00	1983:2
Δ(inventory investment)/GDP	0.91			0.04	1988:1	1987:3–1992:2	0.00	0.10	
Exports	0.09			0.00	1975:4	1975:2–1978:2	0.95	0.75	
Imports	0.00	1972:4	1972:2–1973:2	0.00	1986:2	1986:1–1988:1	0.96	0.05	1986:2
Government spending	0.06			0.45			0.33	0.65	
Production									
Goods (total)	0.92			0.00	1983:4	1983:2–1986:4	0.54	0.03	1983:3
Nondurable goods	0.09			0.00	1983:4	1983:3–1987:1	0.00	0.29	
Durable goods	0.77			0.02	1985:2	1984:3–1989:1	0.33	0.02	1985:2
Services	0.00	1968:3	1968:1–1969:1	0.98			0.69	0.92	
Structures	0.02	1991:3	1991:1–1992:1	0.02	1984:2	1983:4–1988:1	0.42	0.03	1984:2
Nonagricultural employment	0.03	1981:2	1980:4–1981:4	0.00	1983:2	1982:4–1985:3	0.00	0.02	1973:3
Price inflation (GDP deflator)	0.00	1973:2	1972:4–1973:4	0.11			0.00	0.00	1971:2
90-day T-bill rate	0.00	1981:1	1980:3–1981:3	0.01	1984:4	1984:2–1988:1	0.00	0.00	1984:4
10-year T-bond rate	0.02	1981:1	1980:3–1981:3	0.00	1979:3	1972:2–1980:1	0.02	0.00	1979:3

Notes: The test results are based on the QLR test for the changes in the coefficients of an AR(4). The first column shows the p-value for the QLR-test break test statistic. The second column shows the least-squares estimates of the break date (when the QLR statistic is significant at the 5% level), and the final column shows the 67% confidence interval for the break date. The results in the "Conditional Mean" columns correspond to the parameters α and ϕ in equation (1). The results in the "Conditional Variance" columns refer to the variance of ε_t in equation (1), either with or without a time trend in the QLR regression. The tests are described in more detail in Appendix A.

and Kim, Nelson, and Piger (2001). The 67% confidence interval for the break date is precise, 1982:4–1985:3, although (for reasons discussed in footnote 4) the 95% confidence interval is rather wide, 1982:1–1989:4.

The results for the components of GDP indicate that although several series (such as the components of consumption) reveal significant time variation in the conditional-mean coefficients, the estimated break dates and confidence intervals do not coincide with the timing of the reductions in volatility evident in Figure 2. In contrast, for ten of the seventeen NIPA components there are significant changes in the conditional variance, and for eight of those ten series the break in the conditional variance is estimated to be in the mid-1980s. Thus, like Kim, Nelson, and Piger (2001), who use Bayesian methods, we find breaks in the volatility of many components of GDP, not just durable-goods output as suggested by McConnell and Perez-Quiros (2000). Durables consumption, total fixed investment, residential investment, imports, goods production, and employment all exhibit significant breaks in their conditional volatility with break dates estimated in the mid-1980s.

3.1.4 Estimates Based on the Stochastic Volatility Model As another check on this conclusion, we recalculated the estimates of the instantaneous variance based on the stochastic volatility model (the smooth lines in Figure 2), with the restriction that the AR coefficients remain constant at their full-sample OLS estimated values. The resulting estimated instantaneous standard deviations (not reported here) were visually very close to those reported in Figure 2. The most substantial differences in the estimated instantaneous variance was for price inflation, in which changes in the conditional-mean coefficients in the 1960s contributed to changes in the estimated standard deviation. These results are consistent with the conclusion drawn from Table 3 that the reduction in the variance of these series is attributable to a reduction in the conditional variance.

3.1.5 Results for Other Series Results for additional time series are summarized in Table 10 in Appendix A. There is evidence of widespread instability in both the conditional mean and the conditional variance. Half of the 168 series show breaks in their conditional-mean parameters [consistent with the evidence in Stock and Watson (1996)]. Strikingly, the hypothesis of a constant variance is rejected in two-thirds of the series. Sensier and van Dijk (2001) find a similar result in their analysis of 215 U.S. macroeconomic time series. The breaks in the conditional means are mainly concentrated in the 1970s. In contrast, the breaks in the conditional variances are concentrated in the 1980s or, for some series, the early 1990s. Thus, the timing of the reduction in the unconditional variance of these series in the 1980s and 1990s coincides with the estimated breaks in the conditional variance, not with the estimated breaks in the conditional means.

3.2 IS THE MODERATION A TREND OR A BREAK?

Kim and Nelson (1999) and McConnell and Perez-Quiros (2000) modeled the volatility reduction using Markov switching models; like the AR model (1) with coefficient breaks, the Markov switching model treats the moderation as a discrete event, which they independently dated as occurring in 1984:1. After examining evidence on rolling standard deviations, however, Blanchard and Simon (2001) argued that the volatility reduction was better viewed as part of a longer trend decline, in which the high volatility of the late 1970s and early 1980s was a temporary aberration.

To elucidate this trend-vs.-break debate, we conduct some additional tests using a model that nests the two hypotheses. Specifically, the QLR test for a change in the standard deviation in Section 3.1 was modified so that the model for the heteroscedasticity includes a time trend as well as the break. That is, the QLR test is based on the regression $|\hat{\varepsilon}_t| = \gamma_0 + \gamma_1 t + \gamma_2 d_t(\tau) + \eta_t$, where $d_t(\tau)$ is a binary variable that equals 1 if $t \geq \tau$ and equals zero otherwise, and η_t is an error term; the modified QLR test looks for breaks for values of τ in the central 70% of the sample.

The results are reported in the final columns of Table 3. For GDP, the coefficient on the time trend is not statistically significantly different from zero, while the hypothesis of no break (maintaining the possibility of a time trend in the standard deviation) is rejected at the 1% significance level. The estimated break date in GDP volatility is 1983:2, the same whether a time trend is included in the specification or not. For GDP, then, this evidence is consistent with the inference drawn from the estimated instantaneous standard deviation plotted in Figure 2: the sharp decline in the volatility of GDP growth in the mid-1980s is better described as a discrete reduction in the variance than as part of a continuing trend towards lower volatility.

The results in Table 2 suggest that the break model is also appropriate for many of the components of GDP, specifically nondurables consumption, residential fixed investment, imports, total goods production, production of durables, and production of construction. For these series, the estimated break dates fall between 1983:2 and 1987:3. Consumption of durables and production of nondurables, however, seem to be better described by the trend model. A few of the components of GDP, such as exports, are not well described by either model.

These conclusions based on Table 2 are consistent with those based on the smoothed volatility plots in Figure 2: there was a sharp decline, or break, in the volatility of GDP growth and some of its components, most strikingly residential investment, durable-goods output, and output of construction, while other components and time series show more complicated patterns of time-varying volatility.

3.3 MULTIVARIATE ESTIMATES OF BREAK DATES

In theory, a common break date can be estimated much more precisely when multiple-equation methods are used [see Hansen (2001) for a review]. In this section, we therefore use two multivariate methods in an attempt to refine the break-date confidence intervals of Section 3.1, one based on low-dimensional VARs, the other based on dynamic factor models.

3.3.1 Common Breaks in VARs To estimate common breaks across multiple series, we follow Bai, Lumsdaine, and Stock (1998) and extend the univariate autoregression in (1) to a VAR. The procedure is the same as described in Section 3.1, except that, to avoid overfitting, the VAR coefficients were kept constant. The hypothesis of no break is tested against the alternative of a common break in the system of equations using the QLR statistic computed using the absolute values of the VAR residuals. We also report the OLS estimator of the break date in the mean absolute residual and the associated 67% confidence interval, computed using the formulas in Bai, Lumsdaine, and Stock (1998).

The results for three different VARs are summarized in Table 4. The first VAR decomposes GDP by its end-use components, the second de-

Table 4 ESTIMATES OF COMMON BREAK DATES OF VARIANCES OF VAR RESIDUALS

Variables	No. of variables	QLR p-Value	Break date	67% Confidence interval
Consumption, investment, exports, imports, government spending	5	0.01	1982:4	1981:1–1984:3
Output of: durables, nondurables, services, and structures	4	0.00	1984:1	1982:3–1985:3
Consumption of durables, consumption of nondurables, residential fixed investment	3	0.00	1983:2	1982:1–1984:3

Notes: The estimated break dates and confidence intervals are computed using the methods in Bai, Lumsdaine, and Stock (1998).

composes GDP by its production components, and the third focuses on the more durable components of demand by individuals, consumption of nondurables and durables, and residential fixed investment. In each, the hypothesis of a constant variance is rejected at the 1% significance level. The estimated break dates range from 1982:4 to 1984:1, with 67% confidence intervals that are tight and similar to the 67% confidence interval based on the univariate analysis of GDP growth.

3.3.2 Evidence Based on Factor Models Dynamic factor models provide a complementary way to use information on multiple variables to estimate the volatility break date. Chauvet and Potter (2001) use Bayesian methods to analyze a dynamic factor model of nine measures of economic activity (including GDP, industrial production, consumption, sales, and employment). Their model allows for breaks in the autoregressive coefficients and variance of the single common dynamic factor. They find strong evidence for a break in the variance of the common factor, and the posterior distribution for the break date places almost all the mass in 1983 or 1984.

This analysis can be extended to higher-dimensional systems by using the principal components of the data to estimate the space spanned by the postulated common dynamic factors (Stock and Watson, 2001). Previous empirical work (Stock and Watson, 1999, 2001) has shown that the first principal component computed using the series such as those in Appendix B captures a large fraction of the variation in those series, and that the first principal component can be thought of as a real activity factor. Like GDP, this factor has a significant break in its conditional variance, with an estimated break date of 1983:3 and a 67% confidence interval of 1983:2 to 1986:3.

3.4 SUMMARY

The results in this section point to instability both in conditional-mean functions and in conditional variances. The weight of the evidence, however, suggests that the reductions in volatility evident in Table 1 and Figure 2 are associated with changes in conditional variances (error variances), rather than changes in conditional means (autoregressive coefficients). Analysis of the full set of 168 series listed in Appendix B provides evidence of a widespread reduction in volatility, with the reduction generally dated in the mid-1980s. For most series, this conclusion is unchanged when one allows for the possibility that the volatility reduction could be part of a longer trend. Accordingly, we conclude that for most series the preferred model is one of a distinct reduction in volatility rather than a trend decline.

This view of a sharp moderation rather than a trend decline is particularly appropriate for GDP and some of its more durable components. Following McConnell and Perez-Quiros (2000), much of the literature focuses on declines in volatility in the production of durable goods; however, like Kim, Nelson, and Piger (2001), we find significant reductions in volatility in other series. Our results particularly point to large reductions in the variance of residential fixed investment and output of structures, both of which are highly volatile. The finding of a break in volatility in the mid-1980s is robust, and univariate and multivariate confidence intervals for the break date are tightly centered around 1983 and 1984.

4. Impulse or Propagation?

The univariate analysis of Section 3.1 suggests that most of the moderation in volatility of GDP growth is associated with a reduction in its conditional variance, not changes in its conditional mean. But does this conclusion hold when multiple sources of information are used to compute the conditional mean of output growth? Several recent studies (Ahmed, Levin, and Wilson 2001; Boivin and Giannoni, 2002a; 2002b; Primiceri (2002); Simon, 2000) have examined this question using vector autoregressions, and we adopt this approach here. Specifically, in the context of reduced-form VARs, is the observed reduction in volatility associated with a change in the magnitude of the VAR forecast errors (the *impulses*), in the lag dynamics modeled by the VAR (*propagation*), or both?

4.1 THE COUNTERFACTUAL VAR METHOD

Because the results of Sections 3.2 and 3.3 point to a distinct break in volatility in 1983 or 1984, in this section we impose the break date 1984:1 found by Kim and Nelson (1999) and McConnell and Perez-Quiros (2000). Accordingly, we use reduced-form VARs estimated over 1960–1983 and 1984–2001 to estimate how much of the reduction in the variance of GDP is due to changes in the VAR coefficients and how much is due to changes in the innovation covariance matrix. Each VAR has the form

$$X_t = \Phi_i(L)X_{t-1} + u_t, \qquad \text{Var}(u) = \Sigma_i, \tag{2}$$

where X_t is a vector time series and the subscript $i = 1, 2$ denotes the first and second subsample [the intercept is omitted in (2) for notational convenience but is included in the estimation]. Let B_{ij} be the matrix of coefficients of the jth lag in the matrix lag polynomial $B_i(L) = [I -$

$\Phi_i(L)L]^{-1}$. With this notation, the variance of the kth series in X_t in the ith period is

$$\text{Var}(X_{kt}) = \left(\sum_{j=0}^{\infty} B_{ij} \Sigma_i B'_{ij} \right)_{kk} = \sigma_k(\Phi_i, \Sigma_i)^2. \tag{3}$$

By evaluating the expression in (3) for different Φ and Σ, it is possible to compute the counterfactual variance of X_{kt} that would have arisen had either Φ or Σ taken on different values. For example $\sigma_k(\Phi_1, \Sigma_1)$ is the standard deviation of X_{kt} in period 1, and $\sigma_k(\Phi_2, \Sigma_1)$ is the standard deviation of X_{kt} that would have occurred had the lag dynamics been those of the second period and the error covariance matrix been that of the first period. Although these expressions are based on the population parameters, the various counterfactuals can be estimated by replacing the population parameters with sample estimators.

4.2 RESULTS

The results are summarized in Table 5, where, for comparability with the previous tables, the quarterly variances have been temporally aggregated to pertain to annual growth rates of quarterly variables. Table 5a presents results for a four-variable VAR(4) benchmark model consisting of GPD growth, the first difference of inflation (measured by the GDP deflator), the federal funds rate, and the growth rate of commodity prices. The first two columns provide the sample standard deviations of the various series, and the final four columns provide the VAR-based estimates of the standard deviations for the four possible permutations of estimated lag coefficients and covariance matrices. The columns labeled $\sigma(\hat{\Phi}_1, \hat{\Sigma}_1)$ and $\sigma(\hat{\Phi}_2, \hat{\Sigma}_2)$ respectively contain the VAR-based estimate of the first- and second-period sample standard deviations, which (as they should be) are quite close to the respective sample standard deviations. The columns labeled $\sigma(\hat{\Phi}_1, \hat{\Sigma}_2)$ and $\sigma(\hat{\Phi}_2, \hat{\Sigma}_1)$ contain the counterfactual estimates.

First consider the results for GDP. The counterfactual combination of second-period dynamics and first-period shocks [that is, $\sigma(\hat{\Phi}_2, \hat{\Sigma}_1)$] produces an estimated standard deviation of 2.63, essentially the same as the first-period standard deviation. In contrast, the first-period dynamics and second-period shocks produce an estimated standard deviation of 1.48, essentially the same as the second-period standard deviation. According to these estimates, had the shocks of the 1970s occurred in the 1990s, the 1990s would have been almost as volatile as the 1970s. Similarly, had the shocks of the 1990s occurred in the 1970s, the 1970s would have been almost as quiescent as the 1990s. In short, the changes in the covariance

Table 5   IMPLIED STANDARD DEVIATIONS OF FOUR-QUARTER GDP
GROWTH FROM SUBSAMPLE VARs

$$X_t = \Phi(L)X_{t-1} + u_t, \qquad \mathrm{Var}(u_t) = \Sigma$$

First sample period: 1960–1983 [estimated parameters $\hat{\Phi}_1(L)$ and $\hat{\Sigma}_1$]

Second sample period: 1984–2001 [estimated parameters $\hat{\Phi}_2(L)$ and $\hat{\Sigma}_2$]

(a) Four-Variable Benchmark Specification [VAR(4) with GDP Growth,
Change in Inflation, Federal Funds Rate, and the Growth Rate
of Real Commodity Prices]

Variable	*Sample standard deviation*		*Standard deviation of four-quarter GDP growth implied by the VAR*			
	1960–1983	1984–2001	$\sigma(\hat{\Phi}_1, \hat{\Sigma}_1)$	$\sigma(\hat{\Phi}_2, \hat{\Sigma}_2)$	$\sigma(\hat{\Phi}_1, \hat{\Sigma}_2)$	$\sigma(\hat{\Phi}_2, \hat{\Sigma}_1)$
GDP growth	2.71	1.59	2.76	1.43	1.48	2.63
Inflation	1.49	0.59	1.52	0.57	0.95	0.92
Federal funds rate	2.64	1.47	2.67	1.48	1.35	3.03

(b) Sensitivity Analysis: Alternative Specifications

Deviation from benchmark specification	$\sigma(\hat{\Phi}_1, \hat{\Sigma}_1)$	$\sigma(\hat{\Phi}_2, \hat{\Sigma}_2)$	$\sigma(\hat{\Phi}_1, \hat{\Sigma}_2)$	$\sigma(\hat{\Phi}_2, \hat{\Sigma}_1)$
First period is 1960–1978	2.52	1.43	1.46	2.58
VAR(6)	2.78	1.37	1.59	2.45
Levels instead of first differences	2.65	1.61	1.43	2.87
1-year Treasury bill rate instead of FF rate	2.72	1.41	1.42	2.73
Alternative commodity price index (PPI for crude materials)	2.76	1.46	2.13	2.60
Alternative commodity price index (Index of sensitive mat. prices)	2.74	1.44	1.68	2.50
Commodity prices dropped	2.76	1.47	1.34	2.68
GDP replaced with goods output	3.94	2.68	2.55	4.08
GDP replaced with goods sales	3.00	2.23	2.25	3.00
Monthly data (using IP and CPI)	5.50	3.13	3.25	5.53

Note: Entries are various estimates of the square root of the variance of the four-quarter growth in GDP. In the base VAR specification, commodity prices are an index of spot prices, all commodities (PSCCOM). The alternative commodity price indexes are PWCMSA and PSM99Q.

matrix of the unforecastable components of the VARs—the impulses—account for virtually all of the reduction in the observed volatility of output.

4.3 SENSITIVITY ANALYSIS AND COMPARISON WITH THE LITERATURE

The sensitivity of this finding to changes in the model specification or assumptions is investigated in Table 5b. The conclusion from the benchmark model—that it is impulses, not shocks, that are associated with the variance reduction—is robust to most changes reported in that table. For example, similar results obtain when the first period is changed to end in 1978 (the second period remains 1984–2001); when log GDP, inflation, and the interest rate are used rather than their first differences; when monthly data are used; and when GDP is replaced with goods output or sales. Dropping the commodity spot price index does not change the results, nor does using an alternative index of sensitive-materials prices [a smoothed version of which is used by Christiano, Eichenbaum, and Evans (1999)]. Curiously, however, replacing the commodity price index by the produce price index for crude materials does change the conclusions somewhat, giving some role to propagation. The weight of this evidence, however, suggests that changes in the propagation mechanism play at most a modest role in explaining the moderation of economic activity.

The substantive conclusions drawn from Table 5 are similar to Primiceri's (2002), Simon's (2000), and (for the same sample periods) Boivin and Giannoni's (2002a, 2002b). Ahmed, Levin, and Wilson (2002) conclude that most of the reduction in variance stems from smaller shocks, but give some weight to changes in the propagation mechanism. The main source of the difference between our results and theirs appears to be that Ahmed, Levin, and Wilson (2002) measure commodity prices by the producer price index for crude materials.

4.4 CONCLUSIONS

The estimates in Table 5 suggest that most, if not all, of the reductions in the variance of the four-quarter growth of GDP are attributable to changes in the covariance matrix of the reduced-form VAR innovations, not to changes in the VAR lag coefficients (the propagation mechanism). These changes in reduced-form VAR innovations could arise either from reductions in the variance of certain structural shocks or from changes in how those shocks impact the economy, notably through changes in the structure of monetary policy. To sort out these possibilities, however, we need to move beyond reduced-form data description and consider structural economic models, a task taken up in the next section.

5. Explanations for the Great Moderation

What accounts for the moderation in the volatility of GDP growth and, more generally, for the empirical evidence documented in Sections 2–4? In this section, we consider five potential explanations. The first is that the reduction in volatility can be traced to a change in the sectoral composition of output away from durable goods. The second potential explanation, proposed by McConnell and Perez-Quiros (2000), is that the reduction in volatility is due to new and better inventory management practices. The third possibility emphasizes the volatility reduction in residential fixed investment. The fourth candidate explanation is that the structural shocks to the economy are smaller than they once were: we simply have had good luck. Finally, we consider the possibility that the reduction in volatility is, at least in part, attributable to better macroeconomic policy, in particular better policymaking by the Federal Reserve Board.

5.1 CHANGES IN THE SECTORAL COMPOSITION

The service sector is less cyclically sensitive than the manufacturing sector, so, as suggested by Burns (1960) and Moore and Zarnowitz (1986), the shift in the United States from manufacturing to services should lead to a reduction in the variability of GDP. Blanchard and Simon (2001), McConnell and Perez-Quiros (2000), and Warnock and Warnock (2001) investigated this hypothesis and concluded that this sectoral shift hypothesis does not explain the reduction in volatility. The essence of Blanchard and Simon's (2001) and McConnell and Perez-Quiros's (2000) argument is summarized in Table 6a. The standard deviation of annual GDP growth fell from 2.7% during 1960–1983 to 1.6% during 1984–2001; when the output subaggregates of durables, nondurables, services, and structures are combined using constant 1965 shares, the resulting standard deviations for the two periods are 3.1% and 1.8%. Thus, autonomously fixing the output shares of the different sectors yields essentially the same decline in the standard deviation of GDP growth as using the actual, changing shares. Mechanically, the reason for this is that the volatility of output in the different sectors has declined across the board. Moreover, the sectors with the greatest volatility—durables and structures—also have output shares that are essentially constant.

The same result is evident if (like Warnock and Warnock, 2001) one

Table 6   THE EFFECT OF CHANGING SECTORAL COMPOSITION ON THE
VARIANCE OF GDP AND AGGREGATE EMPLOYMENT

Sector	Standard deviation		Shares	
	1960–1983	1984–2001	1960	2001
(a) GDP				
GDP (actual)	.027	.016		
GDP (1965 shares)	.031	.018		
Durables	.084	.053	.18	.18
Nondurables	.030	.018	.31	.19
Services	.012	.008	.39	.53
Structures	.072	.048	.11	.09
(b) Aggregate Employment				
Total (actual)	.020	.013		
Total (1965 shares)	.022	.014		
Mining	.075	.059	.013	.004
Construction	.053	.045	.054	.051
Durable man.	.056	.028	.174	.085
Nondurable man.	.026	.014	.136	.056
Trans. & util.	.023	.014	.074	.053
Trade	.017	.017	.210	.230
FIRE	.013	.020	.049	.057
Services	.011	.012	.136	.307
Government	.019	.008	.154	.157

Notes: The first row of each part shows the standard deviation of the four-quarter changes in the aggregate series. The next row shows the standard deviation of the 1965-share-weighted share of four-quarter changes in the disaggregated series shown in the other rows of the table.

looks instead at employment growth: the standard deviation of employment growth falls by approximately one-third whether one uses actual employment shares or constant employment shares. Here, as discussed further by Warnock and Warnock (2001), it is not just that employment is migrating from a more volatile to a less volatile sector; rather, the volatility of employment within construction and manufacturing has itself declined.[5] Finally, the structural-shift hypothesis has a timing problem: the shift away from manufacturing has taken place gradually over the past

5. A caveat on these accounting-identity calculations is that they ignore general-equilibrium effects of a switch to service production. If, for example, increased stability of employment in services results in more stable incomes, then an increase in the share of services could in equilibrium stabilize demand for all products, including goods and construction. If so, the mechanical calculation in Table 6 could understate the moderating effect of a shift to services.

four decades, whereas the analysis of Sections 2–4 suggests a sharp moderation in volatility in the mid-1980s.

5.2 CHANGES IN INVENTORY MANAGEMENT

McConnell and Perez-Quiros (2000) proposed that new inventory management methods, such as just-in-time inventory management, are the source of the reduction in volatility in GDP; this argument is elaborated upon by Kahn, McConnell and Perez-Quiros (2001, 2002). The essence of their argument is that the volatility of production in manufacturing fell sharply in the mid-1980s, but the volatility of sales did not; they found a statistically significant break in output variability, especially in durables manufacturing, but not in sales variability. They concluded that changes in inventory management must account for this discrepancy. Moreover, they suggested that the decline in the variance of goods production fully accounts for the statistical significance of the decline in GDP, so that understanding changes in inventory behavior holds the key to understanding the moderation in GDP volatility. Unlike the sectoral-shift hypothesis, timing works in favor of this inventory-management hypothesis, for new inventory management methods relying heavily on information technology gained popularity during the 1980s.

This bold conjecture—that micro-level changes in inventory management could have major macroeconomic consequences—has received a great deal of attention. Our reading of this research suggests, however, that upon closer inspection the inventory-management hypothesis does not fare well. The first set of difficulties pertain to the facts themselves. The stylized fact that production volatility has fallen but sales volatility has not is not robust to the method of analysis used or the series considered. Ahmed, Levin, and Wilson (2002) find statistically significant evidence of a break in final sales in 1983:3 using the Bai–Perron (1998) test; Herrera and Pesavento (2002) use the QLR test and find a break in the variance of the growth of sales in nondurables manufacturing (estimated by least squares to be in 1983:3) and in durables manufacturing (in 1984: 1), as well as in many two-digit sectors; and Kim, Nelson, and Piger (2001) find evidence of a decline in volatility of aggregate final sales and in durable goods sales using Bayesian methods.

Our break-test results for sales (see Table 10) are consistent with this more recent literature: we find statistically significant breaks in the variance of total final sales and final sales of durable goods. Like Kim, Nelson, and Piger (2001), we date the break in the variance of durable-goods sales to the early 1990s, whereas the break in the variance of production is dated to the mid-1980s. Although the confidence intervals for the break dates in durables production and sales are wide, the 67% confidence inter-

Figure 3 DURABLE-GOODS PRODUCTION AND SALES: TIME-VARYING
STANDARD DEVIATIONS

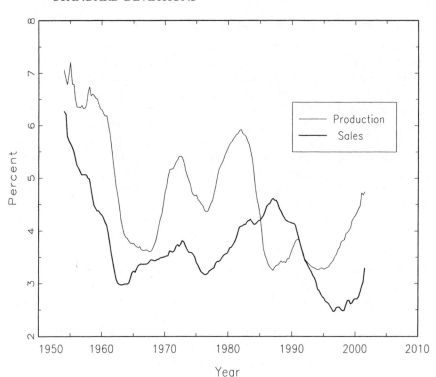

val for the durable-sales break date does not include the mid-1980s. Figure 3 presents the estimated instantaneous variances, computed using the
non-Gaussian smoother described in Appendix A, for the four-quarter
growth in durables production and sales. Both series have a complicated
pattern of time-varying volatility, but the decline in volatility in the 1980s
and 1990s is evident for both series (as is the mismatch in the timing of
this decline).[6]

An additional challenge for the inventory-management hypothesis is
that the finding that the variance of production has fallen proportionately
more than the variance of sales is sensitive to the frequency of the data
considered. As seen in the first columns of Table 7, the standard deviation
of the quarterly growth of production in durables manufacturing fell

6. The variance of final sales of nondurable goods has also experienced a statistically significant decrease, although that decrease appears better characterized by a trend than by a
distinct break.

Table 7 STANDARD DEVIATIONS OF GROWTH OF PRODUCTION, SALES, AND INVENTORIES

Series	One-quarter growth			Four-quarter growth		
	$S_{1960-1983}$	$S_{1984-2001}$	$S_{1984-2001}/$ $S_{1960-1983}$	$S_{1960-1983}$	$S_{1984-2001}$	$S_{1984-2001}/$ $S_{1960-1983}$
GDP	4.32	2.18	.51	2.71	1.59	.59
Total goods:						
Production	7.78	4.58	.59	4.12	2.87	.70
Sales	5.14	3.93	.76	3.05	2.01	.66
$\Delta I/$sales	6.22	4.50	.72	2.09	1.95	.94
Durable goods:						
Production	17.25	8.06	.47	8.46	5.28	.62
Sales	9.86	7.83	.79	5.67	3.67	.65
$\Delta I/$sales	12.10	8.17	.68	4.15	3.15	.76
Nondurable goods:						
Production	7.41	4.69	.63	2.96	1.81	.61
Sales	4.50	2.88	.64	2.35	1.41	.60
$\Delta I/$sales	6.55	3.97	.61	1.89	1.59	.84
Services production	1.71	1.38	.81	1.18	0.80	.68
Structures production	11.80	6.71	.57	7.16	4.79	.67

Notes: $S_{1960-1983}$ denotes the standard deviation computed using the 1960–1983 data, etc. One-quarter growth rates are computed as $400\ln(X_t/X_{t-1})$, where X_t is sales (etc.), except for $\Delta I/$sales, which is computed as 400 times its quarterly first difference ($400\Delta X_t$). Four-quarter growth rates are computed as $100\ln(X_t/X_{t-1})$, except for $\Delta I/$sales, which is computed as 100 times its fourth difference [$100(X_t - X_{t-4})$].

sharply in the latter period, whereas the standard deviation of sales fell proportionately less: the standard deviation of quarterly growth of durable goods sales in the second period is 79% what it was in the first period, while the standard deviation of quarterly growth of durable goods production in the second period was 47% of its first-period value.[7] As the second set of columns show, however, this disproportionate decline disappears at longer horizons: when one considers four-quarter growth rather than one-quarter growth, the standard deviations of production and sales fell by essentially the same amount.[8] Indeed, the striking feature of the final column of Table 7a is that the standard deviation of four-quarter growth in sales and production fell by 30% to 40% across all pro-

7. The entries in first columns of Table 7 closely match those in Table 4 of Kahn, McConnell, and Perez-Quiros (2002), with slight differences presumably attributable to different sample periods and different vintages of data.
8. This is true for other degrees of temporal aggregation. For one-quarter growth, the ratio of the relative standard deviations of durables output to durables sales growth is .79/.47 = 1.70; for two-quarter growth, it falls to 1.35; for three-, four-, six-, and eight-quarter growth, it is respectively 1.15, 1.04, 1.00, and 1.01.

duction sectors: durables, nondurables, services, and structures. This suggests that, to the extent that information technology has facilitated using inventories to smooth production, this effect is one of smoothing across months or across adjacent quarters. At the longer horizons of interest in business-cycle analysis, such as the four-quarter growth rates considered in this paper, the declines in volatility of production and sales have been effectively proportional, suggesting no role for improved inventory management in reducing volatility at longer horizons.

The inventory-management hypothesis confronts other difficulties as well. As emphasized by Blinder and Maccini (1991) and Ramey and West (1999), most inventories in manufacturing are raw materials or work-in-progress inventories, which do not play a role in production smoothing (except avoiding raw-material stockouts). One would expect inventory–sales ratios to decline if information technology has an important impact on aggregate inventories; however, inventory–sales ratios have declined primarily for raw materials and work-in-progress inventories, and in fact have risen for finished-goods inventories and for retail and wholesale trade inventories. Information technology may have improved the management of finished-goods inventories, but this improvement is not reflected in a lower inventory–sales ratio for finished goods.

Ramey and Vine (2001) offer a different explanation of the relative decline in the variance of production at high frequencies, relative to sales. They suggest that a modest reduction in the variance of sales can be magnified into a large reduction in the variance of production because of nonconvexities in plant-level cost functions. In their example, a small reduction in the variance of auto sales means that sales fluctuations can be met through overtime rather than by (for example) adding temporary shifts, thereby sharply reducing the variance of output and employee-hours.

None of this evidence is decisive. Still, in our view it suggests that the reduction of volatility is too widespread across sectors and across production and sales (especially at longer horizons) to be consistent with the view that inventory management plays a central role in explaining the economywide moderation in volatility.

5.3 RESIDENTIAL HOUSING

Although residential fixed investment constitutes a small share of GDP, historically it has been highly volatile and procyclical. The estimated instantaneous variance of the four-quarter growth in residential investment is 14.2 percentage points in 1981, but this falls to 6.0 percentage points in 1985. As is evident in Figure 2, even after weighting by its small share in GDP, the standard deviation fell during the mid-1980s by approximately the same amount as did the share-weighted standard deviation of durable-goods output.

Figure 4 presents estimated instantaneous standard deviations of the four-quarter growth of various series relating to the construction sector (these plots are comparable to those in Figure 2, except that Figure 2 is share-weighted whereas Figure 4 is not). The sharp decline in volatility in the mid-1980s is evident in the residential-sector real activity measures

Figure 4 TIME-VARYING STANDARD DEVIATIONS

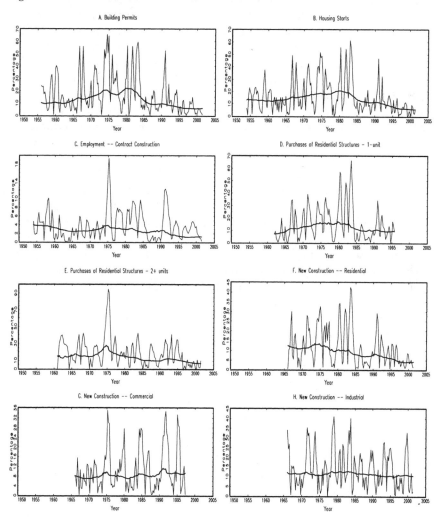

of building permits, housing starts, and real private residential construction put in place. In contrast, nonresidential construction does not show any volatility reduction: the variance of real industrial construction is approximately constant, while the variance of real commercial construction is constant and then increases slightly during the 1990s. As noted by Warnock and Warnock (2001), employment in total contract construction (which includes residential and nonresidential) also shows a decline in volatility, although it is not as sharp as for the output measures. Intriguingly, the decline in volatility of purchases of residential structures is more distinct for single-unit than for multiunit residences.

There are a variety of potential explanations for this marked decline in volatility in the residential sector. One explanation emphasizes structural changes in the market for home loans. As discussed in detail by McCarthy and Peach (2002), the mortgage market underwent substantial regulatory and institutional changes in the 1970s and 1980s. These changes included the introduction of adjustable-rate mortgages, the development of the secondary market for bundled mortgages, and the decline of thrifts and growth of nonthrift lenders. To the extent that these changes reduced or eliminated credit rationing from the mortgage market, so that mortgages became generally available at the stated interest rate for qualified borrowers, they could have worked to reduce the volatility of demand for new housing. According to this explanation, this autonomous decline in the volatility of residential investment in turn spills over into a reduction of volatility of aggregate demand. A difficulty with this explanation, however, is that these institutional developments took time, and the drop in volatility observed in Figure 4 is quite sharp. Moreover, McCarthy and Peach (2002) present evidence that although the impulse response of residential investment to a monetary shock changed in the mid-1980s, the ultimate effect of a monetary shock on residential investment was essentially unchanged; their results are, however, based on a Cholesky-factored VAR, and without a structural identification scheme they are hard to interpret. Additional work is needed to ascertain if there is a relation between the developments in the mortgage market and the stabilization of real activity in residential construction.[9]

9. U.S. financial markets generally, not just mortgage markets, developed substantially from the 1970s to 1990s. Blanchard and Simon (2001) suggest that increased consumer access to credit and equity ownership could have facilitated intertemporal smoothing of consumption, which in turn led to a reduction in aggregate volatility. Bekaert, Harvey, and Lundblad (2002) report empirical evidence based on international data that countries that liberalize equity markets experience a subsequent reduction in the volatility of economic growth. In the U.S., however, general financial market developments, like those in the mortgage market, took place over decades, whereas we estimate a sharp volatility reduction in the mid-1980s: it seems the timing of the financial market developments in the U.S. does not match the timing of the reduction in volatility.

Other explanations suggest a more passive role for housing, that is, the reduction in housing volatility could be a response to the reduction in general shocks to the economy. For example, if the decision to purchase a home is based in part on expected future income, and if expected future income is less volatile, then home investment should be less volatile. A difficulty with this explanation is that, although the volatility of four-quarter GDP growth has diminished, it is not clear that the volatility of changes in permanent income has fallen. In fact, if there is a break in the variance of consumption of services, it is in the early 1970s and we do not find a statistically significant break in durables consumption (see Table 3). To the extent that nondurables consumption is a scaled measure of permanent income, the variance of permanent income does not exhibit a statistically significant break in the 1980s. This argument is quantified by Kim, Nelson, and Piger (2001), who in fact conclude that the reduction in the variance of GDP growth is associated with a decrease in the variance of its cyclical, but not its long-run, component.

A related candidate explanation emphasizes the role of mortgage rates rather than expected incomes: the reduction in volatility of housing investment reflects reduced volatility of expected real long-term rates. This is consistent with the reduction in the volatility of long and short interest rates in Figure 2, at least relative to the late 1970s and early 1980s. It is also consistent with the reduction in the volatility of durable-goods consumption, sales, and production, which in part entail debt financing by consumers. To investigate this hypothesis, however, one would need to develop measures of the expected variance of the ex ante real mortgage rate, to see how these measures changed during the 1980s, and to integrate this into a model of housing investment—topics that are left to future work.

5.4 SMALLER SHOCKS

The reduced-form VAR analysis of Section 4 suggested that most, possibly all, of the decline in the variance of real GDP growth is attributable to changes in the covariance matrix of the VAR innovations. In this section, we attempt to pinpoint some specific structural shocks that have moderated. We consider five types of shocks: money shocks, fiscal shocks, productivity shocks, oil price shocks, and shocks to other commodity prices.

5.4.1 Money Shocks Over the past fifteen years, there has been considerable research devoted to identifying shocks to monetary policy and to measuring their effects on the macroeconomy. Two well-known approaches, both using structural VARs but different identifying assumptions, are Bernanke and Mihov (1998) (BM) and Christiano, Eichenbaum, and Evans (1997) (CEE) [see Christiano, Eichenbaum, and Evans (1999) for a survey]. Using structural VARs, we have implemented the BM and CEE identification strategies and computed the implied money shocks in the early (pre-1984) and late (post-1984) sample periods. Our specifications are the same as used by those authors, although we extend their datasets.[10] Bernanke and Mihov suggest that monetary policy shifted over the sample period, so we include a specification that incorporates this shift.

The standard deviation of the BM and CEE monetary shocks in the 1984–2001 sample period, relative to the standard deviation in the earlier period, are reported in the first block of Table 8. Since the money shocks were very volatile during 1979–1983, results are shown for early sample periods that include and that exclude 1979–1983. The results suggest a marked decrease in the variability of monetary shocks for both CEE and BM identifications. The relative standard deviations over 1984–2001 are roughly 0.50 when the early sample includes 1979–1983, and 0.75 when that period is excluded.

5.4.2 Fiscal Shocks Blanchard and Perotti (2001) identify shocks to taxes and government spending using a VAR together with an analysis of the automatic responses of these variables to changes in real income and inflation. The next two rows of Table 8 show results for their shocks.[11] There has been some moderation in both shocks; the standard deviation of tax shocks has fallen by approximately 20%.

5.4.3 Productivity Shocks Standard measures of productivity shocks, such as the Solow residual, suffer from measurement problems from variations in capacity utilization, imperfect competition, and other sources. While there have been important improvements in methods and models for measuring productivity (for example, see Basu, Fernald, and Kimball, 1999), there does not seem to be a widely accepted series on productivity shocks suitable for our purposes. Instead we have relied on a method suggested by Gali (1999) that, like the money and fiscal shocks, is based on a structural VAR. In particular, Gali associates productivity shocks with those components of the VAR that lead to permanent changes in

---

10. In our version of BM we use industrial production instead of their monthly interpolated GDP, because their series, and the related series in Bernanke, Gertler, and Watson (1997), end in 1997.
11. We thank Roberto Perotti for supplying us with the data and computer programs used to compute these shocks.

Table 8 CHANGES IN THE STANDARD DEVIATION OF VARIOUS
MACROECONOMIC SHOCKS

Shock	Period 1	Period 2	$\frac{S_{period\ 2}}{S_{period\ 1}}$	Relative contribution to GDP variance reduction
Monetary policy:				
Christiano–Eichenbaum–Evans	60:1–83:4	84:1–01:3	0.50	0.10
Christiano–Eichenbaum–Evans	60:1–78:4	84:1–01:3	0.76	0.00
Bernanke–Mihov-1 (monthly)	66:1–83:4	84:1–01:9	0.57	0.23*
Bernanke–Mihov-1 (monthly)	66:1–78:12	84:1–01:9	0.75	0.27*
Bernanke–Mihov-2 (monthly)	66:1–83:12	84:1–01:9	0.39	0.16*
Bernanke–Mihov-2 (monthly)	66:1–78:4	84:1–01:9	0.62	0.05*
Fiscal policy:				
Taxes (Blanchard–Perotti)	60:1–83:4	84:1–97:4	0.83	0.02
Spending (Blanchard–Perotti)	60:1–83:4	84:1–97:4	0.94	0.03
Productivity:				
Gali	60:1–83:4	84:1–01:3	0.75	0.15
Oil prices:				
Nominal price	60:1–83:4	84:1–01:3	2.80	−0.12
Real price	60:1–83:4	84:1–01:3	2.98	−0.15
Hamilton	60:1–83:4	84:1–01:3	1.09	0.05
Commodity prices:				
All	60:1–83:4	84:1–01:3	0.73	0.18
Food	60:1–83:4	84:1–01:3	0.75	0.07
Industrial-material prices	60:1–83:4	84:1–01:3	0.78	0.13
Sensitive-material prices	60:1–83:4	84:1–01:3	0.78	0.14

Notes: Standard deviations were computed for each of the shocks listed in the first column over the sample periods listed in the second and third columns. The relative standard deviation shown in the third column is the period-2 standard deviation divided by the period-1 standard deviation. The final column shows the fraction of the reduction in output variance associated with the change in shock variance. For the quarterly series the output series is the annual growth rate of annual GDP. For the monthly series marked * the output series is the annual growth rate of the index of industrial production. Bernanke–Mihov-1 corresponds to shocks estimated in the Bernanke–Mihov model with constant coefficients over the full sample period. Bernanke–Mihov-2 shocks allow the coefficients to differ in the two sample periods. See the text for description of the shocks.

labor productivity. Gali's (1999) productivity shock shows a 25% reduction in its standard deviation in the second sample period.

5.4.4 Oil Price Shocks The next three rows show results for oil price shocks. The first two rows measure oil shocks by quarterly growth rates in nominal and real oil prices. Since oil prices were much more variable in the post-1984 sample period, these measures show a larger relative standard deviation in the second sample period. Hamilton (1996) argues that oil-price effects are asymmetric, and he proposes a measure that is the larger of zero and the percentage difference between the current price and the maximum price during the past year. Using Hamilton's measure, there has been essentially no change in the variability of oil shocks across the two sample periods.

5.4.5 Other Commodity Price Shocks   The final four rows show results for broader commodity price measures: an aggregate index of commodity prices (the same measure often included in VAR models), an index for food, an index for industrial materials, and an index for sensitive materials. Results are shown for nominal growth rates (commodity price inflation); the results for real growth rates are essentially identical. These series show a marked reduction in volatility, with standard deviations falling between 20% and 30% in the second sample period relative to the first period.

5.4.6 Importance of These Reductions   Whether the reductions in the variances of the structural shocks can explain the moderation in GDP depends on the importance of these shocks in determining output growth. The final column of Table 8 reports the fraction of the reduction in the variance of four-quarter GDP growth that is explained by the change in the variance of the shock in that row. For example, the reduction in the variance of the CEE monetary-policy shock explains 10% of the reduction in the variance of GDP growth when the first period ends in 1983 (but none of the reduction when the first period ends in 1978). The BM shock explains more of the reduction, at least in some specifications, although that percentage reduction is not directly comparable to the other rows because it pertains to industrial production. Fiscal-policy shocks make a negligible contribution, and oil price shocks either make a negligible contribution (the Hamilton shock) or go the wrong way, because oil price volatility increased in the second period. Productivity and commodity price shocks seem to have made modest contributions, in the neighborhood of 15%, to the reduction in the variance of four-quarter GDP growth.

It is tempting to add up the entries in the final column to produce a composite number, but the result would be misleading. If these are true structural shocks, they should be uncorrelated with each other, but they are not; there is, in fact, considerable disagreement about whether these series are plausible proxies for the structural shocks they purport to estimate (e.g. Rudebusch, 1998). This said, although these shocks appear to explain some of the observed reduction in the volatility, most—perhaps three-fourths—of the reduction in volatility is *not* explained by the reduction in volatility of these shocks.

5.5 CHANGES IN POLICY

An important candidate for the moderation in GDP growth is improved monetary policy.[12] Most importantly, the timing is right: empirical studies suggest that monetary policy changed significantly in the Volcker–Greenspan era relative to earlier times. For example, Taylor (1999b), Clarida, Gali, and Gertler (2000), and Boivin and Giannoni (2002b) estimate large increases in the inflation response in Taylor-type monetary policy rules for the short-term interest rate. Moreover, developments in financial markets are consistent with a shift in monetary policy. Although short rates are less variable than they were before 1984, they seem to be more persistent: Watson (1999) reports that the (median unbiased) estimate of the largest AR root for monthly observations of the federal funds rate increased from 0.96 in the 1965–1978 sample period to 1.00 in the 1985–1998 sample period.[13] This increase in persistence has a large effect on the variance of expected future values of the federal funds rate, and hence on the expectations component of long-term rates. Indeed, while the variance of short rates declined in the second sample period, the variance of long rates, relative to that of short rates, increased. Taking this together with the evidence on changing Taylor-rule coefficients, it appears that the Fed has become more responsive to movements in inflation and output and that these responses have led to increases in the variability of (medium- and long-term) interest rates.

There now are a number of studies examining the extent to which this change in monetary policy—more precisely, this change in the rule approximating monetary policy—caused the reduction of the variance of output growth and/or inflation; see Boivin and Giannoni (2002a, 2002b), Clarida, Gali and Gertler (2000), Cogley and Sargent (2001), Gali, Lopez-Salido, and Valles (2002), Primiceri (2002), and Sims and Zha (2002). This is a challenging task: to evaluate the effect of a change in the monetary-policy rule, it is necessary to specify a model of the economy that is arguably invariant to the policy shift, that is, to specify a plausible structural model for the economy. The general strategy in this literature has been to combine some structural reasoning with VARs that permit the model to fit the dynamics in the data, but within this general framework the details of the approach differ widely. In this subsection, we perform these

---

12. As Taylor (2000) argues, fiscal policy is not a likely candidate. For example, Auerbach and Feenberg (2000) show that fiscal automatic stabilizers in 1995 were roughly at their same level as in the early 1960s, and if anything were higher in the late 1970s and early 1980s (because of high inflation and the lack of indexation of the tax code).

13. Similar results, obtained using different methods, are reported by Kim, Nelson, and Piger (2001) and Basistha and Startz (2001).

counterfactual policy evaluation calculations using a four-variable structural VAR with GDP growth (y), GDP deflator inflation (π), the one-year Treasury bill rate (R), and commodity prices (PSCCOM, z).

5.5.1 *Model Specification and Identification* The structural VAR identification scheme is based on a structural model with an IS equation, a forward-looking New Keynesian Phillips curve, a forward-looking Taylor-type monetary-policy rule, and an exogenous process for commodity prices:

$$y_t = \theta r_t + \text{lags} + \varepsilon_{y,t}, \tag{4}$$

$$\pi_t = \gamma Y(\delta)_t + \text{lags} + \varepsilon_{\pi,t}, \tag{5}$$

$$r_t = \beta_\pi \pi_{t+h/t} + \beta_y \bar{y}^{gap}_{t+h/t} + \text{lags} + \varepsilon_{r,t}, \tag{6}$$

$$z_t = \text{lags} + \alpha_y \varepsilon_{y,t} + \alpha_\pi \varepsilon_{\pi,t} + \alpha_r \varepsilon_{r,t} + \varepsilon_{z,t}, \tag{7}$$

where $r_t = R_t - \bar{\pi}_{t+k/t}$ is the real interest rate; $\bar{\pi}_{t+k/t}$ is the expected average inflation rate over the next k periods, where k is the term of the interest rate R; $Y(\delta)_t = \sum_{i=0}^{\infty} \delta^i y^{gap}_{t+1/t}$ is the discounted expected future output gap; and $\bar{y}^{gap}_{t+h/t}$ is the expected future average output gap over the next h periods. We have used generic notation "lags" to denote unrestricted lags of variables in each of these equations.

Equation (4) is an IS relation. Equation (5) is a hybrid New Keynesian Phillips curve. If δ, the discount factor used to construct $Y(\delta)_t$, is equal to 0, then this is a traditional formulation of the relation. More recent formulations based on price stickiness [discussed, for example, in Gali and Gertler (1999), Goodfriend and King (1997), and Rotemberg and Woodford (1997, 1999)] express π_t as a function of the output gap (as a proxy for marginal cost) and expected future inflation. Solving this equation forward yields (5) with $\delta = 1$. Allowing forward-looking and backward-looking price setting yields (5) with δ interpreted as the weight on forward inflation (Gali and Gertler, 1999). Equation (6) is a forward-looking Taylor rule, written in terms of the real interest rate. The parameter h indexes the horizon. For simplicity we use the same interest rate in (4) and (6), although in principle one would like to use long rates in (4) and short rates in (6).[14] We use the 1-year interest rate as a compromise between a long and short rate. Similarly, in our benchmark specification we use a 1-year horizon in (6), so that $h = 4$, but investigate the robustness of this as well. The commodity-price equation (7) plays no structural role

---

14. Both long and short rates could be included by adding a term structure equation as in Bernanke, Gertler, and Watson (1997).

in the analysis, but, as is conventional, commodity prices are included to help forecast future values of inflation and the output gap. As usual, the ε's are taken to be mutually uncorrelated structural shocks.

5.5.2 Estimation   Our estimation strategy relies on *a priori* knowledge of the three key parameters θ (the slope of the IS function), γ (the slope of the Phillips relation), and δ (the parameter governing the forward-looking nature of the Phillips relation). Given these parameters, estimation proceeds as follows. First, projecting all variables on lags produces a version of (4)–(7) in which the variables are replaced by reduced-form VAR residuals. (The forecasts of the output gap and inflation are computed by the VAR, so that innovations in these variables are also functions of the reduced-form VAR innovations.) We suppose that the forecast errors associated with trend output are negligible, so we replace innovations in the expected future gap with innovations in expected future output. Then, with θ, δ and γ given, the errors ε_y and ε_π follow from (4) and (5). These errors are in turn used as instruments to estimate the parameters in the Taylor rule, yielding ε_r. The unknown coefficients in (7) can then be determined by OLS. We assume that the parameters θ, δ, and γ remain constant over the entire sample period, but we allow the parameter of the Taylor rule to change. We also allow the coefficients in equation (7) to change.

There is considerable disagreement about the values of the parameters θ, γ, and δ in the literature [see Rudebusch (2002)]. In our benchmark model, we set $\theta = -0.2$, $\gamma = 0.3$, and $\delta = 0.5$. When simulating small quantitative models, a larger value for θ is sometimes used (e.g. $\theta = -1$), but large values of θ are difficult to reconcile with IS slope estimates computed by traditional methods (which often find values of $\theta = -0.1$ or smaller). The value $\gamma = 0.3$ was used by Clarida, Gali, and Gertler (2000) in their simulations of the effects of changes in monetary policy on output and inflation variability. Traditional estimates of the Phillips curve (for example, Staiger, Stock, and Watson, 2001) suggest values of γ around 0.1. The value of δ has also been the subject of controversy. Backward-looking models (such as Rudebusch, and Svensson 1999) set $\delta = 0$, Gali and Gertler (1999) estimate δ to be approximately 0.6, and many models are simulated with $\delta = 1.0$.

Table 9 summarizes the results for these benchmark parameter values. Results are presented for the 1960–1978 and 1984–2001 sample periods. The estimated Taylor-rule coefficients (Table 9a) are consistent with what others have found. The inflation response in the first period is negative (remember that we specify the Taylor rule using the real interest rate), and the output coefficient is small. In the second period both the inflation and output coefficients are significantly higher.

Table 9 IMPLIED STANDARD DEVIATION FROM SAMPLE-SPECIFIC STRUCTURAL VARs

$$AX_t = A\Phi(L)X_{t-1} + \varepsilon_t \qquad \text{var}(\varepsilon_t) = \Omega$$

Estimated parameters: $\hat{\Phi}_1(L)$, $\hat{A}_1$, and $\hat{\Omega}_1$ (period 1), and $\hat{\Phi}_2(L)$, $\hat{A}_2$, and $\hat{\Omega}_2$ (period 2)

(a) Estimated Taylor-Rule Coefficients, Benchmark Specification
$$\theta = -0.2, \delta = 0.5, \gamma = 0.3$$

Sample period	β_π	β_y
1	−0.25 (0.18)	0.16 (0.18)
2	0.75 (0.31)	0.62 (0.18)

(b) Implied Standard Deviations of Four-Quarter GDP Growth, Benchmark Specification

| | Sample standard deviation | | Standard deviations implied by VAR | | | | | | | | | |
| | | | VAR with $\Phi = \Phi_1$ | | | | | VAR with $\Phi = \Phi_2$ | | | | |
Variable	1960–1978	1984–2001	$\Omega_{1,}$ A_1	$\Omega_{1,}$ A_2	$\Omega_{2,}$ A_1	$\Omega_{2,}$ A_2	Fract. Var_1	$\Omega_{1,}$ A_1	$\Omega_{1,}$ A_2	$\Omega_{2,}$ A_1	$\Omega_{2,}$ A_2	Fract. Var_2
GDP	2.49	1.60	2.54	2.41	1.59	1.50	0.14	2.68	2.30	1.67	1.41	0.18
Inflation	1.37	0.59	1.40	1.32	0.96	0.92	0.13	0.85	0.74	0.63	0.56	0.05
FF rate	1.29	1.51	1.33	1.57	1.07	1.05	1.50	1.89	2.20	1.45	1.49	0.30

(c) Sensitivity Analysis: Alternative Parameter Values

| IS and Phillips-Curve coefficients | | | Estimated Taylor rule coefficients | | | | Standard deviations implied by VAR | | | | | |
| | | | Period 1 | | Period 2 | | Var with $\Phi = \Phi_1$ | | | VAR with $\Phi = \Phi_2$ | | |
θ	γ	δ	β_π	β_y	β_π	β_y	Ω_1, A_2	Ω_2, A_1	Fract. Var_1	Ω_1, A_2	Ω_2, A_1	Fract. Var_2
-0.20	0.30	0.50	-0.25	0.16	0.75	0.63	2.41	1.59	0.14	2.30	1.67	0.18
-0.20	0.30	0.90	0.00	0.06	4.15	0.25	1.86	2.88	0.67	1.87	2.56	1.02
-0.20	0.30	0.10	-0.40	0.22	0.21	0.69	2.41	1.61	0.14	2.32	1.65	0.17
-0.20	0.10	0.50	-0.45	0.24	0.19	0.69	2.39	1.63	0.17	2.30	1.65	0.17
-0.20	0.60	0.50	0.12	0.01	1.55	0.54	2.38	1.62	0.18	2.28	1.67	0.18
-0.10	0.30	0.50	-0.45	0.17	0.39	0.57	2.45	1.58	0.09	2.39	1.58	0.12
-0.50	0.30	0.50	0.87	0.14	1.91	0.81	2.19	1.77	0.36	2.19	1.77	0.26
-0.20	0.10	0.90	-0.11	0.10	2.14	0.47	1.98	1.94	0.57	1.96	1.83	0.30
-0.20	0.30	0.75	-0.04	0.07	1.97	0.49	2.20	1.76	0.36	2.10	1.79	0.27
-0.20	0.10	0.75	-0.29	0.18	0.72	0.63	2.35	1.63	0.21	2.24	1.68	0.19
-0.50	0.10	0.75	0.19	0.31	1.62	0.84	2.19	1.80	0.37	2.02	2.01	0.46
0.00	0.30	0.50	-0.61	0.17	0.05	0.51	2.49	1.59	0.06	2.49	1.51	0.07

Notes: The identifying restrictions for the structural VAR are summarized in equations (4)–(7) in the text. The two sample periods are 1960–1978 and 1984–2001. Fract. Var_1 is the ratio, $[\sigma^2(\Phi_1, \Omega_1, A_1) - \sigma^2(\Phi_1, \Omega_1, A_2)]/[\sigma^2(\Phi_1, \Omega_1, A_1) - \sigma^2(\Phi_2, \Omega_2, A_2)]$, and Fract. $Var_2 = [\sigma^2(\Phi_2, \Omega_2, A_1) - \sigma^2(\Phi_2, \Omega_2, A_2)]/[\sigma^2(\Phi_1, \Omega_1, A_1) - \sigma^2(\Phi_2, \Omega_2, A_2)]$.

Armed with these estimated parameters, we can use the structural VAR to compute the implied variability of output growth, changes in inflation, and interest rates. The calculations are analogous to those carried in Section 4, except now the VAR is characterized by three sets of parameters: Φ, the VAR distributed lag coefficients (just as in Section 4); Ω, the covariance matrix of the structural shocks (ε_y, ε_π, ε_r, ε_z); and A, the structural coefficients (θ, γ, δ, β_π, β_y, α_y, α_π, α_r) that link the structural and reduced form errors. We present results for the triples $\sigma(\Phi_i, \Omega_j, A_k)$, for $i, j, k = 1, 2$ corresponding to the two sample periods.

The results are shown in Table 9b. Using (Φ_1, Ω_1, A_1), the standard deviation of the four-quarter growth rate of GDP is 2.54%. Using (Φ_2, Ω_2, A_2), the corresponding value is 1.41%. These are close to the estimates of the standard deviation of output growth computed directly from the sample moments of GDP. How much of this change in the variability of output can be attributed to shocks (Ω), and how much to policy (A)? The standard deviation of output using (Φ_1, Ω_2, A_1) is 1.59; using (Φ_1, Ω_1, A_2), it is 2.41. These results suggest that 14% of the decrease in variance in output growth is associated with changes in the monetary-policy coefficients.[15] Said differently, most of the reduction in variability in output stems from smaller shocks, not from changes in the monetary-policy coefficients.

The results for other sets of parameter values are shown in Table 9c. To save space, this table only reports the estimated Taylor-rule coefficients for each subsample and the implied variability of output growth for the four counterfactual simulations. Looking across these results, the estimated effect of the change in monetary policy is larger when the IS curve is more elastic (θ is more negative), when the output gap receives more weight in the Phillips curve (γ is larger), and when the New Keynesian Phillips curve is more forward looking (δ is larger).

One notable special case is when $\theta = 0$, so that monetary policy has no effect on output growth within the period; this corresponds to a common VAR-identifying restriction [see the discussion in Christiano, Eichenbaum, and Evans (1999)]. This assumption implies that the change in monetary policy had little to do with the decline in output growth volatility (the estimated contribution to the variance reduction when $\theta = 0$, $\gamma = 0.3$, and $\delta = 0.5$ is approximately 6%). For most of the parameter combinations examined in Table 9c, however, the estimated contribution of the change in monetary policy to the reduction in the variance of four-quarter GDP growth falls in the range of 10% to 25%. Estimates with very large contributions are associated with implausibly large coefficients on infla-

---

15. The total decrease in the variance of output estimated using the VAR is $2.54^2 - 1.41^2$. The estimated decrease associated with the change in A is $2.54^2 - 2.41^2$. The ratio is 0.14.

tion in the estimated second-period Taylor rule (inflation responses of 4 or more).

5.5.3 Other Sensitivity Checks   We performed a number of other sensitivity checks. These included reducing the horizon in the Taylor rule to one quarter; dropping the commodity price index from the VAR; replacing the commodity price index with the estimated first factor (principal component) constructed from the series listed in Appendix B [as suggested by Bernanke and Boivin's (2000) factor-augmented VARs]; and carrying out the counterfactuals holding the parameters α fixed at their period-1 values. The results from these models are similar to results from the specifications reported in Table 9 and, to save space, are not reported.

5.5.4 Summary   Even within the stylized model of equations (4)–(7), there is considerable uncertainty about whether the widely perceived shift in monetary policy in the 1980s produced the moderation of output volatility. For the benchmark parameter values, and for other values that produce estimates of monetary reaction functions consistent with those discussed elsewhere in the literature, our calculations attribute perhaps 10% to 25% of the reduction in the variance of four-quarter GDP growth to improved monetary policy.

6. Conclusions and Remaining Questions

There is strong evidence of a decline in the volatility of economic activity, both as measured by broad aggregates and as measured by a wide variety of other series that track specific facets of economic activity. For real GDP growth, the decline is, we think, best characterized as a sharp drop in the mid-1980s. This sharp decline, or break, in the volatility in real GDP growth is mirrored by declines in the variance of the four-quarter growth rates of consumption and production of durable goods, in residential fixed investment, and in the production of structures. Not all series, however, have exhibited this sharp drop in volatility, and for some series the decline in their variance is better characterized as a trend or, possibly, an episodic return to the relative quiescence of the 1960s.

Our search for the causes of this great moderation has not been completely successful, nor does one find a compelling case in the literature for a single cause. On the positive side, we find some role for improved monetary policy; our estimates suggest that the Fed's more aggressive response to inflation since the mid-1980s has contributed perhaps 10% to 25% of the decline in output volatility. In addition, we find some role for identifiable shocks, such as less volatile productivity shocks and commodity price shocks, in reducing the variance of output growth. But this leaves much—perhaps half—of the decline in volatility unaccounted for. The shift away from manufacturing and towards services does not seem to explain the moderation; nor do improvements in inventory management arising from information technology seem to us to be a source of the reductions in volatility of four-quarter GDP growth, although improved inventory management could help to smooth production within the month or quarter. Our reduced-form evidence suggests that this reduction in volatility is associated with an increase in the precision of forecasts of output growth (and of other macroeconomic variables), but to a considerable extent we have not identified the specific source of the reduced forecast errors.

These results provide some clues for future work. Among the components of GDP, the clearest concomitant declines appear in durable goods (both consumption and production), in output of structures, and in residential investment. The declines in volatility appear in a variety of measures of residential (but not nonresidential) construction, and further investigation of the role of the housing sector in the moderation is warranted.

To the extent that improved policy gets some of the credit, then one can expect at least some of the moderation to continue as long as the policy regime is maintained. But because most of the reduction seems to be due to good luck in the form of smaller economic disturbances, we are left with the unsettling conclusion that the quiescence of the past fifteen years could well be a hiatus before a return to more turbulent economic times.

Appendix A. Time-Series Methods

This appendix describes the stochastic volatility model used to compute the smoothed estimates in Figures 2–4 and the variance-break tests in Tables 3 and 10.

A.1 STOCHASTIC VOLATILITY MODEL

The smoothed instantaneous standard deviations were estimated using a stochastic volatility model with time-varying autoregressive coefficients. Specifically, let y_t follow the time-varying AR process

$$y_t = \sum_{j=1}^{p} \alpha_{jt} y_{t-j} + \sigma_t \varepsilon_t,$$

$$\alpha_{jt} = \alpha_{jt-1} + c_j \eta_{jt},$$

$$\ln \sigma_t^2 = \ln \sigma_{t-1}^2 + \zeta_t,$$

Table 10 BREAK RESULTS FOR UNIVARIATE AUTOREGRESSIONS FOR SELECTED MACROECONOMIC TIME SERIES

Series	Variance			Conditional mean			Conditional variance: break only			Conditional variance: trend and break		
	p-Value	Break date	67% Confidence interval	p-Value	Break date	67% Confidence interval	p-Value	Break date	67% Confidence interval	p-Value: trend	p-Value: break	Break date
GDPQ	0.00	1984:2	1983:3–1987:1	0.98			0.00	1983:2	1982:4–1985:3	0.65	0.00	1983:2
GCQ	0.00	1993:1	1992:3–1996:2	0.55			0.00	1992:1	1991:3–1994:1	0.00	0.12	
GCDQ	0.00	1991:1	1990:4–1994:1	0.04	1987:3	1987:1–1988:1	0.00	1987:3	1987:2–1990:2	0.69	0.02	1987:3
GCNQ	0.38			0.00	1991:4	1991:2–1992:2	0.08			0.96	0.79	
GCSQ	0.03	1993:2	1992:2–1998:4	0.00	1969:4	1969:2–1970:2	0.18			0.03	0.00	1971:3
GPIQ	0.07			0.05			0.13			0.06	0.26	
GIFQ	0.02	1984:2	1982:4–1989:3	0.69			0.01	1983:3	1983:1–1986:4	0.66	0.07	
GINQ	0.84			0.47			0.70			0.69	0.61	
GIRQ	0.01	1983:3	1982:4–1989:1	0.10			0.00	1983:2	1983:1–1985:2	0.08	0.00	1983:2
DGV_GDP	0.26			0.91			0.04	1988:1	1987:3–1992:2	0.00	0.10	
GEXQ	0.03	1973:1	1972:4–1978:1	0.09			0.00	1975:4	1975:2–1978:2	0.95	0.75	
GIMQ	0.00	1985:3	1985:1–1990:2	0.00	1972:4	1972:2–1973:2	0.00	1986:2	1986:1–1988:1	0.96	0.05	1986:2
GGEQ	0.65			0.06			0.45			0.33	0.66	
GOQ	0.01	1984:2	1983:2–1989:3	0.92			0.00	1983:4	1983:2–1986:4	0.54	0.02	1983:4
GODQ	0.04	1984:1	1983:4–1992:2	0.09			0.00	1983:4	1983:3–1987:1	0.00	0.30	
GONQX	0.12			0.77			0.02	1985:2	1984:3–1989:1	0.34	0.02	1985:2
GOOSQ	0.00	1967:1	1965:3–1968:1	0.00	1968:3	1968:1–1969:1	0.98			0.69	0.93	
GOCQ	0.01	1984:2	1983:1–1988:3	0.02	1991:3	1991:1–1992:1	0.02	1984:2	1983:4–1988:1	0.43	0.03	1984:2
LPNAG	0.03	1984:4	1981:1–1987:3	0.03	1981:2	1980:4–1981:4	0.00	1983:2	1982:4–1985:3	0.00	0.01	1973:3
GDPD	0.37			0.00	1973:2	1972:4–1973:4	0.11			0.00	0.00	1971:2
FYGM3	0.71			0.00	1981:1	1980:3–1981:3	0.01	1984:4	1984:2–1988:1	0.00	0.00	1984:4
FYGT10	0.01	1979:3	1975:4–1981:1	0.02	1981:1	1980:3–1981:3	0.00	1979:3	1972:2–1980:1	0.02	0.00	1979:3
GGFENQ	0.49			0.00	1972:2	1971:4–1972:4	0.00	1987:4	1984:2–1989:4	0.00	0.04	1974:3
GOSQ	0.03	1993:4	1993:2–2000:1	0.50			0.39			0.10	0.21	
GODSQ	0.00	1991:1	1990:4–1997:1	0.06			0.05			0.55	0.06	

Table 10 CONTINUED

Series	Variance			Conditional mean			Conditional variance: break only			Conditional variance: trend and break		
	p-Value	Break date	67% Confidence interval	p-Value	Break date	67% Confidence interval	p-Value	Break date	67% Confidence interval	p-Value: trend	p-Value: break	Break date
GONSQX	0.00	1986:2	1984:1–1988:2	0.46			0.01	1986:2	1985:3–1989:3	0.02	0.64	
CONCRED	0.01	1995:1	1994:4–2001:3	0.29			0.19			0.30	0.05	1970:1
FM1	0.02	1979:1	1971:3–1979:2	0.03	1980:4	1980:2–1981:2	0.00	1979:3	1971:2–1980:3	0.00	0.67	
FM2	0.01	1993:2	1992:4–1998:2	0.16			0.27			0.14	0.13	
FM2DQ	0.05			0.00	1975:2	1974:4–1975:4	0.16			0.04	0.00	1989:3
FM3	1.00			0.20			0.11			0.38	0.05	1971:2
FMFBA	0.88			0.03	1981:2	1980:4–1981:4	0.07			0.06	0.88	
FMRRA	0.04	1978:3	1974:4–1982:1	0.02	1972:3	1972:1–1973:1	0.00	1978:3	1974:1–1979:4	0.99	0.37	
FSDXP	0.63			0.01	1979:1	1978:3–1979:3	0.21			0.35	0.07	
FSNCOM	0.32			0.02	1975:3	1975:1–1976:1	0.42			0.25	0.13	
FSPCAP	0.57			0.10			0.60			0.18	0.15	
FSPCOM	0.73			0.00	1978:4	1978:2–1979:2	0.45			0.66	0.35	
FSPIN	0.91			0.00	1995:1	1994:3–1995:3	0.10			0.34	0.04	1991:1
FSPXE	0.41			0.02	1978:4	1978:2–1979:2	0.77			0.61	0.56	
FYAAAC	0.02	1979:3	1974:1–1980:2	0.01	1981:3	1981:1–1982:1	0.00	1979:2	1972:1–1979:4	0.00	0.00	1979:2
FYBAAC	0.02	1979:3	1974:1–1980:2	0.02	1980:4	1980:2–1981:2	0.00	1979:3	1973:1–1980:2	0.00	0.00	1989:1
FYFF	0.53			0.07			0.00	1984:4	1984:3–1987:3	0.00	0.00	1984:4
FYFHA	0.04	1979:3	1973:4–1980:4	0.11			0.00	1979:3	1974:3–1980:1	0.06	0.00	1979:3
FYGT1	0.01	1966:4	1965:4–1967:1	0.00	1981:1	1980:3–1981:3	0.05	1984:4	1984:2–1989:3	0.00	0.00	1984:4
GMCANQ	0.00	1991:1	1990:4–1994:4	0.08			0.03	1991:3	1991:2–1994:4	0.00	0.06	
GMCDQ	0.00	1991:1	1990:4–1994:1	0.04	1987:3	1987:1–1988:1	0.00	1987:3	1987:2–1990:1	0.72	0.03	1987:3
GMCNQ	0.38			0.00	1991:4	1991:2–1992:2	0.09			0.96	0.78	
GMCQ	0.00	1993:1	1992:3–1996:2	0.61			0.00	1992:1	1991:3–1994:1	0.00	0.12	
GMCSQ	0.03	1993:2	1992:2–1998:4	0.00	1969:4	1969:2–1970:2	0.18			0.03	0.00	1971:3
GMPYQ	0.03	1995:2	1994:2–1999:4	0.00	1981:3	1981:1–1982:1	0.03	1995:1	1994:3–1997:3	0.00	0.00	1972:2

	v	d	CI	v	d	CI	v	d	CI	v	v	d
GMYXPQ	0.12			0.33	1992:3	1992:1–1993:1	0.13	1984:3	1983:4–1988:4	0.00	0.00	1970:3
HSBR	0.13			0.01	1991:1	1990:3–1991:3	0.04	1984:3	1983:4–1987:2	0.09	0.00	1984:3
HSFR	0.08			0.00			0.00	1984:1	1983:3–1986:4	0.28	0.00	1984:3
HSMW	0.18			0.71			0.00	1986:1	1985:2–1989:4	0.26	0.00	1984:1
HSNE	0.00	1992:2	1992:1–1997:2	0.08			0.02			0.02	0.20	
HSSOU	0.15	1985:1	1983:2–1989:3	0.02	1995:2	1994:4–1995:4	0.16	1985:1	1984:3–1987:1	0.05	0.00	1983:1
HSWST	0.01	1984:1	1983:3–1988:4	0.00	1991:1	1990:3–1991:3	0.00	1983:3	1983:2–1985:3	0.00	0.00	1966:2
IP	0.00	1983:3	1983:2–1989:3	0.01	1992:1	1991:3–1992:3	0.00	1984:1	1983:3–1986:3	0.00	0.00	1973:4
IPC	0.01			0.36			0.00			0.00	0.13	
IPCD	0.06			0.76			0.02	1983:3	1983:1–1987:3	0.02	0.30	
IPCN	0.23	1984:1	1983:3–1992:1	0.00	1978:2	1977:4–1978:4	0.20	1984:1	1983:3–1987:1	0.01	0.07	
IPD	0.04			0.04	1993:3	1993:1–1994:1	0.00			0.65	0.04	
IPE	0.05			0.74			0.16			0.07	0.24	1983:3
IPF	0.00	1984:2	1983:3–1988:3	0.56			0.00	1983:3	1983:1–1985:4	0.79	0.03	1983:3
IPI	0.58			0.92			0.00	1983:3	1982:3–1986:3	0.00	0.00	1973:3
IPM	0.00	1984:1	1983:4–1989:1	0.00	1993:3	1993:1–1994:1	0.00	1983:3	1983:1–1985:3	0.74	0.01	1983:3
IPMD	0.01	1984:1	1983:3–1989:4	0.10			0.00	1983:1	1982:4–1985:1	0.96	0.07	
IPMFG	0.01	1984:1	1983:3–1989:3	0.02	1992:1	1991:3–1992:3	0.00	1984:1	1983:4–1986:1	0.00	0.01	1973:4
IPMIN	0.01	1986:3	1986:2–1993:3	0.01	1982:2	1981:4–1982:4	0.10			0.03	0.08	
IPMND	0.60			0.01	1974:1	1973:3–1974:3	0.27			0.04	0.00	1974:3
IPN	0.28	1984:1	1982:3–1989:1	0.00	1978:2	1977:4–1978:4	0.00	1983:3	1983:1–1986:4	0.00	0.00	1974:3
IPP	0.02	1980:4	1977:2–1982:1	0.01	1994:3	1994:1–1995:1	0.00	1983:3	1983:1–1985:4	0.00	0.00	1973:4
IPUT	0.00	1983:4	1983:3–1985:3	0.00	1972:4	1972:2–1973:2	0.00	1978:4	1973:4–1980:1	0.00	0.04	1990:2
IPXMCA	0.00	1993:1	1992:3–1997:1	0.31			0.00	1983:1	1983:2–1985:2	0.00	0.08	
IVMFDQ	0.00			0.02	1967:2	1966:4–1967:4	0.00	1967:2	1966:4–1969:1	0.00	0.06	
IVMFGQ	0.10	1985:3	1985:1–1992:1	0.02	1975:1	1974:3–1975:3	0.43			0.15	0.20	1985:3
IVMFNQ	0.01			0.03	1984:3	1984:1–1985:1	0.25			0.23	0.05	
IVMTQ	0.33			0.24			0.74			0.35	0.49	
IVRRQ	0.01	1987:2	1986:3–1992:3	0.27			0.14			0.18	0.73	
IVWRQ	0.01	1984:4	1983:4–1989:2	0.21			0.00	1983:2	1982:2–1985:3	0.00	0.13	

Table 10 CONTINUED

Series	Variance			Conditional mean			Conditional variance: break only			Conditional variance: trend and break		
	p-Value	Break date	67% Confidence interval	p-Value	Break date	67% Confidence interval	p-Value	Break date	67% Confidence interval	p-Value: trend	p-Value: break	Break date
IVSRMQ	0.05	1984:3	1984:2–1993:4	0.57			0.00	1983:4	1983:2–1986:3	0.08	0.00	1983:4
IVSRQ	0.06			0.68			0.00	1983:4	1983:2–1986:3	0.00	0.00	1972:3
IVSRRQ	0.89			0.23			0.42			0.21	0.09	
IVSRWQ	0.01	1984:4	1984:2–1990:4	0.69			0.00	1984:2	1983:2–1986:3	0.92	0.12	
GVSQ	0.28			0.09			0.53			0.16	0.29	
GVDSQ	0.00	1992:4	1992:3–1998:2	0.47			0.08			0.02	0.26	
GVNSQ	0.37			0.00	1974:3	1974:1–1975:1	0.08			0.02	0.00	1985:4
MDOQ	0.03	1984:2	1983:4–1991:2	0.95			0.02	1984:2	1983:4–1988:2	0.18	0.00	1984:2
MOCMQ	0.01	1984:2	1983:3–1990:1	0.44			0.00	1983:3	1983:1–1986:2	0.12	0.00	1983:3
MPCONQ	0.07			0.04	1973:3	1973:1–1974:1	0.20			0.04	0.00	1966:3
MSDQ	0.05	1983:4	1983:3–1992:3	0.81			0.01	1983:4	1983:2–1987:2	0.17	0.00	1983:4
MSMQ	0.00	1983:4	1983:2–1987:1	0.75			0.00	1983:4	1983:2–1985:4	0.16	0.00	1983:4
MSMTQ	0.01	1984:1	1983:3–1990:2	0.30			0.00	1983:4	1983:2–1986:2	0.59	0.01	1983:4
MSNQ	0.02	1983:2	1983:1–1990:4	0.24			0.00	1983:2	1982:4–1985:4	0.09	0.00	1983:2
MSONDQ	1.00			0.33			0.55			0.63	0.41	
LHEL	0.45			0.00	1995:2	1994:4–1995:4	0.00	1983:2	1982:4–1986:2	0.02	0.00	1983:2
LHELX	0.03	1984:2	1982:3–1989:2	0.08			0.00	1983:4	1983:1–1986:4	0.25	0.00	1983:4
LHEM	0.28			0.43			0.00	1984:4	1983:4–1987:4	0.00	0.00	1974:3
LHNAG	0.24			0.23			0.00	1984:4	1983:4–1987:3	0.00	0.00	1972:4
LHU14	0.00	1984:2	1983:4–1989:3	0.97			0.00	1982:2	1981:4–1985:1	0.00	0.46	
LHU15	0.02	1984:3	1983:4–1990:2	0.00	1982:2	1981:4–1982:4	0.00	1977:2	1976:3–1980:2	0.92	0.27	
LHU26	0.07			0.00	1983:3	1983:1–1984:1	0.00	1983:2	1982:1–1986:2	0.19	0.00	1982:1
LHU5	0.07			0.11			0.06			0.02	0.28	
LHU680	0.03	1985:1	1983:2–1990:1	0.00	1994:2	1993:4–1994:4	0.16			0.99	0.72	
LHUR	0.25			0.50			0.01	1983:4	1983:2–1987:2	0.00	0.00	1972:4

Series											
LP	0.01	1984:4	1982:4–1988:2	0.01	1981:3	1981:1–1982:1	0.00	1982:1	1981:4–1984:1	0.01	1970:1
LPCC	0.38	1984:3	1983:1–1987:4	0.01	1966:3	1966:1–1967:1	0.00	1984:1	1983:3–1986:3	0.00	1974:1
LPED	0.00	1984:2	1983:3–1987:2	0.34			0.00	1983:3	1983:2–1985:4	0.06	
LPEM	0.00			0.08			0.00	1983:1	1982:4–1984:4	0.00	1969:3
LPEN	0.07			0.02	1995:1	1994:3–1995:3	0.00	1984:2	1983:4–1986:2	0.00	1984:2
LPFR	0.00	1966:4	1965:3–1967:1	0.00	1987:2	1986:4–1987:4	0.38	1982:1	1981:4–1984:1	0.07	1970:1
LPGD	0.00	1984:2	1983:2–1987:4	0.24			0.00			0.00	
LPGOV	1.00			0.49			0.79			0.37	
LPHRM	0.02	1983:4	1983:3–1990:4	0.04	1995:1	1994:3–1995:3	0.00	1983:3	1982:4–1986:4	0.02	1973:4
LPMOSA	0.00	1984:1	1983:4–1988:3	0.61			0.00	1983:3	1983:1–1985:3	0.01	1983:3
LPS	1.00			0.27			0.05	1978:2	1976:4–1982:4	0.00	1970:1
LPSP	1.00			0.41			0.17			0.26	
LPT	0.04	1992:4	1991:3–1998:2	0.28	1980:4	1980:2–1981:2	0.00	1991:1	1990:3–1993:2	0.00	1974:4
PMCP	0.04	1972:3	1967:3–1974:3	0.01	1994:4	1994:2–1995:2	0.16	1981:4	1981:3–1983:2	0.12	
PMDEL	0.38			0.00			0.00			0.22	
PMEMP	0.17			0.01	1981:1	1980:3–1981:3	0.01	1983:1	1982:3–1986:3	0.73	
PMI	0.10			0.00	1994:4	1994:2–1995:2	0.00	1984:4	1984:2–1987:4	0.06	
PMNO	0.17			0.00	1994:4	1994:2–1995:2	0.19			0.06	
PMNV	0.02	1984:2	1983:3–1990:3	0.00	1979:3	1979:1–1980:1	0.00			0.25	
PMP	0.18			0.00	1994:4	1994:2–1995:2	0.07	1977:1	1976:3–1978:2	0.00	1970:3
R_LEHCC	0.00	1992:1	1991:2–1993:3	0.00	1973:1	1972:3–1973:3	0.41			0.10	1972:1
LEHCC	0.03	1991:2	1989:4–1996:2	0.05	1969:2	1968:4–1969:4	0.08			0.00	1983:1
R_LEHM	0.03	1980:1	1978:2–1985:2	0.00	1972:1	1971:3–1972:3	0.00	1983:1	1981:3–1986:1	0.04	
LEHM	0.02	1975:1	1974:4–1980:2	0.01	1974:2	1973:4–1974:4	0.02	1975:1	1974:3–1978:4	0.62	
GDC	0.05			0.02	1973:2	1972:4–1973:4	0.03	1970:3	1965:4–1972:4	0.00	1970:3
PUNEW	0.12			0.00	1966:1	1965:3–1966:3	0.01	1970:2	1960:1–1970:4	0.00	1991:2
PUXF	0.10			0.00	1975:2	1974:4–1975:4	0.02	1991:1	1990:4–1994:3	0.00	1991:2
PUXHS	0.23			0.08			0.01	1972:4	1960:1–1973:2	0.00	1991:3
PUXM	0.09			0.00	1980:1	1979:3–1980:3	0.03	1991:2	1990:4–1994:4	0.00	1991:2
PW	0.27			0.01	1974:4	1974:2–1975:2	0.00	1972:4	1965:1–1973:4	0.00	1972:4
PSCCOM	0.05	1972:4	1962:2–1973:1	0.21			0.04	1971:4	1962:1–1973:2	0.00	1971:4
R_PSCCOM	0.03	1971:4	1962:4–1972:1	0.13			0.02	1971:4	1963:4–1973:2	0.00	1971:4
PSM99Q	0.04	1973:4	1964:2–1974:1	0.01	1974:4	1974:2–1975:2	0.11			0.00	1973:4
R_PSM99Q	0.05	1971:4	1961:1–1972:1	0.01	1974:1	1973:3–1974:3	0.23			0.00	1973:4
PU83	0.00	1972:2	1970:4–1972:3	0.00	1987:2	1986:4–1987:4	0.00	1972:2	1963:1–1972:3	0.04	1990:2

Table 10 CONTINUED

Series	Variance			Conditional mean			Conditional variance: break only			Conditional variance: trend and break		
	p-Value	Break date	67% Confidence interval	p-Value	Break date	67% Confidence interval	p-Value	Break date	67% Confidence interval	p-Value: trend	p-Value: break	Break date
R_PU83	0.07			0.00	1968:3	1968:1–1969:1	0.00	1973:2	1969:2–1974:1	0.00	0.00	1990:1
PU84	0.05	1979:1	1970:1–1979:2	0.47			0.00	1978:2	1968:4–1979:2	0.00	0.00	1991:4
R_PU84	0.00	1970:3	1965:1–1970:4	0.03	1969:2	1968:4–1969:4	0.02	1973:2	1962:3–1974:2	0.00	0.13	
PU85	0.05			0.55			0.00	1984:2	1984:1–1986:4	0.00	0.00	1966:2
R_PU85	0.00	1992:4	1992:3–1997:3	0.12			0.00	1983:2	1982:4–1985:4	0.00	0.00	1971:3
PUC	0.04	1972:4	1962:3–1973:1	0.00	1972:3	1972:1–1973:1	0.02	1972:4	1962:4–1974:1	0.00	0.00	1992:1
R_PUC	0.00	1972:4	1966:2–1973:1	0.00	1970:3	1970:1–1971:1	0.02	1972:4	1961:1–1973:4	0.02	0.07	
PUCD	0.11			0.00	1978:2	1977:4–1978:4	0.00	1991:1	1990:3–1993:3	0.00	0.00	1969:2
R_PUCD	0.14			0.07			0.10			0.19	0.02	1985:3
PUS	0.15			0.52			0.00	1983:4	1983:3–1987:1	0.00	0.00	1983:4
R_PUS	0.01	1986:2	1986:1–1987:1	0.01	1980:2	1979:4–1980:4	0.00	1986:2	1986:1–1988:2	0.00	0.00	1983:3
PW561	0.00	1985:4	1984:4–1986:3	0.03	1974:1	1973:3–1974:3	0.00	1985:4	1980:4–1986:1	0.72	0.07	
R_PW561	0.00	1985:4	1984:2–1986:3	0.00	1974:1	1973:3–1974:3	0.00	1985:4	1981:2–1986:1	0.73	0.06	
PWFCSA	0.53			0.76			0.02	1972:4	1964:4–1974:2	0.17	0.00	1972:4
R_PWFCSA	0.10			0.41			0.02	1972:4	1964:1–1974:2	0.22	0.00	1972:4
PWFSA	0.41			0.88			0.02	1972:4	1965:2–1974:3	0.08	0.00	1972:4
R_PWFSA	0.11			0.64			0.02	1972:2	1967:1–1974:2	0.26	0.00	1972:2
RTNQ	0.73			0.00	1973:4	1973:2–1974:2	0.12			0.10	0.71	
WTDQ	0.03	1984:2	1984:1–1992:2	0.81			0.00	1982:2	1981:2–1985:2	0.22	0.00	1982:2
WTNQ	0.19			0.31			0.04	1986:3	1985:3–1990:3	0.01	0.07	
WTQ	0.01	1984:2	1984:1–1991:3	0.08			0.00	1982:3	1982:1–1985:1	0.02	0.19	1972:3
IPCAN	0.00	1991:1	1990:4–1996:1	0.04	1974:1	1973:3–1974:3	0.07			0.83	0.21	
IPFR	0.04	1980:4	1980:3–1988:2	0.03	1974:2	1973:4–1974:4	0.15			0.61	0.21	
IPIT	0.01	1983:3	1983:2–1990:3	0.00	1973:2	1972:4–1973:4	0.01	1983:3	1983:1–1987:1	0.00	0.00	1969:2
IPJP	0.24			0.00	1973:1	1972:3–1973:3	0.15			0.01	0.00	1976:2
IPOECD	0.05	1984:3	1983:3–1991:1	0.01	1972:2	1971:4–1972:4	0.00	1984:3	1984:1–1987:2	0.00	0.15	
IPUK	0.10			0.00	1974:3	1974:1–1975:1	0.02	1985:3	1985:2–1989:2	0.00	0.00	1971:4
IPWG	0.32			0.27			0.30			0.98	0.96	

Notes: The first column reports tests of the hypothesis that the variance of the series is constant, against the alternative of a single break. For the remaining columns, the ... to Table 3. The break-test methods are described in the text of the appendix.

where $\varepsilon_t, \eta_{1t}, \ldots, \eta_{pt}$ are i.i.d. $N(0, 1)$ and independently distributed, and where ζ_t is distributed independently of the other shocks. To allow for large jumps in the instantaneous innovation variance σ_t^2 (and thereby capture a possible break in the variance), we use a mixture-of-normals model for ζ_t; specifically, ζ_t is distributed $N(0, \tau_1^2)$ with probability q and $N(0, \tau_2^2)$ with probability $1 - q$. The series y_t is standardized before the computations, and we set $c_j = 7/T$, a value consistent with previous estimates of parameter drift in autoregressions. For these calculations, we set $\tau_1 = 0.04$, $\tau_2 = 0.2$, $q = 0.95$, and $p = 4$.

The non-Gaussian smoother for the time-varying parameters is computed using Markov-chain Monte Carlo (MCMC) methods. Let Y denote $y_1, \ldots, y_T$, let A denote $\{\alpha_{jt}, j = 1, \ldots, p, t = 1, \ldots, T\}$, and let S denote $\sigma_1, \ldots, \sigma_T$. The MCMC algorithm iterates between the three conditional distributions of $Y|A, S$, of $A|Y, S$, and of $S|A, Y$. The first two of these conditional distributions are normal, given the stated assumptions. The third distribution, however, is non-normal and—as suggested by Shephard (1994)—is computed by approximating the distribution of $\ln \varepsilon_t^2$ (which is the distribution of the logarithm of a chi-squared random variable with one degree of freedom) by a mixture-of-normals distribution; the means and variances of the mixture (and the mixture weights) were chosen to match the first four moments of the log χ_1^2 distribution. Initial conditions were set using a flat prior, and a diffuse conjugate prior was used for the parameter values.

Given the smoothed parameter values, the estimated instantaneous autocovariances of y_t are computed using $\sigma_{t|T}^2$ and $a_{jt|T}$, the conditional means of σ_t^2 and α_{jt} given $y_1, \ldots, y_T$. The smoothed instantaneous variances of four-quarter growth rates were computed by temporal aggregation of the instantaneous autocovariance function.

A.2 VARIANCE-BREAK TESTS

To test for a break in the unconditional variance (the first column of Table 10), the absolute value of the demeaned series (e.g., the absolute value of demeaned four-quarter growth in GDP) was regressed against a constant and a binary variable 1 ($t \geq \tau$) for the break date. The QLR statistic is the squared heteroscedasticity- and autocorrelation-robust t-statistic on the break indicator, maximized over τ in the central 70% of the sample.

The tests for a break in the conditional variance were computed as follows. Let $\varepsilon_t(\kappa)$ denote the errors in the autoregression in (1), where the AR coefficients break at date κ, and let $\hat{\varepsilon}_t(\kappa)$ denote the OLS residuals estimated with a break in the AR coefficients at date κ. Under the null hypothesis that there is no break in the variance, $E|\varepsilon_t(\kappa)|$ is constant; under the alternative hypothesis that there is a break at date τ, we have $E|\varepsilon_t(\kappa)| =$

$\sigma_1 + \lambda \, 1(t \geq \tau)$, where σ_1 is the first-period standard deviation and λ is the difference between the standard deviations before and after the break. We therefore test for a break by computing the QLR statistic in the regression of $|\hat{\varepsilon}_t(\hat{\kappa})|$ against a constant and the binary variable $1(t \geq \tau)$, using homoscedastic standard errors (which are valid under the null), where $\hat{\kappa}$ is the least-squares estimator of the break date in the AR coefficients. Table 3 also reports results for a trend-augmented version of this regression, in which $|\hat{\varepsilon}_t(\hat{\kappa})|$ was regressed against a constant, $1(t \geq \tau)$, and the time trend t, as well as the p-value for the test that the coefficient on t is zero in the regression in which $\tau = \hat{\tau}$. Critical values for the QLR statistic [the squared t-statistic on $1(t \geq \tau)$, maximized over τ] in this trend-augmented regression were computed by Monte Carlo simulation. In all cases, the search over τ was conducted in the central 70% of the sample.

Confidence intervals for the conditional-variance break date were computed using the least-squares estimator from the regression of $|\hat{\varepsilon}_t(\hat{\kappa})|$ against a constant and $1(t \geq \tau)$. If there is a break, the variance of the error term in this regression differs before and after the break, requiring a modification to Bai's (1997) limiting distribution for the least-squares break-date estimator. This modification entails scaling the distribution differently on either side of the break, by the appropriate estimated variance. The confidence interval for the break date is then obtained by inverting the test of the break date, based on this distribution. This results in asymmetric confidence intervals that express greater uncertainty about the break date in the low- than in the high-volatility period. The same method applies to the unconditional-variance break date, except the dependent variable is the absolute value of the demeaned series and HAC standard errors are used as discussed in Bai (1997).

Results for all 168 series are summarized in Table 10.

Appendix B. Data

Table 11 lists the time series used in the empirical analysis. The series were either taken directly from the DRI–McGraw Hill Basic Economics database, in which case the original mnemonics are used, or produced by authors' calculations based on data from that database, in which case the authors' calculations and original DRI–McGraw Hill series mnemonics are summarized in the data description field. Following the series name is a transformation code and a short data description. The transformations are (1) level of the series; (2) first difference; (3) second difference; (4) logarithm of the series; (5) first difference of the logarithm; (6) second difference of the logarithm. The following abbreviations appear in the data descriptions: sa = seasonally adjusted; nsa = not seasonally

Table 11   DATA

Series name	Transformation code	Description
NIPA Components		
GDPQ	5	Gross domestic product (chained)
GOQ	5	Gross domestic product—goods
GOSQ	5	Final sales of goods
GODQ	5	Gross domestic product—durable goods
GODSQ	5	Final sales of durables
GONQX	5	Gross domestic product—nondurables
GONSQX	5	Final sales of nondurables
GOOSQ	5	Gross domestic product—services
GOCQ	5	Gross domestic product—structures
GCQ	5	Personal consumption expenditures (chained)—total
GCDQ	5	Personal consumption expenditures (chained)—durables
GCNQ	5	Personal consumption expenditures (chained)—nondurables
GCSQ	5	Personal consumption expenditures (chained)—services
GPIQ	5	Investment, total (chained)
GIFQ	5	Fixed investment, total (chained)
GINQ	5	Fixed investment, nonresidential (chained)
GIRQ	5	Fixed investment, residential (chained)
GEXQ	5	Exports of goods and services (chained)
GIMQ	5	Imports of goods and services (chained)
GGEQ	5	Government consumption expenditures and gross investment (chained)
DGV_GDP	1	Change in Nominal Inventory Investment divided by nominal GDP (ac)
GGFENQ	5	National defense consumption expenditures and gross investment (chained)
GMCANQ	5	Personal consumption expenditures (chained)—new cars (bil. 1996$, saar)
GMCDQ	5	Personal consumption expenditures (chained)—total durables (bil. 1996$, saar)
GMCNQ	5	Personal consumption expenditures (chained)—nondurables (bil. 1992$, saar)
GMCQ	5	Personal consumption expenditures (chained)—total (bil. 1992$, saar)
GMCSQ	5	Personal consumption expenditures (chained)—services (bil. 1992$, saar)
GMPYQ	5	Personal income (chained) (series #52) (bil. 1992$, saar)
GMYXPQ	5	Personal income less transfer payments (chained) (#51) (bil. 1992$, saar)

Table 11 CONTINUED

Series name	Transformation code	Description
Money, Credit, Interest Rates, and Stock Prices		
CONCRED	6	Consumer credit
FM1	6	Money stock: M1 (curr. trav. cks, dem. dep., other ckable dep.) (bil. $, sa)
FM2	6	Money stock: M2 (M1 + overnight rps, euro $, g/p and b/d mmmfs and sav and sm time dep (bil. $)
FM2DQ	5	Money supply—M2 in 1992 dollars (bci)
FM3	6	Money stock: M3 (bil. $, sa)
FMFBA	6	Monetary base, adj for reserve requirement changes (mil. $, sa)
FMRRA	6	Depository inst reserves: total, adj for reserve req chgs (mil. $, sa)
FSDXP	5	S&p's composite common stock: dividend yield (%/yr)
FSNCOM	5	Nyse common stock price index: composite (12/31/65 = 50)
FSPCAP	5	S&p's common stock price index: capital goods (1941–1943 = 10)
FSPCOM	5	S&p's common stock price index: composite (1941–1943 = 10)
FSPIN	5	S&p's common stock price index: industrials (1941–1943 = 10)
FSPXE	5	S&p's composite common stock: price-earnings ratio (%, nsa)
FYAAAC	2	Bond yield: Moody's aaa corporate (%/yr)
FYBAAC	2	Bond yield: Moody's baa corporate (%/yr)
FYFF	2	Interest rate: federal funds (effective) (%/yr, nsa)
FYFHA	2	Secondary market yields on FHA mortgages (%/yr)
FYGM3	2	Interest rate; U.S. Treasury bills, sec mkt, 3-mo. (%/yr, nsa)
FYGT1	2	Interest rate: U.S. Treasury const. maturities, 1-yr. (%/yr, nsa)
FYGT10	2	Interest rate: U.S. Treasury const. maturities, 10-yr. (%/yr, nsa)
Housing		
HSBR	5	Housing authorized: total new priv. housing units (thous., saar)
HSFR	5	Housing starts: nonfarm (1947–1958; total farm and nonfarm (1959–) (thous., sa)
HSMW	5	Housing starts: midwest (thous. u., sa)
HSNE	5	Housing starts: northeast (thous. u., sa)

Table 11   CONTINUED

Series name	Transformation code	Description
HSSOU	5	Housing starts: south (thous. u., sa)
HSWST	5	Housing starts: west (thous. u., sa)

Industrial Production

Series name	Transformation code	Description
IP	5	Industrial production: total index (1992 = 100, sa)
IPC	5	Industrial production: consumer goods (1992 = 100, sa)
IPCD	5	Industrial production: durable consumer goods (1992 = 100, sa)
IPCN	5	Industrial production: nondurable consumer goods (1992 = 100, sa)
IPD	5	Industrial production: durable manufacturing (1992 = 100, sa)
IPE	5	Industrial production: business equipment (1992 = 100, sa)
IPF	5	Industrial production: final products (1992 = 100, sa)
IPI	5	Industrial production: Intermediate products (1992 = 100, sa)
IPM	5	Industrial production: materials (1992 = 100, sa)
IPMD	5	Industrial production: durable-goods materials (1992 = 100, sa)
IPMFG	5	Industrial production: manufacturing (1992 = 100, sa)
IPMIN	5	Industrial production: mining (1992 = 100, sa)
IPMND	5	Industrial production: nondurable-goods materials (1992 = 100, sa)
IPN	5	Industrial production: nondurable manufacturing (1992 = 100, sa)
IPP	5	Industrial production: products, total (1992 = 100, sa)
IPUT	5	Industrial production: utilities (1992 = 100, sa)
IPXMCA	1	Capacity util. rate: manufacturing, total (% of capacity, sa) (frb)

Inventories, Orders, and Sales

Series name	Transformation code	Description
IVMFDQ	5	Inventories, business durables (mil. of chained 1996 dollars, sa)
IVMFGQ	5	Inventories, business, mfg. (mil. of chained 1996 dollars, sa)
IVMFNQ	5	Inventories, business, nondurables (mil. of chained 1996 dollars, sa)
IVMTQ	5	Mfg. and trade inventories: total (mil. of chained 1996) (sa)

Table 11   CONTINUED

Series name	Transformation code	Description
IVRRQ	5	Mfg. and trade inventories: retail trade (mil. of chained 1996 dollars) (sa)
IVWRQ	5	Mfg. and trade inventories: merchant wholesalers (mil. of chained 1996 dollars) (sa)
IVSRMQ	5	Ratio for mfg. and trade: mfg.; inventory/sales (1996$) (s.a.)
IVSRQ	5	Ratio for mfg. and trade: inventory/sales (chained 1996 dollars, sa)
IVSRRQ	5	Ratio for mfg. and trade: retail trade; inventory/sales (1996$) (s.a.)
IVSRWQ	5	Ratio for mfg. and trade: wholesaler; inventory/sales (1996$) (s.a.)
GVSQ	1	(Change in inventories)/sales—goods (ac)
GVDSQ	1	(Change in inventories)/sales—durable goods (ac)
GVNSQ	1	(Change in inventories)/sales—nondurable goods
MDOQ	5	New orders, durable goods industries, 1992 dollars
MOCMQ	5	New orders (net)—consumer goods and materials, 1992 dollars
MPCONQ	5	Contracts and orders for plant and equipment in 1992 dollars
MSDQ	5	Mfg. and trade: mfg.; durable goods (mil. of chained 1996 dollars) (sa)
MSMQ	5	Sales, business—mfg. (chained)
MSMTQ	5	Mfg. and trade: total (mil. of chained 1996 dollars) (sa)
MSNQ	5	Mfg. and trade: mfg.; nondurable goods (mil. of chained 1996 dollars) (sa)
MSONDQ	5	New orders, nondefense capital goods, in 1992 dollars
RTNQ	5	Retail trade: nondurable goods (mil. of 1996 dollars) (sa)
WTDQ	5	Merch wholesalers: durable goods total (mil. of chained 1996 dollars) (sa)
WTNQ	5	Merch wholesalers: nondurable goods (mil. of chained 1996 dollars) (sa)
WTQ	5	Merch wholesalers: total (mil. of chained 1996 dollars) (sa)
Employment		
LHEL	5	Index of help-wanted advertising in newspapers (1967 = 100; sa)
LHELX	5	Employment: ratio; help-wanted ads: no. unemployed

Table 11 CONTINUED

Series name	Transformation code	Description
LHEM	5	Civilian labor force: employed, total (thous., sa)
LHNAG	5	Civilian labor force: employed, nonagric. industries (thous., sa)
LHU14	5	Unemploy. by duration: persons unempl. 5 to 14 wks (thous., sa)
LHU15	5	Unemploy. by duration: persons unempl. 15 wk + (thous., sa)
LHU26	5	Unemploy. by duration: persons unempl. 15 to 26 wk (thous., sa)
LHU5	5	Unemploy. by duration: persons unempl. less than 5 wk (thous., sa)
LHU680	5	Unemploy. by duration: average duration in weeks (sa)
LHUR	2	Unemployment rate: all workers, 16 years and over (%, sa)
LP	5	Employees on nonag payrolls: total, private (thous, sa)
LPCC	5	Employees on nonag. payrolls: contract construction (thous., sa)
LPED	5	Employees on nonag. payrolls: durable goods (thous., sa)
LPEM	5	Employees on nonag. payrolls: manufacturing (thous., sa)
LPEN	5	Employees on nonag. payrolls: nondurable goods (thous., sa)
LPFR	5	Employees on nonag. payrolls: finance, insur. and real estate (thous., sa)
LPGD	5	Employees on nonag. payrolls: goods-producing (thous., sa)
LPGOV	5	Employees on nonag. payrolls: government (thous., sa)
LPHRM	5	Avg. weekly hrs. of prod. wkrs.: manufacturing (sa)
LPMOSA	5	Avg. weekly hrs. of prod. wkrs.: mfg., overtime hrs. (sa)
LPNAG	5	Employees on nonag. payrolls: total (thous., sa)
LPS	5	Employees on nonag. payrolls: services (thous., sa)
LPSP	5	Employees on nonag. payrolls: service-producing (thous., sa)
LPT	5	Employees on nonag. payrolls: wholesale and retail trade (thous., sa)
NAPM indexes		
PMCP	1	Napm commodity prices index (%)
PMDEL	1	Napm vendor deliveries index (%)

Table 11   CONTINUED

Series name	Transformation code	Description
PMEMP	1	Napm employment index (%)
PMI	1	Purchasing managers' index (sa)
PMNO	1	Napm new orders index (%)
PMNV	1	Napm inventories index (%)
PMP	1	Napm production index (%)

Wages and Prices

Series name	Transformation code	Description
R_LEHCC	2	ln(lehcc/gdpd)
LEHCC	6	Avg hourly earnings of constr wkrs: construction ($, sa)
R_LEHM	2	ln(lehm/gdpd)
LEHM	6	Avg hourly earnings of prod wkrs: manufacturing ($, sa)
GDPD	6	Gross domestic product: implicit price deflator (index, 92 = 100)
GDC	6	Implicit price deflator: personal consumption expenditures
PUNEW	6	Cpi-u: all items (82–84 = 100, sa)
PUXF	6	Cpi-u: all items less food (82–84 = 100, sa)
PUXHS	6	Cpi-u: all items less shelter (82–84 = 100, sa)
PUXM	6	Cpi-u: all items less medical care (82–84 = 100, sa)
PW	6	Producer price index: all commodities (82 = 100, nsa)
PSCCOM	6	Spot market price index: bls. & crb.: all commodities (67 = 100, nsa)
R_PSCCOM	2	ln(psccom/gdpd) (ac)
PSM99Q	6	Index of sensitive materials prices (1990 = 100)
R_PSM99Q	2	ln(psm99q/gdpd) (ac)
PU83	6	Cpi-u: apparel & upkeep (82–84 = 100, sa)
R_PU83	2	ln(pu83/gdpd) (ac)
PU84	6	Cpi-u: transportation (82–84 = 100, sa)
R_PU84	2	ln(pu84/gdpd) (ac)
PU85	6	Cpi-u: medical care (82–84 = 100, sa)
R_PU85	2	ln(pu85/gdpd) (ac)
PUC	6	Cpi-u: commodities (82–84 = 100, sa)
R_PUC	2	ln(puc/gdpd) (ac)
PUCD	6	Cpi-u: durables (82–84 = 100, sa)
R_PUCD	2	ln(pucd/gdpd) (ac)
PUS	6	Cpi-u: services (82–84 = 100, sa)
R_PUS	2	ln(pus/gdpd) (ac)
PW561	6	Producer price index: crude petroleum (82 = 100, nsa)
R_PW561	2	ln(pw561/gdpd) (ac)
PWFCSA	6	Producer price index: finished consumer goods (82 = 100, sa)

Table 11   CONTINUED

Series name	Transformation code	Description
R_PWFCSA	2	ln(pwfcsa/gdpd) (ac)
PWFSA	6	Producer price index: finished goods (82 = 100, sa)
R_PWFSA	2	ln(pwfsa/gdpd) (ac)

Industrial Production in Other Countries

IPCAN	5	Industrial production: Canada (1990 = 100, sa)
IPFR	5	Industrial production: France (1987 = 100, sa)
IPIT	5	Industrial production: Italy (1987 = 100, sa)
IPJP	5	Industrial production: Japan (1990 = 100, sa)
IPOECD	5	Industrial production—OECD, European countries (1990 = 100, sa)
IPUK	5	Industrial production: United Kingdom (1987 = 100, sa)
IPWG	5	Industrial production: West Germany (1990 = 100, sa)

Additional Series Shown in Figure 4

GFIRSQ	5	Purchases of residential structures—1 unit
GFIRMQ	5	Purchases of residential structures—2 or more units
CONFRC	5	Construct. put in place: priv residential bldg (mil. 1987$, saar)
CONCC	5	Construct. put in place: commercial bldgs (mil. 1987$, saar)
CONIC	5	Construct. put in place: industrial bldg (mil. 1987$, saar)

adjusted; saar = seasonally adjusted at an annual rate; frb = Federal Reserve Board; ac = authors' calculations.

REFERENCES

Ahmed, S., A. Levin, and B. Wilson. (2002). "Recent U.S. macroeconomic stability: Good luck, good policies, or good practices?" Board of Governors, Federal Reserve Bank. Manuscript.

Andrews, D. W. K. (1993). Tests of parameter instability and structural change with unknown change point. *Econometrica* 61:821–856.

Auerbach, A., and D. Feenberg. (2000). The significance of federal taxes and automatic stabilizers. *Journal of Economic Perspectives*, Summer, 37–56.

Bai, J. (1997). Estimation of a change point in multiple regression models. *Review of Economics and Statistics* 79:551–563.

———, R. Lumsdaine, and J. Stock. (1998). Testing for and dating common breaks in multivariate time series. *The Review of Economic Studies* 65:395–432.

————, and P. Perron. (1998). Estimating and testing linear models with multiple structural changes. *Econometrica* 66:47–78.

Basistha, A., and R. Startz. (2001). Why were changes in the federal funds rates smaller in the 1990s? University of Washington. Manuscript.

Basu, S., J. Fernald, and M. Kimball. (1999). Are technology improvements contractionary? University of Michigan. Manuscript.

Bekaert, G., C. R. Harvey, and C. Lundblad. (2002). Growth volatility and equity market liberalization. Manuscript, Fuqua School of Business, Duke University.

Bernanke, B., and J. Boivin. (2000). Monetary policy in a data-rich environment. *Journal of Monetary Economics*, forthcoming.

————, M. Gertler, and M. W. Watson. (1997). "Systematic monetary policy and the effects of oil price shocks." *Brookings Papers on Economic Activity* 1997:1, 91–142.

————, and I. Mihoy. (1998). Measuring monetary policy. *Quarterly Journal of Economics* 113:869–902.

Blanchard, O., and R. Perotti. (2001). An empirical characterization of the dynamic effects of changes in government spending and taxes on output. Cambridge, MA: MIT. Manuscript.

————, and J. Simon. (2001). The long and large decline in U.S. output volatility. *Brookings Papers on Economic Activity* 2001(1):135–164.

Blinder, A. S., and L. J. Maccini. (1991). Taking stock: A critical assessment of recent research on inventories. *Journal of Economic Perspectives* 5(1):73–96.

Boivin, J. (2000). The Fed's conduct of monetary policy: Has it changed and does it matter? *Essays on the Analysis of Changes in the Conduct of Monetary Policy.* Princeton University. PhD Dissertation, Chapter 3.

————, and M. Giannoni. (2002a). Assessing changes in the monetary transmission mechanism: A VAR approach. *Federal Reserve Bank of New York Monetary Policy Review* 8(1):97–111.

————, and M. Giannoni. (2002b). Has monetary policy become less powerful? Federal Reserve Bank of New York. Staff Paper 144.

Burns, A. (1960). Progress towards economic stability. *American Economic Review* 50(1):2–19.

Chauvet, M., and S. Potter. (2001). Recent Changes in the US Business Cycle. Federal Reserve Bank of New York. Manuscript.

Christiano, L., M. Eichenbaum, and C. Evans. (1997). Sticky price and limited participation models of money: A comparison. *European Economic Review* 41:1201–1249.

————, ————, and ————. (1999). Monetary policy shocks: What have we learned and to what end? Ch. 2 in J. Taylor and M. Woodford (ed.). In *Handbook of Macroeconomics*, Vol. 1A:65–148.

Clarida, R., J. Gali, and M. Gertler. (2000). Monetary policy rules and macroeconomic stability: Evidence and some theory. *Quarterly Journal of Economics*, February, pp. 147–180.

Cogley, T., and T. J. Sargent. (2001). Evolving post-World War II U.S. inflation dynamics. In *NBER Macroeconomics Annual*. Cambridge, MA: The MIT Press, pp. 331–372.

————, and ————. (2002). Drifts and volatilities: Monetary policies and outcomes in the post-WWII U.S. Stanford University. Manuscript.

Feroli, M. (2002). An equilibrium model of inventories with investment-specific technical change. New York University. Manuscript.

Gali, J. (1999). Technology, employment and the business cycle: Do technology shocks explain aggregate productivity. *American Economic Review* 89:249–271.

———, and M. Gertler. (1999). Inflation dynamics: A structural econometric analysis. *Journal of Monetary Economics* 44:195–222.

———, J. D. Lopez-Salido, and J. Valles. (2002). Technology shock and monetary policy: Assessing the Fed's performance. Cambridge, MA: National Bureau of Economic Research. NBER Working Paper 8768.

Gilchrist, S., and A. Kashyap. (1990). Assessing the smoothness of recent GNP growth. Internal memorandum, Board of Governors of the Federal Reserve System.

Golub, J. E. (2000). Post-1984 inventories revitalize the production-smoothing model. University of Missouri–Kansas City. Manuscript.

Goodfriend, M., and R. King. (1997). The New Neoclassical Synthesis and the Role of Monetary Policy. In *NBER Macroeconomics Annual*. Cambridge, MA: The MIT Press.

Hamilton, J. D. (1996). This is what happened to the oil price–macroeconomy relationship. *Journal of Monetary Economics* 38(2):215–220.

Hansen, B. (2001). Testing for structural change in conditional models. *Journal of Econometrics* 97:93–115.

Herrera, A. M., and E. Pesavento. (2002). The decline in US output volatility: Structural changes in inventories or sales? Michigan State University. Manuscript.

Kahn, J., M. M. McConnell, and G. Perez-Quiros. (2001). The reduced volatility of the U.S. economy: Policy or progress? Federal Reserve Bank of New York. Manuscript.

———, ———, and ———. (2002). On the causes of the increased stability of the U.S. economy. *Federal Reserve Bank of New York Economic Policy Review* 8(1):183–202.

Kim, C.-J., and C. R. Nelson. (1999). Has the U.S. economy become more stable? A Bayesian approach based on a Markov-switching model of the business cycle. *The Review of Economics and Statistics* 81:608–616.

———, ———, and J. Piger. (2001). The less volatile U.S. economy: A Bayesian investigation of breadth, and potential explanations. Board of Governors of the Federal Reserve System. International Finance Discussion Paper 707.

McCarthy, J., and R. W. Peach. (2002). Monetary policy transmission to residential investment. *Federal Reserve Bank of New York Economic Policy Review* 8(1):139–158.

McConnell, M. M., and G. Perez-Quiros. (2000). Output fluctuations in the United States: What has changed since the early 1980's? *American Economic Review* 90(5):1464–1476.

Moore, G. H., and V. Zarnowitz. (1986). The development and role of the NBER's business cycle chronologies. In *The American Business Cycle: Continuity and Change*, R. J. Gordon (ed.). Chicago: University of Chicago Press.

Pagan, A. (2000). Some thoughts on trend and cycle. Australian National University. Manuscript.

Pivetta, F., and R. Reis. (2001). The persistence of inflation in the U.S. Department of Economics, Harvard University. Manuscript.

Primiceri, G. (2000). Time varying structural vector autoregressions and monetary policy. Princeton University. Manuscript.

————, and M. Woodford. (1999). Interest rate rules in an estimated sticky price model. In *Monetary Policy Rules*, J. Taylor (ed.). University of Chicago Press.

Quandt, R. E. (1960). Tests of the hypothesis that a linear regression obeys two separate regimes. *Journal of the American Statistical Association* 55:324–330.

Ramey, V. A., and D. J. Vine. (2001). Tracking the source of the decline in GDP volatility: An analysis of the automobile industry. University of California, San Diego. Manuscript.

————, and K. D. West. (1999). Inventories. In *Handbook of Macroeconomics*, J. Taylor and M. Woodford (eds.). Vol. 1B, pp. 863–923.

Rotemberg, J., and M. Woodford. (1997). An optimization-based econometric framework for the evaluation of monetary policy. In *NBER Macroeconomics Annual*. Cambridge, MA: The MIT Press. 297–345.

Rudebusch, G. D. (1998). Do measures of monetary policy in a VAR make sense? *International Economic Review* 39:907–931.

————. (2002). Assessing nominal income rules for monetary policy with model and data uncertainty. *The Economic Journal* 112:402–432.

————, and L. Svensson. (1999). Rules for inflation targeting. In *Monetary Policy Rules*, J. Taylor (ed.). University of Chicago Press.

Sensier, M., and D. van Dijk. (2001). Short-term volatility versus long-term growth: Evidence in US macroeconomic time series. University of Manchester. Manuscript.

Shephard, N. (1994). Partial non-Gaussian state space. *Biometrika* 81(1):115–131.

Simon, J. (2000). The long boom. *Essays in Empirical Macroeconomics*. Cambridge, MA: MIT. PhD Dissertation, Chapter 1.

————. (2001). The decline in Australian output volatility. Reserve Bank of Australia. Manuscript.

Sims, C. (2001). Stability and instability in US monetary policy behavior. Princeton University. Manuscript.

————, and T. Zha. (2002). Macroeconomic switching. Princeton University. Manuscript.

Staiger, D., M. W. Watson, and J. H. Stock. (2001). Prices, wages and the U.S. NAIRU in the 1990s, Ch. 1 in *The Roaring Nineties*, A. Krueger and R. Solow (eds.), Russell Sage Foundation/The Century Fund: New York, 3–60.

Stock, J. H., and M. W. Watson. (1996). Evidence on structural instability in macroeconomic time series relations. *Journal of Business and Economic Statistics* 14:11–29.

————, and ————. (1998). Asymptotically median unbiased estimation of coefficient variance in a time varying parameter model. *Journal of the American Statistical Association* 93:349–358.

————, and ————. (1999). Forecasting inflation. *Journal of Monetary Economics* 44: 293–335.

————, and ————. (2001). Macroeconomic forecasting using diffusion indexes. *Journal of Business and Economic Statistics*, forthcoming.

————. (1999b). An historical analysis of monetary policy rules. In Taylor (1999a).

————. (2000). Remarks for the panel discussion on recent changes in trend and cycle. Stanford University. Manuscript.

Warnock, M. V. C., and F. E. Warnock. (2001). The declining volatility of U.S. employment: Was Arthur Burns right? Board of Governors of the Federal Reserve System. Manuscript.

Watson M. (1999). Explaining the increased variability in the long-term interest rate. *Economic Quarterly* (Federal Reserve Bank of Richmond) 85(Fall).

Comment

JORDI GALÍ
Centre de Recerca en Economia Internacional (CREI) and Universitat
Pompeu Fabra

1. Introduction

In their contribution, Stock and Watson (henceforth, SW) provide a comprehensive statistical account of the changes experienced (or not) by the U.S. business cycle over the postwar period. They also conduct several exercises that aim at understanding what the sources of those changes may be. I believe their paper will be a standard reference on the changing business cycle for years to come, at least until enough new data become available to force us to revisit the issue and, perhaps, reconsider some of the conclusions attained here.

My comments below are just some thoughts provoked by SW's paper. They are meant to complement their analysis or to suggest possible avenues of research, rather than question any of their evidence or conclusions.

2. Two Decompositions of GDP Growth

The paper, like the literature on which it builds, focuses on the volatility of the growth rate of GDP and other macro variables. In that context, authors and readers are often tempted to interpret any decline in those volatility measures as good news, possibly the result of improvements on the policy front. But modern business-cycle theory does not suggest that more GDP stability is something to be desired, always and everywhere—certainly not, at least, in economies that experience continuous shocks to technology, preferences, external demand and investment opportunities, public-good requirements, etc. Hence, by focusing on the volatility of raw measures of GDP one may be overstating (a) the extent of the possible benefits from any observed decline in volatility, and (b) the room left for further, more aggressive stabilization policies.

In order to address the previous concern (at least in theory), one may specify a decomposition like

$$\Delta y_t = \Delta \bar{y}_t + \Delta \tilde{y}_t$$

where y_t denotes (log) output, $\bar{y}_t$ denotes the efficient or target level of (log) output (*potential* output, for short), and $\tilde{y}_t \equiv y_t - \bar{y}_t$ is the distance between actual and potential output (the *output gap*). Accordingly, the standard deviation of output growth, denoted by s, is given by

$$s = \sqrt{\bar{s}^2 + \tilde{s}^2 + 2\rho\bar{s}\tilde{s}},$$

where $\bar{s}$ and $\tilde{s}$ denote, respectively, the standard deviations of $\bar{y}_t$ and $\tilde{y}_t$, and ρ is the correlation between the previous variables. Hence, a reduction in the volatility of GDP growth may be due to a smaller volatility of potential output, a decline in the volatility of the output gap, or a lower correlation between those two variables (or a combination of any of those factors).

To the extent that potential output is independent of policy (or, at least, of the sort of stabilization policies we are interested in), the latter can influence the volatility of output growth only by inducing changes in $\tilde{s}$ and/or ρ. Furthermore, and given our normative interpretation of potential output, only changes in policy that bring about a reduction in the volatility of the output gap could be viewed as a policy improvement.

In order to shed some light on some of the welfare and policy interpretations of the changes in the U.S. business cycle, one would think it might be useful to extend the empirical analysis of SW to each of the two components of GDP. That exercise faces, however, a basic problem: neither potential output nor the output gap is a theory-free variable—certainly, neither is readily observable in the absence of further assumptions.

In order to illustrate how some of the conclusions may depend on one's view of potential output, let me consider two alternative decompositions.

2.1 A TRADITIONAL DECOMPOSITION

The first decomposition, which I will refer to as *traditional*, relies on the Congressional Budget Office (CBO) estimate of potential output, which is itself based on a smooth estimate of the NAIRU. The standard deviations of the quarterly time series for $\Delta\bar{y}_t$ and $\Delta\tilde{y}_t$ constructed on the basis of that decomposition are reported in the panel of Table 1 labeled CBO. In addition to statistics for the full sample period (1959:I–2001:III), the table also reports the corresponding values for two subperiods: 59:I–83:IV (under the heading "Early") and 84:I–01:III (under "Late"), as well as their ratio, their absolute difference, and the contribution of each to the observed decline in the volatility of output growth (all in percentage terms). As a reference, similar statistics are reported for Δy_t in the top row of the table. The choice of break date is motivated by some of the findings in SW and other related papers.

The results of that analysis make clear that both components of output growth have experienced a volatility decline in the second half of the

Table 1 OUTPUT DECOMPOSITIONS AND CHANGES IN VOLATILITY

| | Standard deviation (%) | | | | | |
Quantity	Full	Early	Late	Ratio	Change	Contribution
Δy_t	1.22	1.48	0.72	0.49	−0.76	
CBO:						
$\Delta \bar{y}_t$	0.42	0.48	0.28	0.59	−0.20	22.0%
$\Delta \tilde{y}_t$	0.88	1.06	0.54	0.51	−0.52	65.5%
NK:						
$\Delta \bar{y}_t$	1.01	1.18	0.68	0.58	−0.50	50.3%
$\Delta \tilde{y}_t$	0.75	0.86	0.53	0.62	−0.33	23.0%

postwar period, with volatility ratios of an order of magnitude similar to those found in SW. We notice, however, that given that the traditional decomposition attributes, on average, a much larger volatility to the output-gap component, the contribution of the latter to the absolute decline in the volatility of GDP growth is almost three times that of potential output.

2.2 A NEW KEYNESIAN DECOMPOSITION

The second decomposition analyzed is one consistent with a simple version of an optimizing new Keynesian (NK) model. Following some recent work with coauthors Mark Gertler and David López-Salido,[1] I consider the measure of aggregate inefficiency

$$gap_t = mrs_t - mpn_t$$

where mrs_t denotes the (log) marginal rate of substitution, and mpn_t is the (log) marginal product of labor. For simplicity I assume the following parametrization (consistent with standard specifications of preferences and technology):

$$mrs_t = \sigma c_t + \varphi n_t,$$

$$mpn_t = y_t - n_t,$$

where c_t denotes (log) consumption and n_t (log) hours, while σ and φ respectively denote the elasticities of the marginal utility of consumption and the marginal disutility of labor. Next, let us define *potential* output as

1. Galí, Gertler, and López-Salido (2001).

the level of output that would prevail in equilibrium if markups remained constant at their steady-state levels (e.g., in the absence of wage and price rigidities, and under the assumption of constant desired markups).[2] In that context, and under a few auxiliary assumptions,[3] the following relationship obtains (up to an additive constant):

$$\tilde{y}_t = \frac{\text{gap}_t}{\sigma + \varphi}.$$

Thus, it is straightforward to use the previous relationship to construct a time series for $\Delta \tilde{y}_t$ and (as a residual) $\Delta \bar{y}_t$, conditional on a calibration of σ and φ. In what follows I assume $\sigma = 1$ and $\varphi = 5$, which corresponds to the baseline calibration in Galí, Gertler, and López-Salido (2001). The bottom panel (labeled NK) in Table 1 reports standard deviations of each component based on the decomposition just described, together with statistics summarizing its evolution across the two periods.

As was the case under a traditional decomposition, both components of output growth appear to have experienced a substantial volatility decline. However, the relative contribution of each component to the observed decline in output-growth volatility is now significantly different from the previous case: the greater stability of potential output now accounts for almost two-thirds of that volatility decline, the role left for the output gap being smaller (though far from negligible).

The previous analysis illustrates the extent to which the interpretation that we may want to give to the evidence of a decline in output volatility cannot be model-free. Instead, it will depend critically on one's views regarding how potential output is determined. Thus, by stressing the importance of changes in output-gap volatility, the traditional decomposition allows (at least potentially) for a strong role of policy as a factor behind the milder cycle. By way of contrast, the evidence based on the NK decomposition appears to be easier to reconcile with an interpretation that stresses a reduction in the size of nonpolicy shocks experienced by the U.S. economy (while still leaving some room for a significant policy role).

3. Predictable vs. Unpredictable Components

One of the most interesting exercises in SW's paper is the analysis, in a multivariate framework, of the contribution to the decline in GDP volatility of the predictable and unpredictable components of several macro

2. That definition is consistent, e.g., with the framework of Erceg, Henderson, and Levin (2000), *Journal of Monetary Economics*, October, 281–313.
3. Basically all that is needed is that both labor productivity and the savings ratio be exogenous.

time series. SW conclude that changes in the unpredictable component (reflected in the variance–covariance matrix Σ of reduced-form VAR innovations) seem to have played a dominant role. In a structural VAR framework, however, changes in Σ must be caused by changes in the variance–covariance matrix of *structural* shocks, and/or changes in the matrix of contemporaneous relationships among the different variables. That observation raises an interesting question, which is briefly addressed in Blanchard and Simon (2001), but not in SW's paper: if we agree that monetary policy affects aggregate demand and output only with a lag (an assumption often incorporated in structural VARs), is it possible to reconcile the dominant role of the unpredictable component detected by SW with the policy-improvement hypothesis (e.g., a more aggressive Taylor rule)?

In my opinion that question can only be addressed using an explicit structural model with an embedded policy rule of the sort used by SW in the last section of their paper. The SW model, however, may not be suitable to address the question posed above, since it does not incorporate any policy transmission lags. Perhaps a more realistic model incorporating those lags [like those of Rotemberg and Woodford (1999), or Christiano, Eichenbaum, and Evans (2001)] could be used in future research to reexamine the role of policy, in light of SW's evidence pointing to a dominant role of the unpredictable component as an immediate factor behind the changing volatility of U.S. GDP growth.

4. The Cross-Country Dimension

SW's paper, as well as much of the related literature, studies the phenomenon of changes in the business cycle from a time-series perspective. But measures of macroeconomic volatility appear to vary across countries no less than they vary over time. Can we learn anything from the cross-country evidence regarding the sources of the observed changes (over time) in the U.S. business cycle? Here I just want to point to some evidence reported by Acemoglu and Zilibotti (1997), and whose possible connection with the issue at hand is, to say the least, intriguing. They provide rather strong evidence of a negative relationship across countries between their level of development (measured by per capita GDP) and their cyclical volatility (measured by the standard deviation of GDP growth).[4] Fatás

---

4. Acemoglu and Zilibotti develop a model that explains their evidence as the result of the insufficient diversification of productive activities resulting from project indivisibilities, which is only overcome as an economy develops (possibly thanks to a sequence of favorable shocks). Kraay and Ventura (2001) provide an alternative explanation based on the patterns of specialization during the process of development of an economy. While both stories may help explain the cross-sectional evidence, neither mechanism seems a plausible candidate to explain the taming of the U.S. business cycle over the postwar period.

and Mihov (2001) show, using data for OECD countries and U.S. states, that the negative correlation between income levels and output volatility mentioned above does not go away once they control for variables that are likely to be correlated with both (e.g., the size of government).

To what extent are the two phenomena related? The pattern of variations in the share of services in GDP, across countries and over time, would have seemed a good candidate to reconcile the two dimensions of the evidence, but SW provide a simple, unambiguous rejection of that hypothesis. Similarly, some of the candidate explanations proposed for the U.S. time-series evidence (e.g., policy improvement) do not seem particularly plausible explanations of the cross-country evidence. As macroeconomists we can only hope that a successful explanation is found that can account for both dimensions of the phenomena.

REFERENCES

Acemoglu, D., and F. Zilibotti. (1997). Was Prometheus unbound by chance? Risk, diversification, and growth. *Journal of Political Economy* 105(4):709–751.
Blanchard, O., and J. Simon. (2001). The long and large decline in U.S. output volatility. *Brookings Papers on Economic Activity* 1:135–164.
Christiano, L. J., M. Eichenbaum, and C. L. Evans. (2001). Nominal rigidities and the dynamic effects of a shock to monetary policy. Northwestern University. Mimeo.
Erceg, C., D. Henderson, and A. Levin. (2000). Optimal monetary policy with staggered wage and price contracts. *Journal of Monetary Economics* 46(2):281–313.
Fatás, A., and I. Mihov. (2001). Government size and automatic stabilizers: International and intranational evidence. *Journal of International Economics* 55:3–28.
Galí, J., M. Gertler, and D. López-Salido. (2001). Markups, gaps, and the welfare cost of business fluctuations. CEPR Working Paper 3212.
Kraay, A., and J. Ventura. (2001). Comparative advantage and the cross-section of business cycles. Cambridge, MA: National Bureau of Economic Research. NBER Working Paper 8104.
Rotemberg, J., and M. Woodford. (1999). Interest rate rules in an estimated sticky price model. In *Monetary Policy Rules*, J. B. Taylor (ed.). University of Chicago Press.

Comment

ROBERT E. HALL
Stanford University and National Bureau of Economic Research

Figure 1 displays the type of evidence considered in this paper and shows why the conclusion is compelling. The figure shows the volatility of real GDP, measured as the squared deviation of the one-year growth rate from its average value. Volatility by this measure ended discontinuously in 1984, reappearing only in the recessions of 1990 and 2001. The econometric analy-

Figure 1 VOLATILITY OF REAL GDP OVER ONE-YEAR INTERVALS

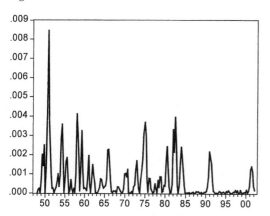

The plot shows the squared values of the one-year change in log of real GDP less its mean, squared.

sis in the paper supports the conclusion of the naked eye. The paper also shows that the decline occurred in many measures and not just in real GDP.

The authors stick relentlessly to a single definition of volatility, namely the one used in Figure 1, the variance of one-year rates of change. Although it is useful to have a standard measure to compare over time periods and across variables, concentration on one-year changes does not tell the whole story of volatility by any means. The persistence of random movements matters. One-year changes look the same for a series subject to white-noise disturbances around a predictable mean as they do for a series that evolves as a random walk. But there is much more uncertainty in the longer run about a random walk. Longer differences are a good way to get at this issue. Figure 2 shows the volatility of five-year rates of change of real GDP. In this plot, the first half of the 1990s was a period of high volatility, as growth from the late 1980s was below par. Notice that recessions—a dominant source of volatility in one-year rates—are not important for five-year rates. The recession years 1975, 1990, and 2001 contribute spikes to Figure 1 but are troughs of volatility in Figure 2. The evidence for diminished volatility is weaker in five-year rates of change. In fact, a better summary would be that the economy is hit by episodes of volatility in five-year rates—mostly from periods of high or low growth— against a background of stability.

Figure 3 shows that the volatility of ten-year changes in real GDP tells yet another story. There were two huge spikes—high growth from the late 1950s to the late 1960s, and low growth from the early 1970s to the early 1980s. At other times, ten-year growth rates have remained at normal levels. In particular, ten-year growth has been normal since 1984, so

Figure 2 VOLATILITY OF REAL GDP OVER FIVE-YEAR INTERVALS

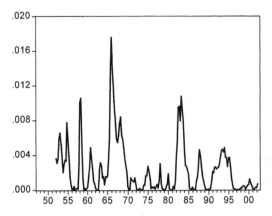

The plot shows the squared values of the five-year change in log of real GDP less its mean, squared.

the hypothesis of a break in 1984 receives more support from ten-year changes than from five-year changes.

One of the conclusions of the paper is that changes in persistence parameters have been an unimportant source of changes in volatility. I believe that this conclusion is special to the one-year framework. Consider the following example, stripped to the basics of the issue. A series—say log real GDP—evolves according to an AR(1) process:

$$y_t = \rho y_t - 1 + \varepsilon_t.$$

Figure 3 VOLATILITY OF REAL GDP OVER TEN-YEAR INTERVALS

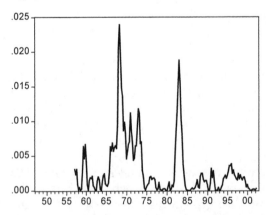

The plot shows the squared values of the ten-year change in log of real GDP less its mean, squared.

The variance of the kth difference is

$$V(y_t - y_{t-k}) = 2 \frac{1 + \rho + \cdots + \rho^{k-1}}{1 + \rho} \sigma^2.$$

Notice that this confirms my earlier statement about the role of persistence in determining the relation between the length of the difference and volatility. If a series is white noise ($\rho = 0$), the variance is $2\sigma^2$ for differences of any length. If a series is a random walk, ($\rho = 1$), the variance is $k\sigma^2$, rising in proportion to the length of the difference.

Stock and Watson are concerned about how changes in the persistence parameter—here ρ—affect volatility, measured as the variance of the difference. Consider the derivative of the variance with respect to ρ, evaluated at $\rho = 1$ (a relevant point, because real GDP and most other series are close to random walks):

$$\frac{dV}{d\rho} = \frac{k(k-2)}{2} \sigma^2.$$

Figure 4 DERIVATIVE OF VOLATILITY WITH RESPECT TO THE
       PERSISTENCE PARAMETER

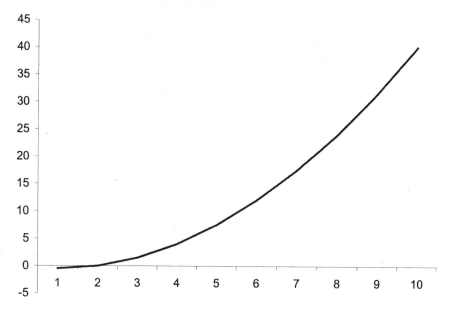

The derivative is *negative* for one-year differences, zero for two-year, and then rises to high positive levels for longer differences. Figure 4 shows the relation.

Thus the finding that changes in persistence parameters have made little contribution to changing volatility is almost automatic for short differences. But the conclusion could be completely different for longer differences. Again, one-year differences tell an incomplete story.

Within the one-year-difference framework, Stock and Watson make many important contributions. In particular, they cast doubt on a number of popular and plausible explanations: that the economy is more stable because its more stable sectors are growing faster, because modern information technology has tamed the inventory cycle, and because financial markets have fewer frictions. They give moderate support to the view that monetary policy is less a generator of shocks and more a tool for moderating other shocks. But the primary conclusion is that key macro variables such as real GDP are more stable because the economy suffers smaller outside shocks now than it did before 1984.

Discussion

Bob Gordon questioned the metric of volatility used by the authors. He suggested using a gap-oriented metric such as the 20-quarter moving average of the absolute value of the GDP gap, following Blanchard and Simon. He noted that using this metric, volatility does not appear to be a step function, but looks more like there was a gradual decline. He took issue with what he saw as a tendency in the paper to look at shocks one at a time, rather than thinking about the interaction of many shocks. As an example, he noted that Volcker's actions were a response to the oil shocks of the 1970s.

On a related point, Mark Gertler suggested that standard linear methods might be biased in favor of finding shifts in volatility instead of regime shifts. He noted that a major difference between the early part of the sample and the later part is that there were a lot of major recessions in the first half, and very few in the second half. He pointed out that if the business cycle is asymmetric in that contractions are sharper than expansions, this might show up as a change in volatility rather than a shift in the propagation mechanism. As an example, he suggested that the recession of 1980–1982 could be plausibly attributed to the Volcker disinflation rather than to bad shocks. On the recession of 1974–1975 he noted that although the consensus view is that it was due to shocks, a recent paper by Robert Barsky has argued otherwise. He was interested to see whether as a general rule the big recessions can be explained by shocks, and if so, what are the shocks. He also commented that any explanation of the reduction in output volatility must be consistent with the reduction in the volatility of inflation.

Jonathan Parker suggested that it might be interesting to see what survey forecast data have to say about reduced volatility. He pointed out that if economic forecasts lag, it might give a sense that the reduction in volatility described in the paper was a surprise. In this case, it could be that a VAR would do a better job of fitting the data than actual expectations over the period of the decline in volatility.

Justin Wolfers suggested a link between Galí and Hall's evidence on the reduction in the volatility of potential output and the output gap, and the debate about the Phillips curve in the session on Nancy Stokey's paper. He said that in order for the Phillips curve to describe the inflation path of the 1990s, it is necessary to have enormous volatility in the natural rate of unemployment which cannot be squared with the observed reduction in volatility. He also remarked that since the sample size used to generate sectoral employment data triples over the period in question, it might be safer to base decisions on sectoral differences on output shares rather than employment shares.

Fabrizio Perri remarked that it might be particularly useful to look at international data when trying to attribute the reduction in volatility to changes in shocks or policy. He noted that there has also been a big decline in volatility in Europe. On this issue, Ken Rogoff mentioned that economists working at the IMF have produced evidence of a decline in the volatility of output and employment across the OECD. However, he noted that the volatility of stock prices has clearly not fallen. He speculated that this could imply that improvements in measurement over time are driving some of the observed reduction in volatility of GDP and employment.

Jean Boivin remarked that the IS curve in the structural model used to evaluate the contribution of policy changes is very reduced-form. He worried that expectations of monetary policy are not sufficiently controlled for, leaving open the possibility that changes in monetary policy could contaminate the estimates of changes in volatility.

In summing up, Mark Watson welcomed the comments of Bob Hall and Bob Gordon on the question of regime break vs. slow decline in volatility. Ideally, he said, the authors would have liked to estimate linear models such as VARs, allowing for stochastic volatility in the shocks and also drift in the regression coefficients. But this is hard to do, and the regime-break approach was chosen for parsimony. He also welcomed Hall's approach of comparing different frequencies of the spectrum in his discussion. He remarked that Ahmed, Levin, and Wilson look at the spectrum of GDP before and after 1984 and find that the entire spectrum shifts down. He noted that this suggests that the finding of declining volatility is robust to which frequency of the spectrum is looked at. Watson also welcomed Jordi Galí's comments on the output gap and potential output as fundamentally important.

On the discussion of regime break vs. slow decline in volatility, Jim Stock remarked that the test for the existence of a break also has power against slowly changing processes, although the dating of the break is less robust. On Ken Rogoff's point on stock price volatility, he suggested that the most important change in measurement in the sample period is a change in accounting rules, which implies that the measurement issues are more likely to be on the stock-price side.

Charles Engel
UNIVERSITY OF WISCONSIN AND NBER

Expenditure Switching and Exchange-Rate Policy

1. Introduction

Exchange-rate flexibility, it has been argued, is useful because it facilitates relative price adjustment among countries. Currency depreciation is a quick and painless way to lower domestic prices relative to foreign prices. Much attention has been paid recently to the benefits of exchange-rate stability in emerging economies. That literature has focused on the potential for greater monetary and financial stability from either fixing exchange rates or taking more extreme measures such as adopting a currency board or dollarizing. But that analysis is not directly applicable to the choices facing many advanced countries—such as the decision to adopt the euro for some European countries. These countries uniformly have stable monetary policies (at least as stable as the policy conducted by the European Central Bank) and have deep, well-regulated financial markets. The economic benefit of adopting the euro lies in the increased efficiency of transactions and the elimination of uninsurable exchange-rate risk. On the other hand, a country adopting the euro cedes its monetary policy to the European Central Bank, and no longer has the option of using monetary policy to respond to local conditions. Furthermore, adopting the euro eliminates one possible avenue for adjustment between countries—the relative price changes induced by exchange-rate movements. It is this latter effect that is the focus of this study.

Recent evidence has found that consumer prices in rich countries are

The National Science Foundation has supported this research through a grant to the University of Wisconsin–Madison. I thank the discussants, Karen Lewis and Pierre Olivier Gourinchas, as well as Mick Devereux and Ken West, for helpful comments, and Akito Matsumoto and Shiu-Sheng Chen for excellent research assistance.

not much affected by nominal exchange-rate changes in the short run.[1] This finding may imply that nominal-exchange-rate changes do not play much of a role in changing relative prices of goods. If consumer prices are not responsive to exchange rates, then a depreciation of the home currency, for example, does not increase much the price that consumers pay for imported goods. However, there are other interpretations of the evidence on exchange rates and consumer prices. For example, there might be important relative price effects but not for final consumer goods. One possibility is that intermediate firms substitute between domestic and foreign goods according to relative price changes, but set prices for consumers in a way that is unresponsive to exchange-rate changes.

The extent to which exchange rates alter relative prices may be important for determining the desirability of exchange-rate flexibility among advanced nations. Milton Friedman (1953), an early advocate of flexible exchange rates, argued that one advantage of floating rates is that they could allow rapid change in relative prices between countries (p. 162):

> A rise in the exchange rate . . . makes foreign goods cheaper in terms of domestic currency, even though their prices are unchanged in terms of their own currency, and domestic goods more expensive in terms of foreign currency, even though their prices are unchanged in terms of domestic currency. This tends to increase imports [and] reduce exports.

This passage makes two assumptions: that goods prices are unchanged in the currency of the producer of the good, and that there is significant passthrough of the exchange-rate change to the buyer of the good. On the nominal-price stickiness, Friedman argues that the choice of exchange-rate regime would matter little if nominal goods prices adjusted quickly to shocks (p. 165):

> If internal prices were as flexible as exchange rates, it would make little economic difference whether adjustments were brought about by changes in exchange rates or by equivalent changes in internal prices. But this condition is clearly not fulfilled. . . . At least in the modern world, internal prices are highly inflexible.

In assessing this relative-price effect and its significance for the choice of exchange-rate regime, Friedman is certainly correct to emphasize the

---

1. I have been the perpetrator of some of this literature: for example, Engel (1993, 1999) and Engel and Rogers (1996, 2001). Other works include Rogers and Jenkins (1995), Obstfeld and Taylor (1997), Parsley and Wei (2001a, 2001b), and Crucini, Telmer, and Zachariadis (2001). Mussa's (1986) classic paper stimulated much of this research.

importance of nominal-goods-price stickiness. As Buiter (1999) has force-fully emphasized, the decision to join a monetary union, or the choice of an exchange-rate regime, is a monetary issue. Relative-price behavior is usually independent of monetary regime in a world of perfect goods-price flexibility. The choice of monetary regime in this case only matters for short-run adjustment problems—the period during which nominal prices are adjusting.

The pioneering work of Obstfeld and Rogoff (1995, 1998, 2000a) has assumed that nominal prices are fixed in the producers' currencies, so that prices for consumers change one for one in the short run with changes in the nominal exchange rate. This is exactly the assumption of Friedman. I shall call this the PCP (for "producer-currency pricing") model. The Obstfeld–Rogoff (hereinafter, OR) models offer a sound analytical foundation for the claim that flexibility of exchange rates is desirable in this setting.[2] They derive three important results: (1) Exchange-rate flexibility achieves relative-price adjustment under PCP pricing. Indeed, in their models, flexible exchange rates are a perfect substitute for flexible nominal prices. That is, the flexible nominal-price allocations are achieved with PCP pricing but flexible exchange rates. (2) The policy that achieves the flexible price allocation is a constrained Pareto optimum. The monetary authorities can do no better. (3) This optimal policy is completely self-oriented. No policy coordination across countries is required or desirable. In this sense, perfectly flexible exchange rates are optimal.

The key role of nominal-exchange-rate flexibility in these models is that it allows for *expenditure switching*. That is, in the presence of real shocks that are specific to one country (productivity shocks, labor supply shocks, government spending shocks, etc.), nominal-exchange-rate changes allow adjustment of relative prices of goods across countries. These changes in relative prices can replicate the changes in relative prices that occur in flexible-price economies. For example, a country that experiences a productivity increase should experience a decline in the price of its output that induces a switch in expenditures toward the domestic product. In the PCP framework, even though nominal prices are sticky in the producers' currencies, this relative-price decline can be accomplished by nominal currency depreciation.

A number of recent papers [Betts and Devereux (1996, 2000), Chari, Kehoe, and McGrattan (2000), and others] have examined OR-style models in which nominal prices are set in advance in the currency of consumers. In that case, nominal-exchange-rate changes do not, in the short run, change any prices—nominal or real—faced by consumers. I shall call this

---

2. See Lane (2001) for an excellent general survey of the work stimulated by OR.

the LCP (for "local-currency pricing") model. Devereux and Engel (2001) have examined monetary policy in this setting, and have concluded that there is no case for nominal-exchange-rate flexibility—indeed, fixed exchange rates are preferred.

The size of the expenditure-switching effect is important in international macroeconomics not only for how it might influence optimal monetary policy. The literature, dating back to Mundell (1968) and earlier,[3] has emphasized the expenditure-switching role of nominal-exchange-rate changes in transmitting business-cycle fluctuations between countries. On the other hand, Krugman (1989) has argued that nominal-exchange-rate volatility might be accentuated if the expenditure-switching effect is small. The smaller the effect of exchange-rate changes on relative prices, and hence on relative demands, the larger the exchange-rate change that is required to reach equilibrium.[4]

Sections 2, 3, 4, and 5 of this paper lay out the framework of the new open-economy macroeconomics. I discuss why floating exchange rates are desirable under PCP, but fixed exchange rates may be optimal under LCP. Empirical evidence supports the notion that consumer prices are not very responsive in the short run to nominal-exchange-rate changes. Section 6 reviews some of that empirical evidence, and adds some new supporting evidence.

But the apparent small response of consumer prices to exchange-rate changes in the short run does not necessarily imply that nominal prices are sticky in consumers' currencies, or that the expenditure-switching effect is small. In OR (2000b), transportation costs and distribution costs increase the cost of imported goods, and serve to segment national markets. Even if imported goods are nearly perfect substitutes for domestically produced goods, they may not be consumed in great quantity because their cost is higher. In that case, an exchange-rate change will have only a small effect on the consumer price index.

A related approach observes that the actual physical good is only a small part of what the consumer buys. The consumer also pays for the nontraded marketing, distribution, and retailing services that bring the good to the buyer. Perhaps these costs are quite large, and dominate the cost of the physical good. If so, the influence of exchange-rate changes on real allocations is likely to be small, since the exchange-rate change only affects a small part of the cost of the good cum service purchased by the consumer. This is the approach taken by McCallum and Nelson (2000).

3. See Obstfeld (2001) for a survey of pre-Mundellian literature.
4. Devereux and Engel (2002) explore this argument and its limitations in the context of new open-economy macro models.

In both of these models, nominal consumer prices of imported goods are not sticky. But some new evidence will be presented in Sections 7 and 8 that suggests these models are, at best, only a small part of the explanation for the lack of responsiveness of consumer prices to exchange-rate changes. It seems likely that there is a significant degree of nominal-consumer-price stickiness. However, sticky consumer prices in themselves do not necessarily rule out an important expenditure-switching effect.

Obstfeld (2001) and Devereux, Engel, and Tille (1999) model imported goods as intermediates in the production of final consumer goods. In Obstfeld, there are domestic substitutes for the import, while in Devereux, Engel, and Tille there are not. When there are substitutes, the importer might switch between the imported intermediate and the locally produced alternative when the exchange rate changes. Obstfeld argues that in this type of economy, there may indeed be a significant expenditure-switching effect. It is not consumers who switch between imports and locally produced goods, but rather local producers who combine intermediate goods to make the final consumer product. It is both the degree of passthrough and the amount of substitutability that determine the strength of the expenditure-switching effect. Section 9 explores these models, and Section 10 sets out some directions for future research.

2. Models of Exchange Rates and Relative Prices

In this and the next three sections, I examine some simple new-open-economy macroeconomic models. These models are fully integrated equilibrium models in which households and firms make optimal choices, but in which some nominal prices are not completely responsive to shocks.

There are two countries in the general model. I will assume that there is a single period, though most of the results I discuss carry over to a multiperiod framework. I assume households in the home country maximize

$$U = \frac{1}{1-\rho} C^{1-\rho} + \chi \ln\left(\frac{M^D}{P}\right) - \psi L.$$

C is a consumption aggregate. Households consume goods produced in the home country and in the foreign country. Assume preferences are homothetic (so consumption aggregates and price indexes are defined.)

Real balances, M^D/P, appear in the utility function, where P is the optimal price index. Households get disutility from work, L.

Foreign households are assumed to have similar utility functions:

$$U^* = \frac{1}{1-\rho} C^{*1-\rho} + \chi \ln\left(\frac{M^{D*}}{P^*}\right) - \psi L^*.$$

Starred (*) variables are the foreign counterparts to the home-country variables.

Money is supplied exogenously through transfers. In equilibrium we have money supply equals money demand in each country $M = M^D$ and $M^* = M^{D*}$. The money supplies are random (as are productivity shocks to be introduced shortly.)

I will assume there are financial markets of the type discussed in Devereux and Engel (2001). Specifically, there are nominal bonds, traded prior to the realization of the state, that have payoffs specific to each possible state of the world. Most of the models we consider have home and foreign consumers facing different prices for the same good on spot markets. That is, the markets are segmented. We assume that it is impossible to make state-contingent trades that allow payoffs in physical goods, as that would allow households to get around paying the price set in their market. Instead, payoffs are specified in nominal terms. Optimal contracts ensure that the marginal utility from an additional unit of currency is proportional between home and foreign consumers in all states (where I have assumed the constant of proportionality is 1):

$$\frac{C^{-\rho}}{P} = \frac{C^{*-\rho}}{SP^*}.$$

S is the nominal exchange rate, expressed as the home-currency price of foreign currency.

Even though there is a nominal bond traded for each state of the world, markets are not complete, because the goods markets are segmented nationally. If the same good sells for different prices in different markets, households cannot arbitrage the goods market. As a result, risk sharing is not perfect unless purchasing-power parity (PPP) holds ($P = SP^*$).

The assumption that so many nominal assets are traded is, of course, unrealistic. It is a useful benchmark, and here it allows us to arrive at a simple flexible model that can be used to analyze relative-price effects in general equilibrium. We can reproduce Friedman's claim that nominal-exchange-rate flexibility allows desirable relative price adjustments to occur rapidly under his assumption of nominal prices fixed in producer's currencies, but we can also analyze other assumptions about how prices are set.

The following equilibrium conditions emerge using the first-order conditions for the household optimization problem:

$$M = \chi PC^\rho, \qquad M^* = \chi P^* C^{*\rho},$$
$$W = \psi PC^\rho, \qquad W^* = \psi P^* C^{*\rho}.$$

Here, W and W^* are the home and foreign wage, respectively.

This framework, while making very specific assumptions about preferences, has the advantage that it is easy to analyze under a variety of assumptions about goods pricing and about preferences over goods. We can derive a solution for the nominal exchange rate that does not depend on any assumptions about the production side of the economy or about how nominal prices are set, without making any further assumptions about consumption utility:

$$S = \frac{M}{M^*}.$$

Now we turn to the production side of the economy. There are a large number of goods produced in each country, each by a monopolist. We will initially consider models in which output for each firm i is produced using only a labor input: $Y_i = \eta L_i$ and $Y_i^* = \eta^* L_i^*$.[5] Here η (η^*) is a productivity shock that is common to all home (foreign) firms. We will consider a variety of possible assumptions about how prices are set. Prices may be flexible—that is, set with full information about the state. Or, in the new open-economy models, firms must set nominal prices in some currency prior to knowledge about the state.

3. Flexible Nominal Prices

It is helpful first to examine some of the properties of this model under completely flexible nominal prices. We shall assume home and foreign households have identical CES preferences over home and foreign aggregates. Each of these aggregates is in turn a CES function over the individual goods produced in the home and the foreign country, respectively. Firms face constant-elasticity demand curves, and therefore set prices as a constant markup over unit costs. We allow firms to discriminate across home and foreign markets. But under our assumptions about preferences

---

5. One of the models we examine later will have an iceberg transportation cost for shipping goods overseas. We will also consider models in which intermediate goods are used as inputs into final-goods production.

and about financial markets, when PPP holds (under flexible prices or under PCP), firms choose the same price for home and foreign consumers.

Aggregating across all home firms, we get

$$P_H = \mu W / \eta,$$

where P_H is the home currency price of home goods, and $\mu > 1$ is the markup. We have also $P_H = SP_H^*$, where P_H^* is the foreign-currency price of home goods. Likewise,

$$P_F^* = \mu W^* / \eta^*,$$

and $P_F = SP_F^*$.

We can also derive these equations for nominal wages in equilibrium:

$$W = \frac{\Psi}{\chi} M, \qquad W^* = \frac{\Psi}{\chi} M^*.$$

It follows from the equilibrium conditions that

$$\frac{P_H}{P_F} = \frac{P_H^*}{P_F^*} = \frac{\eta^*}{\eta}.$$

The relative price of home goods falls when there is an increase in η. When productivity in home firms increases, the cost per unit of home goods declines. Those costs savings are passed on to consumers in the form of lower prices.

I will not undertake a formal welfare analysis of the models presented here. Instead, I will focus on what turns out to be a critical aspect of the welfare analysis: the extent to which an exchange-rate regime is beneficial in achieving the adjustment of the price of home goods relative to foreign goods. Under the Friedman framework, exchange-rate flexibility allows immediate adjustment of that relative price in response to real shocks. But, as we shall see, that finding is a special case that depends critically on how Friedman assumes nominal goods prices are set.

4. Sticky Nominal Prices: PCP Case

Now consider the model when firms must set nominal prices in advance. In the one-period framework here, this means that prices are set in advance of knowledge of the preference shocks and money-supply realizations. Perhaps there are menu costs or some other sorts of costs that make it more profitable to set a non-state-contingent nominal price. First we take up the case in which firms set prices in their own currencies. That is, home firms set prices in the home currency, whether for sale to home or foreign households. We call this the PCP case. The law of one price holds for goods sold at home and in the foreign country, because, as we noted above, under our assumptions about preferences and financial markets, firms do not price-discriminate.

It follows that

$$\frac{P_H}{P_F} = \frac{P_H^*}{P_F^*} = \frac{P_H}{SP_F^*}.$$

Under the PCP assumption, both P_H and P_F^* are fixed ex ante and do not respond to shocks to demand or money supply. Define $\kappa \equiv P_H/P_F^*$. Because these nominal prices are set in advance of the realization of the state, κ does not depend on the outcomes of the random variables. Then the relative price of home to foreign goods varies inversely with the exchange rate:

$$\frac{P_H}{P_F} = \frac{\kappa}{S}.$$

Substituting in the expression for the equilibrium exchange rate, we get, under PCP pricing,

$$\frac{P_H}{P_F} = \kappa\frac{M^*}{M}.$$

Here we can see the gist of Friedman's argument for flexible exchange rates. If the exchange rate were fixed, there would be no channel to translate real demand shocks into a relative-price change. That is, if the exchange rate were held constant at a value of $\bar{S}$, the relative price of home to foreign goods would not depend on the shocks that hit the economy:

$$\frac{P_H}{P_F} = \frac{\kappa}{\bar{S}}.$$

But with exchange-rate flexibility and the correct monetary policy, the real productivity shocks can be translated precisely into the same relative-price effect that occurs under flexible prices. With the monetary policy rules $M = (\chi\eta/\psi\mu)P_H$ and $M^* = (\chi\eta^*/\psi\mu)P_F^*$, the relative price will equal exactly its value under flexible prices:

$$\frac{P_H}{P_F} = \frac{P_H^*}{P_F^*} = \frac{\eta^*}{\eta}.$$

In fact, allocations are identical under PCP with these monetary rules, and under flexible prices. That is very much in accord with Friedman's intuition: flexible exchange rates are a perfect substitute for flexible goods prices in the presence of real shocks.

Moreover, in the models of OR (1998, 2000a), mimicking the flexible price allocation is the constrained globally efficient monetary policy. While the flexible-price equilibrium itself is not Pareto-efficient (because of the monopoly distortions), optimal monetary policy can do no better than to replicate the flexible-price allocation.

The monetary policy I set out above is not only the policy that would be set by a global central planner. It is, as OR (2000a) show, the policy that self-interested national economic planners would follow. That is, there is no gain to international monetary coordination. Central banks following policies that maximize their own country's welfare can achieve the constrained globally efficient outcome. Thus, a system in which central bankers do not cooperate at all and allow the exchange rate to float freely is optimal, as Friedman claimed.[6]

This model, however, has implications that seem counterfactual: that exchange-rate changes are passed through one for one into consumer prices, and that the law of one price holds for all goods. It is this characteristic of the model that has led some researchers to consider the local-currency pricing version of the sticky-nominal-price model.

5. Sticky Prices: LCP Case

An alternative model for price setting is that firms set prices in the currency of consumers of the product. That is, when a home firm sells in the home market, it sets prices in the home currency, but for sales to the foreign market it sets prices in the foreign currency. We call this the LCP (for "local-currency pricing") case.

It follows immediately in this case that a flexible nominal exchange rate cannot achieve the optimal relative-price adjustment. P_h and P_f are both

6. OR (1998, 2000a) have delicate sets of assumptions on preferences and market structure that ensure that markets are actually complete. But OR (2001) show that these basic conclusions are, to first order, robust to market incompleteness.

set in the domestic currency and do not respond to contemporaneous shocks. We cannot replicate the flexible-price solution $P_H/P_F = P_H^*/P_F^* = \eta^*/\eta$ with flexible exchange rates, no matter what the monetary policy. In fact, Devereux and Engel (2001) go further and demonstrate that the optimal monetary policy in this case delivers fixed exchange rates.[7] Or, put another way, if the foreign country is following optimal monetary policy while the home country is using the exchange rate as its policy instrument, the optimal exchange-rate policy is to fix.

There is a simple way to understand the striking difference in optimal policy in the PCP world vs. the LCP world. There are two types of deviations from efficiency which monetary policy might be able to rectify in a sticky-price world. One is that relative prices might not respond in the correct way to real shocks, so that we might not achieve $P_H/P_F = P_H^*/P_F^* = \eta^*/\eta$. In the absence of optimal relative-price changes, consumers do not receive the correct signals and do not alter their demand for goods in the appropriate way when real shocks hit. As a consequence, resources will not be allocated efficiently.

The other type of inefficiency comes because deviations from PPP lead to incomplete risk sharing. As noted above, with a complete set of nominal contingent claims traded, in equilibrium $C^{-\rho}/P = C^{*-\rho}/SP^*$. Asset markets do not deliver complete risk sharing unless PPP holds ($P = SP^*$).

When prices are set in producers' currencies (PCP), PPP does hold, so asset markets do deliver complete risk sharing. In that case, monetary policy can be devoted entirely to ensuring that relative prices respond in the appropriate way to real shocks. But, of course, exchange-rate flexibility is needed to deliver the relative-price response.

Under local-currency pricing, relative prices simply cannot change in the short run in response to real shocks. It is useless for monetary-policy makers to devote any effort to achieving an efficient relative-price response. But, under LCP pricing, both P and P^* are predetermined and not affected by real shocks. If the nominal exchange rate is fixed so that PPP holds ($S = P/P^*$), then asset markets will achieve complete risk sharing.

This model is designed to highlight the role of expenditure switching and deviations from the law of one price for determining optimal monetary policy. The conclusion that fixed exchange rates are optimal, though, arises from some special features of the model: identical preferences, all goods traded, and a nominal state-contingent bond traded for every state

---

7. Bacchetta and van Wincoop (2000) and Devereux and Engel (1998) also examine exchange-rate rules with local-currency pricing. However, those analyses do not examine the real shocks that are at the heart of the issues we discuss here.

of the world. Under these assumptions, it is optimal to target world out-put and, with fixed exchange rates, allow financial markets to share the risk that arises from idiosyncratic shocks.

More generally, there might be a trade-off between the objective of monetary independence and that of minimizing deviations from the law of one price. Suppose that in each economy there is a sector that produces nontraded goods, and there are productivity shocks arising in the non-traded sector. On the one hand, it might be desirable to use monetary policy in this case to target local shocks. But such independent monetary policy will lead to nominal-exchange-rate changes that imply deviations from the law of one price for traded goods. These deviations would in-duce idiosyncratic risk in traded goods consumption.

Corsetti and Pesenti (2001) develop a model of "partial" passthrough of exchange rates to final consumer prices. Ex ante, firms may pass through only a fraction λ (taken to be exogenous) of any exchange-rate change to consumer prices. The PCP model is one extreme, in which $\lambda = 1$, and the LCP is the other extreme, in which $\lambda = 0$. They examine optimal monetary policy and the optimal degree of exchange-rate flexibility in this framework. Since Corsetti and Pesenti assume goods are sold directly to consumers (as do OR, and Devereux and Engel), it seems as though the empirically relevant case is the one in which λ is nearly zero, since passthrough to consumer prices is very small in the short run.

Corsetti and Pesenti show in their model that optimal policy minimizes a function of the *output gap* and deviations from the law of one price. The output gap is "the distance between actual and equilibrium employment levels." It is not always the case that eliminating the output gap is the optimal feasible policy. Corsetti and Pesenti's theorem implies that policymakers can improve welfare by using monetary policy to help elim-inate deviations from the law of one price. Sometimes there is tension between that goal and the goal of eliminating the output gap.

6. Empirical Evidence on Deviations from the Law of One Price

The PCP model and the LCP model differ clearly in one empirical predic-tion. The PCP model predicts that the law of one price holds for consumer goods, while the LCP model predicts that it fails. Under the LCP model the (log) price of good i in the home country relative to the foreign coun-try, $p_i - s - p_i^*$, varies as the nominal exchange rate changes, while in the PCP model this relative price is unaffected by nominal-exchange-rate movements.

That the law of one price (which I shall abbreviate as LOOP in this and subsequent sections) fails for traded-goods prices is a well-established empirical fact. [See, for example, Isard (1977) and Kravis and Lipsey (1978). The recent pricing-to-market literature, surveyed by Goldberg and Knetter (1997), has documented the lack of full response of import prices to exchange-rate changes.] This literature has focused on import and export prices, not on the price of consumer goods. That distinction is important, as will become apparent in subsequent sections of this paper.

Some more recent work has focused on the failure of LOOP for consumer goods. That literature has documented not only that LOOP fails, but that its failure is large.

To say that the failure is "large" requires some metric for judging the size of the deviations from LOOP. One approach, in Engel (1993), was to compare the variance of deviations from LOOP [that is, $\text{Var}(\Delta(p_i - s - p_i^*))$, where Δ is the time difference] with the variance of relative price changes between goods within a single country [$\text{Var}(\Delta(p_i - p_j))$, where i and j are different products]. The idea is to understand what causes the observed large movements in real exchange rates between industrialized nations. One possibility is that real-exchange-rate movements are due largely to deviations from LOOP. But there are major competing theories that assume LOOP holds and attribute real-exchange-rate changes to relative-price changes among different goods. The most prominent of those theories posits that the real exchange rate changes between two countries as the price of nontraded goods relative to traded goods changes. So, if $p_N - p_T$ rises relative to $p_N^* - p_T^*$ [home-country (log) price of nontraded goods relative to traded goods rises relative to the foreign-country (log) relative price], the home-country price level will rise relative to the foreign-country level. That is, there will be a home real appreciation. Another, somewhat less prominent theory is that real exchange rates fluctuate because CPIs weight goods differently in different countries. Even if all goods are traded and LOOP holds for all goods, real exchange rates fluctuate as relative prices change. For example, if the French weight wine heavily in their CPI, then their CPI will rise relative to CPIs in other countries when the price of wine relative to other goods increases.

Engel (1993) compares $\text{Var}(\Delta(p_i - s - p_i^*))$ with $\text{Var}(\Delta(p_i - p_j))$ in some industrialized countries, looking at 1-, 3-, 6-, and 12-month horizons. For some measures, the consumer goods are fairly narrowly defined (potatoes, televisions, wine), although for some other measures the goods are quite aggregated (food, services, energy, rent). That paper simply tabulates $\text{Var}(\Delta(p_i - s - p_i^*))$ for all goods and countries, and $\text{Var}(\Delta(p_i - p_j))$ for all goods and countries, and compares their sizes. In general, the measures of $\text{Var}(\Delta(p_i - s - p_i^*))$ tend to be much larger than $\text{Var}(\Delta(p_i - p_j))$

at all horizons. The median value of $\text{Var}(\Delta(p_i - s - p_i^*))$ is about 6 or 7 times as large as the median value of $\text{Var}(\Delta(p_i - p_j))$ for all measures at all horizons.

Rogers and Jenkins (1995) extend this analysis, with a focus on U.S.–Canadian consumer prices. They confirm the large deviations from LOOP, and in addition find the deviations are very persistent.

Engel (1999) decomposes real-exchange-rate variation into a component attributable to deviations from LOOP and a component attributable to changes in the relative price of nontraded goods. Consider a price index for a country that is a weighted geometric average of traded- and non-traded-goods prices:

$$p_t = (1 - \alpha)p_t^T + \alpha p_t^N.$$

We can also write

$$p_t^* = (1 - \beta)p_t^{T*} + \beta p_t^{N*}.$$

Then the real exchange rate is given by

$$q_t = x_t + y_t, \tag{1}$$

where $q_t \equiv s_t + p_t^* - p_t$, $x_t \equiv s_t + p_t^{T*} - p_t^T$, and $y_t \equiv \beta(p_t^{N*} - p_t^{T*}) - \alpha(p_t^N - p_t^T)$.

The log of the real exchange rate is composed of two parts: the relative price of traded goods between the countries, x_t; and a component that is a weighted difference of the relative price of nontraded- to traded-goods prices in each country, y_t. Engel (1999) then decomposes the mean squared error of changes in U.S. real exchange rates into parts attributable to x_t and y_t (and a part attributed to their comovement, which is small) at different horizons. That study uses four separate measures of prices, and finds that the deviations from LOOP account for over 90% of movements in U.S. real exchange rates relative to almost all countries at all horizons for all measures.

Here I replicate and extend some of that analysis, using consumer-price data from the OECD Main Economic Indicators (available from Datastream). Data are monthly (from 1973:12 to 2001:1) on four components of the consumer price index: food, all commodities less food, rent, and all services less rent, for eleven OECD countries.[8] The first two goods are

---

8. The United States, Canada, Japan, France, Italy, Switzerland, Belgium, Norway, Spain, Denmark, and the Netherlands.

tradables, and the last two are nontradables. I construct price indexes for a consumer that has Cobb–Douglas preferences and weights these items with the same weights they receive in the 2001 U.S. consumer price index.[9] In terms of the formula above, the weights α and β are set equal to 0.587 for all countries. In practice, the U.S. weight for nontraded goods is higher than for almost all OECD countries, but this should only bias the results in favor of finding a significant role for the relative price of nontraded goods (the y_t-component).

The constructed q_t, x_t, and y_t are all very persistent. Even though there are 27 years of monthly data, an augmented Dickey–Fuller (ADF) test is able to reject a unit root at the 5% level for only 9 of the 55 q_t-series, 9 of the 55 x_t-series, and 8 of the 55 y_t-series. At the 1% level, there are rejections only in one case for each of the three series.[10] All of the series had first-order serial correlation over 0.90 and, except in a few cases, over 0.96. So, in examining movements in these series, it makes sense to look at changes rather than levels.

Figure 1 plots

$$\frac{\text{MSE}(x_t - x_{t-j})}{\text{MSE}(x_t - x_{t-j}) + \text{MSE}(y_t - y_{t-j})} \quad \text{for} \quad j = 1, 2, \ldots, 18,$$

where MSE stands for mean squared error. These statistics were calculated for 55 real exchange rates, but plots for only 10 are included because of space considerations.[11] Engel (1999) presents similar plots using these data, but only for five countries, and only for U.S. real exchange rates. Any variance or mean-squared-error decomposition must find a way to deal with comovements. Here, we leave the comovements of x_t and y_t out of both the numerator and denominator of the MSE ratios. In practice the comovements account for very little of the mean squared error of real-exchange-rate changes. The correlation of the series generally was highest in absolute value at short horizons, but at those horizons the correlation was almost always negative—so the sum of the variances of x_t and y_t is greater than the variance of q_t.

The decompositions shown in Figure 1 for the U.S. real-exchange-rate series confirm the findings of Engel (1999). Nearly all of the movements in real exchange rates are attributed to x_t, the component that measures deviations from LOOP. For all but the U.S.–Canada rate, x_t's share of the

---

9. Weights: 0.157 for food; 0.256 for commodities less food; 0.312 for rent; 0.275 for services less rent.
10. All of the ADF tests included a constant, no time trend, and three lags.
11. The NBER working paper version, Engel (2002), includes all 55 plots.

Figure 1 MSE DECOMPOSITION OF REAL-EXCHANGE-RATE CHANGES

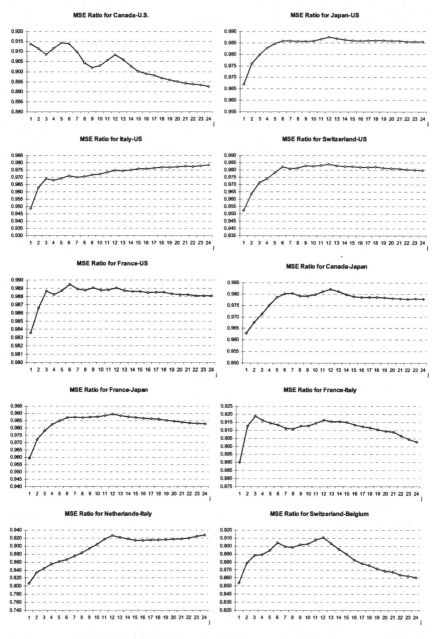

Horizontal axis: horizon (in months). Vertical axis: MSE share due to LOOP violations.

mean squared error is above 0.90 at all horizons. Usually it is above 0.95. Only for the U.S.–Canada rate does it dip below 0.90 at the longer horizons, and then only to 0.893 for 18-month changes.

A similar finding holds for cross-continental real exchange rates—that is, Japanese (relative to North America and Europe) and Canadian (relative to Europe). The x_t-component accounts for over 90% of the MSE share for all real exchange rates at all horizons.[12] Usually the share is well over 95%.

The story for within-Europe real exchange rates is only slightly different. While x_t's share is often less than 90%, for 19 of the 28 European country pairs it is never less than 80% at any horizon. The nine pairs where x_t's share falls below 0.80, and the range at all horizons for x_t's share for those country pairs, are: Spain–Italy, 0.75–0.86; Denmark–France, 0.68–0.87; Norway–Netherlands, 0.73–0.88; Belgium–Netherlands, 0.67–0.89; Switzerland–Netherlands, 0.74–0.89; Denmark–Netherlands, 0.59–0.71; Denmark–Norway, 0.73–0.89; Denmark–Belgium, 0.63–0.71; and Denmark–Switzerland, 0.77–0.89.

The fact that the deviations from LOOP are a slightly smaller share of real-exchange-rate movements for intra-European country pairs suggests that perhaps the deviations from LOOP are not really attributable to sticky consumer prices. Perhaps they arise because transportation costs cause imperfect integration of markets. The somewhat smaller failures of LOOP for the European pairs might reflect the fact that transportation costs are lower for within-European trade than for cross-continental trade. On the other hand, during 1974–2001, intra-European nominal exchange rates have been less volatile than the cross-continental exchange rates. So, the fact that deviations from LOOP are smaller within Europe is consistent with sticky nominal consumer prices and deviations arising from nominal-exchange-rate fluctuations. The next section helps to shed some light on this question.

Betts and Kehoe (2001) recently have performed similar decompositions for a large number of countries, finding somewhat more evidence that the relative price of nontraded goods drives real exchange rates. However, there are two reasons why their results should be treated with a bit of caution. They measure q_t, the real exchange rate, using relative consumer price indexes in essentially the same way as I do.[13] But their

12. Except for the Danish–Canadian share at the 1-month horizon, which is 0.893.
13. One difference is that I construct real exchange rates for consumers who weight the four main components with equal weights in all countries, while they simply used published CPIs. Thus, their real-exchange-rate changes may reflect changes in relative prices that get reflected in real exchange rates because goods receive different weights across national CPIs.

measure of x_t is not a CPI measure of traded goods. Instead they take x_t to be the relative producer price indexes across countries (that is, s + log PPI* − log PPI). This measure of x_t might vary over time even if LOOP held for all traded goods and CPI weights for traded goods were identical. That is because it measures x_t using output weights rather than consumption weights. Output weights can be very different across countries even when CPI weights are not. A more substantial reason why Betts and Kehoe attribute more of real-exchange-rate movements to y_t is that they measure y_t as simply $q_t − x_t$. As I argued in Engel (1999), where I also employed this measure of y_t (as one of the four measures of y_t I considered), a serious bias is introduced by measurement error in this case. Since x_t and q_t are measured from different pricing surveys (PPI and CPI), where no effort is made to reconcile the pricing errors there will be largely uncorrelated measurement errors in the two series. This in turn implies there will be a potentially large negative correlation between the measure of x_t and the measure of y_t ($= q_t − x_t$). Indeed, in Engel (1999), I found that x_t and y_t measured in this way were highly negatively correlated. Decomposing the real exchange rate into x_t and y_t components is problematic because one must find a way to deal with the negative correlation. Although their results are similar to mine, Betts and Kehoe do attribute a larger share of the variance of annual changes in real exchange rates to the nontraded goods (y_t), even for the countries that I consider here. I do not find that the difference in our findings is attributable to differences in methodology, and so I must conclude that they arise from the difference in the way we measure the price of tradable goods.

In essence, Devereux and Engel (2001) take the evidence against LOOP for consumer goods as support for the position that nominal-exchange-rate changes are not passed through to consumer prices because of local-currency pricing. But there are other ways to interpret the evidence that do not rely on LCP behavior. We turn to a few of these alternatives.

7. Shipping Costs

One explanation for why LOOP fails is that home and foreign consumers are consuming slightly different products. That is, suppose a given product can be produced in both the home and the foreign country. Let the per-unit iceberg transport cost for exported goods be δ, as in OR (2000b). Let P_H be the domestic-currency price of the good in the home country, and P_F^* be the foreign-currency price of the good in the foreign country. The two goods are perfect substitutes for households. Then,

$$\frac{1}{1 + \delta} S P_F^* \leq P_H \leq (1 + \delta) S P_F^*.$$

If the home price is within this band, there is no passthrough of exchange rates to domestic prices. On the edges of the band, passthrough is complete. But this model has the untenable implication that zero passthrough occurs only because there is no trade.

A more satisfactory version of the transportation-cost theory is that there are two varieties of the good, one produced in the home country and the other produced in the foreign country. Assume CES utility (and no differences in tastes between home and foreign residents) and an elasticity of substitution between varieties greater than 1. If the elasticity and the per-unit transport costs are high enough, foreign varieties may constitute a small share of overall consumption and thus a small share in the measured price of home-country consumption. The reverse will be true of the foreign country. LOOP may fail grossly for the price index of these two goods.

Let P_i be the price of a particular good. However, P_i is itself an index over the price of two varieties of the good—one produced at home and one in the foreign country. Suppose home and foreign households have the same preferences for the good:

$$C_i = [\alpha C_{iH}^{(\lambda-1)/\lambda} + (1 - \alpha) C_{iF}^{(\lambda-1)/\lambda}]^{\lambda/(\lambda-1)},$$

where the subscript i is for the good, of which there are two types: H for home and F for foreign. Let the per-unit iceberg transport cost for exported goods be δ. The home-country producer is the only producer of the home variety, and the foreign producer the only producer of the foreign variety. LOOP holds exclusive of transport costs. We have $P_{iH}^* = (1 + \delta)P_{iH}/S$ and $P_{iF} = (1 + \delta)SP_{iF}^*$. The rest of the macro model is the same as specified above.

Under flexible nominal prices, P_{iH}/P_{iF} and P_{iH}^*/P_{iF}^* respond to real shocks. If nominal prices are sticky as in the Friedman framework of PCP, it is clear that a flexible exchange rate is necessary to achieve a desirable response of P_{iH}/P_{iF} (or P_{iH}^*/P_{iF}^*) to real shocks. This framework potentially is also consistent with the observation that measured consumer prices do not respond much to exchange-rate changes. We have:

$$P_i = [\alpha^\lambda P_{iH}^{1-\lambda} + (1 - \alpha)^\lambda P_{iF}^{1-\lambda}]^{1/(1-\lambda)}$$
$$= [\alpha^\lambda P_{iH}^{1-\lambda} + (1 - \alpha)^\lambda (1 + \delta)^{1-\lambda} S^{1-\lambda} P_{iF}^{*1-\lambda}]^{1/(1-\lambda)}.$$

The passthrough elasticity for the home country, for example, is

$$\varepsilon = \frac{(1 - \alpha)^\lambda (1 + \delta)^{1-\lambda} S^{1-\lambda} P_{iF}^{*1-\lambda}}{\alpha^\lambda P_{iH}^{1-\lambda} + (1 - \alpha)^\lambda (1 + \delta)^{1-\lambda} S^{1-\lambda} P_{iF}^{*1-\lambda}}.$$

For $\lambda > 1$, we have $\varepsilon \to 0$ as $\delta \to \infty$. If the cost of the foreign good is high enough, there will not be much effect of exchange rates on home consumer prices if the foreign good is a sufficiently high substitute for the domestic good. For foreign prices (in domestic-currency terms);

$$SP_i^* = S[\alpha^\lambda P_{iH}^{*1-\lambda} + (1 - \alpha)^\lambda P_{iF}^{*1-\lambda}]^{1/(1-\lambda)}$$
$$= [\alpha^\lambda(1 + \delta)^{1-\lambda}P_{iH}^{1-\lambda} + (1 - \alpha)^\lambda S^{1-\lambda}P_{iF}^{*1-\lambda}]^{1/(1-\lambda)}.$$

If shipping costs were zero, so $\delta = 0$, LOOP would hold for good i. That is, we would have $P_i / SP_i^* = 1$. But as δ increases above zero, deviations from LOOP for good i (that is, for the index of the price of varieties H and F) increase. Taking a Taylor series expansion, the variance of $\ln(P_i / SP_i^*) = p_i - s - p_i^*$ equals approximately

$$\left(\frac{1}{\lambda - 1}\right)^2 \left(\frac{z - 1}{z + 1}\right)^2 \text{Var}(X), \quad \text{where} \quad z = (1 + \delta)^{\lambda-1}$$

$$\text{and} \quad X = \left(\frac{1 - \alpha}{\alpha}\right)^\lambda \left(\frac{P_{iH}}{SP_{iF}^*}\right)^{\lambda-1}.$$

As the shipping costs increase, the variance of $p_i - s - p_i^*$ increases (holding the variance of X constant.)

Several studies have examined how the variations of deviations from LOOP are related to distance, which is taken to be a proxy for shipping costs. Engel and Rogers (1996) posit that the standard deviation of changes in $p_i - s - p_i^*$ is related to distance. Their comparison is made for 14 disaggregated CPI categories (food at home, food away from home, men's and boy's apparel, etc.) and for 23 cities in North America—9 Canadian cities and 14 U.S. cities. They found that deviations from LOOP were significantly related to distance between locations. But they also found that, even taking into account the distance effect, the deviations from LOOP were much larger when comparing goods prices between U.S. and Canadian cities than when comparing prices for city pairs within the United States or Canada. That is, there is a large *border effect*.

Similar findings have been confirmed for U.S.–Japanese prices (Parsley and Wei 2001a), and intra-European prices (Engel and Rogers, 2001; Parsley and Wei, 2001b). Parsley and Wei's studies used data on very narrowly defined consumer goods (for example, boxes of facial tissues, men's jeans, imported whiskey). Each of these studies confirms that distance between locations is a significant explanatory variable for the standard deviation of $p_i - s - p_i^*$. But these studies go further, and find that volatility of nominal exchange rates plays a much greater role in accounting for the volatility of deviations from LOOP.

Here I shall present some evidence that is similar in spirit to the evidence presented in those papers. My traded-goods price data are not nearly as disaggregated as the data in the other studies: I will use the OECD data on consumer prices for food and for all commodities excluding food that I described in the previous section.

In Table 1, I report cross-section regressions, in which the dependent variable is the standard deviation of changes in $p_i - s - p_i^*$ (for food, and for commodities less food), so there are 55 observations in each cross-section regression, representing the standard deviation of $p_i - s - p_i^*$ for each of the 55 country pairs. The top panel reports regressions for 1-month changes, and the bottom panel for 12-month changes. The shipping costs are captured by DIST, which measures the log of the distance between the capital cities. It is difficult to gauge the correct form of the nonlinear relationship between distance and shipping costs, especially over large intercontinental distances. So the regressions also include a dummy variable that takes on a value of 1 if one of the countries in the country pair is Japan (JADUM), and another dummy that is 1 if the country pair has one country in North America and another in Europe (ATLDUM).

For both food and nonfood goods, the coefficient on log distance is positive and highly significant for both 1-month and 12-month changes. This is in accord with the transportation-cost theory of deviations from LOOP.

Another approach is to take bilateral trade volumes as a measure of integration between two countries. Table 1 reports regressions that use the log of bilateral trade volumes instead of the log of distance as an explanatory variable.[14] Two sets of regressions are reported. The first are OLS in which the bilateral trade volumes are deflated by the product of GDPs of the trading pairs. The second are IV regressions in which the undeflated bilateral trade volumes are explained in a first stage by a gravity model—using the log of distance and the log of the product of GDPs as instruments. For both food and nonfood goods, the coefficient on log of trade is positive and significant for both 1-month and 12-month changes.

However, as was noted in the previous section, countries that are closer together, or that have higher (scaled) bilateral trade volumes, also tend to have lower nominal-exchange-rate volatility. So the transportation-cost effects that Table 1 reports may be overstating the value of distance or trade. In Table 2, the same regressions are run, but also using the standard

---

14. These data were taken from Andrew Rose's Web site, http://haas.berkeley.edu/~arose/RecRes.htm. They are the data used in Frankel and Rose (2002). I take the average of the log of bilateral trade for 1975, 1980, 1985, 1990, and 1995.

Table 1 REGRESSIONS OF RELATIVE PRICE VOLATILITY ON DISTANCE OR TRADE VOLUMES

Standard deviation of relative price of	No.	Estimation method	Log of distance	Log of volume of bilateral trade	Constant	JADUM	ATLDUM	R^2
			One-Month Differences					
Food	1	OLS	0.41 (5.32)		-0.87 (-1.78)	0.58 (2.85)	0.34 (2.04)	0.89
	2	OLS		-0.17 (-3.48)	-2.04 (-1.88)	1.17 (7.88)	0.76 (5.65)	0.85
	3	IV		-0.09 (-2.94)	3.18 (6.37)	1.56 (14.69)	1.09 (11.99)	0.84
Nonfood commodities	4	OLS	0.37 (4.57)		-0.42 (-0.82)	0.25 (1.18)	0.27 (1.58)	0.82
	5	OLS		-0.13 (-2.71)	-1.12 (-1.00)	0.81 (5.30)	0.68 (4.92)	0.78
	6	IV		-0.13 (-4.71)	3.98 (8.94)	1.12 (11.91)	0.92 (11.44)	0.82

Twelve-Month Differences

Food							
7	OLS	0.018 (4.43)		−0.051 (−1.92)	0.027 (2.43)	0.024 (2.65)	0.87
8	OLS		−0.0098 (−4.19)	−0.16 (−2.95)	0.048 (6.62)	0.038 (5.74)	0.86
9	IV		−0.0024 (−1.39)	0.10 (3.84)	0.070 (12.44)	0.058 (11.98)	0.81
Nonfood commodities							
10	OLS	0.022 (5.28)		−0.069 (−2.64)	0.020 (1.84)	0.025 (2.86)	0.88
11	OLS		−0.013 (−6.25)	−0.23 (−4.82)	0.041 (6.22)	0.038 (6.35)	0.84
12	IV		−0.0029 (−1.71)	0.11 (4.21)	0.071 (12.41)	0.065 (13.33)	0.83

t-statistics in parentheses. All regressions use 55 country-pair observations.
Dependent variable in regression is specified in leftmost column. Standard deviations are calculated from monthly data, 1973:12–2001:1. IV estimation uses log of distance and log of products of GDP as instruments.

Table 2 REGRESSIONS OF RELATIVE PRICE VOLATILITY ON DISTANCE OR TRADE VOLUMES AND ON VOLATILITY OF NOMINAL EXCHANGE RATES

Std. dev. of relative price of	No.	Est. method	Log of distance	Log of volume of bilateral trade	Standard deviation of nominal exchange rate	Constant	JADUM	ATLDUM	R^2
				One-Month Differences					
Food	13	OLS	0.041 (1.07)		0.83 (16.25)	0.28 (1.33)	0.33 (3.90)	0.016 (0.23)	0.98
	14	OLS		0.029 (18.76)	0.89 (18.76)	1.09 (2.61)	0.40 (5.87)	0.072 (1.20)	0.98
	15	IV		−0.055 (−6.07)	0.82 (24.16)	1.42 (8.85)	0.44 (8.02)	0.088 (1.80)	0.99
Nonfood commod.	16	OLS	0.17 (1.91)		0.44 (3.80)	0.20 (0.41)	0.11 (0.59)	0.10 (0.62)	0.86
	17	OLS		−0.011 (−0.23)	0.56 (4.91)	0.85 (0.85)	0.33 (2.01)	0.25 (1.73)	0.84
	18	IV		−0.11 (−4.97)	0.49 (5.98)	2.91 (7.49)	0.45 (3.39)	0.32 (2.74)	0.89

Twelve-Month Differences

		Method							R^2
Food	19	OLS	0.026 (1.67)		0.86 (20.62)	−0.0006 (−0.71)	0.0014 (0.37)	−0.0030 (−0.93)	0.99
	20	OLS		−0.0005 (−0.51)	0.88 (20.40)	−0.002 (−0.09)	0.0049 (1.52)	−0.0005 (−0.17)	0.98
	21	IV		−0.0005 (−1.04)	0.88 (23.17)	0.017 (1.90)	0.0058 (1.78)	0.0002 (0.05)	0.98
Nonfood commod.	22	OLS	0.0083 (2.98)		0.72 (9.77)	−0.031 (−1.97)	−0.0014 (−0.21)	0.0027 (0.48)	0.96
	23	OLS		−0.0060 (−4.09)	0.68 (9.73)	−0.11 (−3.60)	0.0075 (1.42)	0.0082 (1.74)	0.96
	24	IV		−0.0012 (−1.29)	0.81 (11.74)	0.033 (2.11)	0.012 (2.01)	0.012 (2.36)	0.95

t-statistics in parentheses. All regressions use 55 observations.
Dependent variable in regression is specified in leftmost column. Standard deviations are calculated from monthly data, 1973:12–2001:1. IV estimation uses log of distance and log of products of GDP as instruments.

deviation of the nominal exchange rate as an explanatory variable. In all cases, the standard deviation of the nominal exchange rate is highly significant. In comparison with Table 1, the absolute values of the coefficients on the trade and distance variables fall greatly, and their statistical significance also falls.

Table 3 reports an analysis of variance for each of the regressions reported in Table 2. The purpose of Table 3 is to show how much of the "explained" variance of the dependent variable is attributable to the standard deviation of nominal exchange rates, the integration variable (distance or trade volume), the dummy variables, and their interaction. Table 3 reveals that distance or trade volume accounts for a small fraction of the explained variance in all of the reported regressions. In eight of the twelve regressions, it accounts for 1% or less of the explained variance. In one regression it accounts for 16.4%, and in the remaining three for less than 10%. In contrast, in all of the regressions, the standard deviation of the nominal exchange rate accounts for a large fraction of the explained variance. In all but one case it is over 50%, and in most cases it is over 80%. So, even though distances or trade volumes are sometimes significant in explaining the standard deviation of $p_i - s - p_i^*$, they do not carry much of the load in explaining it.

In the transportation-cost model, the behavior of nominal exchange rates plays no role in explaining the deviations from the law of one price. The deviations result from a real trading cost. The models make no mention of these costs differing across nominal-exchange-rate regimes. In the LCP model, by contrast, deviations from LOOP are volatile precisely because nominal exchange rates are volatile. The empirical work cited above, and the new work reported here, shows there is a role for both models in explaining the deviations from LOOP. But the implication of the analysis of variance in Table 3 is that the proxies for trading costs account for a very small fraction of the variation in prices across countries compared to nominal-exchange-rate fluctuations.

These empirical studies certainly do not perfectly measure transportation costs, or their effects on deviations from LOOP. However, even if transportation costs were much more significant, this model actually would not support a strong expenditure-switching effect. The reason there is so little passthrough of exchange rates to consumer prices in the home country in the transportation-cost model is that foreign varieties are a small share of total consumption. In fact, ε measures not only the elasticity of consumer prices with respect to a change in the price of foreign goods; it also measures the share of foreign goods in expenditures. So passthrough can only be small in this model if the expenditure share on foreign varieties is small. The case for floating rates is weak in this

Table 3   ANALYSIS OF VARIANCE OF REGRESSIONS FROM TABLE 2

Regression no.	Variance of s.d. of exchange-rate component	Variance of distance or trade component	Covariance of ex. rate and trade or distance component	Variance of dummies	Covariance of dummies with nondummies
			1-month changes		
13	80.6	0.5	9.7	3.4	9.7
14	87.8	0.3	-4.5	4.5	12.0
15	77.8	1.0	1.4	5.9	13.8
16	46.1	16.4	25.4	1.2	10.9
17	67.9	0.1	2.1	8.3	21.7
18	50.6	7.4	3.0	14.6	24.4
			12-month changes		
19	92.8	0.8	7.7	0.2	-1.5
20	95.8	0.0	1.5	0.3	2.4
21	96.0	0.0	0.3	0.4	3.3
22	69.0	8.0	21.5	0.2	1.3
23	64.2	6.1	17.1	1.5	11.1
24	81.7	0.2	0.6	3.1	14.4

Cell entries are the percentage of total explained sum of squares from corresponding regressions in Table 2 that are explained by each component.

case. Floating rates might be needed to achieve optimal relative-price adjustments, but those adjustments are not very important to the functioning of the economy in this model.

In fact, OR (2000b) reason that the low passthrough to consumer prices cannot be fully explained by transportation costs, and that some other factors must be at play.

8. Nontraded Distribution Services and PCP

One possible explanation for the apparent nonresponsiveness of consumer prices to exchange-rate changes is that CPIs measure the price of a basket of both consumer goods and the distribution services that bring the goods to consumers. LOOP might very well hold for the actual physical good (as in PCP models), but the measured consumer price includes the price of the distribution service, which is nontraded and for which LOOP need not hold. Recent examples of papers that have adopted this type of model are McCallum and Nelson (2000), Burstein, Neves, and Rebelo (2000), and Burstein, Eichenbaum, and Rebelo (2002).[15] None of these papers provide direct evidence on the role of distribution costs in accounting for real-exchange-rate changes.

Let the home price of imported good i be a composite of a traded-goods price $\bar{P}_i$ for which LOOP holds ($\bar{P}_i = S\bar{P}_i^*$) and the price of a nontraded distribution service (P_{iS}). If output of the final consumer product is a CES function of the traded good and the distribution service (with elasticity equal to λ), the price of the final product can be written as

$$P_i = [\alpha^\lambda P_{iS}^{1-\lambda} + (1 - \alpha)^\lambda \bar{P}_i^{1-\lambda}]^{1/(1-\lambda)} = [\alpha^\lambda P_{iS}^{1-\lambda} + (1 - \alpha)^\lambda S^{1-\lambda} \bar{P}_i^{*1-\lambda}]^{1/(1-\lambda)}. \quad (2)$$

If $\bar{P}_i^*$ is fixed in foreign-currency terms, the passthrough of exchange rates is given by:

$$\varepsilon = \frac{(1 - \alpha)^\lambda S^{1-\lambda} \bar{P}_i^{*1-\lambda}}{\alpha^\lambda P_{iS}^{1-\lambda} + (1 - \alpha)^\lambda S^{1-\lambda} \bar{P}_i^{*1-\lambda}}.$$

As $\alpha \to 1$, $\varepsilon \to 0$. That is, as the share of the nontraded distribution service increases toward unity, the passthrough elasticity falls toward zero.

We cannot usually observe $\bar{P}_i$ and $\bar{P}_i^*$ directly, but we might be able to examine this hypothesis using only measures of the consumer price and

---

15. The model of OR (2000a) could be interpreted this way. The final good in that type of model is a composite of a traded home-produced good, a traded foreign-produced good, and a nontraded distribution service.

a measure of the price of services. To simplify matters, let the production function be Cobb–Douglas [so $\lambda \to 1$ in (2)]. The price of good i in the home compared to the foreign country is

$$p - s - p^* = k + \alpha x + (1 - \alpha)u, \tag{3}$$

where lowercase letters mean logs, the subscripts i are dropped, k is a constant, α is the cost share of nontraded distribution services, $x \equiv p_s - s - p_s^*$ is the price of services in the home country relative to the foreign country, and $u \equiv \bar{p} - s - \bar{p}^*$ is the price deviation for the traded good. Under the null LOOP, u should in principle be zero, but the null might allow for a small i.i.d. error. So equation (3) could be estimated. It should have a good fit and yield a tight estimate of α if the distribution cost model is true.

But estimating this equation is not useful for distinguishing between the model in which prices are equalized for the traded good and the model in which there is local-currency pricing for the traded good. To allow for this alternative, let $u = -\gamma s + \varepsilon$. Under LOOP for the traded good, $\gamma = 0$. Under LCP, $\gamma = 1$. The quantity $1 - \gamma$ is the degree of pass-through. Assume that ε is uncorrelated with s and has a small variance. Also, define $v = p_s - p_s^*$, and assume for purposes of exposition that it is also uncorrelated with s. Then $x \equiv v - s$. Under these assumptions, the probability limit of the OLS estimate of α from equation (3) is given by

$$\alpha + \frac{(1 - \alpha)[\text{Cov}(\varepsilon, v) + \gamma \, \text{Var}(s)]}{\text{Var}(v) + \text{Var}(s)}.$$

Under the hypothesis that LOOP holds for the traded good ($\gamma = 0$), the asymptotic bias is small, since $\text{Cov}(\varepsilon, v)/\text{Var}(s)$ is likely to be small. But when $\gamma = 1$, the asymptotic bias of the estimate of α from this regression could be large. As $\text{Var}(s)$ gets large, the probability limit of the estimate of α approaches $\alpha + (1 - \alpha) = 1$. Under the alternative of LCP, estimating equation (3) would return a large estimate of α. The equation would fit well and appear to attribute most of the variation of $p - s - p^*$ to the relative services component. Estimating (3) is not a good way to test for the model in which LOOP holds for the traded good (and the services component accounts for all of the deviations in the CPI prices across countries), vs. the LCP model.

Suppose, however, we could group u with x and estimate

$$p - s - p^* = k + \alpha(x - u) + u. \tag{4}$$

The probability limit of the estimate of α from this regression is given by

$$\alpha + \frac{\text{Cov}(\varepsilon, v) - \text{Var}(\varepsilon) - \gamma(1 - \gamma)\,\text{Var}(s)}{\text{Var}(v) + \text{Var}(\varepsilon) - 2\,\text{Cov}(\varepsilon, v) + (1 - \gamma)^2\text{Var}(s)}.$$

When $\gamma = 0$, the asymptotic bias is small because $\text{Var}(s)$ is large relative to the other variances and covariances. The R^2 from the regression should be high, because $x - u = v - \varepsilon + s$ in this case, which has a high variance relative to the regression error, $u = \varepsilon$. But under LCP ($\gamma = 1$) the asymptotic bias is much higher, and likely to be negative if $\text{Cov}(\varepsilon, v)$ is near zero. Moreover, the R^2 will be low, since $x - u = v - \varepsilon$ has small variance and the regression error $u = -s + \varepsilon$ has large variance. So, if LCP were important, the coefficient estimate and R^2 from this regression would be very different than if LOOP held for the traded good. This might be a useful approach to distinguish the models.

Fortunately, we can observe $x - u$ up to a constant of proportionality, because $x - u = [1/(1 - \alpha)][p_s - p - (p_s^* - p^*)]$. Substituting into equation (8.3), we arrive at the equation we propose to estimate:

$$p - s - p^* = k + \frac{\alpha}{1 - \alpha}\,[p_s - p - (p_s^* - p^*)] + u. \tag{5}$$

To sum up the previous discussion: Under the hypothesis that nontraded distribution services account for the observed deviations across countries in consumer prices, while LOOP holds well for the actual traded good, the slope coefficient in the regression should be strongly positive and the R^2 should be high. Alternatively, if there is LCP for the traded good, the slope coefficient is biased downward (and may be negative), and the R^2 will be low [especially if $\text{Var}(s)$ is high].

We do not observe the cost of the distribution services, p_s, directly. But we can use as a proxy the OECD prices of services (excluding rent) described above in Section 6. We use as our measure of the observable traded-goods price, p, the traded-goods price that was constructed from the OECD data on food prices and prices of nonfood commodities.

As we noted above, the measures of $p - s - p^*$ are highly persistent for all 55 country pairs, and we fail to reject a unit root in almost all cases. Similarly, $p_s - p - (p_s^* - p^*)$ is persistent. We reject a unit root at the 5% level for only nine of the 55 country pairs, and at the 1% level for only two. So we will examine the relationship between changes in $p - s - p^*$ and changes in $p_s - p - (p_s^* - p^*)$. We regress 1-month (2-month, 3-month, ..., 24-month) changes in $p - s - p^*$ on 1-month (2-month, 3-month, ..., 24-month) changes in $p_s - p - (p_s^* - p^*)$.

Figure 2 presents plots of the estimated slope coefficient from the regressions for the 24 horizons, with one graph for 10 of the 55 country pairs. Figure 3 plots the R^2's from those regressions.[16]

The results indicate poor performance for the distribution-services model at the shortest horizons. For horizons less than 6 months, there are no cases in which the coefficient is positive and the R^2 is greater than 0.07. In many instances, the coefficient on the relative price of services is negative. For all of the intra-European country pairs, which have low nominal-exchange-rate volatility, the coefficient is negative at horizons of 1 to 6 months. In some cases the R^2 is high (in the range of 0.15 to 0.45) in these regressions. As we would expect under LCP, the lowest R^2's are for the country pairs that have the highest nominal-exchange-rate volatility—country pairs involving the U.S., Japan, and Canada with overseas partners.

At the longest horizons, the distribution-services model fares only slightly better. It is still the case that the coefficient estimates is negative at the longer horizons for almost all of the European country pairs. Of the 28 European country pairs, only nine display positive coefficients at all of the horizons from 19 to 24 months. Two more have positive coefficients at the 23- and 24-month horizons. In only one of these eleven cases (Belgium–Norway) is the R^2 above 0.20. The distribution-services model appears to explain a bit more for the 27 country pairs that are not intra-European. In 14 cases, the regression coefficient is positive at all of the longer horizons (19 to 24 months), and in 2 additional cases it is positive for some of the longer horizons. Of these 16 country pairs with positive coefficient estimates at longer horizons, only 3 (Belgium–U.S., Belgium–Canada, and Netherlands–U.S.) have R^2's greater than 0.20.

Goldberg and Verboven (2001a) (hereinafter referred to as GV) have a related empirical study that appears to find much stronger evidence in favor of the distribution-services approach. GV use extremely detailed data for automobile prices sold in five European countries. They have prices of specific models for 15 years, data on characteristics of the automobiles (horsepower, size, luxury features, etc.), production location of each model, and some data on income of buyers. They use tax data, and make use of data on import restrictions. In short, their data are comprehensive and much better than the data used here.

In essence, GV estimate a version of equation (3). However, they do not simply allow the deviation from LOOP for the traded good to appear as an error term in the regression. They are not able to observe u. But they build a highly complex model of automobile demand and the pricing-

16. The NBER working paper version, Engel (2002), presents plots for all 55 country pairs.

Figure 2 COEFFICIENT ESTIMATES FOR REGRESSION OF TRADED PRICES
ON SERVICE PRICES

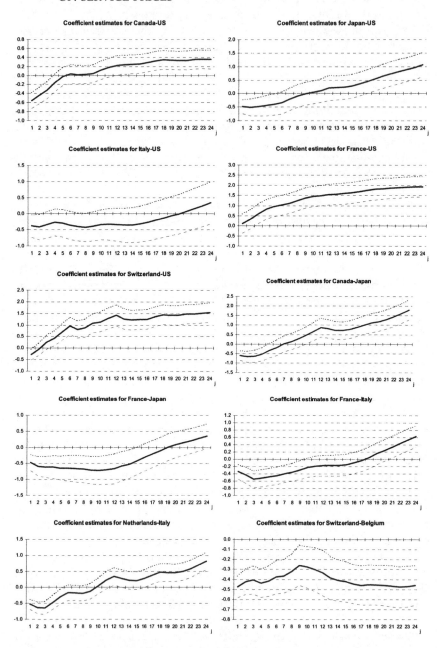

Horizontal axis: horizon (in months). Plotted is slope coefficient of regression of relative traded prices
on service price, and 95% confidence interval.

Figure 3 R^2 FROM REGRESSIONS REPORTED IN FIGURE 2

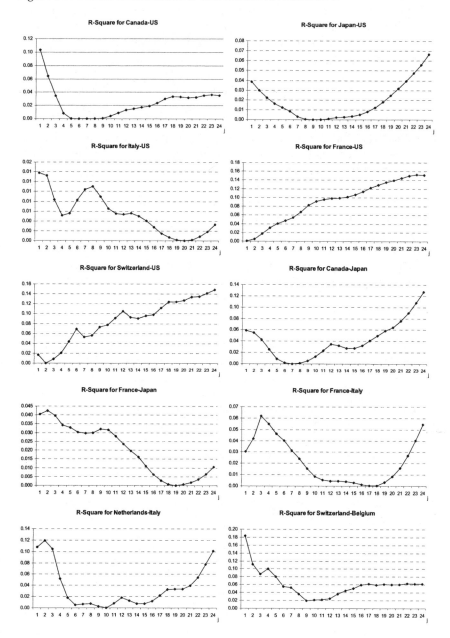

to-market behavior of automobile producers. Combining these, they use sophisticated nonlinear methods to come up with a measure of the desired degree of price discrimination by firms. Although this does not do justice to GV's work, in essence their empirical model could be expressed as an extension of (3):

$$p - s - p^* = k + \alpha x + y + \eta.$$

Relative to (3), the term y represents the sophisticated estimate of desired price discrimination by firms. The error term η represents all the elements not captured by y, so $\eta \equiv (1 - \alpha)u - y$.

GV's approach is a reasonable and very admirable attempt to deal with the unobservability of u. My hunch—and this obviously deserves further study—is that GV still do not capture the full degree of price discrimination. In fact, if producers are simply setting prices in local currencies (because, say, of menu costs), the model of GV will certainly underpredict the degree of desired local-currency price stability for the imported good. So the residual remaining in the GV regression will still be highly negatively correlated with s, and therefore highly positively correlated with x. As a result, GV will tend to attribute too much to the distribution services component x.

GV believe they rule out the possibility of transitory price stickiness by estimating their equation in levels over a 15-year period—to capture the long-run pricing equation. However, real exchange rates are extremely persistent (see Rogoff, 1996). Chari, Kehoe, and McGrattan (2000) show that when price setting is asynchronized, the adjustment can be very slow. Rogoff cites a half-life for the real exchange rate of 3–5 years. With such slow adjustment of prices, the 15-year sample that GV use may not be sufficient to capture only long-run pricing behavior.

Even if the distribution-services hypothesis is correct, it might imply that the role for nominal-exchange-rate flexibility is small. In this approach, the reason that nominal exchange rates have low passthrough to consumer prices is that the distribution services are a large component of the cost of consumer goods. As in the model with transportation costs, if the nontraded marketing services are such a large component of the cost of consumer goods that we barely observe any effect of exchange-rate passthrough, then the physical import must not be a very important component of our consumer basket. Exchange-rate flexibility is desirable for achieving relative price adjustments, but these relative price adjustments may not be very significant. The cost of the physical traded good is a small component of the overall cost of consumer goods, so achieving the optimal relative-price change for this component may not influence welfare much.

9. Imports as Intermediate Goods

Obstfeld (2001) models imported goods as intermediate products. They are combined with products produced locally to make final consumer goods (which are nontraded). There is complete passthrough of exchange rates to imported-goods prices in this framework. That is, the price of imported goods is set in the producers' currencies, so the imported price varies one for one with the exchange rate. But imported goods are not sold directly to consumers. The price of the final good is set in the consumers' currencies.

This model, then, is completely consistent with the observation that consumer prices do not respond much to exchange-rate changes in the short run. But there is still an important role for exchange-rate flexibility in changing relative prices. The final-goods producer faces a *sourcing* decision—to use imported intermediates or locally produced intermediates. There is not perfect substitutability between the two, but there is some.[17] So a nominal-exchange-rate adjustment can change the price of imported relative to locally produced intermediates.

There is a single final consumer good, sold by a monopolist that buys intermediate inputs in competitive markets. The price of the final good in the home country is P, and it is fixed in home currency.

The cost of producing the good is not fixed ex ante. The cost is given by

$$\Gamma = [\alpha^\lambda P_H^{1-\lambda} + (1 - \alpha)^\lambda S^{1-\lambda} P_F^{*1-\lambda}]^{1/(1-\lambda)}.$$

Here, P_H is the price of the home-produced intermediate good. That good is produced using a variety of labor inputs. In the Obstfeld setup, each household is a monopoly supplier of a unique type of labor. Nominal wages are fixed ex ante. The intermediate-goods market is competitive with free entry. The price P_H is in principle flexible, but under competitive conditions it is equal to the ex ante fixed nominal wage. (In Obstfeld's model, there are no productivity shocks, but there are labor-supply shocks. The labor input per unit of output is fixed at unity.)

Likewise, P_F^* is the price of the foreign-produced intermediate in the foreign currency. The structure of the foreign intermediate market is the same as that of the home market, which implies that P_F^* is fixed ex ante

---

17. Specifically, in Obstfeld's framework there is unit elasticity of substitution.

in the foreign currency. The home-currency price, $P_F = SP_F^*$, changes with the exchange rate.

Under flexible nominal prices, using the general model of Section 2, we find

$$\frac{P_H}{P_F} = \frac{P_H^*}{P_F^*} = \frac{\eta^*}{\eta}.$$

(Here, an increase in η represents an increase in home labor supply, which would reduce the wage and cost per unit of the home product under flexible prices and wages.)

With fixed nominal wages, we have for example in the home country $P_H/P_F = P_H/SP_F^*$. Since P_H and P_F^* will be fixed under the market conditions described, we need exchange-rate flexibility to allow relative price adjustment. Indeed, since $S = M/M^*$, with a suitably designed monetary policy of the form $M = k\eta$ and $M^* = k^*\eta^*$ the flexible price equilibrium can be mimicked. Indeed, Obstfeld demonstrates that prices and allocations are the same under flexible prices as under sticky nominal wages with this inward-looking monetary policy that has exchange-rate flexibility.[18]

OR (2000) present evidence that shows there is much more passthrough of exchange rates to imported-goods prices than to final-consumer prices. While the passthrough is certainly not 100% (as in the model just described), there appears to be a sufficient degree of passthrough to allow for a significant expenditure-switching effect following from nominal-exchange-rate changes. Goldberg and Knetter (1997) and Goldberg and Campa (2001) offer evidence that while passthrough to import prices is far from complete, it is significantly greater than passthrough to final-consumer prices.

An important aspect of the Obstfeld (2001) model is the idea that there are final-goods producers or distributors who can substitute between locally produced and imported intermediates. Devereux, Engel, and Tille (1999) take an approach that is quite similar to Obstfeld (2001). However, they take the limiting case of the cost function in which the elasticity of substitution is zero. That is, their model can be interpreted as one in which the distributor combines imported goods and locally produced goods in fixed proportion.[19] In that case, of course, there is no possibility of substi-

---

18. In fact, in terms of real variables and prices of output, the model is isomorphic to the PCP model of OR (2000a).
19. That is not exactly the set-up in Devereux, Engel, and Tille, but there is little difference in substance between the model I describe here and theirs.

tution between imported goods and local goods when the exchange rate changes, even though there is complete passthrough of the exchange rate to imported prices.

Potentially there are wealth effects from exchange-rate changes in this case. The demand for imported goods is fixed, because their price is fixed in consumers' currencies and the distributor cannot substitute toward locally produced goods. When the home currency depreciates, it raises the price that local distributors must pay for imported goods and lowers their profits. Foreign distributors have a windfall gain. In Devereux, Engel, and Tille (1999), these profit effects are not consequential, because of their assumption that there are state-contingent nominal bonds traded for each possible state. But Tille (2000) investigates the importance of these wealth effects for equilibrium demands when only non-state-contingent bonds can be traded. These wealth effects are a completely different channel through which exchange rates affect equilibrium than the relative price effects that are so important to the Friedman analysis.

The model of Devereux, Engel, and Tille (1999) is best described as one in which imports are primarily branded final goods. The distributor cannot substitute any local product for that brand. For example, a Toyota dealer cannot substitute a Chevrolet Lumina for a Camry if the yen becomes too expensive. The Obstfeld (2001) model is best thought of as a model in which the consumer cannot differentiate between local and imported sources of inputs. Perhaps the typical product in this setup is auto parts. The automobile may itself be assembled in the country in which it is consumed (in fact, many Toyota Camrys purchased in the United States are manufactured there), but using parts that may be imported or produced locally.

The empirical question is to what extent substitution occurs at some stage before the good reaches the consumer. For the question of exchange-rate flexibility, the key is whether substitution can occur between imported and local products. For example, if the United Kingdom is considering adopting the euro vs. keeping an independent pound, the question is whether in response to a pound depreciation the British can substitute toward British goods. Let me clarify what this means by way of an example. Suppose the imported good is wine. If the euro appreciates relative to the pound and dollar and thereby raises the pound price of French wine (as in the PCP specification), then the British might substitute away from French wine toward American wine. But for that margin of substitution, the flexibility of the pound–euro rate does not matter at all. Even if the pound–euro rate were fixed, the price of French wine would rise relative to that of American wine. The question is the degree to which a euro appreciation leads U.K. distributors to substitute away from goods produced on the continent toward U.K.-produced goods. If a large degree of such substitution occurs (as in the Obstfeld (2001) model), then exchange-rate flexibility is desirable. If little such substitution occurs (as in Devereux, Engel, and Tille (1999)), then there is not so strong a case for an independent currency with freely floating rates.

10. Conclusions

The famous case for flexible exchange rates advanced by Friedman (1953) is based on a view that appears at odds with empirical evidence. Friedman's approach assumes that nominal prices are set in producers' currencies and exchange-rate changes are passed through completely to final users of the goods. Thus an exchange-rate change delivers a relative price adjustment between foreign and domestically produced goods.

Recent theoretical papers confirm Friedman's policy prescription under his assumption about goods pricing. Empirical evidence, however, appears to contradict this assumption, because consumer prices are not very responsive to exchange rates. If there is no effect of exchange rates on prices that are paid by demanders of goods, then the exchange rate does not play the role in adjusting relative prices that Friedman posits. The jury is still out on whether we can reconcile the evidence of low exchange-rate pass-through to consumer prices with a significant expenditure-switching effect.

Even for advanced countries that have credible monetary policies and stable financial markets, expenditure switching is only one of several factors that are important in the choice of fixed vs. floating. As has been noted, one traditional argument in favor of floating exchange rates is that countries are able to follow independent monetary policies that allow monetary policy to react to local conditions. In the model of Devereux and Engel (2001), independent monetary policies are strictly suboptimal—they lead to undesirable deviations from LOOP, and do not yield any gains. But the structure of their model rules out possible gains from monetary policy, because it assumes a full set of nominal state-contingent claims, identical preferences for home and foreign households, and that all goods are traded.

On the other hand, there is evidence that fixed exchange rates, or currency unions, confer gains that are not addressed in the models discussed here. Rose (2000) and Frankel and Rose (2002) find empirical evidence that joining currency unions will increase the volume of trade between union members, and the increased trade will stimulate growth. These papers do not explain why currency unions increase trade, but presumably the unions somehow foster more tightly integrated markets. Indeed, Parsley and Wei (2001b), Rogers (2001), and GV (2001b) find that deviations from LOOP are small for currency-union members—even smaller than for countries that have fixed exchange rates but separate currencies. So the choice of exchange-rate regime, and particularly the choice to join a currency union, might influence how prices are set.

The models discussed here assume that the exchange rate is driven by monetary and real factors, and there is no significant role for speculative bubbles. If bubbles are important in determining exchange rates, then perhaps a stronger case for fixed exchange rates or currency union can be made. Jeanne and Rose (2002) advance the view that fixed exchange rates are desirable on the grounds that they help reduce the role of pure noise in exchange rates.

Missing from my survey of empirical work has been evidence concerning quantities: trade flows or employment, for example. Integrating such evidence is important, but beyond the scope of this paper. Microeconomic studies that examine how imports of particular types of goods, or how employment in specific industries, are affected by changes in import prices must be applied with a dollop of caution. That is because there is a missing link that must be supplied before one can use these studies to judge the quantitative significance of the expenditure-switching effect: the degree of passthrough. Import demand may be fairly elastic with respect to price changes, but if the import price is inelastic with respect to the nominal exchange rate, the overall effect on import demand may be small.

Aggregate studies that link employment or aggregate imports or sectoral employment to real exchange rates suffer less from this problem, because we know that for advanced countries the real exchange rate moves closely with the nominal exchange rate. Hooper, Johnson, and Marquez (2000) estimate short-run aggregate import and export elasticities for the G-7 countries. They find these elasticities are uniformly small, and generally statistically indistinguishable from zero. They conclude, "The evidence suggests that . . . changes in relative prices play a lesser role as a short-run international conduit."

On the other hand, studies of the effects of real exchange rates on employment, such as Gourinchas (1998, 1999) and Goldberg and Tracy (2000), do find statistically significant effects. It is difficult to judge, however, the economic significance of their findings for the importance of the expenditure-switching effect without placing them in the context of a general equilibrium model. For example, Gourinchas (1998) finds "an average 0.27% contraction in tradable employment over the 3 quarters following a mild 10% appreciation of the real exchange rate." Gourinchas (1999) finds "a 1 percent appreciation of the real exchange rate destroys 0.95 percent of tradable jobs over the next two years." It is difficult to judge whether such changes imply that nominal-exchange-rate flexibility has large or small effects on welfare unless these findings can be integrated into a full general equilibrium model.

The new open-economy macroeconomics has given us a structured way to think about the issues that are important when considering the desirability of floating exchange rates vs. currency union. Unfortunately for policymakers facing a near-term deadline for choosing an exchange-rate system, our knowledge has not advanced far enough to offer a firm recommendation backed up by appropriate theory.

REFERENCES

Bacchetta, P., and E. van Wincoop. (2000). Does exchange rate stability increase trade and welfare? *American Economic Review* 90:1093–1109.
Betts, C., and M. B. Devereux. (1996). The exchange rate in a model of pricing-to-market. *European Economic Review* 40:1007–1021.
———, and ———. (2000). Exchange rate dynamics in a model of pricing-to-market. *Journal of International Economics* 50:215–244.
———, and T. J. Kehoe. (2001). Real exchange rate movements and the relative price of nontraded goods. University of Minnesota. Mimeo.
Buiter, W. (1999). The EMU and the NAMU: What is the case for North American monetary union? *Canadian Public Policy* 25:285–305.
Burstein, A., J. C. Neves, and S. Rebelo. (2000). Distribution costs and exchange rate dynamics during exchange-rate-based stabilizations. Cambridge, MA: National Bureau of Economic Research. NBER Working Paper 7862.
———, M. Eichenbaum, and S. Rebelo. (2002). Why are rates of inflation so low after large devaluations? Cambridge, MA: National Bureau of Economic Research. NBER Working Paper 8748.
Chari, V. V., P. J. Kehoe, and E. R. McGrattan. (2000). Can sticky price models generate volatile and persistent exchange rates? Cambridge, MA: National Bureau of Economics Research. NBER Working Paper 7869.
Corsetti, G., and P. Pesenti. (2001). International dimensions of optimal monetary policy. University of Rome III. Manuscript.
Crucini, M. J., C. I. Telmer, and M. Zachariadis. (2001). Understanding European real exchange rates. Vanderbilt University. Mimeo.
Devereux, M. B., and C. Engel. (1998). Fixed vs. floating exchange rates: How price setting affects the optimal choice of exchange-rate regime. Cambridge, MA: National Bureau of Economic Research. NBER Working Paper 6867.
———, and ———. (2001). Monetary-policy in the open economy revisited: Exchange rate flexibility and price setting behavior. University of Wisconsin–Madison. Manuscript.
———, and ———. (2002). Exchange rate passthrough, exchange rate volatility, and exchange rate disconnect. *Journal of Monetary Economics*, 49:913–940.
———, ———, and C. Tille. (1999). Exchange rate pass-through and the welfare effects of the euro. Cambridge, MA: National Bureau of Economic Research. NBER Working Paper 7382.
Engel, C. (1993). Real exchange rates and relative prices: An empirical investigation. *Journal of Monetary Economics* 32:35–50.
———. (1999). Accounting for U.S. real exchange rate changes. *Journal of Political Economy* 107:507–538.

———. (2002). Expenditure switching and exchange rate policy. Cambridge. MA: National Bureau of Economic Research. NBER Working Paper.

———, and J. H. Rogers. (1996). How wide is the border? *American Economic Review* 86:1112–1125.

———, and ———. (2001). Deviations from the purchasing power parity: Causes and welfare costs. *Journal of International Economics* 55:29–57.

Frankel, J. A., and A. K. Rose. (2002). An estimate of the effect of currency unions on trade and growth. *Quarterly Journal of Economics*, 117:437–466.

Friedman, M. (1953). The case for flexible exchange rates. In *Essays in Positive Economics*. Chicago: University of Chicago Press, pp. 157–203.

Goldberg, L., and J. Campa. (2001). Exchange rate pass-through into import prices: A macro or micro phenomenon? Federal Reserve Bank of New York. Mimeo.

———, and J. Tracy. (2000). Exchange rates and local labor markets. In *Trade and Wages* (Robert Feenstra, ed.). Chicago: National Bureau of Economic Research and University of Chicago Press.

Goldberg, P. K., and M. M. Knetter. (1997). Goods prices and exchange rates: What have we learned? *Journal of Economic Literature* 35:1243–1272.

———, and F. Verboven. (2001a). The evolution of price dispersion in the European car market. *Review of Economic Studies* 68:811–848.

———, and ———. (2001b). Market integration and convergence to the law of one price: Evidence from the European car market. Cambridge, MA: National Bureau of Economic Research. NBER Working Paper 8402.

Gourinchas, P.-O. (1998). Exchange rates and jobs: What do we learn from job flows? In *NBER Macroeconomics Annual 1998*, B. S. Bernanke (ed.). Cambridge, MA: National Bureau of Economic Research, pp. 183–208.

———. (1999). Exchange rates do matter: French job reallocation and exchange rate turbulence, 1984–1992, *European Economic Review* 43:1279–1316.

Hooper, P. K. Johnson, and J. Marquez. (2000). Trade elasticities for the G-7 countries. Princeton Studies in International Economics 87.

Isard, P. (1977). How far can we push the law of one price? *American Economic Review* 67:942–948.

Jeanne, O., and A. K. Rose. (2002). Noise and exchange rate regimes. *Quarterly Journal of Economics*, 117:537–569.

Kravis, I. B., and R. E. Lipsey. (1978). Price behavior in light of balance of payments theories. *Journal of International Economics* 12:201–223.

Krugman, P. (1989). *Exchange Rate Instability*. Cambridge: The MIT Press.

Lane, P. R. (2001). The new open economy macroeconomics: A survey. *Journal of International Economics* 54:235–266.

McCallum, B. T., and E. Nelson. (2000). Monetary policy for an open economy: An alternative framework with optimizing agents and sticky prices. *Oxford Review of Economic Policy* 16:74–91.

Mundell, R. (1968). *International Economics*. New York: MacMillan.

Mussa, M. (1986). Nominal exchange rate regimes and the behavior of real exchange rates: Evidence and implications. *Carnegie-Rochester Conference Series on Public Policy* 25:117–213.

Obstfeld, M. (2001). International macroeconomics: Beyond the Mundell–Fleming model. *IMF Staff Papers* 47 (special issue):1–39.

———, and K. Rogoff. (1995). Exchange rate dynamics redux. *Journal of Political Economy* 103:624–660.

————, and ————. (1998). Risk and exchange rates. Cambridge, MA: National Bureau of Economic Research. NBER Working Paper 6694.

————, and ————. (2000a). New directions for stochastic open economy models. *Journal of International Economics* 50:117–153.

————, and ————. (2000b). The six major puzzles in international macroeconomics: Is there a common cause? In *NBER Macroeconomics Annual 2000*, B. S. Bernanke (ed.). Cambridge, MA: National Bureau of Economic Research, pp. 339–390.

————, and ————. (2001). Global implications of self-oriented national monetary rules. Department of Economics, University of California, Berkeley. Manuscript.

————, and A. M. Taylor. (1997). Non-linear aspects of goods market arbitrage and adjustment: Heckscher's commodity points revisited. *Journal of the Japanese and International Economies* 11:441–479.

Parsley, D. C., and S.-J. Wei. (2001a). Explaining the border effect: The role of exchange rate variability, shipping costs and geography. *Journal of International Economics* 55:87–105.

————, and ————. (2001b). Limiting currency volatility to stimulate goods market integration: A price based approach. Owens Graduate School of Management, Vanderbilt University. Manuscript.

Rogers, J. H. (2001). Price level convergence, relative prices, and inflation in Europe. Board of Governors of the Federal Reserve System. International Finance Discussion Paper 699.

————, and M. Jenkins. (1995). Haircuts or hysteresis? Sources of movements in real exchange rates. *Journal of International Economics* 38:339–360.

Rogoff, K. (1996). The purchasing power parity puzzle. *Journal of Economic Literature* 34:647–668.

Rose, A. K. (2000). One money, one market: The effect of common currencies on trade. *Economic Policy* 15:7–46.

Tille, C. (2000). "Beggar-thy-Neighbor" or "beggar-thyself"? The income effect of exchange rate fluctuations. Federal Reserve Bank of New York. Staff Report 112.

Comment

KAREN K. LEWIS
The Wharton School of the University of Pennsylvania

1. Introduction

This paper by Charles Engel is a very useful survey on what the new-open-economy literature and empirical evidence on real-exchange-rate behavior have to say about Milton Friedman's (1953) case for floating exchange rates. Friedman argued that when prices are sticky, floating exchange rates are preferable to fixed exchange rates because the nominal exchange rate can move to bring the real exchange rate in line with the equilibrium relative price between domestic and foreign goods. As Engel demonstrates, however, this question hinges upon the degree to which exchange-rate changes are passed through into imported-goods prices in domestic currencies. After describing this result, Engel examines the current empirical literature on real-exchange-rate behavior. The evidence suggests that domestic prices are rather unresponsive to exchange rates. Engel argues that fixed, not flexible, exchange rates are optimal in this case. Engel also looks at other explanations for the insensitivity of domestic prices to exchange-rate changes and concludes that more research needs to be done to arrive at a definitive answer.

As a status report on the literature, this paper fills an important niche in emphasizing what we have learned so far. However, the paper also highlights some issues that remain on the table to understand the significance of both the specific arguments in the paper and how they bear on the literature as a whole. Some of these issues are described by Engel. Therefore, I focus below on some of the issues not mentioned in the paper. I divide my comments into two broad categories: first, issues arising from the argument in the paper itself; and second, issues that remain for the literature to confront in the future.

2. Issues Arising from the Paper

The basic premise of this paper is derived in Devereux and Engel (2001). The model is a *new-open-economy macro* model with two countries populated by monopolistic competitors facing constant markups and representative consumers. In the basic model, consumers have the same utility function, although generalizations are described later in the paper. Importantly, markets are incomplete, so that agents cannot undo the effects of sticky prices, a critical factor in Friedman's case for floating exchange rates. The nature of market incompleteness assumed here is that state-contingent assets have nominal, not real, payouts. This assumption turns out to be key to the welfare implications, as I describe below.

With this model, Engel examines three regimes with different exchange-rate passthrough assumptions. First, it is assumed that prices are completely flexible. In this case, it is shown that whether the exchange rate is fixed or flexible, the constrained optimum can be achieved. In this optimum, relative prices of home to foreign goods are equal to the ratio of endowment supplies, so that

$$P_H/P_F = P_H^*/P_F^* = \eta^*/\eta. \tag{1}$$

The second regime Engel examines is the *producer currency pricing* (PCP) regime, in which there is 100% passthrough. The price is set in the exporting country's currency, and under floating exchange rates any change in exchange rates is completely passed through into changes in the importing country's price of the imported good. Purchasing-power parity (PPP) holds for each individual good. In this case, the same constrained optimum can be achieved, since relative prices change with the exchange rate. It is this channel that generates the optimum under both the flexible goods and the PCP case. This is a version of Friedman's argument for flexible exchange rates under sticky prices.

This result is reversed in the third case Engel examines, however. Under *local currency pricing* (LCP) the price is set in the importing country's currency. In this case, there is no passthrough. Since prices are unrelated to exchange-rate movements, there is no adjustment to changes in goods supplies even under flexible exchange rates. Therefore, it is not possible to achieve the constrained optimum. In fact, Engel argues that the optimal policy is to fix the exchange rate at the level implied by PPP.

The intuition for this result illustrates why the asset-markets assumption is so critical when there is no passthrough (LCP). First, the channel for relative prices to respond to real shocks is missing. Therefore, relative prices do not attain the constrained optimum, so that equation (1) does not hold, even under floating exchange rates.

Second, since PPP does not hold and since contingent claims pay out in nominal (not real) contracts, there is an additional source of distortion. In particular, nominal contingent contracts imply that asset markets achieve the following first-order condition:

$$U'(C)/P = U'(C)^*/SP^*, \tag{2}$$

where $U'(C)$ [$U'(C)^*$] is the marginal utility of consumption to the domestic [foreign] consumer, and P, P^*, and S are the domestic price, foreign price, and nominal exchange rate, respectively. As is well known, the standard complete-markets optimum would generate[1]

$$U'(C) = U'(C)^*. \tag{3}$$

Therefore, asset markets would achieve optimal risk sharing only if $P = SP^*$, since in this case the asset-market condition (2) also generates (3). In other words, the risk-sharing optimum holds only if PPP holds.

This distortion does not arise in the 100%-passthrough (PCP) regime,

---

1. In the standard model with isoelastic utility, the growth rates of marginal utilities are equalized. In this simple single-period model, parameters are normalized so that marginal-utility levels are equalized.

since PPP holds, resulting in the risk-sharing optimum automatically. However, in the no-passthrough (LCP) regime with nominal contingent contracts, there is an additional lack of risk-sharing distortion arising from deviations from PPP. In fact, in this regime the optimal policy is to give up on responding to supply shocks and instead target risk sharing by fixing the exchange rate at the level that will imply PPP.

While this policy is the best the authorities can accomplish under no passthrough (LCP), it is still Pareto-inferior to the optimum under 100% passthrough (PCP), since the economy is still left with the relative price distortion under no passthrough.

Given this background, I now describe questions arising from the argument.

2.1 WHAT TYPE OF ASSET MARKETS ARE THESE?

As explained above, the nature of the welfare hierarchy of the exchange-rate policies in the presence of different degrees of exchange-rate pass-through depends critically on the asset-market structure. However, there is little motivation for this market. Why are there state-contingent claims in nominal, but not real, payoffs? Many critics of the complete-markets assumption focus upon the state-contingent nature of the payoffs. Recent studies find that only a small proportion of risks measured by consumption outcomes are spanned by financial returns.[2] Given the substantial stickiness of prices documented by Engel, it seems unlikely that adjusting by the nominal price levels would affect this result. By contrast, it could be argued that liquid markets exist for real-index bonds for which assets pay out in real terms. Another approach that has been taken in the literature is to assume that state-contingent assets do not trade at all, but that risk-free bonds can be used to smooth consumption intertemporally.[3] It would be interesting to see how these more conventional assumptions about incomplete markets would affect the results from the analysis.

Whatever the result, it is clear that the assumed asset structure is key to the outcome in the paper. Therefore, it deserves more discussion. Why can't people trade at least some assets with real payouts if they can trade in what would seem like much more complex asset markets that pay off nominal returns in *all* states? What kind of market is this, and where do we see examples in the real world? How robust are the implications for fixed vs. floating exchange rates to the specific assumptions of the form of market incompleteness?

2. See for example Davis, Nalewaik, and Willen (2000).
3. See Heaton and Lucas (1995, 1996), and Baxter and Crucini (1995), to name a few.

2.2 HOW IMPORTANT QUANTITATIVELY ARE THESE INEFFICIENCIES?

Taking the asset market structure as given, the other question lurking behind the welfare hierarchy is: "How big are the welfare distortions?" Recall that under 100% passthrough the constrained optimum can be achieved where two potential distortions can be eliminated: (a) misallocation of relative goods supplies, and (b) inefficient sharing of risks across countries. Under the no-passthrough (LCP) regime, only the risk-sharing inefficiency (b) can be eliminated. Therefore, the obvious question is: how large is this inefficiency (b) compared to the inefficiency (a)?

If risk-sharing welfare costs (b) are large and the supply allocation welfare costs (a) are small, then it would seem that the difference between the optimal exchange-rate regimes under no passthrough and 100% passthrough would not be very great. Under no passthrough (LCP), the economy would be left with a small resource-allocation distortion after fixing exchange rates, but in either case, the risk-sharing costs are eliminated. This would imply that the welfare costs of having no passthrough are not large.

On the other hand, if risk-sharing welfare costs (b) are significantly smaller than supply allocation costs (a), then there is a significant welfare loss under fixed exchange rates arising from the exporters' practice of fixing prices in local currencies and not passing through exchange-rate changes. In this case, the choice of exchange-rate regime would be a less important policy issue than this practice by exporters and importers. This is because, whether exchange rates are fixed or floating, there is a large welfare loss from supply misallocation (a) that arises purely from the practice of not passing exchange-rate changes through to exporting prices. Therefore, a more important policy might be to encourage exporters and importers to pass exchange-rate changes through to local-currency prices, thereby getting the economy closer to a constrained optimum.

As this discussion makes clear, without some quantification, we cannot know how critical the degree of exchange-rate passthrough is to Friedman's argument for fixed vs. floating exchange rates.

2.3 IS THE FOCUS UPON THE FRIEDMAN ARGUMENT FOR FLOATING RATES TOO NARROW?

In this paper, Engel asks what this version of the new open-economy model has to say about Friedman's argument for floating exchange rates. Given the discussion above, it is clear that this leads to an argument not for fixed exchange rates necessarily, but for a *PPP rule*. Moreover, the rationale behind this PPP rule in the model is expressly to eliminate a distortion of international risk sharing.

On the other hand, countries that have adopted a PPP exchange-rate rule, such as Latin American countries and Israel, do not appear to have had international risk sharing as a major policy objective. Rather, the PPP rule seems to coincide with announced concerns about reducing inflation and generating credibility in financial markets.

Thus, it appears that by choosing to focus upon Friedman's argument, Engel has narrowed the discussion of fixed vs. floating rates to risk sharing. This particular consideration does not seem to be a major concern to policymakers faced with this decision, however.

3. Issues Ahead for the Literature

Above, I have restricted my comments to the specifics of the model and empirical evidence outlined by Engel in his paper. In this section, I describe some issues that lie ahead for the literature to confront if the new open-economy model is to be used to make welfare statements about Friedman's argument for fixed vs. floating rates.

3.1 HOMOGENEOUS PASSTHROUGH ACROSS INDUSTRIES

The model described in the paper relies upon fixed markups and passthrough across industries at the aggregate economy level. However, the empirical evidence on passthrough has found both assumptions to be counterfactual at the industry level. For example, Knetter (1993) finds significant differences in markups across industries. In fact, he finds that there is greater variation in markups across industries than across countries. Furthermore, Bodnar, Dumas, and Marston (2002) examine a duopoly model of domestic and foreign exporters in Japan in which the markups not only are time-varying, but depend upon the exchange rate. Table 1 reproduces some of the estimates of passthrough across indus-

Table 1   PASSTHROUGH ESTIMATES BY INDUSTRY FROM BODNAR, DUMAS, AND MARSTON (2002)

Industry	Passthrough coefficient
Construction machinery	0.806
Measuring equipment	0.750
Camera	0.471
Copies	0.294
Motor vehicles	0.262
Electronic parts	0.244
Magnetic recording	0.218
Film	0.148

Figure 1 MOTOR VEHICLE PRICES IN YEN

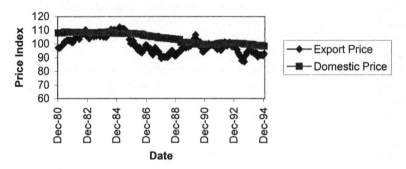

Figure 2 CAMERA PRICES IN YEN

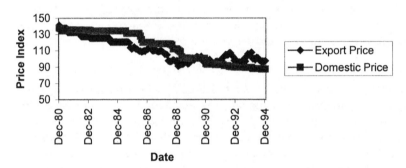

tries. The passthrough coefficients of exchange rates to Japanese export goods differ from about 81% for construction machinery to about 15% for film. To illustrate the relationship between the domestic and foreign prices, Figures 1 and 2 show the domestic price index and the export price index, both in Japanese yen, for motor vehicles and cameras, respectively.[4] While these figures are not the most extreme differences in passthrough shown in Table 1, there are clearly differences in the amount of variability in the deviations from the law of one price in these goods.

Thus, before the model outlined in the paper can be used to make policy statements that hinge critically on the degree of passthrough, more research must be done to understand the behavior of aggregate passthrough. In particular, the literature must tackle the question of how differences in markups and / or passthrough at the industry level (perhaps

4. I thank Dick Marston for providing me with the data from the Bank of Japan to generate these figures.

even the firm level) aggregate up to the macroeconomic response of goods pricing.

3.2 CONSTANT PASSTHROUGH OVER TIME

In the literature, a standard assumption is that passthrough is constant over time. Accordingly, in the paper by Engel, passthrough is either 100% or zero all the time, although these extremes are clearly meant as benchmark assumptions. While this assumption makes for tractable analysis and results, it is at odds with standard business practice. Companies involved in international trade differ in their approaches to exchange-rate risk, but most international financial officers claim to use a variety of strategies to manage this risk. These strategies include a combination of hedging the risk with financial instruments and adjusting the local-currency price as the exchange rate changes.

Some evidence on these business practices is provided in a survey of 399 firms' use of derivatives (Bodnar, Marston, and Hayt (1998). These firms were from diverse industries coming from three different sectors: primary products, manufacturing, and services. Moreover, the firms ranged from small (sales less than $150 million) to large (sales more than $1.2 billion). Of the large firms, 83% responded that they used financial derivatives to hedge risk; of the medium-sized firms, 45%; of the small firms, 12%. This suggests that much of the international trade transactions at the macro level in the United States is hedged to some degree with derivatives.

What does hedging have to do with passthrough? Financial officers suggest that they often view hedging and adjusting their local-currency price as substitute strategies for protecting profits from adverse exchange-rate changes. When profits are protected from exchange-rate movements by existing hedges, exporters feel less need to adjust prices in local currency and tend not to pass through exchange-rate changes. On the other hand, when there are no hedges or existing hedges have expired, exchange-rate movements are felt more directly in profit lines and there is a more immediate need to consider a price change.

On this issue, the survey by Bodnar, Marston, and Hayt (1998) is again illuminating. Of the firms that use derivatives to hedge currency risk, 85% replied that they hedged anticipated transactions less than a year, and only 57% said that they hedge anticipated transactions more than a year. This evidence is consistent with anecdotal evidence that suggests firms hedge short-term exposures more actively than longer-term exposures. Moreover, 60% of the firms said that while they faced foreign-exchange exposure, the net exposure was only plus or minus 5% of net revenues.

This suggests that many firms have multiple exposures so that they are operationally hedged.

If firms are hedged with either derivatives or a mix of operations, then it is likely that many international financial officers do not alter local-currency prices in the near term. Therefore, short-term passthrough is likely to be low. However, as hedging instruments expire, these same international officers are forced to pass through the changes at least partially in order to preserve profit lines. Clearly, the degree of competition and the mix of operations are key factors in this decision.

Overall, it is difficult to envision a model that brings empirics on exchange-rate passthrough together with welfare analysis of Friedman's argument for fixed exchange rates without considering the passthrough decision as an endogenous variable to the firm.

4. Conclusions

This paper is an insightful survey of what the new-open-economy macro literature and empirical evidence on the real exchange rate jointly have to say about Friedman's argument for fixed vs. floating exchange rates. It should be useful to any researcher who wants to learn more about the area.

At the same time, I was left with the wish list of research items posed above. This list includes: (1) quantifying the importance of the welfare costs; and (2) analyzing the robustness of the results to (a) the asset market assumptions and (b) heterogeneity and time variation in passthrough across industries. I look forward to reading about such further research.

REFERENCES

Baxter, M. and M. J. Crucini. (1995). Business cycles and the asset structure of foreign trade. *International Economic Review* 36:821–854.
Bodnar, G., R. Marston, and G. Hayt. (1998). Survey of derivatives usage by U.S. non-financial firms. Weiss Center for International Financial Research, Wharton School.
———, B. Dumas, and R. C. Marston. (2002). Pass-through and exposure. *Journal of Finance* 57:199–231.
Davis, S. J., J. Nalewaik, and P. Willen. (2000). On the gains to international trade in risky financial assets. Cambridge, MA: National Bureau of Economic Research. NBER Working Paper 7796.
Devereux, M. B., and C. Engel. (2001). Monetary policy in the open economy revisited: Exchange rate flexibility and price setting behavior. University of Wisconsin–Madison. Manuscript.
Friedman, M. (1953). The case for flexible exchange rates. *Essays in Positive Economics*. Chicago: University of Chicago Press, pp. 157–203.
Heaton J., and D. Lucas. (1995). The importance of investor heterogeneity and

financial market imperfections for the behavior of asset prices. *Carnegie-Rochester Conference Series on Public Policy* 42:1–32.

——, and ——. (1996). Evaluating the effects of incomplete markets on risk sharing and asset pricing. *Journal of Political Economy* 104:443–487.

Knetter, M. M. (1993). International comparisons of price-to-market behavior. *American Economic Review* 83:473–486.

Comment[1]

PIERRE-OLIVIER GOURINCHAS
Princeton University, NBER, and CEPR

1. Introduction

It is a pleasure to discuss this paper by Charles Engel. In recent years, Engel has been a major contributor to the new-open-economy macro (NOEM) literature. This literature, pioneered by Obstfeld and Rogoff (1995), aims to build models of the open economy in the New Keynesian tradition while retaining solid micro foundations and a rigorous intertemporal approach. Engel's empirical and theoretical papers have shaped and greatly influenced the direction that this research has taken.

This paper offers two contributions. The first part is a survey of recent developments in the literature, both theoretical and empirical. This is most welcome. The field is starting to look a lot like a restaurant menu with 150 different entrees, all made from the same 20 basic ingredients. In the end, and without a little clarification for the layman inside all of us, they all taste the same. The second part of the paper provides additional empirical evidence that prices are sticky in consumers' currency, evidence that is used to discriminate further between alternative models.

I like the first part. I am somewhat less convinced by the second one, as my comments will now explain.

2. A (Selective) Review of the Literature: What We Have Learned

A key issue is the impact of exchange-rate movements on relative prices and quantities. In the traditional Mundell–Fleming framework, domestic-currency prices of domestically produced goods are given, and the pass-through from exchange rates to prices is unitary. A depreciation of the domestic currency lowers the price of exports in the foreign currency and

1. Thanks to Richard Friberg, Helene Rey, and Lars Svensson for helpful discussions and comments.

increases the price of imports in the domestic currency. This relative-price change affects the allocation of expenditure—the *expenditure-switching mechanism*—which is at the heart of the adjustment process and is the key to the potency of monetary policy under flexible exchange rates.

2.1 EARLY NEW OPEN-ECONOMY MODELS: PRODUCER CURRENCY PRICING

The early NOEM models of Obstfeld and Rogoff (1995, 1998, 2000, 2002) have incorporated this mechanism by assuming that prices are fixed in the currency of the producer (*producer currency pricing*, or PCP). Not surprisingly, perhaps, these models retain the flavor of the old Mundell–Fleming framework. In contrast, though, one can now ask normative questions such as (1) "What are the optimal exchange-rate regime and monetary policy?" and (2) "Should there be monetary cooperation?" In Obstfeld and Rogoff (2002), the answers are (1) to float, and to set monetary policy to respond to domestic real shocks only, and (2) no.

This paper provides a nice intuition for these results: under a complete set of *nominal* claims, the marginal utility of a unit of domestic currency is proportional between domestic and foreign consumers. Full insurance—equating marginal utilities—requires that PPP hold. This happens when the exchange rate is flexible. On the other hand, country-specific shocks require an adjustment in relative prices. When prices are sticky in the producer's currency, this is achieved by a flexible exchange rate, provided monetary policy targets domestic real shocks. This is the rationale for flexible exchange rates in Mundell's classical analysis of optimum currency areas, and this also underlies Friedman's celebrated argument for flexible exchange rates. In the Obstfeld–Rogoff setup, therefore, Friedman meets Mundell, and they both conclude that flexible exchange rates do the trick. Together with an appropriately chosen monetary policy (one that focuses exclusively on the task at hand, i.e. stabilizing domestic fluctuations), this implements the constrained Pareto-efficient allocation and replicates the flexible price allocation.

It is useful to note that this result does not depend too much on the assumption that markets for nominal contingent claims are complete. Indeed, as Obstfeld and Rogoff (2002) have shown, even when markets are incomplete, the gains from cooperation are likely to be very small compared to the potential gains from stabilization of domestic disturbances. This is so because in this class of models the welfare gains from international risk sharing are not very large.

2.2 BUT THE LAW OF ONE PRICE DOES NOT HOLD

So, what more could we ask for?

Well, it turns out that a critical assumption in this class of models is the

PCP assumption and the associated expenditure-switching mechanism. In its simplest form, it implies that the law of one price (LOOP) holds for consumer prices. Yet, as Engel and others demonstrated in a series of very influential papers (Engel, 1993, 1999; Engel and Rogers, 1996, 2001; Parsley and Wei, 2001), and as he shows anew in this paper (see his Figure 1), domestic and foreign consumer markets are very segmented. Put simply, LOOP does not hold, and the passthrough to retail prices is closer to zero than to one. Engel (1999) demonstrates an even stronger result. He decomposes movements in the CPI real exchange rate into two components (up to some empirically small covariance term): the relative price of traded goods, and a weighted difference of the relative price of traded to nontraded goods at home and abroad. Under standard theories of exchange-rate determination, tradable goods satisfy LOOP, so movements in the real exchange rate should be accounted for by fluctuations in the relative price of traded to nontraded goods at home and abroad. Yet, Engel finds that up to 90% of the variability in real exchange rates, even at long horizons, is explained instead by deviations from LOOP.

This result is consistent with a combination of two assumptions. First, firms can price-discriminate across markets (*price to market*, or PTM). Second, they set prices in advance in local currency (*local currency pricing*, or LCP). As Devereux and Engel (1998) and this paper show, these assumptions deliver starkly different results. Since prices are now sticky in the importer's currency, relative-price adjustments do not take place, even with a flexible exchange rate. A flexible exchange rate just causes profit risk for exporters. A fixed exchange rate is therefore the optimal policy. In this framework, both Mundell and Friedman are wrong, the former because there is no expenditure-switching effect, the latter because there are no relative-price adjustments.

2.3 YET THERE IS EVIDENCE OF EXPENDITURE SWITCHING

Given the extensive evidence of the failures of LOOP, is the debate settled?

Not quite. Obstfeld and Rogoff (2000) and Obstfeld (2001) show that the LCP assumption has some implications for the comovements of the terms of trades and the nominal exchange rate that are rejected by the data. Suppose, as Devereux and Engel do, that prices are fixed in the importer's currency. Denote the domestic currency price of imported foreign goods by P_F. Denote the foreign currency price of exported domestic goods by P_H^*. Both are fixed. The terms of trade, the relative price of home imports in terms of home exports, is simply $P_F/\varepsilon P_H^*$, where ε denotes the nominal exchange rate quoted as units of domestic currency per unit of foreign currency. Under LCP, a currency depreciation—an increase in ε—*improves* the terms of trade.

Conversely, under PCP, the domestic price of imports, $P_F = \varepsilon P_F^*$, increases one for one with the exchange rate, while the domestic-currency price of domestic exports, P_H, remains unchanged. Hence the terms of trade are $\varepsilon P_F^* / P_H$ and *deteriorate* with a currency depreciation.

As Obstfeld and Rogoff show, terms-of-trade deteriorations are, if anything, positively correlated with nominal-exchange-rate depreciations. Figures 1 and 2 report scatterplots of the 12-month change in the relative price of exports—a proxy for P_F / P_H—against the 12-month change in the nominal exchange rate for Japan and Germany against the United States. The correlation is positive and very high in both cases (0.86 for Japan–U.S. and 0.95 for Germany–U.S.), indicating substantial deterioration in the terms of trade when the currency depreciates.

As Obstfeld (2001, p. 19) argues, "because the ultimate consumer is several steps removed from the port of entry of import goods, however, findings such as Engel's (1999) have only an indirect bearing on the height of barriers to international trade between firms, which accounts for most of international trade." Indeed, empirical studies of passthrough surveyed in Goldberg and Knetter (1997) indicate substantial but not 100% passthrough at the firm level.

To summarize, the overwhelming evidence assembled by Engel in this

Figure 1 YEN–DOLLAR RELATIVE EXPORT PRICES VS. NOMINAL EXCHANGE RATE (12-MONTH PERCENTAGE CHANGE), 1974–2002

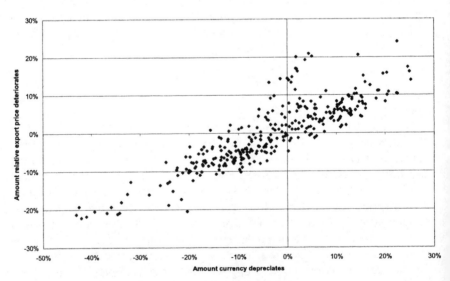

Figure 2 DEUTSCHE-MARK–DOLLAR RELATIVE EXPORT PRICE VS. NOMINAL EXCHANGE RATE (12-MONTH PERCENTAGE CHANGE), 1974–2002

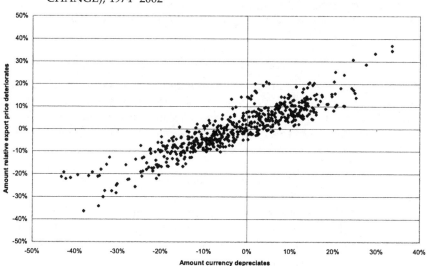

and previous papers indicates that consumer markets are very segmented, even for tradable goods. Yet terms of trade and export prices do respond to exchange rates. This opens up the possibility that expenditure-switching channels are present at the importer level, yet do not affect the consumer level much.

3. What Should Come Next

What can account for the different behavior of import and consumer prices? The paper considers three possibilities. First, trading costs may lead domestic consumers to substitute for domestic alternatives (Obstfeld and Rogoff, 2000). If so, the share of foreign goods in the price index may be small, and fluctuations in the exchange rate may not affect the CPI much. Second, deviations of LOOP could arise from the nontraded component in each traded good—local production and distribution costs such as rent, advertising, etc. (McCallum and Nelson, 2000; Burstein, Neves, and Rabelo, 2000). Lastly, intermediate inputs represent the bulk of international trade between developed economies. If domestic and foreign intermediates are substitutes, a fluctuation in the exchange rate may not affect the overall CPI much, even with a high passthrough at the import level (Obstfeld, 2001).

The substantive part of the paper considers all three alternatives and argues that explanations based on trading costs and on nontradable services and distribution do not hold up to the data. Before I comment on this part, it is important to log a few remarks on the general research agenda.

3.1 INVOICING: PRACTICE AND THEORY

Clearly, price discrimination and invoicing practices can have a large effect on the transmission mechanism and optimal monetary policy. This raises two questions, one positive and one normative: What do we know about invoicing practices? In which currency should exporters set their prices?

3.1.1 Invoicing in Practice   The empirical evidence is sparse. Obstfeld and Rogoff (2000), as well as most of the literature, refer to a 1995 Institute study concluding that most exports tend to be invoiced in the currency of the exporter. There is one notable exception: exports to the United States are generally invoiced in dollars.

Table 1 reports some more recent evidence on the currency of denomination of exports and imports of some industrialized countries between 1992 and 1996, from Tavlas (1997). The U.S. special status is still there:

Table 1   CURRENCY DENOMINATION OF SELECTED INDUSTRIAL COUNTRIES, 1992–1996

Country	Fraction (%)		
	U.S. Dollar	DM	Yen
Exports			
United States	98.0	0.4	0.4
Germany	9.8	76.4	0.6
Japan	52.7	—	35.7
United Kingdom	22.0	5.0	0.7
France	18.6	10.6	1.0
Italy	23.0	18.0	—
Imports			
United States	88.8	3.2	3.1
Germany	18.1	53.3	1.5
Japan	70.4	2.8	22.5
United Kingdom	22.0	11.9	2.4
France	23.1	10.1	1.0
Italy	28.0	13.0	—

Source: Tavlas (1997)

98% of exports and 88% of imports are invoiced in dollars. For other countries, the picture is more mixed. For instance, the U.S. dollar is used to invoice more than half of Japanese exports, and about 20% of French and Italian exports. Lastly, Germany is comparable to the United States, invoicing more than 50% of its imports in its own currency. This last fact does not fit well with either the PCP or the LCP assumption. Take the extreme case where all international transactions with the United States are invoiced in dollars, at set prices in the short run. Neither the U.S. terms of trade, $P_F/\varepsilon P_H^*$, nor the U.S. CPI responds to nominal exchange rates, and the exchange-rate risk falls squarely on foreigners.

Table 2 in Friberg (2001)—reproduced here as Table 2—provides some additional data for Sweden for 1968 and 1995. Less than 50% of exports is now invoiced in Swedish krona. In contrast, the fraction of imports invoiced in krona has increased from 26% to 33%.

One can conclude that the pattern of the ECU study has not remained stable over time, as more firms appear to rely on international currencies or the importing-country currency for international transactions. One may legitimately ask whether this change has been accompanied by similar changes in the passthrough or associated with some of the changes in

Table 2   CURRENCY DENOMINATION OF SWEDISH TRADE 1995 AND 1968

	Fraction (%)				Share in Swedish exports (%)
	Imports		Exports		
Currency	1995	1968	1995	1968	
SEK	33.1	25.8	43.8	66.1	—
USD	21.9	22	18.4	12.3	8
DEM	14.4	17.4	9.8	3.8	13.3
GBP	5.4	17.3	5.4	11.2	10.2
NLG	5.1	NA	3.2	NA	5.3
FRF	4.1	2.5	3.7	0.8	5.1
DKK	3	3.9	2.6	1.8	6.9
NOK	2	2.2	2.8	0.7	8.1
ITL	1.7	1.8	1.4	0.3	3.8
JPY	1.7	NA	1.4	NA	2.7
FIM	1.6	NA	1.7	NA	4.8
CHF	1.5	NA	NA	0.5	1.9
Other	4.3	4.7	4.6	2.5	29.9
Total	100	100	100	100	100

Source: Friberg (2001). Data from 1995 are taken from the settlement reports of Sveriges Riksbank—all payments for goods above a threshold of SEK 100,000 and going through Swedish banks are reported. The data from 1968 are from Grassman (1973). Data on exports are from 1994; source: Statistics Sweden.

the structure and patterns of international trade between developed countries (outsourcing, intrafirm trade, etc.), and of financial flows (globalization, international currencies, etc.). But more importantly, this evidence highlights the perils of assessing the merits of various monetary-policy and exchange-rate regimes if we do not have a clear understanding of the determinants of invoicing practices.

3.1.2 Invoicing in Theory At a theoretical level, the invoicing decision need not be neutral. The choice of currency can affect the variability of profits through exchange-rate risk. Consider for instance the case where an exporter sets its price P_H^* in the importer's currency. Assume that import demand depends only upon the import price $[Q(P_H^*)]$ and that forward markets are available and efficient. The exporter can hedge fully any fluctuation in future revenues by selling $P_H^* Q(P_H^*)$ of the foreign-currency forward. On the other hand, if a price P_H is set in the exporter's currency, the future demand $Q(P_H/\varepsilon)$ becomes uncertain and may be more difficult to hedge. This intuition underlies Friberg's (1998) result that invoicing in the importer's currency maximizes ex ante profits when the latter are concave in exchange-rate surpises.

But these results are obtained in partial equilibrium, and therefore somewhat unsatisfactory. After all, it is likely that the volatility of the exchange rate will depend upon the equilibrium currency invoicing that we observe. To paraphrase Krugman (1989), high exchange-rate volatility may be a telltale sign that exchange rates do not matter much, a situation that is much more likely when prices are set in the importer's currency. Further, a firm's decision to invoice in a given currency may not be independent of what other firms are doing. Strategic complementarities can be important.

One recent paper considers the invoicing question in a general-equilibrium framework: Bacchetta and Van Wincoop (2001). They show that exporters have a greater preference to invoice in their own currency the higher their market share and the lower the elasticity of substitution with competing products.

It is a bit early to tell whether these results are robust, or what optimal monetary policy would be like, and how it would depend upon the degree of market incompleteness. But this is clearly an area that deserves further investigation.

3.2 BEYOND EXPENDITURE SWITCHING

In modern economies, exchange-rate movements have complex effects that cannot be reduced to a simple expenditure-switching effect. Consider

Devereux and Engel's (2002) careful attempt at *disconnecting* the exchange rate from other macro fundamentals. Under LCP, relative export prices will not change. Yet external adjustment will come through at least two other channels. First, a depreciation of the domestic currency will reduce markups on foreign goods sold domestically. This decreases profits for local distributors and/or foreign producers, depending on the vertical pricing structure of the industry. As foreign goods become generally less profitable, one should expect a gradual improvement over time in the external accounts. Second, an *expected* depreciation leads to a compensating interest-rate differential. A higher domestic interest rate induces a higher growth rate of consumption, which can also increase current net exports. The general message from Devereux and Engel's paper is that it takes quite a bit of work, and a number of not so appealing assumptions, to disconnect the exchange rate.

Given the empirical evidence on the disconnect, i.e. of "weak feedback links between the exchange rate and the rest of the economy" (Obstfeld and Rogoff, 2000), this may indicate that expenditure switching—and all the other channels—are not very operational. *A contrario*, this reinforces the view that the expenditure effect is not so crucial anyway.

3.2.1 Quantities and J-Curve What does the empirical evidence say? One way to make progress is to look at the evidence on the effect of exchange rates on quantities. After all, it is not enough to measure the effect of nominal exchange rate on relative prices or terms of trade. The ultimate importance of expenditure switching can only be measured by its effect on quantities: goods imported or exported, demand for factors of production, etc.

Engel correctly argues that "microeconomic studies that examine how imports of particular types of goods, or how employment in specific industries, are affected by changes in import prices must be applied with a dollop of caution. That is because there is a missing link that must be supplied before one can use these studies to judge the quantitative significance of the expenditure-switching effect: the degree of passthrough." But similarly, one should apply caution in interpreting studies that show a low degree of passthrough without looking at the effect on quantities. What if import demand is very elastic? Even with a low passthrough, adjustments may be substantial.

The first piece of evidence comes from Figure 3, from Backus, Kehoe, and Kydland's (1994) classic study on the J-curve. The cross-correlation function between terms of trade and the ratio of the trade balance to output indicates that the trade balance tends to improve following an improvement in competitiveness (a worsening in the terms of trade).

Figure 3 CROSS-CORRELATION FUNCTIONS FOR THE TRADE BALANCE
AND THE TERMS OF TRADE IN 11 COUNTRIES.

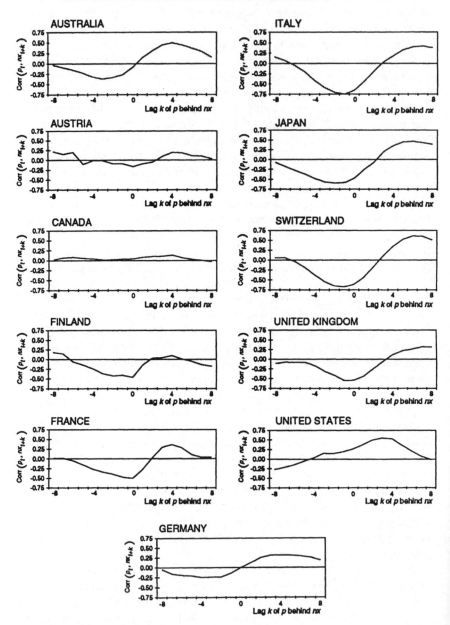

From Backus, Kehoe, and Kydland (1994).

But these cross-correlations do not tell us how large is the effect of the exchange rate on the trade balance or factor demands. In Gourinchas (1998), I looked directly at the impact of exchange-rate movements on the labor market. An important methodological innovation in that paper was to focus on disaggregated data and to construct industry-specific exchange rates from bilateral real exchange rates based on the wholesale price index, using as weights the trade shares of the major trading partners. While changes in exchange rate appear to have little effect at the aggregate level, they have important effects on export-oriented and import-competing industries. Importantly for Engel's paper, these results do not look at the effect of changes in relative export or import prices. The reason for doing so is simple: export prices are choice variables for firms. Issues of simultaneity and exogeneity are thus likely to be important. On the other hand, most firms are likely to take the bilateral exchange rate as given and unlikely to be influenced by their individual production decisions.[2]

This has the important consequence that I am estimating a *net* exchange-rate effect on employment, after being filtered into import prices, markups, wealth and profits.[3] The results, reproduced in Table 3, indicate that a 10% depreciation of the exchange rate (a high value of λ) leads to an increase in tradable manufacturing employment of 0.27% over the next three quarters. The evidence indicates that these exchange-rate movements account for between 9% and 11% of the fluctuations of employment at the four-digit level, on average. While not a major source of fluctuation, they are nonetheless significant. Goldberg and Tracy (2002, 2000) and Campa and Goldberg (2001), in a series of papers, argue further that exchange-rate changes also affect wages significantly, especially for low-skill workers.

These results indicate that exchange rates do matter, although the evidence is not detailed enough to indicate whether it is through an expenditure-switching effect or any other channel.

4. What We Cannot Conclude (Yet)

With these comments made, let me return to the second part of the paper. Sections 7–9 consider three models that can potentially explain the low

2. The issue of simultaneity is more delicate to handle, since exchange rates could move in response to monetary and fiscal determinants that affect labor markets directly. I show in my paper that this is not likely to be a serious issue for the United States: in effect, the paper uses the disconnect to identify the response of employment to exchange-rate movements that are not connected with monetary or aggregate activity.
3. Since I also include direct controls for monetary policy, the effect of exchange rates does not include their indirect effect on domestic interest rates.

Table 3 EMPLOYMENT RESPONSE TO REAL-EXCHANGE-RATE DEVIATIONS

| Sector: Regressor | Timing | Two-digit | | All | | Traded | | | | | |
| | | | | | | Exports | | Import comp. | | Nontraded | |
		Coeff.	SE	Coeff.	SE	Coeff.	SE	Coeff.	SE	Coeff.	SE
λ_t	Cont.	1.40	1.65	4.97	2.47	2.72	3.32	4.58	3.18	6.24	3.38
	1 lag	−0.64	2.29	5.47	3.40	2.60	4.70	8.24	4.32	−3.13	4.45
	2 lags	−0.37	1.76	−7.73	2.58	−4.28	3.49	−9.84	3.31	−0.92	3.49
	Sum:	0.39	0.76	2.71	1.13	1.03	1.38	2.96	1.03	2.18	1.88
$\hat{E}_t$	Cont.	0.68	0.03	0.66	0.06	0.48	0.07	0.77	0.08	0.52	0.08
	1 lag	0.01	0.04	0.08	0.06	0.12	0.08	0.03	0.08	0.02	0.08
	2 lags	0.17	0.03	0.28	0.05	0.37	0.07	0.18	0.07	0.06	0.07
	Sum:	0.85	0.04	1.02	0.07	0.98	0.10	0.98	0.10	0.60	0.10
i_t	Cont.	0.05	0.03	0.05	0.05	0.18	0.07	−0.08	0.07	−0.03	0.07
	1 lag	−0.12	0.03	−0.05	0.06	−0.10	0.08	0.01	0.08	−0.06	0.08
	2 lags	0.02	0.03	0.01	0.06	−0.07	0.07	0.04	0.08	0.07	0.07
	Sum:	−0.06	0.02	0.01	0.03	0.01	0.05	−0.03	0.04	−0.01	0.04

Source: Gourinchas (1998, Table 3).

passthrough to consumer prices, together with higher passthrough to import prices and a significant expenditure-switching effect. Among these models, Engel argues that the shipping costs and the nontradable component of tradable goods are not the full answer. I want to revisit his arguments and offer a few comments.

4.1 SHIPPING COSTS AND DISCONNECT

Shipping costs reduce the weight on foreign goods in the CPI, and if domestic and foreign goods are substitute, this lowers the passthrough to consumer prices. To measure the importance of the shipping-cost argument, Engel runs regressions of the volatility of the bilateral real exchange rates for food and for commodities less food against a measure of distance and the volatility of the nominal exchange rate. Distance proxies for shipping costs, as is traditional in the gravity-equation literature. When both variables are introduced in the regression, only the volatility of the nominal exchange rate comes in significantly, which the author interprets as a rejection of the shipping-cost theory.

Yet it is possible to interpret the results somewhat differently. High volatility of the nominal exchange rate could also be evidence of large transaction or shipping costs, as in Dumas (1992). In that model, deviations from LOOP reflect the presence of nonconvex adjustment costs. The larger the costs, the larger the zone of inaction. The argument does not require that prices be set in the currency of the importer.

In other words, we would expect more variability in the nominal and real exchange rates if shipping costs are higher. The endogenous variance of the nominal exchange rate implies that regressions reported in Table 1 of the paper do not allow a separation between the shipping cost theory and the LCP alternative. The volatility of the nominal exchange rate may be picking up those components of the costs that are not already captured by geographical distance.

One may be tempted to dummy exchange-rate regimes. After all, Mussa (1986) showed that there is much less nominal and real exchange-rate variability under fixed than under flexible exchange rates. However, this may fail for another reason: if indeed differences in shipping costs account for the difference in volatility, it is the long-run volatility that matters. A rigid fixed-exchange-rate regime may suffer an ignominious fate—and the ensuing bout of volatility—if the peg does not allow for adjustments in real exchange rates. Though in the short run volatility may be low, in the long run it may be substantially higher.

More generally, nominal-exchange-rate volatility is likely to reflect the volatility of the underlying monetary policy as well as the impediments to trade in goods and the degree of price stickiness. An alternative approach would directly use measures of the volatility of the nonsystematic part of monetary policy—since the systematic part may also be geared to offset exchange-rate fluctuations, as in the case of fixed exchange rates.

As they stand, the empirical results from Section 7 do not provide a tight case that shipping costs are not an important part of the explanation.

4.2 NONTRADABLES AND LOCAL DISTRIBUTION COSTS

The paper argues that nontradables are relatively unimportant in explaining deviations from LOOP. Denote by p^* the foreign-currency price (in logs) of a good sold in the foreign country. If the good is produced at home, the price of exports in home currency is $e + p^*$. As a matter of decomposition, we can write

$$e + p^* = mc(z, y^*, e) + \mu(x^*, e),$$

where $mc(z, y^*, e)$ represents the marginal cost in domestic currency of production *and distribution*, and depends upon the domestic input costs z, as well as the foreign local costs y^* and the exchange rate e. The term $\mu(x^*, e)$ represents the markup and depends upon foreign demand x^* as well as the exchange rate e, if the firm is pricing to market. We observe that the exchange rate appears both in the marginal-cost term, reflecting the importance of the local nontradable component, and in the markup, reflecting pricing to market.

Similarly, let's write the price of the good in the source country as

$$p = mc(z, y, 1) + \mu(x, 1),$$

where both the marginal cost and the markup depend only upon domestic factors, as emphasized by the 1 in both terms. The marginal costs differ to the extent that the distribution part differs as well. The relative price of the good is simply

$$e + p^* - p = [mc(z, y^*, e) - mc(z, y, 1)] + [\mu(x^*, e) - \mu(x, 1)]. \qquad (1)$$

This expression contains two terms. The first one reflects the differences in marginal costs, expressed in a common currency. One can think of this term as measuring the importance of local costs. The second term reflects the fact that firms can price-discriminate and apply different markups to different countries. The exchange rate appears in both terms.

Equation (1) is what Goldberg and Verboven (2001) estimate in their study of the European car market. They first estimate a semistructural demand system and use it to derive own- and cross-price derivatives that determine the optimal price markups. They then estimate a supply system similar to equation (1). They use their estimate to derive the relative importance of the exchange-rate component for the marginal cost and for the markup term. Their results indicate that roughly ⅔ of the deviations from LOOP arise from the local cost component.

By contrast, Engel writes the price of the good in the foreign market as

$$p^* = \alpha\, p_s^* + (1 - \alpha)\bar{p}^*,$$

where p_s^* represents the price of the local—nontradable—components and $\bar{p}^*$ the price of the tradable part. α represents the (constant) share of the costs arising from the local cost component. Using this decomposition, he obtains the following expression for the relative price:

$$e + p^* - p = \frac{\alpha}{1 - \alpha}\,[(p_s^* - p^*) - (p_s - p)] + [e + \bar{p}^* - \bar{p}]. \qquad (2)$$

The first term represents the domestic-vs.-foreign relative price of services, or more generally the nontradable component. Engel interprets this term as capturing the local cost component. The second term represents the relative price of the tradable component. Under the PTM, it should be zero. Engel interprets this term as capturing the relative markup.

Using data on the relative price of services as a proxy for p_s and p_s^*, and data on the price of food and nonfood commodities as a proxy for the price of the tradable component, Engel concludes that most of the variation arises from deviations in the (unobserved) relative price of the tradable component, $e + \bar{p}^* - \bar{p}$. In other words, there is little evidence in the OECD sectoral price data that deviations from LOOP arise from the foreign vs. domestic price of services relative to tradable goods.

Should we conclude that local costs are unimportant, and unaffected by exchange rates, as the paper does?

At face value, this paper's approach has a number of advantages: it relies on a simple decomposition, and does not require the potentially costly auxiliary assumptions on the market structure or the shape of the demand system that Goldberg and Verboven must make. However, it is also unclear that one can map equation (2) simply into equation (1). Ultimately, it is equation (1) that we are interested in, and equation (2) may have little to say about it.

Consider the following counterexample. Suppose there is perfect competition both at home and abroad, so that $\mu(x^*, e) = \mu(x, 1) = 0$. All variations in the relative price must come from the local cost component and relative marginal costs. Assume further that input prices are constant in their own currency. If there is substitution between local and home inputs, and marginal costs are not constant, a fluctuation in the exchange rate will affect the price of the tradable component less or more than one for one, leading to a fluctuation in $e + \bar{p}^* - \bar{p}$. Yet, by construction, this would simply reflect the effect of the exchange rate on relative marginal costs $mc(z, y^*, e) - mc(z, y, 1)$. It would be incorrect to attribute the variation to markup fluctuations.

5. Conclusions and Suggestions

This is a stimulating paper written by an expert in the field. It asks an important question, one that has gathered substantial attention of late: Is there an expenditure-switching effect, and if so, through which channels? In so doing, it provides a very valuable and insightful survey of recent developments on new open economy macro models. It then offers some new empirical evidence aimed at discriminating amongst the recent models that feature both low passthrough at the consumer level and higher passthrough at the import level. I find that part of the paper somewhat less convincing. The empirical evidence is exciting and will undoubtedly provoke further rounds. But I do not think that it addresses squarely the empirical questions raised by the models. The field has matured considerably in the past few years, and I believe it is now ripe for a careful look at the sort of microeconomic evidence that will deliver the next set of stylized facts. I am quite certain that Engel will be among the major contributors to this endeavor.

REFERENCES

Bacchetta, P., and E. Van Wincoop. (2001). A theory of currency denomination of international trade. University of Virginia. Mimeo.
Backus, D., P. Kehoe, and F. Kydland. (1994). Dynamics of the trade balance and the terms of trade: The J-curve? *American Economic Review* 84(1):84–103.
Burstein, A., J. Neves, and S. Rebelo. (2000). Distribution costs and exchange rate dynamics during exchange-rate-based stabilizations. Cambridge, MA: National Bureau of Economic Research. NBER Working Paper 7862.
Campa, J., and L. Goldberg. (2001). Employment versus wage adjustment and the U.S. dollar. *Review of Economics and Statistics* 83(3):477–489.
Devereux, M., and C. Engel. (1998). Fixed vs. floating exchange rates: How price setting affects the optimal choice of exchange-rate regime. Cambridge, MA: National Bureau of Economic Research. NBER Working Paper 6867.
———, and ———. (2002). Exchange rate pass-through, exchange rate volatility, and exchange rate disconnect. *Journal of Monetary Economics* 49(5):913–940.
Dumas, B. (1992). Dynamic equilibrium and the real exchange rate in a spatially separated world. *Review of Financial Studies* 5(2):153–180.

Engel, C. (1993). Real exchange rates and relative prices: An empirical investigation. *Journal of Monetary Economics*, pp. 35–50.

———. (1999). Accounting for U.S. real exchange rate changes. *Journal of Political Economy*, pp. 507–538.

———, and J. Rogers. (1996). How wide is the border? *American Economic Review* 86:1112–1125.

———, and ———. (2001). Deviation from the purchasing power parity: Causes and welfare costs. *Journal of International Economics* 55:29–57.

Friberg, R. (1998). In which currency should exporters set their prices? *Journal of International Economics* 45:59–76.

———. (2001). Comment on Paul Mizen: The euro and the changing role of currencies as transactions vehicles, *Swedish Economic Policy Review* 6:223–230.

Goldberg, L., and J. Tracy. (2000). Exchange rates and local labor markets. In *Trade and Wages*, R. Feenstra (ed.). Chicago: NBER and University of Chicago Press.

———, and ———. (2002). Exchange rates and wages. Cambridge, MA: National Bureau of Economic Research. NBER Working Paper.

Goldberg, P. K. and M. Knetter. (1997). Goods prices and exchange rates: What have we learned? *Journal of Economic Literature* 35:1243–1272.

———, and F. Verboven. (2001). The evolution of price dispersion in the European car market. *Review of Economic Studies* 68:811–848.

Gourinchas, P.-O. (1998). Exchange rates and jobs: What do we learn from job flows. In Ben Bernanke and Julio Rotemberg (eds.), *NBER Macroeconomics Annual 1998*. Cambridge, MA: The MIT Press, pp. 153–208.

Grassman, S. (1973). A fundamental symmetry in international payment patterns. *Journal of International Economics* 3(2):105–116.

Institute, ECU. (1995). *International Currency Competition and the Future Role of the Single European Currency*. London: Kluwer Law International.

Krugman, P. (1989). *Exchange-Rate Instability*. Cambridge, MA: The MIT Press.

McCallum, B., and E. Nelson. (2000). Monetary policy for an open economy: An alternative framework with optimizing agents and sticky prices. *Oxford Review of Economic Policy* 16:74–91.

Mussa, M. (1986). Nominal exchange rate regimes and the behavior of real exchange rates: Evidence and implications. In *Carnegie-Rochester Conference Series on Public Policy*, pp. 117–213.

Obstfeld, M. (2001). International macroeconomics: Beyond the Mundell–Fleming model. *IMF Staff Papers* 47(special issue):1–39.

———, and K. Rogoff. (1995). Exchange rate dynamics redux. *Journal of Political Economy* 103:624–660.

———, and ———. (1998). Risk and exchange rates. Cambridge, MA: National Bureau of Economic Research. NBER Working Paper 6694.

———, and ———. (2000). New directions for stochastic open economy models. *Journal of International Economics* 50:117–153.

———, and ———. (2002). Global implications of self-oriented national monetary rules. *Quarterly Journal of Economics* 117(2):503–536.

Parsley, D., and S.-J. Wei. (2001). Explaining the border effect: The role of exchange rate variability, shipping costs and geography. *Journal of International Economics* 55:87–105.

Tavlas, G. (1997). The international use of the US dollar: An optimal currency area perspective. *World Economy* 20(6):709–747.

Discussion

Alan Stockman remarked that the literature tends to focus on the details of price stickiness and price setting, and pays less attention to the consequences for quantities. He felt that micro-level work on this issue would be interesting, though it should not violate the Flood–Rose disconnect puzzle. He suggested that the disconnect puzzle may be connected with the fact that a fraction of trade is intrafirm trade, which involves transfer pricing for tax purposes. This implies that many prices do not have any economic content. He also questioned whether prices matter for quantities when trade takes place under implicit long-term contracts between firms. He noted that in his work on J-curves, he had found that in the longer term, the J-curve exists, but that it does not have the standard consequences for GDP. Rather than exchange-rate depreciation leading to higher net exports and an increase in GDP, depreciation leads to a statistically significant decrease in GDP.

Ken Rogoff noted that Engel's work provides strong evidence that consumer prices don't respond to exchange-rate changes. He added that Goldberg and Knetter show that passthrough is much greater into wholesale prices, but that recent work by Giovanni Olivei shows that passthrough into wholesale prices has declined both in the developed world and in the developing world. He commented that this is a mystery, and suggested that it might be connected with the fact that intrafirm trade is growing as a share of total trade. He pointed out that intrafirm trade is now over 50% of trade for many countries. He also cited work by Jim Rauch showing that interfirm trade often takes place as part of a network. However, he remarked that while the importance of intrafirm trade might suggest how exchange-rate risk is shared, how firms react to exchange-rate changes is still a puzzle. He noted that some firms, such as Ikea, seem to be good at matching sourcing behavior to exchange-rate changes, but that expenditure switching on a large scale doesn't seem to result.

Ariel Burstein mentioned that in exploring the links between passthrough and expenditure switching, it might be instructive to look at large devaluations, where nominal rigidities are unlikely to play a major role. He noted that in work where he looked at nine large devaluations in the 1990s, import prices move closely with the exchange rate, but consumer prices do not.

Charles Engel noted that the international setting demonstrates that menu costs cannot be the only explanation for nominal price stickiness, as menu costs are incurred no matter which currency prices are set in. Following up on this point, Ken Rogoff remarked that this literature could be very useful for closed-economy macroeconomics. He said that international data confirm what Kimball, Barro, and Hall said in relation to the closed economy: Wage stickiness is not enough; prices also have to be a bit sticky.

Lars Svensson was troubled by the fact that the currency in which firms set prices is taken as exogenous in the paper, and asked Charles Engel whether he had considered endogenizing this choice. On a related point, Bob Hall pointed out that in many cases, particularly in intermediate-product markets, pricing is not the unilateral decision of the seller, but the result of an interaction between buyer and seller. He suggested that the literature should take this into account.

Lars Svensson also asked whether there is evidence of different responses of prices to transitory and permanent changes to the exchange rate, and suggested that VAR evidence might be informative on this point. Engel replied that the evidence suggests that the behavior of real exchange rates and deviations from the law of one price is remarkably similar at short and long horizons. On this point, Alan Stockman remarked that work on the differences across countries in the extent of exchange-rate passthrough would be desirable. He agreed with Karen Lewis that cross-country differences could be due to differences across industries in passthrough and differences across countries in industrial composition. However, he noted that the implications for expenditure switching do not depend on where cross-country heterogeneity in passthrough comes from.

Charles Engel summed up the thrust of his paper as a rejection of the simple Devereux–Engel zero-expenditure-switching local-currency-pricing approach. He noted that the evidence favors considerable consumer price stickiness, except in high-inflation emerging markets as mentioned by Ariel Burstein. But it also favors considerable passthrough to import prices, and he saw the determination of the resulting magnitude of expenditure switching as the next challenge for the literature.

Alberto Alesina, Robert J. Barro,
and Silvana Tenreyro
HARVARD UNIVERSITY, NBER, AND CPER; HARVARD
UNIVERSITY, HOOVER INSTITUTION, AND NBER; AND FEDERAL
RESERVE BANK OF BOSTON

Optimal Currency Areas

1. Introduction

Is a country by definition an optimal currency area? If the optimal number of currencies is less than the number of existing countries, which countries should form currency areas?

This question, analyzed in the pioneering work of Mundell (1961) and extended in Alesina and Barro (2002), has jumped to the center stage of the current policy debate, for several reasons. First, the large increase in the number of independent countries in the world led, until recently, to a roughly one-for-one increase in the number of currencies. This proliferation of currencies occurred despite the growing integration of the world economy. On its own, the growth of international trade in goods and assets should have raised the transactions benefits from common currencies and led, thereby, to a decline in the number of independent moneys. Second, the memory of the inflationary decades of the seventies and eighties encouraged inflation control, thereby generating consideration of irrevocably fixed exchange rates as a possible instrument to achieve price stability. Adopting another country's currency or maintaining a currency board were seen as more credible commitment devices than a simple fixing of the exchange rate. Third, recent episodes of financial turbulence have promoted discussions about "new financial architectures." Although this dialogue is often vague and inconclusive, one of its interesting facets

We are grateful to Rudi Dornbusch, Mark Gertler, Kenneth Rogoff, Andy Rose, Jeffrey Wurgler, and several conference participants for very useful comments. Gustavo Suarez provided excellent research assistance. We thank the NSF for financial support through a grant with the National Bureau of Economic Research.

302 · ALESINA, BARRO, & TENREYRO

is the question of whether the one-country–one-currency dogma is still adequate.[1]

Looking around the world, one sees many examples of movement toward multinational currencies: twelve countries in Europe have adopted a single currency; dollarization is being implemented in Ecuador and El Salvador; and dollarization is under active consideration in many other Latin American countries, including Mexico, Guatemala, and Peru. Six West African states have agreed to create a new common currency for the region by 2003, and eleven members of the Southern African Development Community are debating whether to adopt the dollar or to create an independent monetary union possibly anchored to the South African rand. Six oil-producing countries (Saudi Arabia, United Arab Emirates, Bahrain, Oman, Qatar, and Kuwait) have declared their intention to form a currency union by 2010. In addition, several countries have maintained currency boards with either the U.S. dollar or the euro as the anchor. Currency boards are, in a sense, midway between a system of fixed rates and currency union, and the recent adverse experience of Argentina will likely discourage the use of this approach.

Currency unions typically take one of two forms. In one, which is most common, client countries (which are usually small) adopt the currency of a large anchor country. In the other, a group of countries creates a new currency and a new joint central bank. The second arrangement applies to the euro zone.[2] The Eastern Caribbean Currency Area (ECCA) and the CFA zone in Africa are intermediate between the two types of unions. In both cases, the countries have a joint currency and a joint central bank.[3] However, the ECCA currency (Caribbean dollar) has been linked since 1976 to the U.S. dollar (and, before that, to the British pound), and the CFA franc has been tied (except for one devaluation) to the French franc.

1. In principle, an optimal currency area could also be smaller than a country, that is, more than one currency could circulate within a country. However, we have not observed a tendency in this direction.
2. Some may argue that the European Monetary Union is, in practice, a German mark area, but this interpretation is questionable. Although the European central bank may be particularly sensitive to German preferences, the composition of the board and the observed policies in its first few years of existence do not show a German bias. See Alesina et al. (2001).
3. There are actually two regional central banks in the CFA zone. One is the BCEAO, grouping Benin, Burkina Faso, Ivory Coast, Guinea-Bissau, Mali, Niger, Senegal, and Togo, where the common currency is the *franc de la Communaute Financière de l'Afrique* or CFA franc. The other is the BEAC, grouping Cameroon, Central African Republic, Chad, Republic of Congo, Equatorial Guinea, and Gabon, with the common currency called the *franc de la Cooperation Financière Africaine*, also known as the CFA franc. The two CFA francs are legal tender only in their respective regions, but the two currencies have maintained a fixed parity. Comoros issues its own form of CFA franc but has maintained a fixed parity with the other two.

The purpose of this paper is to evaluate whether natural currency areas emerge from an empirical investigation. As a theoretical background, we use the framework developed by Alesina and Barro (2002), which discusses the trade-off between the costs and benefits of currency unions. Based on historical patterns of international trade and of comovements of prices and outputs, we find that there seem to exist reasonably well-defined dollar and euro areas but no clear yen area. However, a country's decision to join a monetary area should consider not just the situation that applies ex ante, that is, under monetary autonomy, but also the conditions that would apply ex post, that is, allowing for the economic effects of currency union. The effects on international trade have been discussed in a lively recent literature prompted by the findings of Rose (2000). We review this literature and provide new results. We also find that currency unions tend to increase the comovement of prices but are not systematically related to the comovement of outputs.

We should emphasize that we do not address other issues that are important for currency adoption, such as those related to financial markets, financial flows, and borrower–lender relationships.[4] We proceed this way not because we think that these questions are unimportant, but rather because the focus of the present inquiry is on different issues.

The paper is organized as follows. Section 2 discusses the broad evolution of country sizes, numbers of currencies, and currency areas in the post–World War II period. Section 3 reviews the implications of the theoretical model of Alesina and Barro (2002), which we use as a guide for our empirical investigation. Section 4 presents our data set. Section 5 uses the historical patterns in international trade flows, inflation rates, and the comovements of prices and outputs to attempt to identify optimal currency areas. Section 6 considers how the formation of a currency union would change bilateral trade flows and the comovements of prices and outputs. The last section concludes.

2. Countries and Currencies

In 1947 there were 76 independent countries in the world, whereas today there are 193. Many of today's countries are small: in 1995, 87 countries had a population less than 5 million. Figure 1, which is taken from Alesina, Spolaore, and Wacziarg (2000), depicts the numbers of countries created and eliminated in the last 150 years.[5] In the period between World Wars I and II, international trade collapsed, and international borders

4. For a recent theoretical discussion of these issues, see Gale and Vives (2002).
5. The initial negative bar in 1870 represents the unification of Germany.

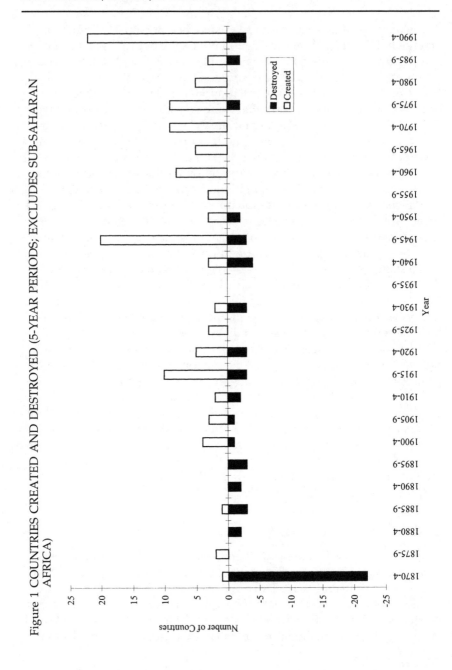

Figure 1 COUNTRIES CREATED AND DESTROYED (5-YEAR PERIODS; EXCLUDES SUB-SAHARAN AFRICA)

were virtually frozen. In contrast, after the end of World War II, the number of countries almost tripled, and the volume of international trade and financial transactions expanded dramatically. We view these two developments as interrelated. First, small countries are economically viable when their market is the world, in a free-trade environment. Second, small countries have an interest in maintaining open borders. Therefore, one should expect an inverse correlation between average country size and the degree of trade openness and financial integration.

Figure 2, also taken from Alesina, Spolaore, and Wacziarg (2000), shows a strong positive correlation over the last 150 years between the detrended number of countries in the world and a detrended measure of the volume of international trade. These authors show that this correlation does not just reflect the relabeling of interregional trade as international trade when countries split. In fact, a similar pattern of correlation holds if one measures world trade integration by the volume of international trade among countries that did not change their borders. Alesina and Spolaore (2002) discuss these issues in detail and present current and historical evidence on the relationship between country formation and international trade.

The number of independent currencies has increased substantially, until recently almost at the same pace as the number of independent countries. In 1947, there were 65 currencies in circulation, whereas in 2001 there were 169. Between 1947 and 2001, the ratio of the number of currencies to the number of countries remained roughly constant at about 85%. Twelve of these currencies, in Europe, have now been replaced by the euro, so we now have 158 currencies.

The increase in the number of countries and the deepening of economic integration should generate a tendency to create multicountry currency areas, unless one believes that a country always defines the optimal currency area. One implication of Mundell's analysis is that political borders and currency boundaries should not always coincide. In fact, as discussed in Alesina and Spolaore (2002), small countries can prosper in a world of free trade and open financial markets. Nevertheless, these small countries may lack the size needed to provide effectively some public goods that are subject to large economies of scale or to substantial externalities. A currency may be one of these goods: a small country may be too small for an independent money to be efficient. To put it differently, an ethnic, linguistic, or culturally different group can enjoy political independence by creating its own country. At the same time, this separate country can avoid part of the costs of being economically small by using other countries to provide some public goods, such as a currency.

A country constitutes, by definition, an optimal currency area only if one views a national money as a critical symbol of national pride and identity.

Figure 2 TRADE OPENNESS AND THE NUMBER OF COUNTRIES

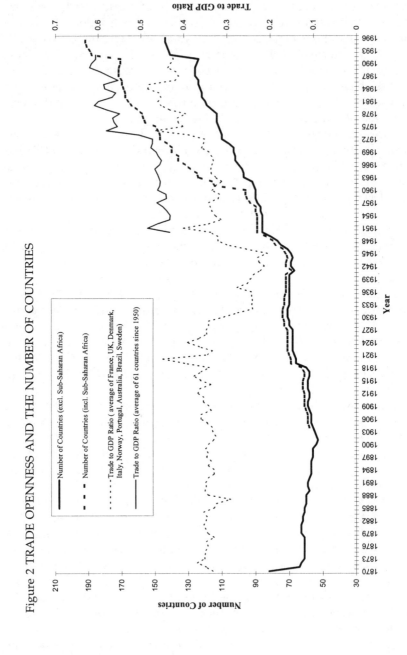

However, sometimes forms of nationalistic pride have led countries into disastrous courses of action. Therefore, the argument that a national currency satisfies nationalistic pride does not make an independent money economically or politically desirable. In fact, why a nation would take pride in a currency escapes us; it is probably much more relevant to be proud of an Olympic team. As for national identity, language and culture seem much more important than a currency, yet many countries have willingly retained the language of their former colonizers. Moreover, many countries undergoing extreme inflation, such as in South America, tended to change the names of their moneys frequently, so even a sentimental attachment to the name "peso" or "dollar" seems not to be so important.

In any event, as already mentioned, one can detect a recent tendency toward formation of multicountry monetary areas. In the next decade, the ratio of currencies to independent countries may decrease substantially, beginning with the adoption of the euro in 2002.

3. The Costs and Benefits of Currency Unions

We view this analysis from the perspective of a potential client country that is considering the adoption of another country's money as a nominal anchor.

3.1 TRADE BENEFITS

Country borders matter for trade flows: two regions of the same country trade much more with each other than they would if an international border were to separate them. McCallum (1995) looked at U.S.–Canadian trade in 1988 and suggested that this effect was extremely large: trade between Canadian provinces was estimated to be a staggering 2200% larger than that between otherwise comparable provinces and states. More recent work by Anderson and van Wincoop (2001) argues that this effect from the U.S.–Canada border was vastly exaggerated but is still substantial: the presence of an international border is estimated to reduce trade among industrialized countries by 30%, and between the United States and Canada by 44%. The question is why national borders matter so much for trade even when there are no explicit trade restrictions in place. Among other things, country borders tend to be associated with different currencies. Therefore, given that border effects are so large, the elimination of one source of border costs—the change of currencies— might have a large effect on trade.[6]

Alesina and Barro (2002) investigate the relationship between currency

6. Obstfeld and Rogoff (2000) argue that these border effects on trade may have profound effects on a host of financial markets and may explain a lot of anomalies in international financial transactions.

unions and trade flows. They model the adoption of a common currency as a reduction of iceberg trading costs between two countries. They find that, under reasonable assumptions about elasticities of substitution between goods, countries that trade more with each other benefit more from adopting the same currency.[7]

Thus, countries that trade more with each other stand to gain more from adopting the same currency. Also, smaller countries should, *ceteris paribus*, be more inclined to give up their currencies. Hence, as the number of countries increases (and their average size shrinks), the number of currencies in the world should increase less than proportionately.[8]

3.2 THE BENEFITS OF COMMITMENT

If an inflation-prone country adopts the currency of a credible anchor, it eliminates the inflation-bias problem pointed out by Barro and Gordon (1983). This bias may stem from two non-mutually-exclusive sources: an attempt to overstimulate the economy in a cyclical context, and the incentive to monetize budget deficits and debts.

A fixed-exchange-rate system, if totally credible, could achieve the same commitment benefit as a currency union. However, the recent world history shows that fixed rates are not irrevocably fixed; thus, they lack full credibility. Consequently, fixed exchange rates can create instability in financial markets. To the extent that a currency union is more costly to break than a promise to maintain a fixed exchange rate, the currency adoption is more credible. In fact, once a country has adopted a new currency, the costs of turning back are quite high, certainly much higher than simply changing a fixed parity to a new one. The ongoing situation in Argentina demonstrates that the government really had created high costs for breaking a commitment associated with a currency board and widespread dollarization of the economy. However, the costs were apparently not high enough to deter eventual reneging on the commitment.

A country that abandons its currency receives the inflation rate of the

---

7. The intuition for why this result does not hold unambiguously is the following. If two countries do not trade much with each other initially, the likely reason is that the trading costs are high. Hence, the trade that does occur must have a high marginal value. Specifically, if the trade occurs in intermediate inputs, then the marginal product of these inputs must be high, because the trade occurs only if the marginal product is at least as high as the marginal cost. In this case, the reduction of border costs due to the implementation of a currency union would expand trade in the intermediate goods that have an especially high marginal product. Hence, it is possible that the marginal gain from the introduction of a currency union would be greater when the existing volume of international trade is low.

8. Alesina and Barro (2002) show that, under certain conditions, an even stronger result holds: as the number of countries increases, the equilibrium number of currencies decreases.

anchor plus the change (positive or negative) in its price level relative to that of the anchor. In other words, if the inflation rate in the United States is 2%, then in Panama it will be 2% plus the change in relative prices between Panama and the United States. Therefore, even if the anchor maintains domestic price stability, linkage to the anchor does not guarantee full price stability for a client country.

The most likely anchors are large relative to the clients. In theory, a small but very committed country could be a perfectly good anchor. However, ex post, a small anchor may be subject to political pressure from the large client to abandon the committed policy. From an ex ante perspective, this consideration disqualifies the small country as a credible anchor.

In summary: The countries that stand to gain the most from giving up their currencies are those that have a history of high and volatile inflation. This kind of history is a symptom of a lack of internal discipline for monetary policy. Hence, to the extent that this lack of discipline tends to persist, such countries would benefit the most from the introduction of external discipline. Linkage to another currency is also more attractive if, under the linked system, relative price levels between the countries would be relatively stable.

3.3 STABILIZATION POLICIES

The abandonment of a separate currency implies the loss of an independent monetary policy. To the extent that monetary policy would have contributed to business-cycle stabilization, the loss of monetary independence implies costs in the form of wider cyclical fluctuations of output.

The costs of giving up monetary independence are lower the higher the association of shocks between the client and the anchor. The more the shocks are related, the more the policy selected by the anchor will be appropriate for the client as well. What turns out to matter is not the correlation of shocks per se, but rather the variance of the client country's output expressed as a ratio to the anchor country's output. This variance depends partly on the correlation of output (and, hence, of underlying shocks) and partly on the individual variances of outputs. For example, a small country's output may be highly correlated with that in the United States. But, if the small country's variance of output is much greater than that of the United States, then the U.S. monetary policy will still be inappropriate for the client. In particular, the magnitude of countercyclical monetary policy chosen by the United States will be too small from the client's perspective.

The costs implied by the loss of an independent money depend also on the explicit or implicit contract that can be arranged between the anchor and its clients. We can think of two cases. In one, the anchor does not change its monetary policy regardless of the composition and experience of its clients. Thus, clients that have more shocks in common with the anchor stand to lose less from abandoning their independent policy but have no influence on the monetary policy chosen by the anchor country. In the other case, the clients can compensate the anchor to motivate the selection of a policy that takes into account the clients' interests, which will reflect the shocks that they experience. The ability to enter into such contracts makes currency unions more attractive. However, even when these agreements are feasible, the greater the association of shocks between clients and anchor, the easier it is to form a currency union. Specifically, it is cheaper for a client to buy accommodation from an anchor that faces shocks that are similar to those faced by the clients.[9] The allocation of seignorage arising from the client's use of the anchor's currency can be made part of the compensation schemes.

The European Monetary Union is similar to this arrangement with compensation, because the monetary policy of the union is not targeted to a specific country (say Germany), but rather to a weighted average of each country's shocks, that is, to aggregate euro-area shocks. In the discussion leading up to the formation of the European Monetary Union, concerns about the degree of association among business cycles across potential members were critical. In practice, the institutional arrangements within the European Union are much more complex than a compensation scheme, but the point is that the ECB does not target the shocks of any particular country, but rather the average European shocks.[10]

In the case of developing countries, the costs of abandoning an independent monetary policy may not be that high, because stabilization policies are typically not well used when exchange rates are flexible. Recent work by Calvo and Reinhart (2002) and Hausmann, Panizza, and Stein (1999) suggests that developing countries tend to follow procyclical monetary policies; specifically, they tend to raise interest rates in times of distress to defend the value of their currency.[11] To the extent that monetary policy is not properly used as a stabilization device, the loss of monetary independence is not a substantial cost (and may actually be a benefit) for

9. Note that, in theory, a small country could be an ideal anchor because it is cheaper to compensate such an anchor for the provision of monetary services that are tailored to the interests of clients. However, as discussed before, a small anchor may lack credibility.
10. The European Union also has specific prescriptions about the allocation of seignorage. The amounts are divided according to the share of GDP of the various member countries. For a discussion of the European Central Bank policy objectives and how this policy relates to individual country shocks, see Alesina et al. (2001).
11. A literature on Latin America, prompted mostly by a paper by Gavin and Perotti (1997), has also shown that fiscal policy has the wrong cyclical properties. That is, surpluses tend to appear during recessions, and deficits during expansions.

developing countries. However, recent work by Broda (2001) shows that countries with floating-exchange-rate systems show superior performance in the face of terms-of-trade shocks. This pattern may reflect the benefits from independent monetary policies.

To summarize, the countries that have the largest comovements of outputs and prices with potential anchors are those with the lowest costs of abandoning monetary independence.

3.4 TRADE, GEOGRAPHY, AND COMOVEMENTS

Countries that trade more can benefit more from currency unions for the reasons already discussed. Increased trade may also raise the comovements of outputs and prices. In this case, there is a second reason why countries that trade more would have a greater net benefit from adopting a currency union.

An established literature on the gravity model of trade shows that bilateral trade volumes are well explained by a set of geographical and economic variables, such as the distance between the countries and the sizes and incomes of the countries. Note that the term "distance" has to be interpreted broadly to include not only literal geographical distance, but also whether the countries share a common language, legal system, and so on. In addition, some geographical variables may influence comovements of outputs and prices beyond their effects through trade. For example, locational proximity and weather patterns may relate to the nature of underlying shocks, which in turn influence the comovements.

Whether more trade always means more comovements of outputs and prices is not a settled issue. On the theoretical side, the answer depends largely on whether trade is interindustry or intraindustry. In the latter case, more trade likely leads to more comovements. However, in the former case, increased trade may stimulate sectoral specialization across countries. This heightened specialization likely lowers the comovements of outputs and prices, because industry-specific shocks become country-specific shocks.[12] The type of trade between two countries is also likely influenced by the levels of per capita GDP; for example, intraindustry trade tends to be much more important for rich countries.

In summary, geographical or gravity variables affect bilateral trade and, as a result, the costs and benefits of currency unions. Some geographical variables may have an effect on the attractiveness of currency unions beyond those operating through the trade channel.

---

12. See Frankel and Rose (1998) for the argument that more trade favors more correlated business cycles. See Krugman (1993) for the opposite argument. For an extensive theoretical and empirical discussion of these issues, see Ozcan, Sorensen, and Yosha (2001, 2002) and Imbs (2000).

4. Data and Methodology

4.1 DATA DESCRIPTION AND SOURCES

Data on outputs and prices come from the World Bank's World Development Indicators (WDI) and Penn World Tables 5.6. Combining both sources, we form a panel of countries with yearly data on outputs and prices from 1960 to 1997 (or, in some cases, for shorter periods). For output, we use real per capita GDP expressed in 1995 U.S. dollars. To compute relative prices, we use a form of real exchange rate relating to the price level for gross domestic products. The measure is the purchasing-power parity (PPP) for GDP divided by the U.S. dollar exchange rate.[13] In the first instance, this measure gives us the price level in country i relative to that in the United States, $P_{i,t}/P_{US,t}$. We then compute relative prices between countries i and j by dividing the value for country i by that for country j. Inflation is computed as the continuously compounded (log-difference) growth rate of the GDP deflator, coming from WDI.

Bilateral trade information comes from Glick and Rose (2002), who in turn extracted it from the International Monetary Fund's *Direction of Trade Statistics*. These data are expressed in real U.S. dollars.[14]

To compute bilateral distances, we use the great-circle-distance algorithm provided by Gray (2002). Data on location, as well as contiguity, access to water, language, and colonial relationships come from the *CIA World Fact Book 2001*. Data on free-trade agreements come from Glick and Rose (2002) and are complemented with data from the World Trade Organization Web page.

4.2 THE COMPUTATION OF COMOVEMENTS

We pair all countries and calculate bilateral relative prices, P_{it}/P_{jt}. (This ratio measures the value of one unit of country i's output relative to one unit of country j's output.) This procedure generates 21,321 ($207 \times 206/2$) country pairs for each year. For every pair of countries, (i, j), we use the annual time series $\{\ln(P_{it}/P_{jt})\}_{t=1960}^{t=1997}$ to compute the second-order autoregression[15]:

---

13. P_i = (PPP of GDP)/(ex. rate) measures how many units of U.S. output can be purchased with one unit of country i's output, that is, it measures the relative price of country i's output with respect to that of the United States. By definition, this price is always 1 when i is the United States.
14. Glick and Rose (2002) deflated the original nominal values of trade by the U.S. consumer price index, with 1982–1984 = 100. We use the same index to express trade values in 1995 U.S. dollars.
15. We use fewer observations when the full time series from 1960 to 1997 is unavailable. However, we drop country pairs for which fewer than 20 observations are available.

$$\ln \frac{P_{it}}{P_{jt}} = b_0 + b_1 \ln \frac{P_{i,t-1}}{P_{j,t-1}} + b_2 \ln \frac{P_{i,t-2}}{P_{j,t-2}} + \varepsilon_{tij}.$$

The estimated residual, $\hat{\varepsilon}_{t,i,j}$, measures the relative price that would not be predictable from the two prior values of relative prices. We then use as a measure of (lack of) comovement of relative prices the root-mean-square error:

$$VP_{ij} \equiv \sqrt{\frac{1}{T-3} \sum_{t=1}^{T} \hat{\varepsilon}_{tij}^2}.$$

The lower VP_{ij}, the greater the comovement of prices between countries i and j.

We proceed analogously to compute a measure of output comovement. The value of VY_{ij} comes from the estimated residuals from the second-order autoregression on annual data for relative per capita GDP:

$$\ln \frac{Y_{it}}{Y_{jt}} = c_0 + c_1 \ln \frac{Y_{i,t-1}}{Y_{j,t-1}} + c_2 \ln \frac{Y_{i,t-2}}{Y_{j,t-2}} + u_{tij}.$$

The estimated residual $\hat{u}_{tij}$ measures the relative output that would not be predictable from the two prior values of relative output. We then use as a measure of (lack of) comovement of relative outputs the root-mean-square error:

$$VY_{ij} \equiv \sqrt{\frac{1}{T-3} \sum_{t=1}^{T} \hat{u}_{tij}^2}.$$

The lower VY_{ij}, the greater the comovement of outputs between countries i and j.

For most countries all of the data are available. We exclude from the computation of comovements country pairs for which we do not have at least 20 observations. Note that this limitation implies that we cannot include in our analysis most of central and eastern Europe, a region in which some countries are likely clients of the euro.

5. Which Currency Areas?

In this section, we sketch "natural" currency areas, based on the criteria discussed above. For anchor currencies, we consider the U.S. dollar, the euro, and the yen. We are not assuming that all countries have to belong to one of the unions centered around these three currencies. In fact, many countries turn out not to be good clients for any of the anchors and seem to be better off keeping their own currency. Therefore, we are addressing the question of which countries would be better served by joining some currency union, as well as the question of which anchor should be chosen if one is needed.

5.1 INFLATION, TRADE, AND COMOVEMENTS

We begin in Table 1 by showing the average inflation rate, using the GDP deflator, for selected countries and groups in our sample from 1970 to 1990. We stopped at 1990 because in the 1990s several countries adopted currency arrangements, such as the EMS, that contributed to reduced inflation. We are interested here mostly in capturing inflation rates that would arise in the absence of a monetary anchor. We take the 1970s and 1980s (that is, after Bretton Woods and before the recent emphasis on nominal anchors) as a period with few true monetary anchors. We show the 20 countries with the highest average inflation rates, along with the averages for industrialized countries and for regional groups of developing countries.

The top average rates of inflation are all Latin American countries, and 7 Latin American countries are in the top 11. The top 5 countries had an average annual inflation rate above 280%. Despite its poor economic performance in other dimensions, Africa does not have a very high average inflation rate. While there are 6 African countries in the top 20, the average for the continent is brought down by the countries in the CFA franc zone, which have relatively low inflation records. The Middle East is the second highest inflation group, with two countries, Israel and Lebanon, in the top 13 with inflation rates of 78% and 44%, respectively. In the euro zone, Greece and Italy lead in the rankings, with inflation rates of 16% and 13%, respectively. Overall, 11 countries had an average annual inflation rate above 50%, 30 countries above 20%, and 72 countries above 10%.

Table 2 shows inflation variability and is organized in the same way as Table 1. Since average inflation and inflation variability are strongly positively correlated, 16 of the top 20 countries in Table 1 are also in the top 20 of Table 2. However, in some cases, such as Chile, the high average inflation rate (107%) reflected one episode of hyperinflation followed by relative stability. In others, such as Colombia, the fairly high average in-

Table 1   MEAN ANNUAL INFLATION
RATE 1970–1990[a]

Region	Rate (%/yr)
High-Inflation Countries[b]	
Nicaragua	1168
Bolivia	702
Peru	531
Argentina	431
Brazil	288
Vietnam	213
Uganda	107
Chile	107
Cambodia	80
Israel	78
Uruguay	62
Congo, Dem. Rep.	49
Lebanon	44
Lao PDR	42
Mexico	41
Mozambique	41
Somalia	40
Turkey	39
Ghana	39
Sierra Leone	34
Industrial Countries[c]	
All	9.8
Developing Countries[c]	
Africa	16.3
Asia	17.4
Europe	6.9
Middle East	19.6
Western Hemisphere	98.6

[a] Based on GDP deflators. Source: WDI 2001.
[b] This group includes only countries with 1997 population above 500,000. Ranked by inflation rate.
[c] Unweighted means.

flation rate (22%) resulted from a long period of moderate, double-digit inflation.

Tables 3, 4, and 5 list for selected countries and groups the average trade-to-GDP ratios[16] over 1960–1997 with three potential anchors for currency areas: the United States, the euro area (based on the twelve mem-

16. The trade measure is equivalent to the average of imports and exports. Glick and Rose's (2002) values come from averaging four measures of bilateral trade (as reported for imports and exports by the partners on each side of both transactions).

Table 2   INFLATION-RATE VARIABILITY
1970–1990[a]

Region	Variability (%/yr)
Countries with High Inflation Variability[b]	
Nicaragua	3197
Bolivia	2684
Peru	1575
Argentina	749
Brazil	589
Chile	170
Vietnam	160
Israel	95
Cambodia	63
Uganda	63
Mozambique	52
Somalia	50
Oman	46
Lebanon	41
Kuwait	38
Uruguay	38
Guinea-Bissau	37
Mexico	37
Guyana	36
Congo, Dem. Rep	36
Industrial Countries[c]	
All	4.6
Developing Countries[c]	
Africa	13.9
Asia	14.0
Europe	6.6
Middle East	28.4
Western Hemisphere	251.2

[a] Standard deviation of annual inflation rates, based on GDP deflators. Source: WDI 2001.
[b] This group includes only countries with 1997 population above 500,000. Ranked by standard deviation of inflation.
[c] Unweighted means.

Table 3   AVERAGE TRADE-TO-GDP
RATIO WITH THE UNITED
STATES, 1960–1997[a]

Region	Ratio (%)
High-Trade-Ratio Countries[b]	
Trinidad and Tobago	29.6
Honduras	24.3
Guyana	23.0
Jamaica	19.4
Angola	19.0
Canada	18.3
Dominican Republic	16.8
Nigeria	15.0
Singapore	13.2
Panama	12.2
Nicaragua	12.1
Venezuela	11.7
Costa Rica	11.3
Hong Kong	11.0
Ecuador	9.9
Haiti	9.6
Mexico	8.7
Gabon	8.0
Congo, Rep.	7.9
Guatemala	7.5
Industrial Countries[c]	
All	2.5
Developing Countries[c]	
Africa	3.3
Asia	3.7
Europe	0.8
Middle East	4.2
Western Hemisphere	12.9

[a] Trade is the average of imports and exports. (Imports is the average of the values reported by the importer and the exporter. Idem for exports.) Averages are for 1960–1997 (when GDP data are not available, the average corresponds to the period of availability). The equations for comovement include only one observation for each pair, corresponding to the period 1960–1997. The explanatory variables then refer to averages over time. Source: Glick and Rose (trade values; WDI 2001 (GDP).
[b] This group includes only countries with 1997 population above 500,000.
[c] Unweighted means.

Table 4   AVERAGE TRADE-TO-GDP
RATIO WITH THE EURO
12, 1960–1997[a]

Region	Ratio (%)
High Trade-Ratio Countries[b]	
Mauritania	34.8
Congo, Rep.	28.3
Guinea-Bissau	27.5
Côte d'Ivoire	24.5
Algeria	24.4
Belgium-Lux.	23.4
Gabon	23.0
Togo	22.9
Nigeria	22.8
Tunisia	20.9
Gambia, The	20.6
Senegal	20.4
Comoros	19.3
Netherlands	18.2
Oman	17.7
Cameroon	17.3
Congo, Dem. Rep.	17.0
Slovenia	16.9
Angola	15.6
Syrian Arab Republic	15.2
Industrial Countries[c]	
Ali	7.3
Developing Countries[c]	
Africa	14.2
Asia	4.3
Europe	7.0
Middle East	11.6
Western Hemisphere	8.3

[a] Trade is the average of imports and exports. (Imports is the average of the values reported by the importer and the exporter. Idem for exports.) Averages are for 1960–1977 (when GDP data are not available, the average corresponds to the period of availability). Source: Glick & Rose (trade values); WDI 2001 (GDP). For a Euro 12 country, the trade ratios apply to the other 11 countries.
[b] This group includes only countries with 1997 population above 500,000.
[c] Underweight means.

Table 5   AVERAGE TRADE-TO-GDP
RATIO WITH JAPAN,
1960–1997[a]

Region	Ratio (%)
High-Trade-Ratio Countries[b]	
Oman	16.0
United Arab Emirates	15.7
Panama	14.1
Singapore	12.8
Kuwait	9.5
Malaysia	9.5
Papua New Guinea	9.2
Bahrain	8.4
Saudi Arabia	8.0
Hong Kong, China	7.9
Indonesia	7.8
Swaziland	6.5
Thailand	5.6
Gambia, The	5.5
Mauritania	5.4
Iran, Islamic Rep.	5.4
Philippines	4.8
Korea, Rep.	4.1
Nicaragua	3.9
Fiji	3.7
Industrial Countries[c]	
All	0.8
Developing Countries[c]	
Africa	1.4
Asia	5.5
Europe	0.3
Middle East	6.1
Western Hemisphere	2.0

[a] Trade is the average of imports and exports. (Imports is the average of the values reported by the importer and the exporter. Idem for exports.) Averages are for 1960–1997 (when GDP data are not available, the average corresponds to the period of availability). Source: Glick and Rose (trade values); WDI 2001 (GDP).
[b] This group includes only countries with 1997 population above 500,000.
[c] Unweigted means.

bers), and Japan. The GDP value in the denominator of these ratios refers to the country paired with the potential anchor.

The tables show that Japan is an economy that is relatively closed; moreover, in comparison with the United States and the euro region, Japan's trade is more dispersed across partners. Hence, few countries exhibit a high trade-to-GDP ratio with Japan. Notably, industrial countries' average trade share with Japan is below 1%. Among developing countries, oil exporters have a high trade share with Japan, but still below that with the Euro 12. Singapore, Malaysia, Hong Kong, and Indonesia exhibit relatively high trade-to-GDP ratios with Japan (above 7%), but Singapore and Hong Kong trade even more with the United States. For the United States, aside from Hong Kong and Singapore, a good portion of Latin America has a high ratio of trade to GDP. Canada is notable for trading almost exclusively with the United States; its trade ratio is 18%, compared with 1.7% for the Euro 12 and 1.4% for Japan. African countries, broadly speaking, trade significantly more with Europe, but some of them, such as Angola and Nigeria, are also closely linked with the United States.

Tables 6, 7, and 8 report our measures of the comovements of prices for selected countries with the United States, the Euro 12 area, and Japan.[17] Remember that a larger number means less comovement. Panama and Puerto Rico, which use the U.S. dollar, have the highest comovements of prices with the United States. These two are followed by Canada and El Salvador, which has recently dollarized. Members of the OECD have fairly high price comovements with all three of the potential anchors (which are themselves members of the OECD). For Japan, the countries that are most closely related in terms of price comovements lack a clear geographical distribution. For the Euro 12, the euro members and other western European countries have a high degree of price comovement. African countries also have relatively high price comovements with the Euro 12, higher than that with the United States.

Tables 9, 10, and 11 report our measures of the comovements of outputs (per capita GDPs) for selected countries with the United States, the Euro 12 area, and Japan.[18] The general picture is reasonably similar to that for prices. Note that all of the OECD countries have relatively high output comovements with the three anchors, particularly with the Euro 12. Japan's business cycle seems to be somewhat less associated with the rest of the world: even developing countries in Asia tend to exhibit, on average, higher output comovements with the Euro 12. The regional patterns

---

17. Recall that we compute comovements only for pairs of countries for which we have at least 20 annual observations.
18. As for prices, we consider only pairs of countries for which we have at least 20 observations.

Table 6   COMOVEMENT OF PRICES
WITH THE UNITED
STATES, 1960–1997[a]

Region	VP
High-Comovement Countries[b]	
Puerto Rico	0.0193
Panama	0.0244
Canada	0.0335
El Salvador	0.0340
Singapore	0.0444
Thailand	0.0529
Guinea	0.0545
Bahrain	0.0563
Hong Kong, China	0.0566
Honduras	0.0571
Malaysia	0.0609
Saudi Arabia	0.0646
Australia	0.0664
Fiji	0.0666
Hungary	0.0673
Egypt, Arab Rep.	0.0681
Cyprus	0.0687
Tunisia	0.0689
New Zealand	0.0691
Norway	0.0671
Industrial Countries[c]	
All	0.0830
Developing Countries[c]	
Africa	0.1445
Asia	0.0913
Europe	0.1107
Middle East	0.1348
Western Hemisphere	0.1040

[a] The table shows the value *VP*, the standard error of the residual for the AR(2) regression for the log of the real exchange rate. In some cases, the sample differs from 1960–1997.
[b] This group includes only countries with 1997 population above 500,000.
[c] Unweighted means.

Table 7 COMOVEMENT OF PRICES
WITH THE EURO 12,
1960–1997[a]

Region	VP
High-Comovement Countries[b]	
Austria	0.0196
Netherlands	0.0217
Denmark	0.0219
Belgium	0.0242
Germany	0.0328
France	0.0338
Norway	0.0363
Switzerland	0.0395
Ireland	0.0397
Morocco	0.0426
Italy	0.0478
Portugal	0.0480
Sweden	0.0489
Spain	0.0491
Greece	0.0510
Tunisia	0.0529
Cyprus	0.0536
Finland	0.0552
United Kingdom	0.0616
New Zealand	0.0678
Industrial Countries[c]	
All	0.0507
Developing Countries[c]	
Africa	0.1403
Asia	0.1103
Europe	0.1152
Middle East	0.1607
Western Hemisphere	0.1350

[a] The table shows the value of *VP*, the standard error of the residual for the ARC(2) regression for the log of the real exchange rate. For a member of the Euro 12, the comovement is in relation to the other 11 countries. In some cases, the sample differs from 1960–1997.
[b] This group includes only countries with 1997 population above 500,000.
[c] Unweighted means.

Table 8   COMOVEMENT OF PRICES
WITH JAPAN, 1960–1997[a]

Region	VP
High-Comovement Countries[b]	
Switzerland	0.0713
Austria	0.0719
Germany	0.0776
New Zealand	0.0791
Netherlands	0.0805
Denmark	0.0810
Belgium	0.0816
Papua New Guinea	0.0827
Thailand	0.0841
Cyprus	0.0845
Singapore	0.0866
France	0.0883
Norway	0.0883
Morocco	0.0918
United States	0.0924
Australia	0.0940
Panama	0.0944
Malaysia	0.0947
Tunisia	0.0960
Puerto Rico	0.0961
Industrial Countries[c]	
All	0.0919
Developing Countries[c]	
Africa	0.1647
Asia	0.1237
Europe	0.1307
Middle East	0.1730
Western Hemisphere	0.1465

[a] The table shows the value of *VP*, the standard error of the residual for the AR(2) regression for the log of the real exchange rate. In some cases, the sample differs from 1960–1997.
[b] This group includes only countries with 1997 population above 500,000.
[c] Unweighted means.

Table 9 COMOVEMENT OF
OUTPUTS WITH THE
UNITED STATES,
1960–1997[a]

Region	VY
High-Comovement Countries[b]	
Canada	0.0135
United Kingdom	0.0150
Australia	0.0175
Germany	0.0196
Netherlands	0.0197
France	0.0200
Colombia	0.0205
Puerto Rico	0.0216
Denmark	0.0217
Norway	0.0224
Italy	0.0230
Spain	0.0238
Honduras	0.0251
Belgium	0.0253
Sweden	0.0254
Switzerland	0.0256
Costa Rica	0.0258
Austria	0.0261
Japan	0.0265
Guatemala	0.0265
Industrial Countries[c]	
All	0.0251
Developing Countries[c]	
Africa	0.0591
Asia	0.0524
Europe	0.0449
Middle East	0.0749
Western Hemisphere	0.0442

[a] The table shows the value of VY, the standard error of the residual for the AR(2) regression for the log of the ratio of real per capita GDPs. In some cases, the sample differs from 1960–1997.
[b] This group includes only countries with 1997 population above 500,000.
[c] Unweighted means.

Table 10   COMOVEMENT OF
OUTPUTS WITH THE
EURO 12, 1960–1997[a]

Region	VY
High-Comovement Countries[b]	
France	0.0094
Belgium	0.0108
Netherlands	0.0116
Austria	0.0131
Colombia	0.0145
Italy	0.0154
Germany	0.0154
Sweden	0.0165
Spain	0.0165
Switzerland	0.0168
United Kingdom	0.0170
Denmark	0.0177
United States	0.0185
Canada	0.0187
Japan	0.0202
Puerto Rico	0.0205
Norway	0.0210
Guatemala	0.0220
Australia	0.0222
Cyprus	0.0227
Industrial Countries[c]	
All	0.0198
Developing Countries[c]	
Africa	0.0557
Asia	0.0500
Europe	0.0421
Middle East	0.0713
Western Hemisphere	0.0426

[a] The table shows the value of *VY*, the standard error of the residual for the AR(2) regression for the log of the ratio of real per capita GDPs. In some cases, the sample differs from 1960–1997. For a member of the Euro 12, the comovement is in relation to the other 11 countries.
[b] This group includes only countries with 1997 population above 500,000.
[c] Unweighted means.

Table 11   COMOVEMENT OF
OUTPUTS WITH JAPAN,
1960–1997[a]

Region	VY
High-Comovement Countries[b]	
France	0.0214
United Kingdom	0.0217
Germany	0.0229
Austria	0.0234
Netherlands	0.0235
Italy	0.0236
Belgium	0.0243
Colombia	0.0252
Australia	0.0254
Sweden	0.0256
Greece	0.0260
Switzerland	0.0262
Puerto Rico	0.0262
Denmark	0.0265
United States	0.0265
Sri Lanka	0.0271
Spain	0.0272
Thailand	0.0282
Cyprus	0.0286
Canada	0.0296
Industrial Countries[c]	
All	0.0282
Developing Countries[c]	
Africa	0.0596
Asia	0.0541
Europe	0.0443
Middle East	0.0748
Western Hemisphere	0.0463

[a] The table shows the value of VY, the standard error of the residual for the AR(2) regression for the log of the ratio of real per capita GDPs. In some cases, the sample differs from 1960–1997.
[b] This group includes only countries with 1997 population above 500,000.
[c] Unweighted means.

show that Africa is generally more associated with the Euro 12, whereas there is more ambiguity for Latin America.

Overall, Japan is a worse anchor than the United States and the Euro 12, in that fewer countries are associated with Japan in price and output comovements, and trade flows to Japan are more dispersed across partners. Africa is more associated in price and output comovements with the Euro 12 than with the United States, and Africa also trades more with the euro zone. North America is highly associated with the United States. As for Latin America, this region trades overall more with the United States than with the euro zone or Japan. However, comovements of prices and outputs for this region are not much higher with the United States than they are with the Euro 12. An interesting case is Argentina. In comovements of prices and outputs, Argentina is more associated with the euro area than with the United States. Mexico, in contrast, is much more associated in its price and output comovements with the United States. In Asia, Hong Kong and Singapore are more associated with the United States than with Japan.

Looking at the tables, the patterns of trade and price and output comovements suggest geographically connected areas that are linked to the U.S. dollar (North and part of South America) and the euro (Europe and Africa). For Japan, at most a small part of east Asia seems to apply.

5.2 WHICH CURRENCY UNIONS?

This subsection brings together the data already presented to discuss which currency unions appear most attractive in terms of the criteria suggested by the underlying theory. The natural clients, with respect to the three proposed anchors, are those countries that have no ability to commit to low inflation (as evidenced by a history of high and variable inflation), that trade a lot (at least potentially) with the anchor, and that have high price and output comovements with the anchor. The implicit assumption here is that the patterns for trade and comovements that apply ex ante (under monetary autonomy) would also apply at least in a relative sense ex post (under a currency union).

We begin in Table 12 by listing the 28 countries in our sample with average inflation rates of at least 15% per year from 1970 to 1990.[19] We suggest that these countries are likely to have a high demand for an external nominal anchor because of their evident lack of commitment to low inflation. We then list for these countries their trade shares and measures of price and output comovements with the three potential anchors.

---

19. We restrict this analysis to countries with populations larger than 500,000 in 1997. The analysis is also constrained by data availability: only countries with data on comovements of output and prices are considered.

Table 12 HIGH-INFLATION COUNTRIES[a]: TRADE RATIOS AND COMOVEMENTS WITH THE UNITED STATES, THE EURO 12, AND JAPAN

Country	Mean annual inflation rate (%)	Trade ratio with U.S.	Trade ratio with Euro 12	Trade ratio with Japan	VP with U.S.	VP with Euro 12	VP with Japan	VY with U.S.	VY with Euro 12	VY with Japan
Nicaragua	1168	0.121	0.079	0.039	0.521	0.530	0.551	0.078	0.077	0.082
Bolivia	702	0.053	0.032	0.014	0.105	0.155	0.150	0.043	0.043	0.049
Peru	531	0.035	0.024	0.011	0.135	0.134	0.157	0.057	0.055	0.060
Argentina	431	0.009	0.017	0.003	0.255	0.230	0.251	0.060	0.056	0.062
Brazil	288	0.015	0.015	0.004	0.122	0.133	0.155	0.042	0.035	0.041
Chile	107	0.047	0.051	0.021	0.116	0.139	0.140	0.050	0.052	0.058
Israel	78	0.052	0.069	0.007	0.092	0.099	0.124	0.038	0.032	0.039
Uruguay	62	0.014	0.027	0.002	0.158	0.154	0.174	0.038	0.038	0.043
Congo, Dem. Rep.	49	0.033	0.170	0.010	0.170	0.163	0.179	0.054	0.052	0.057
Mexico	41	0.087	0.013	0.006	0.111	0.160	0.165	0.036	0.036	0.036
Turkey	39	0.011	0.046	0.003	0.116	0.113	0.138	0.036	0.038	0.042
Ghana	39	0.056	0.108	0.024	0.231	0.248	0.253	0.047	0.042	0.048

Sierra Leone	34	0.049	0.123	0.025	0.207	0.254	0.249	0.058	0.050	0.056
Guinea-Bissau	30	0.014	0.275	0.018	0.156	0.142	0.174	0.063	0.063	0.062
Ecuador	25	0.099	0.043	0.017	0.072	0.114	0.113	0.042	0.040	0.041
Colombia	23	0.045	0.027	0.006	0.071	0.098	0.116	0.020	0.014	0.025
Guyana	22	0.230	0.094	0.035	0.117	0.155	0.151	0.058	0.058	0.062
Costa Rica	20	0.113	0.049	0.013	0.109	0.110	0.141	0.026	0.029	0.040
Venezuela, RB	18	0.117	0.040	0.010	0.112	0.144	0.147	0.044	0.040	0.043
Paraguay	18	0.024	0.034	0.008	0.109	0.119	0.125	0.037	0.034	0.040
Nigeria	18	0.150	0.228	0.025	0.160	0.195	0.213	0.082	0.070	0.079
Jamaica	17	0.194	0.031	0.011	0.113	0.135	0.145	0.050	0.046	0.044
Portugal	16	0.011	0.077	0.003	0.083	0.048	0.096	0.035	0.028	0.030
Iran, Islamic Rep.	16	0.031	0.123	0.054	0.479	0.467	0.497	0.073	0.066	0.069
Oman	16	0.036	0.177	0.160	0.125	0.145	0.162	0.120	0.118	0.112
Greece	16	0.008	0.061	0.006	0.075	0.051	0.097	0.029	0.024	0.026
Dominican Republic	15	0.168	0.031	0.011	0.096	0.114	0.134	0.057	0.053	0.056
Indonesia	15	0.040	0.028	0.078	0.122	0.148	0.151	0.031	0.030	0.033

[a] Only countries with population above 500,000 are considered. For Euro 12 members, comovements are computed in relation to the other 11 countries. High-inflation countries with no data on VY or VP are not reported in the table.

Table 13 HIGH-INFLATION COUNTRIES: BEST ANCHOR BASED ON THE
THREE CRITERIA

Country	Mean annual inflation rate (%)	Trade	VP	VY
Nicaragua	1168.4	**U.S.**	U.S.	Euro
Bolivia	702.4	U.S.	**U.S.**	U.S.
Peru	530.7	U.S.	Euro	Euro
Argentina	430.8	Euro	Euro	Euro
Brazil	288.4	U.S.	U.S.	**Euro**
Chile	106.9	Euro	U.S.	U.S.
Israel	78.2	Euro	U.S.	**Euro**
Uruguay	62.2	Euro	Euro	U.S./Euro
Congo, Dem. Rep.	48.7	**Euro**	Euro	Euro
Mexico	41.0	**U.S.**	**U.S.**	Euro/Japan
Turkey	39.4	Euro	Euro	U.S.
Ghana	38.7	**Euro**	U.S.	Euro
Sierra Leone	34.2	**Euro**	**U.S.**	**Euro**
Guinea-Bissau	30.5	**Euro**	Euro	Japan
Ecuador	25.0	**U.S.**	**U.S.**	Euro
Colombia	22.7	**U.S.**	**U.S.**	**Euro**
Guyana	22.3	**U.S.**	**U.S.**	Euro
Costa Rica	20.0	**U.S.**	U.S.	U.S.
Venezuela	18.5	**U.S.**	**U.S.**	Euro
Paraguay	17.8	Euro	U.S.	Euro
Nigeria	17.5	**Euro**	**U.S.**	**Euro**
Jamaica	16.6	U.S.	U.S.	Japan
Portugal	16.2	**Euro**	**Euro**	Euro
Iran	16.1	**Euro**	Euro	Euro
Oman	16.0	Euro	U.S.	**Japan**
Greece	15.6	**Euro**	Euro	Euro
Dominican Republic	15.1	**U.S.**	U.S.	Euro
Indonesia	15.0	Japan	**U.S.**	Euro

The table excludes countries with 1997 population below 500,000 and countries for which *VP* or *VY* is
not available. Bold values apply if (1) highest trade share less second-highest trade exceeds 0.04,
(2) magnitude of difference between lowest *VP* and next-lowest *VP* exceeds 0.025, or (3) magnitude of
difference between lowest *VY* and next-lowest *VY* exceeds 0.005.

Table 13 summarizes the information from Table 12 by listing for each
of the three criteria (trade, price comovement, and output comovement)
which of the three anchors is best. A boldface entry means that the chosen
anchor is much superior to the other two; a lightface entry means that
the difference from at least one other anchor is small. More specifically,
a bold entry in the trade column means that the highest trade share with
one of the three potential anchors is more than 4 percentage points higher

than that of the second of the three. In the case of price comovements, a bold entry means that the absolute value of the difference between the most associated of the three and the second one is larger that 0.025. For the output comovement, the same definition applies with a cutoff of 0.005. These cutoff choices are arbitrary, but the reader, using the data reported in Table 12, can calculate another cutoff. These criteria emphasize the choice among potential anchors, rather than the choice of whether to retain an independent currency.

Several interesting observations emerge from Table 13. First, Japan is not an attractive anchor for virtually any of the high-inflation countries. Out of 96 entries in the table, only 8 (which includes one tie) are for Japan. No case has more than one of the criteria in favor of Japan.

Second, high-inflation Latin American countries are by no means a clear dollarization bloc. In fact, Brazil might be better served by adopting the euro. (Although there is no clear superiority in terms of trade or price comovements, the euro performs better in terms of comovement of output.) The case of Argentina is interesting: having one of the highest inflation rates, this country seems to be one of the best examples of a place with a high demand for an external currency anchor. However, as shown in Table 12, Argentina has been largely closed to international trade, and its output and price comovements are not high with any of the three potential anchors. So, other than its lack of commitment ability, Argentina does not appear to be an obvious member of a currency union with the euro or the U.S. dollar. In contrast, Mexico and Ecuador look much closer to the U.S. dollar than to the euro. The same conclusion applies to the Dominican Republic. Nicaragua has low comovements with all three anchors, but its exports go mostly to Europe. Hence, the euro might be a better choice than the U.S. dollar. Chile and Uruguay have higher exports to Europe, but they have larger comovements with the United States.

Third, looking at countries at the geographical boundaries of Europe, in some cases their natural anchor is the euro: this conclusion applies to Greece (which has joined the euro zone) and Turkey. Israel might be a good candidate for the euro, although it could also be well served by the U.S. dollar. As for Africa, trade shares are much higher with Europe. Comovements are, however, just as high with the United States. Ghana, Guinea-Bissau, and Sierra Leone seem to be natural euro clients, but other African countries are less clear.

We have measured lack of ability to commit according to past inflation experience. One could also look at institutional measures of potential commitment, such as the degree of central-bank independence. However, although this measure has some explanatory power for inflation performance among OECD countries, it does not seem to explain much for developing countries.[20]

High-inflation countries are not the only potential clients of an anchor. If a country trades extensively with a potential anchor, then adopting the anchor currency may be a good strategy even if the inflation rate under autonomy is low. In Table 14, we report all the countries that have a trade share with at least one of the potential anchors of at least 9% of GDP. In the first column we report the name of the anchor that has the highest trade share; when more than one anchor has a share of at least 9%, we report all in decreasing order. For example, if country X's trade share was 15% of its GDP with the United States and 9% with the Euro 12, the entry will read U.S./Euro. In the next column, we report the name of the anchor with the highest comovements of prices and output, with the same convention as before concerning the bold entries.

The first inference from Table 14 is that the countries forming the Euro 12 area do seem to belong together. The same observation applies to other European countries that are not currently members of the Euro 12, such as Sweden and Switzerland. Second, African countries trade more with Europe than with the United States or Japan, so, by and large, the best potential anchor for Africa is the euro. Note that the CFA franc zone is already tied to the euro. Third, Central American countries trade much more with the United States. Fourth, for several East Asian countries, such as Hong Kong and Singapore, the U.S. dollar appears to be superior to the yen as a potential anchor. These Asian countries trade more with the United States than with Japan and are more closely associated with the U.S. business cycle. Canada is extremely tied to the United States in every dimension.[21]

Overall, we find that geographically connected currency areas tend to emerge with the U.S. dollar and the euro as the anchor. However, Japan does not emerge as much of an anchor. Putting together the results from Table 14 with those of Tables 12 and 13, we draw the following conclusions: (1) There seems to be a fairly clear dollar area including Canada, Mexico, most of Central America, and parts of South America (excluding Argentina and Brazil). Farther afield geographically, the dollar zone seems also to encompass some Asian countries, such as Hong Kong and Singapore. (2) The euro area includes all of western Europe and most of Africa. Argentina might actually be better served by joining the euro area than the dollar area. However, the only reason for Argentina to be seeking

---

20. See Alesina and Summers (1993) for OECD country evidence, and Cukierman (1992) for evidence on developing countries.
21. See Buiter (1999) for a discussion of this point.

Table 14   HIGH-TRADE-SHARE COUNTRIES: BEST ANCHOR BASED ON
THE THREE CRITERIA

Country	Best anchor		
	Trade[a]	VP[b]	VY[b]
Algeria	Euro	Euro	Euro
Austria	Euro	**Euro**	**Euro**
Belgium–Luxembourg	Euro	**Euro**	**Euro**
Benin	Euro	**Euro**	Euro
Cameroon	Euro	Euro	U.S.
Canada	U.S.	**U.S.**	U.S.
Central African Republic	Euro	**Euro**	Euro
Chad	Euro	Euro	Euro
Congo, Dem. Rep.	Euro	Euro	Euro
Congo, Rep	Euro	Euro	Euro
Costa Rica	U.S.	U.S.	U.S.
Côte d'Ivoire	Euro	**Euro**	Japan
Cyprus	Euro	Euro	**Euro**
Dominican Republic	U.S.	U.S.	Euro
Ecuador	U.S.	**U.S.**	Euro
Gabon	Euro	Euro	**Euro**
Gambia, The	Euro	U.S.	Euro
Ghana	Euro	U.S.	Euro
Guinea-Bissau	Euro	Euro	Japan
Guyana	U.S./Euro	**U.S.**	Euro
Haiti	U.S.	U.S.	**Euro**
Honduras	U.S.	**U.S.**	**U.S.**
Hong Kong, China	U.S.	U.S.	Euro
Iran, Islamic Rep.	Euro	Euro	Euro
Ireland	Euro	**Euro**	**Euro**
Jamaica	U.S.	U.S.	Japan
Jordan	Euro	U.S.	Euro
Kenya	Euro	Euro	U.S./Euro
Madagascar	Euro	Euro	Euro
Malaysia	Japan	U.S.	Euro
Mauritania	Euro	Euro	**Euro**
Mauritius	Euro	Euro	U.S.
Morocco	Euro	**Euro**	**Euro**
Netherlands	Euro	**Euro**	**Euro**
Nicaragua	U.S.	U.S.	Euro
Niger	Euro	**Euro**	Euro
Nigeria	Euro/U.S.	**U.S.**	**Euro**
Oman	Euro/Japan	US	**Japan**
Panama	Japan/U.S.	**U.S.**	Euro
Papua New Guinea	Japan	U.S.	Japan
Romania	Euro	U.S.	Euro
Saudi Arabia	Euro	**U.S.**	U.S./Euro
Senegal	Euro	**Euro**	Euro

Table 14   CONTINUED

Country	Best anchor		
	Trade[a]	VP[b]	VY[b]
Sierra Leone	Euro	**U.S.**	**Euro**
Singapore	U.S./Japan	**U.S.**	Euro
Sweden	Euro	**Euro**	**Euro**
Switzerland	Euro	**Euro**	**Euro**
Syrian Arab Republic	Euro	**U.S.**	**Euro**
Togo	Euro	**Euro**	Euro
Trinidad and Tobago	U.S.	U.S.	Euro
Tunisia	Euro	Euro	Euro
United Arab Emirates	Japan/Euro	**U.S.**	Euro
Venezuela, RB	U.S.	**U.S.**	Euro

[a] The table excludes countries with 1997 population below 500,000 and countries for which VP or VY is not available. The best anchor according to the trade criterion is shown only when the trade share exceeds 9%. When there is more than one anchor country for which the trade share exceeds 9%, we list the anchors in descending order of the trade shares.
[b] Bold values apply if the magnitude of the difference between the lowest VP and the next-lowest VP exceeds 0.025 or the magnitude of the difference between the lowest VY and the next-lowest VY exceeds 0.005.

any anchor is her history of high inflation. (3) There does not seem to be any clear yen area. (4) There are several countries that do not appear in Tables 12–14. These are countries with low inflation that do not trade much with any of the three potential anchors. Primary examples are India, Australia, and New Zealand.

It is worthwhile to compare our results briefly with those of Ghosh and Wolf (1994), who use a different approach to assess the pros and cons for regions and countries to form currency unions. They argue that optimal currency areas are typically formed by countries that are geographically disconnected. For example, they conclude that Europe and the states of the United States are not optimal currency areas. We have not examined the U.S. states, but Europe does present a good case for a currency union based on our examination of the patterns of trade and comovements of prices and outputs. More generally, despite some exceptions, geographical proximity typically fits well with our criteria for currency unions. The differences between our findings and those of Ghosh and Wolf seem to arise because they do not emphasize the link between currency unions and trade and because they assume a very high cost from imperfect synchronization of business cycles.

Ideally, we would go beyond the simple criteria thus far advanced to evaluate the relative costs and benefits of the trade-off leading to the choice of currency adoption. For example, should a country such as

Argentina with high inflation but low comovements with the United States and the euro zone remain autonomous or use the dollar or the euro? How much can trade benefits of a currency union compensate for the loss of monetary autonomy? To answer these questions, we need more quantitative information than we have yet generated.

6. What Changes with Currency Adoption?

Thus far, we have discussed the possible configuration of currency areas based on the behavior of inflation, trade, and the comovements of prices and outputs that prevail (in most cases) before the creation of a currency union. In choosing whether to join a monetary area, a potential entrant would have to estimate the values of trade and comovements that would apply after the entry. In practice, this calculation is difficult—for the potential entrant and also for the econometrician.[22] In the next section, we discuss estimates of effects from joining a currency union on international trade flows. Then we discuss some new estimates of effects of currency union on trade and on comovements of prices and outputs.

6.1 CURRENCY UNIONS AND INTERNATIONAL TRADE: THE AVAILABLE EVIDENCE

Most of the existing empirical work on the effects of currency unions on trade flows has been framed in the context of the standard *gravity model.* According to this approach, the bilateral trade between a pair of countries is increasing in their GDPs and is inversely related to their distance, broadly construed to include all factors that create "trade resistance." The gravity equation is then augmented with a dummy variable indicating whether or not the countries share the same currency. The estimate of the coefficient on this dummy is interpreted as the currency-union effect. In the seminal paper in this area, Rose (2000) reports that bilateral trade between two countries that use the same currency is, controlling for other effects, over 200% larger than bilateral trade between countries that use different currencies.

The apparently large effect of currency unions on trade is surprising, because estimates of the effect of reduced exchange-rate volatility on trade are small [see, for example, De Grauwe and Skudelny (2000), Frankel and Wei (1992), and Eichengreen and Irwin (1995)]. Moreover, fees on currency conversion are typically a small percentage of total transaction

---

22. Issing (2001) argues that one should expect that prices and outputs will move more closely together in the European Union after the adoption of the euro.

Table 15 EMPIRICAL STUDIES OF THE EFFECT OF CURRENCY UNION ON TRADE

Authors	Significance[a]	Point estimate of increased trade from currency union
Rose (2000)	s	≈ 240%
Frankel and Rose (1998)	s	≈ 290%
Engel and Rose (2002)	s	≈ 240%
Persson (2001)	ns	≈ 40%
Tenreyro (2001)	ns	≈ 60%
Pakko and Wall (2001)	ns	≈ −55%
Glick and Rose (2002)	s	≈ 100%
Rose and van Wincoop (2001)	s	≈ 140%
Rose (2002)	ns, s	−68% to +708%
Lopez-Cordova and Meissner (2001)	s	≈ 100%
Levy (2001)	s	≈ 50%
Nitsch (2002)	s	≈ 85%
Flandreau and Maurel (2001)	s	≈ 220%
Klein (2002)	s	≈ 50%

[a] s = statistically significantly different from zero, ns = not significant.

costs.[23] On the other hand, as already discussed, border effects on trade are large, and perhaps these large effects can be explained by the necessity to use different currencies on the two sides of a border.

Numerous empirical studies, summarized in Table 15, have examined and extended Rose's research. Pakko and Wall (2001) focus on time-series variation, which involves cases in which currency union is either implemented or abandoned. Their findings reveal a negative, though insignificant, effect of currency union on trade. However, Glick and Rose (2002) use an expanded panel data set that includes more episodes of regime switching. With this set, they find large and positive estimates from the time-series variation.

Rose (2002) provides new estimates of the effect of currency unions on trade, making use of the time-series as well as cross-sectional variation in the data. This study reports a wide range of estimates, using different samples and techniques. Point estimates range from a negative, though insignificant, effect of −68%, using fixed effects in the original sample, to a 708% effect using a matching sample technique and a much broader database.

Rose and van Wincoop (2001), Nitsch (2002), Melitz (2001), Klein (2002),

23. The argument that currency conversion fees are low may not apply to trade in capital, where the currency turnover is extremely high and hence small proportionate costs can translate into large disbursements.

and Levy (2001) address problems of aggregation bias, arguing that pooling different currency unions may mask differential effects. Yet, all these studies point toward a significantly positive effect on trade. Thom and Walsh (2002) present a case study on Ireland's break with sterling, finding no significant effect on trade. Other studies, including Flandreau and Maurel (2001) and Lopez-Cordova and Meissner (2001), focus on pre-W.W. I data.

The underlying assumption in the various empirical studies is that currency unions are randomly chosen. Standard endogeneity problems can, however, confound the estimates. For example, the presence of currency union may encourage trade, but the presence or potential for substantial trade may also stimulate the formation of a currency union. The use of country-pair fixed effects, employed in some of the studies, may not alleviate this simultaneity problem, because a shift at some point in trade linkages may be related to the change in the propensity to form a currency union.

Similarly, the existence of a currency union may reflect unmeasured characteristics that also influence the volume of bilateral international trade. The currency-union dummy can get credit for the effects of these unobserved variables. As examples, compatibility in legal systems, greater cultural links, and tied bilateral transfers may increase the propensity to form a currency union as well as strengthen trade links between two countries. In these cases, the OLS estimate of the currency-union effect on trade tends to be biased upward. Other omitted variables may bias OLS estimates in the opposite direction. For example, a higher level of monopoly power means higher markups, which tend to deter trade. At the same time, a greater degree of monopoly distortion may lead to higher inflation rates under discretion and thereby increase the desire to join a currency union as a commitment device to reduce inflation.

Persson (2001) voices a different critique based on the potential for self-selection in the decision to form a currency union. Among other distinctive features, countries that have been engaged in currency unions during the past decades are typically small and poor, tend to be geographically close, and are likely to share tight cultural links. Examples are the 15 countries of the CFA-franc zone in Africa, the seven members of the Eastern Caribbean Currency Area, and the unilaterally dollarized Panama, Puerto Rico, and Bermuda. Systematic differences in observable characteristics can distort OLS estimates when the effect of using the same currency differs across groups or when there are other types of nonlinearities in the trade relation that have been ignored. Using semiparametric methods, Persson's study finds little support for a currency-union effect on trade; his point estimates, ranging from 13% to 45%, are not statistically significantly different from zero. This result is not surprising, however, because the matching procedure—designed to deal with nonlinearities in observable variables—throws out much of the information in the sample. Moreover, as already noted, when Rose (2002) applies the matching approach to a broader data set, he obtains an enormous estimate for the effect of currency union on trade.

Another concern is a mechanical problem caused by sample selection. Previous estimates of the currency-union effect were based on a sample of countries with positive bilateral trade flows. Pairs of countries with zero trade flows—typically pairs of small countries—were excluded from the sample to satisfy the log specification of the gravity equation. This issue may be important, because roughly half of the annual country-pair observations exhibit zero trade.

6.2 THE EFFECTS OF CURRENCY UNIONS: NEW RESULTS

To address the various estimation issues, Tenreyro (2002) begins by studying the empirical determinants of past and present currency unions.[24] She uses a probit analysis for all country pairings from 1960 to 1997 with four potential currency anchors: Australia, France, the United Kingdom, and the United States.[25] The anchors used here are different from the hypothetical ones considered before for obvious reasons: the euro did not exist before 2002, and the now defunct French franc was historically an important anchor currency. Interestingly, the yen was never an anchor for anyone.

The main results, reported in Table 16, are that a currency union with one of the four candidate anchors is more likely if the client country (1) is closer geographically to the anchor, (2) has the same language as the anchor, (3) is a former or current colony of the anchor, (4) is poorer in terms of per capita GDP, and (5) is smaller in population size. The probability is increasing in the per capita GDP of the anchor (among the four considered). Elements that do not matter significantly include island or land-locked status and a common border with the potential anchor.

Our general idea is to use the estimated model for the propensity of a country to enter into a currency union to form an instrumental variable for the currency-union dummy. However, it does not work to use the estimates from the probit equation directly, because the determinants of the probability of currency union (such as distance and other gravity vari-

---

24. Persson (2001) also modeled the choice of currency union, but he did not use this analysis to construct instrumental variables.
25. Her analysis, unlike Rose's (2000), treats the CFA countries as in a currency union with France. She also departs from Rose in treating the ECCA countries as in a currency union with the United States since 1976 and with the United Kingdom before that.

Table 16   PROPENSITY TO ADOPT THE CURRENCY OF MAIN ANCHORS

Statistic	*Coefficient*	*Std. error*	*Marginal effect at mean*
min(log per capita GDP in pair)	−0.1586*	0.061	−0.0015
max(log per capita GDP in pair)	1.7167*	0.385	0.0163
min(log population in pair)	−0.1352*	0.048	−0.0013
max(log population in pair)	0.2372	0.127	0.0023
min(log area in pair)	−0.0546	0.046	−0.0005
max(log area in pair)	0.2181*	0.072	0.0021
Regional-trade-agreement dummy	−0.8864*	0.277	−0.0032
log distance (km)	−0.8766*	0.143	−0.0083
Border contiguity dummy	−1.2398*	0.619	−0.0033
Landlocked-client dummy	−0.1522	0.242	−0.0013
One-island-in-pair dummy	0.0226	0.240	0.0002
Two-islands-in-pair dummy	1.1880*	0.437	0.0512
Common-language dummy	0.7487*	0.216	0.0124
Ex-colony–colonizer dummy	1.8799*	0.285	0.1369
Current-colony (or territory) dummy	0.8491*	0.239	0.0253
Pseudo R^2	0.473		
Number of observations	29,564		

Dependent variable: currency-union dummy. The sample consists of country pairs that include the four candidate anchors: Australia, France, the United Kingdom and the United States. The equations are for annual data from 1960 to 1997, include year effects, and allow for clustering over time for country pairs. The definition of currency union treats the CFA franc countries as linked to France and treats the ECCA countries as linked to the United States since 1976 and to the United Kingdom before 1976. The mean of the currency-union dummy for this is 0.051. For the sample that regards the CFA countries as unlinked to France and the ECCA countries as unlinked to the United States or the United Kingdom, the mean is 0.024. The last column shows the marginal effect, evaluated at the sample mean, of each explanatory variable on the estimated probability of a currency union. For dummy variables, the effect refers to a shift from zero to one.
* Statistically significant at 1% level.

ables) also enter directly into the determinants of bilateral trading volume. Hence, Tenreyro (2002) adopts an indirect approach.

Consider any potential client country, i, which is evaluating the adoption of a currency with one of the four anchors considered, denoted by $k = 1, 2, 3, 4$. The probit regression determines the estimated probability, $p(i, k)$, of the currency adoption. This probability depends on the distance between i and k and the other variables mentioned above. If the countries take their currency-union decisions independently, then the joint probability that i and j use the currency of anchor k will be given by

$$J^k(i, j) = p(i, k)p(j, k).$$

Note that $J^k(i, j)$ will be high if countries i and j are both close to potential anchor k. The idea, for example, is that Ecuador and El Salvador currently share a common money (the U.S. dollar) not because they are close to each other, but rather because each is close to the United States, and hence each was independently motivated to adopt the U.S. dollar.

The joint probability that i and j use the same foreign currency (among the four candidates considered) will then be given by the sum of the joint probabilities over the support of potential anchors k:[26]

$$J(i, j) = \sum_{k=1}^{4} J^k(i, j) = \sum_{k=1}^{4} p(i, k)p(j, k)$$

One can then use the variable $J(i, j)$ as an instrument for the currency-union dummy, for example, in equations for bilateral trade between countries i and j. The underlying assumption for the validity of this instrument is that the bilateral trade between countries i and j depends on bilateral gravity variables for i and j but not on gravity variables involving third countries, notably those associated with the potential anchor countries k. These gravity variables involving third countries affect the propensity of countries i and j to be part of the same currency zone and thereby influence bilateral trade between i and j through that channel. However, these variables do not (by assumption) directly influence the bilateral trade between i and j.

Tenreyro (2002) uses the new instrument for the currency-union dummy to estimate relations for pairs of countries for trading volume, comovement of prices, and comovement of outputs. We present some of these results in Table 17, which, for brevity, reports only the estimated coefficients of the currency-union variable.

For bilateral trade, the results use annual data from 1960 to 1997 for all pairs of countries. Taking account of data availability, this system comprises over 300,000 observations (when we include the roughly half of the sample that has zeros for bilateral trade). The dependent variable is measured as log(trade + positive constant), where the presence of the positive constant allows us to include the zero-trade observations in the regressions. For the results shown in Table 17, the constant is set to 100 1995 U.S. dollars. The system includes as independent variables a set of usual gravity measures—log of geographical distance, membership in a regional trade agreement, common language, former and current colonial relationship, common colonizer, common border, and island and land-locked status—along with the logs of GDP per capita, population, and

---

26. For a pair of anchors, say, k_1 and k_2, the probability is $J(k_1, k_2) = p(k_1, k_2)[1 - p(k_1, k_3) - p(k_1, k_4)] + p(k_1, k_2)[1 - p(k_2, k_3) - p(k_2, k_4)] + \sum_{s=3}^{4} p(k_1, k_3)p(k_2, k_3)$.

Table 17   ESTIMATED COEFFICIENTS OF CURRENCY-UNION DUMMY IN
VARIOUS SYSTEMS

System	Coefficient (standard error)			
	OLS	OLS with country effects	IV	IV with country effects
log(bilateral trade + 100),	0.75	0.91	1.56	2.70
N = 348,295	(0.20)	(0.18)	(0.44)	(0.44)
Comovement of prices,	0.0690	0.0456	0.2433	0.0874
mean = −0.16,	(0.0058)	(0.0028)	(0.0243)	(0.0080)
N = 9027				
Comovement of outputs,	0.0029	0.0000	0.0119	−0.0020
means = −0.07,	(0.0026)	(0.0011)	(0.0061)	(0.0022)
N = 7610				

The equations for bilateral trade use annual data from 1960 to 1997, include year effects, and allow for clustering of the error terms over time for country pairs. The dependent variable is log(trade + 100), where trade is measured in 1995 U.S. dollars. The value 100 is close to the maximum-likelood estimate of the constant in the expression log(trade + constant). The explanatory variables included, aside from the currency-union dummy, are log(distance); dummy variables for contiguity, common language, colonial relationships, landlocked, and island; and the values for each country in the pair of log(per capita GDP), log(population), and log(area). The definition of currency union treats the CFA franc countries as linked to France and treats the ECCA countries as linked to the United States since 1976 and to the United Kingdom before 1976. Country effects refer to each member of the pair (not to a country pair). The instrumental variable (IV) systems include as an instrument for the currency-union dummy the variable described in the text. The equations for comovement include only one observation for each pair, corresponding to the period 1960–1997. The explanatory variables then refer to averages over time. Standard errors are in parentheses.

area for each country in a pair.[27] The OLS estimates of the gravity variables are typically significant.[28]

Table 17 shows that the estimated coefficient on the currency-union dummy variable is 0.75 (s.e. = 0.20) when country fixed effects are excluded, and 0.91 (0.18) when country fixed effects (not country-pair effects) are included. These results accord reasonably well with those presented by Rose (2000), despite two major differences in the approaches. First, since he used log(trade) as the dependent variable, he discarded all of the zero-trade observations (which, as mentioned, constitute roughly half of the sample). Second, we defined the currency-union dummy more liberally than Rose, in that we treated the CFA franc countries as in a union with the French franc and the ECCA countries as in a union with the U.S. dollar or the British pound (depending on the period).

27. See the footnote to Table 17 for the list of independent variables.
28. The error terms in the systems are allowed to be correlated over time for a given country pair.

The estimated effect of the currency-union dummy variable is larger if we adopt Rose's more restrictive definition of a currency union.[29]

More interestingly, the estimated effects of currency union on bilateral trade become larger when we estimate by instrumental variables, using the instrument discussed before. As shown in Table 17, the estimated coefficient on the currency-union dummy variable becomes 1.56 (0.44) when country fixed effects are excluded, and 2.70 (0.44) when they are included.[30] Hence, these results support the argument that currency union has an important positive effect on bilateral trade. Moreover, these instrumental estimates provide some reason to believe that the causality runs from currency union to trade, rather than the reverse.

The comovement of prices is measured by the negative of the standard error VP_{ij} discussed before. In this case, the sample consists of one observation (estimated for 1960–1997) on each country pair for pairs that have the necessary data. We relate this measure of price comovement to the gravity variables already mentioned and to various measures of country size (logs of per capita GDP, population, and area). Most of the gravity variables turn out to be statistically insignificant in the estimates, although common language and a common colonial heritage are associated with greater price comovement. Comovement also rises with the log of per capita GDP of each country but falls with the log of area of each country.

Table 17 shows that the currency-union dummy is significantly positive for price comovement, with an estimated coefficient of 0.069 (s.e. = 0.006) when country fixed effects are excluded, and 0.046 (0.003) when they are included. These estimated effects are substantial relative to the mean of the comovement variable (the negative of the price-equation standard deviation), which is −0.16. The positive estimated effect of currency union on price comovement may emerge because currency-union countries avoid the sometimes volatile inflation rates and nominal exchange rates that characterize other regimes. The instrumental estimates are even higher than those generated by OLS. In this case, the estimated coefficients are 0.24 (0.02) when country fixed effects are excluded, and 0.087 (0.008) when they are included.

The comovement of outputs is measured by the negative of the standard error VY_{ij} discussed before. The sample again comprises one observation (estimated for 1960–1997) on each country pair with the available

29. The OLS estimates become 1.24 (0.25) without country fixed effects, and 1.06 (0.23) with country fixed effects.
30. The estimated effects are even larger if we adopt Rose's (2000) more restrictive definition of currency unions. In the instrumental estimation, the estimated coefficients of the currency-union dummy variable are then 2.72 (0.75) when country fixed effects are excluded, and 4.68 (0.79) when they are included.

data. The explanatory variables are the same as those used for price co-movements. The main effects from the gravity variables turn out to be positive relationships with a common border, a common language, and prior and current colonial linkages. However, Table 17 shows that the estimated coefficients on the currency-union dummy variable are typically insignificantly different from zero. These results may arise because, as discussed before, the theoretical link between currency union and output comovement is ambiguous.

7. Conclusions

The basic message of this paper is twofold. First, based on the historical data on inflation, trade, and comovements of prices and outputs, we argued that there exist well-defined dollar and euro areas but no clear yen area. Second, it is likely that the adoption of another country's currency increases bilateral trade and raises the comovement of prices. These responses suggest that our examination of the trade patterns and comovements that applied before the adoption of a common currency would underestimate the potential benefits from joining a currency union.

Several issues should be considered in future empirical research. First, the results of the instrumental estimation for the effects of currency union need to be analyzed more fully. Second, these results can be used to estimate how the introduction of a currency union would affect trade and the comovements of prices and outputs for individual country pairs under the hypothetical adoption of a currency union with a specified anchor country. These results would then feed back into our previous analysis of the desirable pattern of world currency unions. Third, using methods analogous to those used in this paper, we can assess the formation of currency unions that are not linked to a major anchor. For example, we can evaluate a Latin American currency union or the proposed unions in southern Africa and among the Persian Gulf states. Fourth, we expect to make particular use of the evidence that accumulates from the experience of the European Monetary Union.

REFERENCES

Alesina, A., and R. Barro. (2002). Currency unions. *Quarterly Journal of Economics*, May, 409–436.
———. O. Blanchard, J. Gali, F. Giavazzi, and H. Uhlig. (2001). *Defining Macroeconomic Policy for Europe*. London: CEPR.
———, and E. Spolaore. (2002). *The Size of Nations*. Cambridge, MA: The MIT Press.
———, and R. Wacziarg. (2000). Economic integration and political disintegration. *American Economic Review*, December, 1276–1296.

———, and L. Summers. (1993). Central bank independence and macroeconomic performance. *Journal of Money, Credit and Banking*, May.

Anderson, J. and E. van Wincoop. (2001). Borders, trade and welfare. In *Brookings Trade Forum 2001*.

Barro, R. J., and D. B. Gordon (1983). Rules, discretion, and reputation in a model of monetary policy. *Journal of Monetary Economics*, July, 101–121.

Broda, C. (2001). Terms of trade and exchange rate regimes in developing countries. *American Economic Review*, May.

Buiter, W. (1999). The EMU and the NAMU: What is the case for North American monetary union. CEPR Working Paper 2181.

Calvo, G., and C. Reinhart. (2002). Fear of floating. *Quarterly Journal of Economics*, forthcoming.

Cukierman, A. (1992). *Central Bank Strategy, Credibility, and Independence: Theory and Evidence*. Cambridge, MA: The MIT Press.

De Grauwe, P., and F. Skudelny. (2000). The impact of EMU on trade flows. *Weltwirtschaftliches Archiv*, 136:381–402.

Eichengreen, B., and D. Irwin. (1995). Trade blocs, currency blocs and the disintegration of world trade in the 1930s. *Journal of International Economics*, February.

Engel, C., and A. Rose. (2002). Currency unions and international integration. *Journal of Money, Credit and Banking*.

Flandreau, M., and M. Maurel. (2001). Monetary union, trade integration and business cycles in 19th century Europe: Just do it. CEPR Discussion Paper 3087.

Frankel, J. and A. Rose. (1998). The endogeneity of the optimum currency area criteria. *Economic Journal*, July, 1009–1025.

———, and S. J. Wei. (1992). Trade blocs and currency blocs. Cambridge, MA: National Bureau of Economic Research. NBER Working Paper 4335. Also in *The Monetary Future of Europe*, G. de la Dehesa et al. (eds.). London: CEPR, 1993.

Gale, D., and X. Vives. (2002). Dollarization, bailouts, and the stability of the banking system. *Quarterly Journal of Economics*, May, 467–502.

Gavin, M. and R. Perotti. (1997). Fiscal policy in Latin America. *NBER Macroeconomics Annual 1997*. Cambridge, MA: The MIT Press.

Ghosh, A. and H. Wolf. (1994). How many monies? A generic approach to finding optimal currency areas. Cambridge, MA: National Bureau of Economic Research. NBER Working Paper 4805.

Glick, R., and A. Rose. (2002). Does a currency union affect trade? The time series evidence. *European Economic Review*, June, 1125–1151.

Gray, A. (2002). Formula available at http://argray.fateback.com/dist/dodist.html.

Hausmann, R., U. Panizza, and E. Stein. (1999). Why do countries float the way they float? Interamerican Development Bank Working Paper 418.

Imbs, J. (2000). Co-fluctuations. London Business School. Unpublished.

Issing, O. (2001). The single monetary policy of the European Central Bank: One size fits all. *International Finance* 4:441–462.

Klein, M. (2002). Dollarization and Trade. Unpublished.

Krugman, P. (1993). Lessons of Massachusetts for EMU. In *The Transition to Economic and Monetary Union in Europe*, F. Giavazzi and F. Torres (eds). Cambridge: Cambridge University Press.

Levy, Y. E. (2001). On the impact of a common currency on bilateral trade. Universidad Di Tella. Unpublished.

Lopez-Cordova, J., and C. Meissner. (2001). Exchange-rate regimes and international trade: Evidence from the classical gold standard era. Berkeley: University of California. Unpublished.

McCallum, J. (1995). National borders matter: Canadian–U.S. regional trade patterns. *American Economic Review*, June, 615–623.

Melitz, J. (2001). Geography, trade and currency unions. CEPR Discussion Paper 2987.

Mundell, R. (1961). A theory of optimum currency areas. *American Economic Review*, September, 657–665.

Nitsch, V. (2002). Honey, I shrunk the currency union effect on trade. *World Economy*, April, 457–474.

Obstfeld, M. and K. Rogoff. (2000). The six major puzzles in international macroeconomics: Is there a common cause. In *NBER Macroeconomics Annual 2000*. Cambridge, MA: The MIT Press.

Ozcan, S., B. Sorensen, and O. Yosha. (2001). Economic integration, industrial specialization and the asymmetry of macroeconomic fluctuations. *Journal of International Economics*, October, 107–137.

———, ———, and ———. (2002). Risk sharing and industrial specialization: Regional and international evidence. Unpublished. University of Houston.

Pakko, M., and H. Wall. (2001). Reconsidering the trade creating effect of currency unions. *Federal Reserve Bank of St. Louis Review*, September/October.

Persson, T. (2001). Currency union and trade, how large is the treatment effect? *Economic Policy*, 335–348.

Rose, A. (2000). One money one market: Estimating the effect of common currencies on trade. *Economic Policy*, April: 7–46.

———. (2002). The effect of common currencies on international trade: A meta-analysis. Berkeley: University of California. Unpublished.

———, and E. van Wincoop. (2001). National money as a barrier to international trade: The real case for currency union. *American Economic Review*, May, 386–390.

Tenreyro, S. (2001). On the causes and consequences of currency unions. Harvard University. Unpublished.

———. (2002). Economic effects of currency unions. Harvard University. Unpublished.

Thom, R., and B. Walsh. (2002). The effect of a currency union on trade: Lessons from the Irish experience, *European Economic Review*, June, 1111–1123.

Comment

RUDI DORNBUSCH
Massachusetts Institute of Technology

This is a very very aggressive paper, and accordingly, a great pleasure to discuss. Andy called me and asked: "How about I discuss the empirical issues and you focus on the rest?" Little did I know that the little bugger had read the paper and I hadn't. But let me stand by our agreement.

This paper says Iraq is part of a U.S. currency union, and it pays a lot of attention to the Comoro Islands, wherever they are. I think this is like looking under the light for the keys. You focus on trade because you have the trade data, and all other considerations must take second place. But the authors are not shy about assigning countries to currency unions. So I want to ask how sturdy those results might be if you looked at a few extra considerations.

But before getting there they have acerbic remarks about nationalism. They say there are 100 extra countries and why the hell do they need a money? They ought to have a soccer team—or, even more expensive, an Olympic team—but why a money? I think they should go further and ask, why should we have these countries? Once we have these countries, don't be surprised they have a money, and a flag, and all the junk that goes with it. I think it's a reality that people who are very poor attach an unusual importance to nationalism. They have nothing else. So I would say, once you have the countries, take for granted that there has to be a compelling reason for them to give up their money—either many humiliating experiences with trying to manage their own, or the total ascendancy of bureaucrats. I say that because the paper ambitiously says that Mexico is actively considering a monetary union or currency union with the United States. I don't think anyone in Mexico is actively thinking about that. They say it would be a really good idea, but forget about it, simply because of this nationalism issue. And I think the same is true in Peru. I was part of putting Peru on the dollar once, for three and a half hours. We had it there, and dessert was served and I had to go to the airport, and in the morning, it hadn't happened. I think that's sort of the likelihood of Peru, Mexico, and many others soon being on the dollar, after the Argentine example takes away the powerful credibility of dollarization and gives nationalism the upper hand. So on the remarks about nationalism, I agree that countries don't need their own money, but be sure that nationalism is an enormously powerful argument, and will stand.

A more technical concern I have with their allocation of countries is, let's say Poland doesn't belong in the euro zone. Now do the experiment, a slightly different experiment, and have the seven accession countries joining the euro zone. And in that experiment, what would happen? Well, my guess is that Poland would shift over and belong in the euro zone, because we go from the bilateral to the cross effects of all the countries who have more of a trade integration with Europe than Poland does. I think this is an interesting question to ask with this model in hand. What happens if you look at a group of three or four countries contemplating where they belong? Then the cross effects between them will matter, and Poland—once the effects of Hungary, the Czech Republic, and God knows what are included—will be much more Europe-oriented, and on that basis likely to get a bold letter that says Europe. But if that isn't true, it is interesting in itself and is a much stronger argument against Poland joining the euro zone (as it will in the next two or three years).

My next concern is Lucas's critique. We look at 1970 or 1950 to 1990, and out of that we get comovements, and those comovements are used to assign countries. But what do they have to do with what a country would look like once it is in a currency union? The second part of the paper addresses that very issue by saying that you would expect to see more comovement of output and prices. But is that enough for the assignment? I think on some issues, like the answer on the yen area, this is very wrong. We have intra-Asian trade growing at two to three times the rate of trade with the rest of the world, so the last thirty years therefore are not really a good representation of what is going to be the case ten years from now. If you join a monetary union or a currency area, you would really like to know what it feels like ten years from now and not just on the wedding night. So I would like to make a more forward-looking, less passionate analysis and ask, does the assignment of countries hold up? And it may well do so; but in the Asian instance, because the growth rates are so high, it is very likely that the picture today would look different. Whether the yen emerges as a natural anchor is open, but I would like to know the answer to that.

The next point is, for a currency union, you need the other side to agree. This paper asks only whether a particular country has an interest in joining the euro or the dollar or the yen. But we could turn the question around and ask: is it in the interest of the United States to have Liberia join a currency union? And if the answer to that is no, then Liberia probably isn't going to join. Think of Canada as an example. You might argue that there are important terms-of-trade changes between the United States and Canada. Part of the welfare analysis of making a decision to have Canada or not to have Canada is to ask what happens to the terms of trade in that change of regime, and whether that is welfare-enhancing or welfare-reducing for the United States. So the extra perspective ought to be there, and perhaps the pieces that are on the table are enough to answer that question already, but certainly it is worth asking.

The next concern I have is that this is sort of like the Club of Rome. Prices don't make a dominant entry into the discussion. We get assigned to a currency area depending on comovements and inflation rates. If the inflation rate is high and the comovement is high, then what you need is good discipline, and not having a central bank (meaning not having an exchange rate) isn't a big loss, so go to the dollar or go to the euro as a result. But there is the third option, of course, of being alone. Is it better to go to the second best, the euro—even though that match on trade, for example, may not be very substantial—than to float alone and be your awful self? I'd like to see a bit of a calibration there for countries that don't have extremely high inflation. A country with extremely high inflation ought to peg to anything, including Singapore. But if a country doesn't have extremely high inflation, is it better to have any currency union, or to have only the best, and if that isn't possible, forget it? I think there is an issue there, because if we have important trade creation and trade diversion effects, I'd like to know how it works when you do the second choice.

I have a technical question on comovements of prices: whether I really think the PPP–GDP deflators are the right measure, or would much better like the terms of trade. What we see in the output and price comovements is sort of an omelet of shocks and structure. And the shocks are likely to be different in a currency union, and so is the structure, and therefore it is very very doubtful that we come back with exactly the same kind of results. The terms of trade are more primitive drivers and as a result have a better chance of surviving into a currency union; they will give us a more stable indicator of what to look at.

In the same context, Mundell's name is often invoked in vain, and is here too. His "optimal currency area" had to do with mobility. Mobility doesn't appear here as a discussion item. But clearly, in looking at a currency union, you would, as the Europeans did, look at the fiscal situation, at whether there is sufficient convergence there. Is there substantial flexibility, so that applying the same policy is not going to be a major challenge to the monetary union? Is mobility in fact a shock absorber? None of these things are there. Trade is the only thing that matters. I think trade is sort of the only thing that doesn't matter, ultimately. So I would change the balance towards structure and finance and away from trade. It's true that Mexico thinks of nothing else other than the United States and that that is its reference, not only for trade, but for everything. But I think that is an extraordinarily narrow point of view. Just let me give one example. Suppose we did direct investment and looked at the regressions we saw before and decided whether currency unions promote direct investment. Do we find the same results as for trade? If we don't then of course you can choose whether an extra dollar of exports is your thing, or whether you are more interested in direct investment as a by-product of a currency union.

In passing, a lot of the discussion about borders and currencies in Europe is coming up now with the hope that the introduction of the euro will somehow equalize prices throughout Europe. Every newspaper has a long article on how tomatoes are cheap in Italy and expensive in Germany, and with the euro this cannot last. Of course the Germans drive the *Kombis* to Italy to fill them with tomatoes and bring them home. But in the end we are really looking at retail prices, and that stuff isn't happening. Do it for automobiles, and you will find that the problem is anticompetitive practices. The issue isn't borders per se, but rather that borders are a hook on which to hang anticompetitive practices, and I think that is an important difference.

Let me ask four questions to finish, maybe three. Since the authors are happy to go forward and make currency unions out of the past correlations, let's go backward and ask, was the sterling area an optimal currency area? I think that's easy to do, it's interesting to do, and I don't really know what to believe. The second question is, poor Korea. I see those islands, the Comoro Islands prominently. I don't see Korea. And Korea searches its soul to know where it belongs. Does it belong in NAFTA? Does it belong in the Japanese monetary area that is actively being discussed, actively being promoted, a north Asia monetary union? And the paper doesn't really get to that. I think that is the interesting question: the yen story. It involves China and Korea; it doesn't really have much to do with Indonesia. So that would be an interesting direction to look. Lastly, Canada is supposed to be in the dollar area, but Canada is very happy not to be, and people like Chrétien get up every morning and say that it is really wonderful that they are not on the dollar because they get the extra cushion that a commodity currency needs of having some movements in the exchange rate. Switzerland every morning wakes up and says thanks be to God we are not in the European monetary union because we would have one percent higher interest rates if we were in and everybody would go bankrupt.

So I think that finance is really three-quarters of the story, the terms of trade are ten percent, and the past correlations are sort of the residual. I think the paper is very challenging, and I think it is a good exercise to piece the world together and find out that 60 percent of the extra 100 countries are orphans, don't belong anywhere on the criterion we have, and are therefore an unsolved problem for international financial architecture.

Comment

ANDREW K. ROSE
University of California at Berkeley and NBER

1. What's Here

Currency unions are all the rage in international policy circles these days. But suppose a country—say Argentina (the crisis du jour)—decides that it needs to adopt a foreign currency. Which one should it pick? Alesina, Barro, and Tenreyro provide the methodology, or at least most of it, to answer this important and interesting question.

Their methodology is reasonable in a number of aspects. First, it is based on solid, standard theory. Second, it seems to yield mostly sensible results in practice. And third, the authors deal with the endogeneity issue carefully; that is, the potential ex post effect of currency union itself on the criteria used to judge the ex ante desirability of currency union. They focus on three key issues: (1) the benefits from enhanced international trade that currency unions bring; (2) the low inflation that clients get from joining a currency union with a low-inflation anchor; and (3) the potential effects of currency union on price and output comovements, which represent the cost of more imperfectly stabilized business cycles. All this I find eminently plausible and valuable.

2. What's Not

All modeling relies on abstraction, and this paper is no exception. There are some omissions which have been made deliberately but which may affect the results in practice. In particular, there are at least four potentially important issues that are absent from the analysis of Alesina, Barro, and Tenreyro. Least important is the fact that the authors do not consider the issue of factor mobility. Labor mobility in practice is glacial, both within country and across countries, for most of the world. Thus it is generally not considered as a response to the sorts of business-cycle shocks that monetary policy might handle (outside a currency union, that is). Still, homage to Mundell's original idea is appropriate for a paper with this title.

A slightly more important consideration is the fact that monetary sovereignty is the fiscal policy of last resort. Any country with its own currency retains the option of monetizing its national debt. This issue has not attracted much attention in the literature, but is clearly important for a number of the Latin-American countries that the authors are most interested in.

A more important omission is the issue of insurance. Regions (whether countries or areas within countries) may be insulated from idiosyncratic productivity shocks with an appropriate insurance system. At least two are widely considered to be important: a federal system of taxes and transfers of the type that we usually see within countries; and the private exchange of financial claims. Growing international financial integration may alleviate the costs of national business cycles, especially if currency union spurs financial integration. I expect this issue to grow in importance over time, and I encourage the authors to pursue it.

The most striking issue is the intentional avoidance of financial issues such as liquidity, bailouts, moral hazard, corporate finance and banking issues, and the lender of last resort. As the authors show, there is no clear reason why Argentina and Brazil are part of the dollar bloc, if one does not consider the level of financial integration. Yet these countries are clearly members of the dollar zone, presumably because of their strong financial ties with the United States. Indeed, these issues have obsessed much of the recent literature on currency unions, mostly on a theoretical basis only. I would be more comfortable with the generality of the results here if they had considered financial issues.

3. What's the Question

The results are mostly quite sensible. Using the criteria of inflation, trade, and price and output comovements, the authors find well-defined dollar and euro areas, although a few countries fall through the cracks. Their most striking result is that there is little evidence of any yen zone. Fine. But at least two issues arise immediately. The first is that there is no obvious way to weigh the various criteria when they disagree about which currency union to join. What should be done when the criteria give conflicting signals, as they do in certain important cases such as Brazil?

Even more important is the question itself. Usually the issue is not *which* currency union to join but *whether* to join. Countries like Denmark, Sweden, and the United Kingdom know that the issue is whether or not to join EMU. Similarly for Argentina, Canada, and Mexico, which are (at least vaguely) considering dollarization. The big payoff in this literature will be a methodology which allows a country to decide in practice, on the basis of quantitative economic criteria, when it makes sense for a country to join. Alesina et al. have certainly made progress on this issue, but the work has not yet been finished.

4. What's Up

While I believe most of the results in this paper, some are more plausible than others. The authors find larger effects than others (like me) have found in the nexus of price comovements, and smaller than those of others on business-cycle comovements. Fair enough; they use a new methodology and a better dependent variable. Their results become the new target.

But speaking of targets, I cannot resist emphasizing the estimated effects of currency union on trade that the authors tabulate in Table 17. These are large compared to those in the literature (summarized in Table 15). But mostly they are just large—enormous, in fact. The (preferred) instrumental-variable estimates are 1.56 (without country effects) and 2.70

(with them); both are statistically significant. They are even higher using a stricter version of currency unions, as note 30 shows. Even the smallest estimate, 1.56, implies that currency union is associated with extra trade to the tune of 475% [since $4.75 \approx \exp(1.56)$]. My original estimate that currency union tripled trade seems positively moderate by comparison.

5. What's More

The authors pursue their analysis as if currency unions were all unilateral: a client country adopts the currency of a large anchor, or not. But in fact there are a number of multilateral currency unions, such as the East Caribbean Currency Area and the CFA franc zones in Africa. These exist without any clear center country, though both are moored externally via exchange-rate pegs. Above and beyond those of small countries considering joining G-3 currencies, it would be nice to extend the analysis of Alesina et al. to multilateral currency unions. This is especially important for Latin-American countries, Africans, and the Gulf states. The benefits of regional currency unions are likely to be at least as high as any involving the G-3, at least with respect to trade integration and price and output comovements.

But do multilateral currency unions have as much monetary discipline as unilateral currency unions based on G-3 countries? Yes. In practice, inflation for ECCA and the CFA averaged 6.7% between 1960 and 1996, while inflation for unilateral CU joiners was significantly higher at 8.9%. I conclude multilateral currency unions are certainly worthy of more research.

6. What's Down

The most innovative contribution of this work is its exploitation of the new instrumental variable developed by Tenreyro. This allows the authors in principle to estimate the effect of currency union on phenomena like trade, taking into account the potential for measurement error, reverse causality, and the like. As the authors realize, this instrument requires that bilateral trade between countries i and j depend on bilateral gravity variables for i and j but not on gravity variables involving third countries. Is this a legitimate assumption to make?

Not generally. A number of authors include *remoteness* in trade equations. Remoteness is usually measured as the (inverse of) distance-weighted GDP, so that New Zealand is usually the most remote country, Luxembourg the least remote. Remoteness violates the identifying assumption made in the paper.

Above and beyond remoteness, the instrumental variable seems a little fishy, since it is almost a combination of variables that are already in the equation. To use the example of the paper, Ecuador and El Salvador speak a common language and are therefore more likely to be in a currency union, as is clear from Table 16. That is, the two countries are "close" to each other and engage in more trade. They will also both be "far" from anchors that do not speak Spanish. This makes me somewhat uncomfortable with the instrumental variable, especially in the context of multilateral currency unions, where no obvious anchor exists.[1] Further, there are a number of odd coefficients in Table 9 in any case, which shows that contiguous countries and countries in a common regional trade agreement are less likely to be in a currency union, somewhat contrary to (at least EMU-based) intuition.

7. What's Good

Mine are essentially petty objections—mostly requests for even more work. Alesina, Barro, and Tenreyro have made progress on an important and interesting topic, and I look forward to more of their research.

Discussion

Several participants took up the question of the optimal number of countries and currencies. Ken Rogoff pursued Rudi Dornbusch's claim that the fixed costs of running a country are large and there are too many small countries by asking him what he thought should be the world's countries. He also asked Dornbusch to what extent he thought that developing-country problems are due to the quality of governance in general, and to what extent due to having monetary autonomy.

Alberto Alesina disagreed with Dornbusch that having lots of small countries is a bad thing. Alesina was of the opinion that in a world with a lot of trade and financial integration, having a lot of small countries could be very useful in preventing conflicts such as civil wars. He noted that under free trade, economic growth is not systematically related to country size. However he agreed that some public goods, such as curren-

---

1. The fact that the procedure seems intuitively more plausible for unilateral than for multilateral currency unions may explain why the authors make some implausible assumptions about multilateral currency unions. The CFA was never really in a currency union with France. It was pegged to the franc at 50 per franc before the 1994 devaluation to 100 (except for Comoros). And the ECCA is not in a currency union with the United States; rather it is pegged at 2.7 per dollar (and was pegged at 4.8 per pound before 1976).

cies, might be better provided on a larger scale, and speculated that nationalist sentiment about currencies might be changing.

Ken Rogoff asked Alberto Alesina which public goods he thought of as most subject to substantial economies of scale. He was particularly curious about the ranking of currency on the list. Alesina replied that there is a trade-off between economies of scale and sharing policy with people with different preferences. The point of the paper is to try to measure the exact trade-off between the two forces as regards monetary policy.

Greg Mankiw asked how large countries with federal governments can be distinguished from small countries with shared public goods provided by supranational organizations. Alesina replied that decentralization can be thought of as a continuum, with a menu of policies that might be decided at different levels of aggregation. Bob Hall remarked on this point that California had its own currency for a long period of time.

A number of participants voiced concern about endogeneity and the Lucas critique. Pointing to the instability of the coefficient on GDP comovements in Table 17, Alan Stockman said he was particularly concerned that output comovements might be substantially affected by domestic monetary policy, and also that other domestic policies might be correlated with membership of a currency union. He noted that, ideally for the empirical strategy, one would like comovements to be generated by factors such as movements in international commodity prices.

On this point, Eric van Wincoop responded that he did not think that endogeneity due to monetary policy is likely to be very serious. He said that the evidence points towards regions within countries comoving much more than countries not because of monetary policy, but because of the greater extent of trade within countries than across countries.

Jonathan Parker took up Alan Stockman's concern about endogeneity. He asked whether the EU is unique in the extensive legal and regulatory changes that took place at the same time as EMU. He remarked that simultaneous important changes in many spheres would make identification difficult.

Pierre-Olivier Gourinchas remarked that the EU is one of the few places where economic reasons rather than historical accident drove the move towards a currency union. Silvana Tenreyro responded that, on the contrary, there are other examples, such as Guinea-Bissau, which joined the CFA in 1987 in order to reduce inflation.

Ken Rogoff raised the question of the irreversibility of currency unions. He noted that although in the past currency boards had been seen as irreversible, it had been proven that this is not the case.

On a related point, Mark Gertler suggested that the output and price comovement variables used by the authors might look very different if they were calculated over the period 1980–2000 instead of 1960–1997. In particular, he was worried that among OECD countries, comovements in the 1970s might have been driven mainly by oil shocks, and he also cited Stock and Watson's evidence of declining volatility in output and prices over the sample period. Alberto Alesina responded that comovements calculated over 1975–1997 do not differ much from those calculated over 1958–1997. He agreed that as a further robustness check, it might be interesting to look at comovements in the more recent past. He also noted that client–anchor comovements are the crucial variable in the paper, so the evidence on the OECD is not necessarily relevant.

Gian-Maria Milesi-Ferretti commented that the fact that the data on bilateral trade are mainly on trade in goods, and do not include trade in services, could be affecting the results. He speculated that the tendency of some small countries to have large service exports in tourism and financial services could be biasing the results in one direction or another. He suggested that it might be possible to check this using better-quality data from industrial countries.

Rudi Dornbusch raised the possibility of "special effects" currency unions, giving the example of a potential union of commodity currencies such as those of Australia, New Zealand, and Canada. He noted that the benefits of such a union would be more on the financial side than on the trade side. He commented that this is another way to think about countries facing common shocks sharing a currency.

Pierre-Olivier Gourinchas asked what is the evidence on trade diversion in the literature with regard to the effects of currency unions on bilateral trade. Silvana Tenreyro replied that Frankel and Rose had tested for trade diversion and found no evidence that it was present. Andy Rose responded that even if there were trade diversion, it would not have negative welfare consequences, as the loss of transactions costs within a currency union would result in efficiency gains.

Takero Doi wondered whether Japan should join the dollar zone rather than create its own currency union. Alberto Alesina answered that the authors had not considered Japan as a client in search of an anchor. He noted that although Europe, the United States, and Japan have business cycles that are fairly highly correlated, the authors do not find plausible the idea that they would form a currency union.

Lars Svensson was curious about the organization of central banks and the goals of monetary policy in small currency unions. Andy Rose said that it depends on the currency union, but that the ECCA and the CFA have multilateral central banks, similar to the European Central Bank.

Silvana Tenreyro responded that as regards goals, small currency unions such as the ECCA and the CFA tend to peg their exchange rates rather than float.

Finally, the authors responded to comments made by the discussants and other participants. Robert Barro addressed in particular the comments of Andy Rose. He agreed that currency unions without major anchors are possible, and indeed being proposed in Southern Africa, the Gulf states, and Australia and New Zealand. But he disagreed that the CFA zone and the ECCA should be thought of as being without an anchor. He felt that the fact that they are linked to a major currency is central to their continued existence. He remarked that the methodology for analyzing currency unions without anchors would be similar to that used in the paper, although more difficult to implement. Barro also responded to Rose's comment that monetary policy is a fiscal instrument that governments might like to retain control of. He said that there are good reasons for precluding governments from using monetary policy as a fiscal instrument. In response to Rudi Dornbusch on the question of whether joining a currency union requires agreement from both sides, he said that while agreement might be favorable, it is not necessary, and that unilateral joining has occurred.

On the issue of Japan, Alberto Alesina said that the authors agree with Andy Rose that the data do not support the existence of a natural yen zone, but disagree with Dornbusch on the matter. He said that Korea's low inflation means that it is not in search of an anchor country, rather than it being a country with no anchor to turn to.